MARCEL PROUST

Modern Critical Views

These and other titles in preparation

Modern Critical Views

MARCEL PROUST

Edited and with an introduction by
Harold Bloom
Sterling Professor of the Humanities
Yale University

CHELSEA HOUSE PUBLISHERS ◇ 1987
New York ◇ New Haven ◇ Philadelphia

© 1987 by Chelsea House Publishers,
a division of Chelsea House Educational Communications, Inc.,
  95 Madison Avenue, New York, NY 10016
  345 Whitney Avenue, New Haven, CT 06511
  5014 West Chester Pike, Edgemont, PA 19028

Introduction © 1987 by Harold Bloom

Printed and bound in the United States of America

∞ The paper used in this publication meets the minimum
requirements of the American National Standard for Permanence
of Paper for Printed Library Materials, Z39.48-1984.

Library of Congress Cataloging-in-Publication Data
Marcel Proust.
  (Modern critical views)
  Bibliography: p.
  Includes index.
  Summary: Critical essays n the work of Marcel
Proust, major twentieth-century French novelist.
  1. Proust, Marcel, 1871–1922—Criticism and
interpretation. [1. Proust, Marcel, 1871–1922—Criticism
and interpretation. 2. French literature—History and
criticism] I. Bloom, Harold. II. Series.
PQ2631.R63Z718   1987   843'.912   86-29911
ISBN 0-87754-726-2 (alk. paper)

Contents

Editor's Note

This book gathers together a representative selection of the best criticism available in English on the work of Marcel Proust, universally regarded as the major novelist of our century. The critical essays are reprinted here in the chronological order of their original publication. I am grateful to Olga Popov for her erudition and judgment in helping me to edit this volume.

My introduction contrasts Proust and Freud on the psychosexual contours of jealousy and then studies the jealousy of Swann and of Marcel in *Remembrance of Things Past,* where the search for lost time frequently is the search for the unfindable "historical" truth of deceptions, betrayals, infidelities.

The chronological sequence of criticism begins fittingly with Samuel Beckett, at this time the most distinguished Western writer, who combines in his own fiction the legacies of Proust, Joyce, and Kafka. Beckett fuses memory, habit, and time as Wordsworth and Ruskin fused them, Ruskin being one of Proust's acknowledged precursors.

Germaine Brée, a lifelong student of Proust's writings, centers on *The Captive* in order to portray the extraordinary resistance to psychological analysis of Proust's characters, complete and closed off, each in herself or himself. The celebrated modern critic of the Sublime, the German-Jewish Walter Benjamin, presents an overview image of Proust as an artist who surmounted his malady not by defying it, but by incarnating it in his work.

Our most influential student of mediated desire in literature, René Girard, traces in Proust the pattern by which a great novelist obsessively represents the desires of a social elite and in doing so prophesies the future desires of an entire culture or nation. Girard contrasts usefully with two American scholars of Proust's optics, the poet Howard Moss, who finds in the bedroom window at Combray the trope for Marcel's magic lantern of sexual imagination, and the critic Roger Shattuck, who explores two perspectives that make up "Proust's binoculars."

The philosopher Gilles Deleuze, combining the heritage of Nietzsche with our modern awareness of signs, finds in Proust a Jewish humor as opposed to the Greek irony of Plato, a humor presumably like Freud's, which holds that to think is to interpret. Another contemporary French rhetorician, Gérard Genette, finds in Proust different orders both of time and of narrative, orders that govern Proust's discourse. Leo Bersani usefully distinguishes between Proust and his truest precursor, Flaubert, by observing that Flaubert's estrangement of art from life is answered by Proust's quest for a more artful life.

Our much-missed foremost theorist of reading, Paul de Man, uncovers in Proust the ultimate consequence of truth's not being able to coincide with itself, which is precisely what we learn to call lost time. An early story in Proust's *Pleasure and Days* is read by Walter Kasell as an anticipation of *Remembrance's* structure and theme.

A psychoanalytic investigation by Randolph Splitter juxtaposes Proust and Joyce in terms of their different ways of utilizing the logic of metaphor. Jean Ricardou, in a retrospective overview, finds in Proust the perpetual New Novel, since Proust is too comprehensive to be surpassed. In this book's final essay, Diana Festa-McCormick finds in the clothes of Proust's characters the masks that help constitute Proust's language of deception. Deception, with its inevitable consequence in jealousy, returns us to this volume's introduction, with its meditation upon Proust's most pervasive and obsessive concern, the imagination of betrayal and infidelity.

Introduction

Sexual jealousy is the most novelistic of circumstances, just as incest, according to Shelley, is the most poetical of circumstances. Proust is the novelist of our era, even as Freud is our moralist. Both are speculative thinkers, who divide between them the eminence of being the prime wisdom writers of the age.

Proust died in 1922, the year of Freud's grim and splendid essay, "Certain Neurotic Mechanisms in Jealousy, Paranoia, and Homosexuality." Both of them great ironists, tragic celebrants of the comic spirit, Proust and Freud are not much in agreement on jealousy, paranoia, and homosexuality, though both start with the realization that all of us are bisexual in nature.

Freud charmingly begins his essay by remarking that jealousy, like grief, is normal, and comes in three stages: *competitive* or normal, *projected, delusional.* The *competitive* or garden variety is compounded of grief, due to the loss of the loved object, and of the reactivation of the narcissistic scar, the tragic first loss, by the infant, of the parent of the other sex to the parent of the same sex. As normal, *competitive* jealousy is really normal Hell, Freud genially throws into the compound such delights as enmity against the successful rival, some self-blaming, self-criticism, and a generous portion of bisexuality.

Projected jealousy attributes to the erotic partner one's own actual unfaithfulness or repressed impulses, and is cheerfully regarded by Freud as being relatively innocuous, since its almost delusional character is highly amenable to analytic exposure of unconscious fantasies. But *delusional* jealousy proper is more serious; it also takes its origin in repressed impulses towards infidelity, but the object of those impulses is of one's own sex, and this, for Freud, moves one across the border into paranoia.

What the three stages of jealousy have in common is a bisexual component, since even *projected* jealousy trades in repressed impulses, and

1

these include homosexual desires. Proust, our other authority on jealousy, preferred to call homosexuality "inversion," and in a brilliant mythological fantasia traced the sons of Sodom and the daughters of Gomorrah to the surviving exiles from the Cities of the Plain. Inversion and jealousy, so intimately related in Freud, become in Proust a dialectical pairing, with the aesthetic sensibility linked to both as a third term in a complex series.

On the topos of jealousy, Proust is fecund and generous; no writer has devoted himself so lovingly and brilliantly to expounding and illustrating the emotion, except of course Shakespeare in *Othello* and Hawthorne in *The Scarlet Letter*. Proust's jealous lovers—Swann, Saint-Loup, above all Marcel himself—suffer so intensely that we sometimes need to make an effort not to empathize too closely. It is difficult to determine just what Proust's stance towards their suffering is, partly because Proust's ironies are both pervasive and cunning. Comedy hovers nearby, but even tragicomedy seems an inadequate term for the compulsive sorrows of Proust's protagonists. Swann, after complimenting himself that he has not, by his jealousy, proved to Odette that he loves her too much, falls into the mouth of Hell:

> He never spoke to her of this misadventure, and ceased even to think of it himself. But now and then his thoughts in their wandering course would come upon this memory where it lay unobserved, would startle it into life, thrust it forward into his consciousness, and leave him aching with a sharp, deep-rooted pain. As though it were a bodily pain, Swann's mind was powerless to alleviate it; but at least, in the case of bodily pain, since it is independent of the mind, the mind can dwell upon it, can note that it has diminished, that it has momentarily ceased. But in this case the mind, merely by recalling the pain, created it afresh. To determine not to think of it was to think of it still, to suffer from it still. And when, in conversation with his friends, he forgot about it, suddenly a word casually uttered would make him change countenance like a wounded man when a clumsy hand has touched his aching limb. When he came away from Odette he was happy, he felt calm, he recalled her smiles, of gentle mockery when speaking of this or that other person, of tenderness for himself; he recalled the gravity of her head which she seemed to have lifted from its axis to let it droop and fall, as though in spite of herself, upon his lips, as she had done on the first evening in the carriage, the languishing

looks she had given him as she lay in his arms, nestling her head against her shoulder as though shrinking from the cold.

But then at once his jealousy, as though it were the shadow of his love, presented him with the complement, with the converse of that new smile with which she had greeted him that very evening—and which now, perversely, mocked Swann and shone with love for another—of that droop of the head, now sinking on to other lips, of all the marks of affection (now given to another) that she had shown to him. And all the voluptuous memories which he bore away from her house were, so to speak, but so many sketches, rough plans like those which a decorator submits to one, enabling Swann to form an idea of the various attitudes, aflame or faint with passion, which she might adopt for others. With the result that he came to regret every pleasure that he tasted in her company, every new caress of which he had been so imprudent as to point out to her the delights, every fresh charm that he found in her, for he knew that, a moment later, they would go to enrich the collection of instruments in his secret torture-chamber.

Jealousy here is a pain experienced by Freud's bodily ego, on the frontier between psyche and body: "To determine not to think of it was to think of it still, to suffer from it still." As the shadow of love, jealousy resembles the shadow cast by the earth up into the heavens, where by tradition it ought to end at the sphere of Venus. Instead, it darkens there, and since the shadow is Freud's reality principle, or our consciousness of our own mortality, Proust's dreadfully persuasive irony is that jealousy exposes not only the arbitrariness of every erotic object-choice but also marks the passage of the loved person into a teleological overdetermination, in which the supposed inevitability of the person is simply a mask for the inevitability of the lover's death. Proust's jealousy thus becomes peculiarly akin to Freud's death drive, since it, too, quests beyond the pleasure/unpleasure principle. Our secret torture-chamber is furnished anew by every recollection of the beloved's erotic prowess, since what delighted us has delighted others.

Swann experiences the terrible conversion of the jealous lover into a parody of the scholar, a conversion to an intellectual pleasure that is more a deviation than an achievement, since no thought can be emancipated from the sexual past of all thought (Freud), if the search for truth is nothing but a search for the sexual past:

Certainly he suffered as he watched that light, in whose golden atmosphere, behind the closed sash, stirred the unseen and detested pair, as he listened to that murmur which revealed the presence of the man who had crept in after his own departure, the perfidy of Odette, and the pleasures which she was at that moment enjoying with the stranger. And yet he was not sorry he had come; the torment which had forced him to leave his own house had become less acute now that it had become less vague, now that Odette's other life, of which he had had, at that first moment, a sudden helpless suspicion, was definitely there, in the full glare of the lamp-light, almost within his grasp, an unwitting prisoner in that room into which, when he chose, he would force his way to seize it unawares; or rather he would knock on the shutters, as he often did when he came very late, and by that signal Odette would at least learn that he knew, that he had seen the light and had heard the voices, and he himself, who a moment ago had been picturing her as laughing with the other at his illusions, now it was he who saw them, confident in their error, tricked by none other than himself, whom they believed to be far away but who was there, in person, there with a plan, there with the knowledge that he was going, in another minute, to knock on the shutter. And perhaps the almost pleasurable sensation he felt at that moment was something more than the assuagement of a doubt, and of a pain: was an intellectual pleasure. If, since he had fallen in love, things had recovered a little of the delightful interest that they had had for him long ago—though only in so far as they were illuminated by the thought or the memory of Odette—now it was another of the faculties of his studious youth that his jealousy revived, the passion for truth, but for a truth which, too, was interposed between himself and his mistress, receiving its light from her alone, a private and personal truth the sole object of which (an infinitely precious object, and one almost disinterested in its beauty) was Odette's life, her actions, her environment, her plans, her past. At every other period in his life, the little everyday activities of another person had always seemed meaningless to Swann; if gossip about such things was repeated to him, he would dismiss it as insignificant, and while he listened it was only the lowest, the most commonplace part of his mind that was engaged; these were the moments when he felt at his most inglorious. But in this strange phase of love the personality of another person becomes so enlarged, so deepened, that the curiosity which he now felt stirring inside him with regard to the smallest details of a woman's daily life, was the same thirst for knowledge with which he had once studied history. And all manner of actions from which hitherto he would have recoiled in shame, such as spying, to-night, outside a window, to-morrow perhaps, for all he knew, putting adroitly provocative questions to casual witnesses, bribing servants, listening at doors, seemed to him now to be precisely on a level with the deciphering of manuscripts, the weighing of evidence, the interpretation of old monuments—so many different methods of scientific investigation with a genuine intellectual value and legitimately employable in the search for truth.

In fact, poor Swann is at the wrong window, and the entire passage is therefore as exquisitely painful as it is comic. What Freud ironically called the overevaluation of the object, the enlargement or deepening of the beloved's personality, begins to work not as one of the enlargements of life (like Proust's own novel) but as the deepening of a personal Hell. Swann plunges downwards and outwards, as he leans "in impotent, blind, dizzy anguish over the bottomless abyss" and reconstructs the petty details of Odette's past life with "as much passion as the aesthete who ransacks the extant documents of fifteenth-century Florence in order to penetrate further into the soul of the Primavera, the fair Vanna or the Venus of Botticelli."

The historicizing aesthete, John Ruskin say, or Walter Pater, becomes the archetype of the jealous lover, who searches into lost time not for a person, but for an epiphany or moment-of-moments, a privileged fiction of duration:

When he had been paying social calls Swann would often come home with little time to spare before dinner. At that point in the evening, around six o'clock, when in the old days he used to feel so wretched, he no longer asked himself what Odette might be about, and was hardly at all concerned to hear that she had people with her or had gone out. He recalled at times that he had once, years ago, tried to read through its envelope a letter addressed by Odette to Forcheville. But this memory was not pleasing to him, and rather than plumb the depths of shame that he felt in it he preferred to indulge in a little grimace, twisting up the corners of his mouth and adding, if need be, a shake of the head which signified "What do I care about it?" True, he considered now that the hypothesis on which he had often dwelt at that time, according to which it was his jealous imagination alone that blackened what was in reality the innocent life of Odette—that this hypothesis (which after all was beneficent, since, so long as his amorous malady had lasted, it had diminished his sufferings by making them seem imaginary) was not the correct one, that it was his jealousy that had seen things in the correct light, and that if Odette had loved him more than he supposed, she had also deceived him more. Formerly, while his sufferings were still keen, he had vowed that, as soon as he had ceased to love Odette and was no longer afraid either of vexing her or of making her believe that he loved her too much, he would give himself the satisfaction of elucidating with her, simply from his love of truth and as a point of historical interest, whether or not Forcheville had been in bed with her that day when he had rung her bell and rapped on her window in vain, and she had written to Forcheville that it was an uncle of hers who had called. But this so interesting problem, which he was only waiting for his jealousy to subside before clearing up, had precisely lost all interest in Swann's eyes when he had ceased to be jealous. Not immediately, however. Long after he had ceased to feel any jealousy with regard to Odette, the memory of that day, that afternoon spent knocking vainly at the little house in the Rue La Pérouse, had continued to torment him. It was as though his jealousy, not dissimilar in that respect from those maladies which appear to have their seat, their centre of contagion, less in certain persons than in certain places, in certain houses, had had for its object not so much Odette herself as that day, that hour in the irrevocable past when Swann had knocked at every entrance to her house in turn, as though that day, that hour alone had caught and preserved a few last fragments of the amorous personality which had once been Swann's, that there alone could he now recapture them. For a long time now it had been a matter of indifference to him whether Odette had been, or was being, unfaithful to him. And yet he had continued for some years to seek out old servants of hers, to such an extent had the painful curiosity persisted in him to know whether on that day, so long ago, at six o'clock, Odette had been in bed with Forcheville. Then that curiosity itself had disappeared, without, however, his abandoning his investigations. He went on trying to discover what no longer interested him, because his old self, though it had shrivelled to extreme decrepitude, still acted mechanically, in accordance with preoccupations so utterly abandoned that Swann could not now succeed even in picturing to himself that anguish—so compelling once that he had been unable to imagine that he would ever be delivered from it, that only the death of the woman he loved (though death, as will be shown later on in this story by a cruel corroboration, in no way diminishes the sufferings caused by jealousy) seemed to him capable of smoothing the path of his life which then seemed impassably obstructed.

Jealousy dies with love, but only with respect to the former beloved. Horribly a life-in-death, jealousy renews itself like the moon, perpetually trying to discover what no longer interests it, even after the object of desire has been literally buried. Its true object is "that day, that hour in the irrevocable past," and even that time was less an actual time than a temporal fiction, an episode in the evanescence of one's own self. Paul de Man's perspective that Proust's deepest insight is the nonexistence of the self founds itself upon this temporal irony of unweaving, this permanent parabasis of meaning. One can remember that even this deconstructive perspective is no more or less privileged than any other Proustian trope, and so cannot give us a truth that Proust himself evades.

The bridge between Swann's jealousy and Marcel's is Saint-Loup's jealousy of Rachel, summed up by Proust in one of his magnificently long, baroque paragraphs:

> Saint-Loup's letter had come as no surprise to me, even though I had had no news of him since, at the time of my grandmother's illness, he had accused me of perfidy and treachery. I had grasped at once what must have happened. Rachel, who liked to provoke his jealousy (she also had other causes for resentment against me), had persuaded her lover that I had made sly attempts to have relations with her in his absence. It is probable that he continued to believe in the truth of this allegation, but he had ceased to be in love with her, which meant that its truth or falsehood had become a matter of complete indifference to him, and our friendship alone remained. When, on meeting him

again, I tried to talk to him about his accusations, he merely
gave me a benign and affectionate smile which seemed to be a
sort of apology, and then changed the subject. All this was not
to say that he did not, a little later, see Rachel occasionally
when he was in Paris. Those who have played a big part in
one's life very rarely disappear from it suddenly for good. They
return to it at odd moments (so much so that people suspect a
renewal of old love) before leaving it for ever. Saint-Loup's
breach with Rachel had very soon become less painful to him,
thanks to the soothing pleasure that was given him by her
incessant demands for money. Jealousy, which prolongs the
course of love, is not capable of containing many more ingredients than the other products of the imagination. If one takes
with one, when one starts on a journey, three or four images
which incidentally one is sure to lose on the way (such as the
lilies and anemones heaped on the Ponte Vecchio, or the Persian
church shrouded in mist), one's trunk is already pretty full.
When one leaves a mistress, one would be just as glad, until
one had begun to forget her, that she should not become the
property of three or four potential protectors whom one pictures in one's mind's eye, of whom, that is to say, one is
jealous: all those whom one does not so picture count for
nothing. Now frequent demands for money from a cast-off
mistress no more give one a complete idea of her life than
charts showing a high temperature would of her illness. But the
latter would at any rate be an indication that she was ill, and
the former furnish a presumption, vague enough it is true, that
the forsaken one or forsaker (whichever she be) cannot have
found anything very remarkable in the way of rich protectors.
And so each demand is welcomed with the joy which a lull
produces in the jealous one's sufferings, and answered with the
immediate dispatch of money, for naturally one does not like to
think of her being in want of anything except lovers (one of the
three lovers one has in one's mind's eye), until time has enabled
one to regain one's composure and to learn one's successor's
name without wilting. Sometimes Rachel came in so late at
night that she could ask her former lover's permission to lie
down beside him until the morning. This was a great comfort
to Robert, for it reminded him how intimately, after all, they
had lived to-together, simply to see that even if he took the

greater part of the bed for himself it did not in the least interfere with her sleep. He realised that she was more comfortable, lying close to his familiar body, than she would have been elsewhere, that she felt herself by his side—even in an hotel—to be in a bedroom known of old in which one has one's habits, in which one sleeps better. He felt that his shoulders, his limbs, all of him, were for her, even when he was unduly restless from insomnia or thinking of the things he had to do, so entirely usual that they could not disturb her and that the perception of them added still further to her sense of repose.

The heart of this comes in the grandly ironic sentence: "Jealousy, which prolongs the course of love, is not capable of containing many more ingredients than the other products of the imagination." That is hardly a compliment to the capaciousness of the imagination, which scarcely can hold on for long to even three or four images. Saint-Loup, almost on the farthest shore of jealousy, has the obscure comfort of having become, for Rachel, one of those images not quite faded away, when "he felt that his shoulders, his limbs, all of him, were for her," even when he has ceased to be there, or anywhere, for her, or she for him. Outliving love, jealousy has become love's last stand, the final basis for a continuity between two former lovers.

Saint-Loup's bittersweet evanescence as a lover contrasts both with Swann's massive historicism and with the novel's triumphant representation of jealousy, Marcel's monumental search after lost time in the long aftermath of Albertine's death. Another grand link between magnificent jealousies is provided by Swann's observations to Marcel, aesthetic reflections somewhat removed from the pain of earlier realities:

> It occurred to me that Swann must be getting tired of waiting for me. Moreover I did not wish to be too late in returning home because of Albertine, and, taking leave of Mme de Surgis and M. de Charlus, I went in search of my invalid in the card-room. I asked him whether what he had said to the Prince in their conversation in the garden was really what M. de Bréauté (whom I did not name) had reported to us, about a little play by Bergotte. He burst out laughing: "There's not a word of truth in it, not one, it's a complete fabrication and would have been an utterly stupid thing to say. It's really incredible, this spontaneous generation of falsehood. I won't ask who it was that told you, but it would be really interesting,

in a field as limited as this, to work back from one person to another and find out how the story arose. Anyhow, what concern can it be of other people, what the Prince said to me? People are very inquisitive. I've never been inquisitive, except when I was in love, and when I was jealous. And a lot I ever learned! Are you jealous?" I told Swann that I had never experienced jealousy, that I did not even know what it was. "Well, you can count yourself lucky. A little jealousy is not too unpleasant, for two reasons. In the first place, it enables people who are not inquisitive to take an interest in the lives of others, or of one other at any rate. And then it makes one feel the pleasure of possession, of getting into a carriage with a woman, of not allowing her to go about by herself. But that's only in the very first stages of the disease, or when the cure is almost complete. In between, it's the most agonising torment. However, I must confess that I haven't had much experience even of the two pleasures I've mentioned—the first because of my own nature, which is incapable of sustained reflexion; the second because of circumstances, because of the woman, I should say the women, of whom I've been jealous. But that makes no difference. Even when one is no longer attached to things, it's still something to have been attached to them; because it was always for reasons which other people didn't grasp. The memory of those feelings is something that's to be found only in ourselves; we must go back into ourselves to look at it. You mustn't laugh at this idealistic jargon, but what I mean to say is that I've been very fond of life and very fond of art. Well, now that I'm a little too weary to live with other people, those old feelings, so personal and individual, that I had in the past, seem to me—it's the mania of all collectors—very precious. I open my heart to myself like a sort of showcase, and examine one by one all those love affairs of which the rest of the world can have known nothing. And of this collection, to which I'm now even more attached than to my others, I say to myself, rather as Mazarin said of his books, but in fact without the least distress, that it will be very tiresome to have to leave it all. But, to come back to my conversation with the Prince, I shall tell one person only, and that person is going to be you."

We are in the elegy season, ironically balanced between the death of jealousy in Swann and its birth in poor Marcel, who literally does not know that the descent into Avernus beckons. When the vigor of an affirmation has more power than its probability, clearly we are living in a fiction, the metaphor or transference that we call love, and might call jealousy. Into that metaphor, Marcel moves like a sleepwalker, with his obsessions central to *The Captive* and insanely pervasive in *The Fugitive.* A great passage in *The Captive,* which seems a diatribe against jealousy, instead is a passionately ironic celebration of jealousy's aesthetic victory over our merely temporal happiness:

> However, I was still at the first stage of enlightenment with regard to Léa. I was not even aware whether Albertine knew her. No matter, it came to the same thing. I must at all costs prevent her from renewing this acquaintance or making the acquaintance of this stranger at the Trocadéro. I say that I did not know whether she knew Léa or not; yet I must in fact have learned this at Balbec, from Albertine herself. For amnesia obliterated from my mind as well as from Albertine's a great many of the statements that she had made to me. Memory, instead of being a duplicate, always present before one's eyes, of the various events of one's life, is rather a void from which at odd moments a chance resemblance enables one to resusci-tate dead recollections; but even then there are innumerable little details which have not fallen into that potential reservoir of memory, and which will remain forever unverifiable. One pays no attention to anything that one does not connect with the real life of the woman one loves; one forgets immediately what she has said to one about such and such an incident or such and such people one does not know, and her expression while she was saying it. And so when, in due course, one's jealousy is aroused by these same people, and seeks to ascertain whether or not it is mistaken, whether it is indeed they who are responsible for one's mistress's impatience to go out, and her annoyance when one has prevented her from doing so by returning earlier than usual, one's jealousy, ransacking the past in search of a clue, can find nothing; always retrospective, it is like a historian who has to write the history of a period for which he has no documents; always belated, it dashes like an enraged bull to the spot where it will not find the dazzling, arrogant creature who is tormenting it and whom the crowd admire for his splendour and cunning. Jealousy thrashes around in the void, uncertain as we are in those dreams in which we

are distressed because we cannot find in his empty house a
person whom we have known well in life, but who here perhaps is another person and has merely borrowed the features of
our friend, uncertain as we are even more after we awake when
we seek to identify this or that detail of our dream. What was
one's mistress's expression when she told one that? Did she not
look happy, was she not actually whistling, a thing that she
never does unless she has some amorous thought in her mind
and finds one's presence importunate and irritating? Did she
not tell one something that is contradicted by what she now
affirms, that she knows or does not know such and such a
person? One does not know, and one will never know; one
searches desperately among the unsubstantial fragments of a
dream, and all the time one's life with one's mistress goes on, a
life that is oblivious of what may well be of importance to one,
and attentive to what is perhaps of none, a life hagridden by
people who have no real connexion with one, full of lapses of
memory, gaps, vain anxieties, a life as illusory as a dream.

Thrashing about in the void of a dream in which a good friend
perhaps is another person, jealousy becomes Spenser's Malbecco: "who
quite/Forgot he was a man, and jealousy is hight." Yet making life "as
illusory as a dream," hagridden by lapses and gaps, is Marcel's accomplishment, and Proust's art. One does not write an other-than-ironic
diatribe against one's own art. Proust warily, but with the sureness of a
great beast descending upon its helpless prey, approaches the heart of his
vision of jealousy, his sense that the emotion is akin to what Freud named
as the defense of isolation, in which all context is burned away, and a
dangerous present replaces all past and all future.

Sexual jealousy in Proust is accompanied by a singular obsessiveness
in regard to questions of space and of time. The jealous lover, who, as
Proust says, conducts researches comparable to those of the scholar, seeks
in his inquiries every detail he can find as to the location and duration of
each betrayal and infidelity. Why? Proust has a marvelous passage in *The
Fugitive* volume of *Remembrance*:

> It is one of the faculties of jealousy to reveal to us the extent to
> which the reality of external facts and the sentiments of the
> heart are an unknown element which lends itself to endless
> suppositions. We imagine that we know exactly what things are
> and what people think, for the simple reason that we do not
> care about them. But as soon as we have a desire to know, as

the jealous man has, then it becomes a dizzy kaleidoscope in which we can no longer distinguish anything. Had Albertine been unfaithful to me? With whom? In what house? On what day? On the day when she had said this or that to me, when I remembered that I had in the course of it said this or that? I could not tell. Nor did I know what her feelings were for me, whether they were inspired by self-interest or by affection. And all of a sudden I remembered some trivial incident, for instance that Albertine had wished to go to Saint-Martin-le-Vêtu, saying that the name interested her, and perhaps simply because she had made the acquaintance of some peasant girl who lived there. But it was useless that Aimé should have informed me of what he had learned from the woman at the baths, since Albertine must remain eternally unaware that he had informed me, the need to know having always been exceeded, in my love for Albertine, by the need to show her that I knew; for this broke down the partition of different illusions that stood between us, without having ever had the result of making her love me more, far from it. And now, since she was dead, the second of these needs had been amalgamated with the effect of the first: the need to picture to myself the conversation in which I would have informed her of what I had learned, as vividly as the conversation in which I would have asked her to tell me what I did not know; that is to say, to see her by my side, to hear her answering me kindly, to see her cheeks become plump again, her eyes shed their malice and assume an air of melancholy; that is to say, to love her still and to forget the fury of my jealousy in the despair of my loneliness. The painful mystery of this impossibility of ever making known to her what I had learned and of establishing our relations upon the truth of what I had only just discovered (and would not have been able, perhaps, to discover but for her death) substituted its sadness for the more painful mystery of her conduct. What? To have so desperately desired that Albertine—who no longer existed— should know that I had heard the story of the baths! This again was one of the consequences of our inability, when we have to consider the fact of death, to picture to ourselves anything but life. Albertine no longer existed; but to me she was the person who had concealed from me that she had assignations with women at Balbec, who imagined that she had succeeded in keeping me in ignorance of them. When we try to consider what will happen to us after our own death, is it not still our living self which we mistakenly project at that moment? And is it much more absurd, when all is said, to regret that a woman who no longer exists is unaware that we have learned what she was doing six years ago than to desire that of ourselves, who will be dead, the public shall still speak with approval a century hence? If there is more real foundation in the latter than in the former case, the regrets of my retrospective jealousy proceeded none the less from the same optical error as in other men the desire for posthumous fame. And yet, if this impression of the solemn finality of my separation from Albertine had momentarily supplanted my idea of her misdeeds, it only succeeded in aggravating them by bestowing upon them an irremediable character. I saw myself astray in life as on an endless beach where I was alone and where, in whatever direction I might turn, I would never meet her.

"The regrets of my retrospective jealousy proceeded none the less from the same optical error as in other men the desire for posthumous fame"—is that not as much Proust's negative credo as it is Marcel's? Those "other men" include the indubitable precursors, Flaubert and Baudelaire, and Proust himself as well. The aesthetic agon for immortality is an optical error, yet this is one of those errors about life that are necessary for life, as Nietzsche remarked, and is also one of those errors about art that is art. Proust has swerved away from Flaubert into a radical confession of error; the novel is creative envy, love is jealousy, jealousy is the terrible fear that there will not be enough space for oneself (including literary space), and that there never can be enough time for oneself, because death is the reality of one's life. A friend once remarked to me, at the very height of her own jealousy, that jealousy was nothing but a vision of two bodies on a bed, neither of which was one's own, where the hurt resided in the realization that one body ought to have been one's own. Bitter as the remark may have been, it usefully reduces the trope of jealousy to literal fears: where was one's body, where will it be, when will it not be? Our ego is always a bodily ego, Freud insisted, and jealousy joins the bodily ego and the drive as another frontier concept, another vertigo whirling between a desperate inwardness and the injustice of outwardness. Proust, like Freud, goes back after all to the prophet Jeremiah, that uncomfortable sage who proclaimed a new inwardness for his mother's people. The law is written upon our inward parts for Proust also, and the law is justice, but the god of law is a jealous god, though he is certainly not the god of jealousy.

Freud, in "The Passing of the Oedipus Complex," writing two years after Proust's death, set forth a powerful speculation as to the difference between the sexes, a speculation that Proust neither evades nor supports, and yet illuminates, by working out of the world that Freud knows only in the pure good of theory. Freud is properly tentative, but also adroitly forceful:

> Here our material—for some reason we do not understand— becomes far more shadowy and incomplete. The female sex develops an Oedipus-complex, too, a super-ego and a latency period. May one ascribe to it also a phallic organization and a castration complex? The answer is in the affirmative, but it cannot be the same as in the boy. The feministic demand for equal rights between the sexes does not carry far here; the morphological difference must express itself in differences in the development of the mind. "Anatomy is Destiny," to vary a saying of Napoleon's. The little girl's clitoris behaves at first just like a penis, but by comparing herself with a boy play-fellow the child perceives that she has "come off short," and takes this fact as ill-treatment and as a reason for feeling inferior. For a time she still consoles herself with the expecta-tion that later, when she grows up, she will acquire just as big an appendage as a boy. Here the woman's "masculine com-plex" branches off. The female child does not understand her actual loss as a sex characteristic, but explains it by assuming that at some earlier date she had possessed a member which was just as big and which had later been lost by castration. She does not seem to extend this conclusion about herself to other grown women, but in complete accordance with the phallic phase she ascribes to them large and complete, that is, male, genitalia. The result is an essential difference between her and the boy, namely, that she accepts castration as an established fact, an operation already performed, whereas the boy dreads the possibility of its being performed.
>
> The castration-dread being thus excluded in her case, there falls away a powerful motive towards forming the super-ego and breaking up the infantile genital organization. These changes seem to be due in the girl far more than in the boy to the results of educative influences, of external intimidation threatening the

loss of love. The Oedipus-complex in the girl is far simpler, less equivocal, than that of the little possessor of a penis; in my experience it seldom goes beyond the wish to take the mother's place, the feminine attitude towards the father. Acceptance of the loss of a penis is not endured without some attempt at compensation. The girl passes over—by way of a symbolic analogy, one may say—from the penis to a child; her Oedipus-complex culminates in the desire, which is long cherished, to be given a child by her father as a present, to bear him a child. One has the impression that the Oedipus-complex is later gradually abandoned because this wish is never fulfilled. The two desires, to possess a penis and to bear a child, remain powerfully charged with libido in the unconscious and help to prepare the woman's nature for its subsequent sex rôle. The comparative weakness of the sadistic component of the sexual instinct, which may probably be related to the penis-deficiency, facilitates the transformation of directly sexual trends into those inhibited in aim, feelings of tenderness. It must be confessed, however, that on the whole our insight into these processes of development in the girl is unsatisfying, shadowy and incomplete.

Anatomy is destiny in Proust also, but this is anatomy taken up into the mind, as it were. The exiles of Sodom and Gomorrah, more jealous even than other mortals, become monsters of time, yet heroes and heroines of time also. The Oedipus complex never quite passes, in Freud's sense of passing, either in Proust or in his major figures. Freud's castration complex, ultimately the dread of dying, is a metaphor for the same shadowed desire that Proust represents by the complex metaphor of jealousy. The jealous lover fears that he has been castrated, that his place in life has been taken, that true time is over for him. His only recourse is to search for lost time, in the hopeless hope that the aesthetic recovery of illusion and of experience alike, will deceive him in a higher mode than he fears to have been deceived in already.

SAMUEL BECKETT

Memory, Habit, Time

The Proustian equation is never simple. The unknown, choosing its weapons from a hoard of values, is also the unknowable. And the quality of its action falls under two signatures. In Proust each spear may be a spear of Telephus. This dualism in multiplicity will be examined more closely in relation to Proust's "perspectivism." For the purposes of this synthesis it is convenient to adopt the *inner* chronology of the Proustian demonstration, and to examine in the first place that double-headed monster of damnation and salvation—Time.

The scaffolding of his structure is revealed to the narrator in the library of the Princesse de Guermantes (one time Mme. Verdurin), and the nature of its materials in the matinée that follows. His book takes form in his mind. He is aware of the many concessions required of the literary artist by the shortcomings of the literary convention. As a writer he is not altogether at liberty to detach effect from cause. It will be necessary, for example, to interrupt (disfigure) the luminous projection of subject desire with the comic relief of features. It will be impossible to prepare the hundreds of masks that rightly belong to the objects of even his most disinterested scrutiny. He accepts regretfully the sacred ruler and compass of literary geometry. But he will refuse to extend his submission to spatial scales, he will refuse to measure the length and weight of man in terms of his body instead of in terms of his years. In the closing words of his book he states his position:

From *Proust in the Collected Works of Samuel Beckett.* © 1970 by Grove Press, Inc.

But were I granted time to accomplish my work, I would not fail to stamp it with the seal of that Time, now so forcibly present to my mind, and in it I would describe men, even at the risk of giving them the appearance of monstrous beings, as occupying in Time a much greater place than that so sparingly conceded to them in Space, a place indeed extended beyond measure, because, like giants plunged in the years, they touch at once those periods of their lives—separated by so many days—so far apart in Time.

Proust's creatures, then, are victims of this predominating condition and circumstance—Time; victims as lower organisms, conscious only of two dimensions and suddenly confronted with the mystery of height, are victims: victims and prisoners. There is no escape from the hours and the days. Neither from tomorrow nor from yesterday. There is no escape from yesterday because yesterday has deformed us, or been deformed by us. The mood is of no importance. Deformation has taken place. Yesterday is not a milestone that has been passed, but a daystone on the beaten track of the years, and irremediably part of us, within us, heavy and dangerous. We are not merely more weary because of yesterday, we are other, no longer what we were before the calamity of yesterday. A calamitous day, but calamitous not necessarily in content. The good or evil disposition of the object has neither reality nor significance. The immediate joys and sorrows of the body and the intelligence are so many superfoetations. Such as it was, it has been assimilated to the only world that has reality and significance, the world of our own latent consciousness, and its cosmography has suffered a dislocation. So that we are rather in the position of Tantalus, with this difference, that we allow ourselves to be tantalised. And possibly the perpetuum mobile of our disillusions is subject to more variety. The aspirations of yesterday were valid for yesterday's ego, not for today's. We are disappointed at the nullity of what we are pleased to call attainment. But what is attainment? The identification of the subject with the object of his desire. The subject has died—and perhaps many times—on the way. For subject B to be disappointed by the banality of an object chosen by subject A is as illogical as to expect one's hunger to be dissipated by the spectacle of Uncle eating his dinner. Even suppose that by one of those rare miracles of coincidence, when the calendar of facts runs parallel to the calendar of feelings, realisation takes place, that the object of desire (in the strictest sense of that malady) is achieved by the subject, then the congruence is so perfect, the time-state of attainment eliminates so accurately the time-state of aspiration, that the actual seems the inevitable, and, all conscious intellectual effort to reconstitute the invisible and unthinkable as a reality being fruitless, we are incapable of appreciating our joy by comparing it with our sorrow. Voluntary memory (Proust repeats it ad nauseam) is of no value as an instrument of evocation, and provides an image as far removed from the real as the myth of our imagination or the caricature furnished by direct perception. There is only one real impression and one adequate mode of evocation. Over neither have we the least control. That reality and that mode will be discussed in their proper place.

But the poisonous ingenuity of Time in the science of affliction is not limited to its action on the subject, that action, as has been shown, resulting in an unceasing modification of his personality, whose permanent reality, if any, can only be apprehended as a retrospective hypothesis. The individual is the seat of a constant process of decantation, decantation from the vessel containing the fluid of future time, sluggish, pale and monochrome, to the vessel containing the fluid of past time, agitated and multicoloured by the phenomena of its hours. Generally speaking, the former is innocuous, amorphous, without character, without any Borgian virtue. Lazily considered in anticipation and in the haze of our smug will to live, of our pernicious and incurable optimism, it seems exempt from the bitterness of fatality: in store for us, not in store in us. On occasions, however, it is capable of supplementing the labours of its colleague. It is only necessary for its surface to be broken by a date, by any temporal specification allowing us to measure the days that separate us from a menace—or a promise. Swann, for example, contemplates with doleful resignation the months that he must spend away from Odette during the summer. One day Odette says: "Forcheville (her lover, and, after the death of Swann, her husband) is going to Egypt at Pentecost." Swann translates: "I am going with Forcheville to Egypt at Pentecost." The fluid of future time freezes, and poor Swann, face to face with the *future* reality of Odette and Forcheville in Egypt, suffers more grievously than even at the misery of his present condition. The narrator's desire to see La Berma in *Phèdre* is stimulated more violently by the announcement "Doors closed at two o'clock" than by the mystery of Bergotte's "Jansenist pallor and solar myth." His indifference at parting from Albertine at the end of the day in Balbec is transformed into the most horrible anxiety by a simple remark addressed by her to her aunt or to a friend: "Tomorrow, then, at half-past eight." The tacit understanding that the future can be controlled is destroyed. The future event cannot be focussed, its implications cannot be seized, until it is definitely situated and a date assigned to it. When Albertine was his prisoner, the possibility of her escape did not seriously disturb him, because it was indistinct and abstract, like the possibility of death. Whatever opinion we may be pleased to hold on the subject of death, we may be sure that it is meaningless and valueless. Death has not required us to keep a day free. The art of publicity has been revolutionised by a similar consideration. Thus I am exhorted, not merely to try the aperient of the Shepherd, but to try it at seven o'clock.

So far we have considered a mobile subject before an ideal object, immutable and incorruptible. But our vulgar perception is not concerned with other than vulgar phenomena. Exemption from intrinsic flux in a given object does not change the fact that it is the correlative of a subject that does not enjoy such immunity. The observer infects the observed with his own mobility. Moreover, when it is a case of human intercourse, we are faced by the problem of an object whose mobility is not merely a function of the subject's, but independent and personal: two separate and immanent dynamisms related by no system of synchronisation. So that whatever the object, our thirst for possession is, by definition, insatiable. At the best, all that is realised in Time (all Time produces), whether in Art or Life, can only be possessed successively, by a series of partial annexations— and never integrally and at once. The tragedy of the Marcel-Albertine liaison is the type-tragedy of the human relationship whose failure is preordained. My analysis of that central catastrophe will clarify this too abstract and arbitrary statement of Proust's pessimism. But for every tumour a scalpel and a compress. Memory and Habit are attributes of the Time cancer. They control the most simple Proustian episode, and an understanding of their mechanism must precede any particular analysis of their application. They are the flying buttresses of the temple raised to commemorate the wisdom of the architect that is also the wisdom of all the sages, from Brahma to Leopardi, the wisdom that consists not in the satisfaction but in the ablation of desire:

> "In noi di cari inganni
> non che la speme, il desiderio è spento."

The laws of memory are subject to the more general laws of habit. Habit is a compromise effected between the individual and his environment, or between the individual and his own organic eccentricities, the guarantee of a dull inviolability, the lightning-conductor of his existence. Habit is the ballast that chains the dog to his vomit. Breathing is habit. Life is habit. Or rather life is a succession of habits, since the individual is a succession of individuals; the world being a projection of the individual's consciousness (an objectivation of the individual's will, Schopenhauer would say), the pact must be continually renewed, the letter of safe-conduct brought up to date. The creation of the world did not take place once and for all time, but takes place every day. Habit then is the generic term for the countless treaties concluded between the countless subjects that constitute the individual and their countless correlative objects. The periods of transition that separate consecutive adaptations (because by no expedient of macabre transubstantiation can the grave-sheets serve as swaddling-clothes) represent the perilous zones in the life of the individual, dangerous, precarious, painful, mysterious and fertile, when for a moment the boredom of living is replaced by the suffering of being. (At this point, and with a heavy heart and for the satisfaction or disgruntlement of Gideans, semi and integral, I am inspired to concede a brief parenthesis to all the analogivorous, who are capable of interpreting the "Live danger-ously," that victorious hiccough in vacuo, as the national anthem of the true ego exiled in habit. The Gideans advocate a habit of living—and look for an epithet. A nonsensical bastard phrase. They imply a hierarchy of habits, as though it were valid to speak of good habits and bad habits. An automatic adjustment of the human organism to the conditions of its existence has as little moral significance as the casting of a clout when May is or is not out; and the exhortation to cultivate a habit as little sense as an exhortation to cultivate a coryza.) The suffering of being: that is, the free play of every faculty. Because the pernicious devotion of habit para-lyses our attention, drugs those handmaidens of perception whose co-opera-tion is not absolutely essential. Habit is like Françoise, the immortal cook of the Proust household, who knows what has to be done, and will slave all day and all night rather than tolerate any redundant activity in the kitchen. But our current habit of living is as incapable of dealing with the mystery of a strange sky or a strange room, with any circumstance unforeseen in her curriculum, as Françoise of conceiving or realising the full horror of a Duval omelette. Then the atrophied faculties come to the rescue, and the maximum value of our being is restored. But less drastic circumstances may produce this tense and provisional lucidity in the nervous system. Habit may not be dead (or as good as dead, doomed to die) but sleeping. This second and more fugitive experience may or may not be exempt from pain. It does not inaugurate a period of transition. But the first and major mode is inseparable from suffering and anxiety—the suffering of the dying and the jealous anxiety of the ousted. The old ego dies hard. Such as it was, a minister of dulness, it was also an agent of security. When it ceases to perform that second function, when it is opposed by a phenomenon that it cannot reduce to the condition of a comfortable and familiar concept, when, in a word, it betrays its trust as a screen to spare its victim the spectacle of reality, it disappears, and the victim, now an ex-victim, for a moment free, is exposed to that reality—an exposure that has its advantages and its disadvantages. It disappears—with wailing and gnashing of teeth. The mortal microcosm cannot forgive the relative immortality of the macrocosm. The whisky bears a grudge against the decanter. The narrator cannot sleep in a strange room, is tortured by a high ceiling, being used to a low ceiling. What is taking place? The old pact is out of date. It contained no clause treating of high ceilings. The habit of friendship for the low ceiling is ineffectual, must die in order that a habit of friendship for the high ceiling may be born. Between this death and that birth, reality, intolerable, absorbed feverishly by his consciousness at the extreme limit of its intensity, by his total consciousness organised to avert the disaster, to create the new habit that will empty the mystery of its threat—and also of its beauty. "If Habit," writes Proust, "is a second nature, it keeps us in ignorance of the first, and is free of its cruelties and its enchantments." Our first nature, therefore, corresponding, as we shall see later, to a deeper instinct than the mere animal instinct of self-preservation, is laid bare during these periods of abandonment. And its cruelties and enchantments are the cruelties and enchantments of reality. "Enchantments of reality" has the air of a paradox. But when the object is perceived as particular and unique and not merely the member of a family, when it appears independent of any general notion and detached from the sanity of a cause, isolated and inexplicable in the light of ignorance, then and then only may it be a source of enchantment. Unfortunately Habit has laid its veto on this form of perception, its action being precisely to hide the essence—the Idea—of the object in the haze of conception—preconception. Normally we are in the position of the tourist (the traditional specification would constitute a pleonasm), whose aesthetic experience consists in a series of identifications and for whom Baedeker is the end rather than the means. Deprived by nature of the faculty of cognition and by upbringing of any acquaintance with the laws of dynamics, a brief inscription immortalises his emotion. The creature of habit turns aside from the object that cannot be made to correspond with one or other of his intellectual prejudices, that resists the propositions of his team of syntheses, organised by Habit on labour-saving principles.

Examples of these two modes—the death of Habit and the brief suspension of its vigilance—abound in Proust. I will transcribe two incidents in the life of the narrator. Of these the first, illustrative of the pact renewed, is extremely important as preparing a later incident that I will have occasion to discuss in relation to Proustian memory and Proustian revelation. The second exemplifies the pact waived in the interests of the narrator's via dolorosa.

The narrator arrives at Balbec-Plage, a holiday resort in Normandy, for the first time, accompanied by his grandmother. They are staying at the Grand Hotel. He enters his room, feverish and exhausted after his journey. But sleep, in this inferno of unfamiliar objects, is out of the question. All his faculties are on the alert, on the defensive, vigilant and taut, and as painfully incapable of relaxation as the tortured body of La Balue in his cage, where he could neither stand upright nor sit down. There is no room for his body in this vast and hideous apartment, because his attention has peopled it with gigantic furniture, a storm of sound and an agony of colour. Habit has not had time to silence the explosions of the clock, reduce the hostility of the violet curtains, remove the furniture and lower the inaccessible vault of this belvedere. Alone in this room that is not yet a room but a cavern of wild beasts, invested on all sides by the implacable strangers whose privacy he has disturbed, he desires to die. His grandmother comes in, comforts him, checks the stooping gesture that he makes to unbutton his boots, insists on helping him to undress, puts him to bed, and before leaving him makes him promise to knock on the partition that separates her room from his, should he require anything during the night. He knocks, and she comes again to him. But that night and for many nights he suffered. That suffering he interprets as the obscure, organic, humble refusal on the part of those elements that represented all that was best in his life to accept the possibility of a formula in which they would have no part. This reluctance to die, this long and desperate and daily resistance before the perpetual exfoliation of personality, explains also his horror at the idea of ever living without Gilberte Swann, of ever losing his parents, at the idea of his own death. But this terror at the thought of separation—from Gilberte, from his parents, from himself—is dissipated in a greater terror, when he thinks that to the pain of separation will succeed indifference, that the privation will cease to be a privation when the alchemy of Habit has transformed the individual capable of suffering into a stranger for whom the motives of that suffering are an idle tale, when not only the objects of his affection have vanished, but also that affection itself; and he thinks how absurd is our dream of a Paradise with retention of personality, since our life is a succession of Paradises successively denied, that the only true Paradise is the Paradise that has been lost, and that death will cure many of the desire for immortality.

The second episode that I have chosen as an illustration of the pact

waived engages the same two characters, the narrator and his grandmother. He has been staying at Doncières with his friend Saint-Loup. He
telephones to his grandmother in Paris. (After reading the description of
this telephone call and its hardly less powerful corollary, when, years later,
he speaks over the telephone with Albertine on returning home late after
his first visit to the Princesse de Guermantes, Cocteau's *Voix Humaine*
seems not merely a banality but an unnecessary banality.).After the conventional misunderstanding with the Vigilant Virgins (*sic*) of the central
exchange, he hears his grandmother's voice, or what he assumes to be her
voice, because he hears it now for the first time, in all its purity and reality,
so different from the voice that he had been accustomed to follow on the
open score of her face that he does not recognise it as hers. It is a grievous
voice, its fragility unmitigated and undisguised by the carefully arranged
mask of her features, and this strange real voice is the measure of its
owner's suffering. He hears it also as the symbol of her isolation, of their
separation, as impalpable as a voice from the dead. The voice stops. His
grandmother seems as irretrievably lost as Eurydice among the shades.
Alone before the mouthpiece he calls her name in vain. Nothing can
persuade him to remain at Doncières. He must see his grandmother. He
leaves for Paris. He surprises her reading her beloved Mme. de Sévigné.
But he is not there because she does not know that he is there. He is
present at his own absence. And, in consequence of his journey and his
anxiety, his habit is in abeyance, the habit of his tenderness for his
grandmother. His gaze is no longer the necromancy that sees in each
precious object a mirror of the past. The notion of what he should see has
not had time to interfere its prism between the eye and its object. His eye
functions with the cruel precision of a camera; it photographs the reality
of his grandmother. And he realises with horror that his grandmother is
dead, long since and many times, that the cherished familiar of his mind,
mercifully composed all along the years by the solicitude of habitual
memory, exists no longer, that this mad old woman, drowsing over her
book, overburdened with years, flushed and coarse and vulgar, is a stranger
whom he has never seen.

The respite is brief. "Of all human plants," writes Proust, "Habit
requires the least fostering, and is the first to appear on the seeming
desolation of the most barren rock." Brief, and dangerously painful. The
fundamental duty of Habit, about which it describes the futile and stupefy-
ing arabesques of its supererogations, consists in a perpetual adjustment
and readjustment of our organic sensibility to the conditions of its worlds.
Suffering represents the omission of that duty, whether through negligence

or inefficiency, and boredom its adequate performance. The pendulum oscillates between these two terms: Suffering—that opens a window on the real and is the main condition of the artistic experience, and Boredom—with its host of top-hatted and hygienic ministers, Boredom that must be considered as the most tolerable because the most durable of human evils. Considered as a progression, this endless series of renovations leaves us as indifferent as the heterogeneity of any one of its terms, and the inconsequence of any given me disturbs us as little as the comedy of substitution. Indeed, we take as little cognisance of one as of the other, unless, vaguely, after the event, or clearly, when, as in the case of Proust, two birds in the bush are of infinitely greater value than one in the hand, and because—if I may add this nox vomica to an apéritif of metaphors—the heart of the cauliflower or the ideal core of the onion would represent a more appropriate tribute to the labours of poetical excavation than the crown of bay. I draw the conclusion of this matter from Proust's treasury of nutshell phrases: "If there were no such thing as Habit, Life would of necessity appear delicious to all those whom Death would threaten at every moment, that is to say, to all Mankind."

Driving to the Guermantes Hotel the narrator feels that everything is lost, that his life is a succession of losses, devoid of reality because nothing survives, nothing of his love for Gilberte, for the Duchesse de Guermantes, for his grandmother, and now nothing of his love for Albertine, nothing of Combray and Balbec and Venice except the distorted images of voluntary memory, a life all in length, a sequence of dislocations and adjustments, where neither mystery nor beauty is sacred, where all, except the adamantine columns of his enduring boredom, has been consumed in the torrential solvent of the years, a life so protracted in the past and so meaningless in the future, so utterly bereft of any individual and permanent necessity, that his death, now or tomorrow or in a year or in ten, would be a termination but not a conclusion. And he thinks how empty is Bergotte's phrase: "the joys of the spirit." For art, which he had so long believed the one ideal and inviolate element in a corruptible world, seems now, whether because of his incurable lack of talent or its own inherent artificiality, as unreal and sterile as the constructions of a demented imagination—"that insane barrel-organ that always plays the wrong tune"; and the materials of art—Beatrice and Faust and the "azur du ciel immense et ronde" and the seagirt cities—all the absolute beauty of a magic world, as vulgar and unworthy in their reality as Rachel and Cottard, and pale and weary and cruel and inconstant and joyless as Shelley's moon. So, after years of fruitless solitude, it is without enthusiasm that he drags himself back to a society that has long since ceased to interest him. And now, on the outskirts of this futility, favoured by the very depression and fatigue that had appeared to his disgust as the aftermath of a minute and sterile lucidity (favoured, because the pretensions of a discouraged memory are for the moment reduced to the most immediate and utilitarian presentification), he is to receive the oracle that had invariably been denied to the most exalted tension of his spirit, which his intelligence had failed to extract from the seismic enigma of tree and flower and gesture and art, and suffer a religious experience in the only intelligible sense of that epithet, at once an assumption and an annunciation, so that at last he will understand the promise of Bergotte and the achievement of Elstir and the message of Vinteuil from his paradise and the dolorous and necessary course of his own life and the infinite futility—for the artist—of all that is not art.

This matinée is divided into two parts. The mystical experience and meditation of the narrator in the Cartesian hotcupboard of the Guermantes library, and the implications of that experience applied to the work of art that takes shape in his mind in the course of the reception itself. From the victory over Time he passes to the victory of Time, from the negation of Death to its affirmation. Thus, at the end as in the body of his work, Proust respects the dual significance of every condition and circumstance of life. The most ideal tautology presupposes a relation and the affirmation of equality involves only an approximate identification, and by asserting unity denies unity.

Crossing the courtyard he stumbles on the cobbles. His surroundings vanish, wattmen, stables, carriages, guests, the entire reality of the place in its hour, his anxiety and doubts as to the reality of life and art disappear, he is stunned by waves of rapture, saturated in that same felicity that had irrigated so sparingly the desolation of his life. Drabness is obliterated in an intolerable brightness. And suddenly Venice emerges from the series of forgotten days, Venice whose radiant essence he had never been able to express because it had been rejected by the imperious vulgarity of a working-day memory, but which this chance reduplication of a precarious equilibrium in the Baptistry of San Marco has lifted from its Adriatic shore and set down, a bright and vehement interloper, in the courtyard of the Princesse de Guermantes. But already the vision has faded and he is free to resume his social functions. He is ushered into the library, because ex-Mme. Verdurin, at once the Norn and Victim of Harmonic Megrims, is enthroned in the midst of her guests, passionately absorbing Rino-Gomenol in the interests of her mucous membrane and suffering the most atrocious ecstasies of Stravinskian neuralgia. While he is waiting alone for the music to be over, the miracle of the courtyard is renewed under four different forms. They have [elsewhere] been referred to. A servant strikes a spoon against a plate, he wipes his mouth with a heavily starched napkin, the water cries like a siren in the pipes, he takes down *François le Champi* from the shelves. And just as the Piazza di San Marco burst its way into the courtyard and there asserted its luminous and fleeting domination, so now the library is successively invaded by a forest, the high tide breaking on the shore at Balbec, the vast dining room of the Grand Hotel flooded, like an aquarium, with the sunset and the evening sea, and lastly Combray and its "ways" and the deferential transmission of a sour and distinguished prose, shaped and stated by his mother's voice, muted and sweetened almost to a lullaby, unwinding all night long its reassuring foil of sound before a child's insomnia.

The most successful evocative experiment can only project the echo of a past sensation, because, being an act of intellection, it is conditioned by the prejudices of the intelligence which abstracts from any given sensation, as being illogical and insignificant, a discordant and frivolous intruder, whatever word or gesture, sound or perfume, cannot be fitted into the puzzle of a concept. But the essence of any new experience is contained precisely in this mysterious element that the vigilant will rejects as an anachronism. It is the axis about which the sensation pivots, the centre of gravity of its coherence. So that no amount of voluntary manipulation can reconstitute in its integrity an impression that the will has—so to speak— buckled into incoherence. But if, *by accident,* and given favourable circum- stances (a relaxation of the subject's habit of thought and a reduction of the radius of his memory, a generally diminished tension of consciousness following upon a phrase of extreme discouragement), if by some miracle of analogy the central impression of a past sensation recurs as an immediate stimulus which can be instinctively identified by the subject with the model of duplication (*whose integral purity has been retained because it has been forgotten*), then the total past sensation, not its echo nor its copy, but the sensation itself, annihilating every spatial and temporal restriction, comes in a rush to engulf the subject in all the beauty of its infallible proportion. Thus the sound produced by a spoon struck against a plate is subcon- sciously identified by the narrator with the sound of a hammer struck by a mechanic against the wheel of a train drawn up before a wood, a sound that his will had rejected as extraneous to its immediate activity. But a subconscious and disinterested act of perception has reduced the object—the wood—to its immaterial and spiritually digestible equivalent, and the record of this pure act of cognition has not merely been associated with this sound of a hammer struck against a wheel, but centralised about it. The mood, as usual, has no importance. The point of departure of the Proustian exposition is not the crystalline agglomeration but its kernel—the crystallised. The most trivial experience—he says in effect—is encrusted with elements that logically are not related to it and have consequently been rejected by our intelligence: it is imprisoned in a vase filled with a certain perfume and a certain colour and raised to a certain temperature. These vases are suspended along the height of our years, and, not being accessible to our intelligent memory, are in a sense immune, the purity of their climatic content is guaranteed by forgetfulness, each one is kept at its distance, at its date. So that when the imprisoned microcosm is besieged in the manner described, we are flooded by a new air and a new perfume (new precisely because already experienced), and we breathe the true air of Paradise, of the only Paradise that is not the dream of a madman, the Paradise that has been lost.

The identification of immediate with past experience, the recurrence of past action or reaction in the present, amounts to a participation between the ideal and the real, imagination and direct apprehension, symbol and substance. Such participation frees the essential reality that is denied to the contemplative as to the active life. What is common to present and past is more essential than either taken separately. Reality, whether approached imaginatively or empirically, remains a surface, hermetic. Imagination, applied—a priori—to what is absent, is exercised in vacuo and cannot tolerate the limits of the real. Nor is any direct and purely experimental contact possible between subject and object, because they are automatically separated by the subject's consciousness of perception, and the object loses its purity and becomes a mere intellectual pretext or motive. But, thanks to this reduplication, the experience is at once imaginative and empirical, at once an evocation and a direct perception, real without being merely actual, ideal without being merely abstract, the ideal real, the essential, the extratemporal. But if this mystical experience communicates an extratemporal essence, it follows that the communicant is for the moment an extratemporal being. Consequently the Proustian solution consists, in so far as it has been examined, in the negation of Time and Death, the negation of Death because the negation of Time. Death is dead because Time is dead. (At this point a brief impertinence, which consists in considering *Le Temps retrouvé* almost as inappropriate a description of the Proustian solution as *Crime and Punishment* of a master-piece that contains no allusion to either crime or punishment. Time is not recovered, it is obliterated. Time is recovered, and Death with it, when he leaves the library and joins the guests, perched in precarious decrepitude on the aspiring stilts of the former and preserved from the latter by a miracle of terrified equilibrium. If the title is a good title the scene in the library is an anticlimax.) So now in the exaltation of his brief eternity, having emerged from the darkness of time and habit and passion and intelligence, he understands the necessity of art. For in the brightness of art alone can be deciphered the baffled ecstasy that he had known before the inscrutable superficies of a cloud, a triangle, a spire, a flower, a pebble, when the mystery, the essence, the Idea, imprisoned in matter, had solic-ited the bounty of a subject passing by within the shell of his impurity, and tendered, like Dante his song to the "ingegni storti e loschi," at least an incorruptible beauty:

"Ponete mente *almen* com'io son bella."

And he understands the meaning of Baudelaire's definition of reality as "the adequate union of subject and object," and more clearly than ever the grotesque fallacy of a realistic art—"that miserable statement of line and surface," and the penny-a-line vulgarity of a literature of notations.

He leaves the library and is confronted by the spectacle of Time made flesh. And whereas a moment ago the bright cymbals of two distant hours, paralysed at arm's length by the rigid spread of intervening years, had obeyed an irresistible impulse of mutual attraction, and clashed, like storm clouds, in a flash and a brazen peal, now the measure of their span from tip to tip is written on the face and frailty of the dying, curved, like Dante's proud, under the load of their years—"unwieldy, slow, heavy and pale as lead."

"e qual più pazienza avea negli atti
piangendo parea dicer:—Più non posso."

We say farewell to M. de Charlus, the Baron Palamède de Charlus, Duke of Brabant, Squire of Montargis, Prince of Oléron, Carency, Viareggio and the Dunes, the unspeakably insolent Charlus, now a humble and convulsive Lear, crowned by the silver torrent of his hair, Oedipus, senile and annulled, stooped over a missal or scraping and bowing before the astonishment of Mme. de Sainte-Euverte, scorned in the full strength of his terrible pride as the Duchesse de Caca or the Princesse de Pipi, the Archangel Raphael in his latter days, still furtively pursuing all the sons of

Toby, escorted by the faithful Jupien, Lord of the Temple of Shameless-
ness. And the dirge of his sepulchral whisper falls like clay from the spade
of a gravedigger. "Hannibal de Bréauté—dead! Antoine de Mouchy—dead!
Charles Swann—dead! Adalbert de Montmorency—dead! Baron de
Talleyrand—dead! Sosthène de Doudeauville—dead!" The narrator
accomplishes a series of identifications, of voluntary and arduous
identifications—balancing those of the library, involuntary and spontaneous.
From one sniggering and abject puppet, something between a beggarly
hawker and a moribund buffoon, he elicits his enemy, M. d'Argencourt,
as he knew him, starched and haughty and impeccable: from a stout
dowager, whom he takes at first for Mme. de Forcheville, Gilberte herself.
So they drift past, Oriane and the Duc de Guermantes, Rachel and Bloch,
Legrandin and Odette, and many others, carrying the burden of Saturn
towards the light that will rise, towards Uranus, the Sabbath star.

In Time creative and destructive Proust discovers himself as an artist:
"I understood the meaning of death, of love and vocation, of the joys of
the spirit and the utility of pain." Allusion has been made to his contempt
for the literature that "describes," for the realists and naturalists worship-
ping the offal of experience, prostrate before the epidermis and the swift
epilepsy, and content to transcribe the surface, the façade, behind which
the Idea is prisoner. Whereas the Proustian procedure is that of Apollo
flaying Marsyas and capturing without sentiment the essence, the Phrygian
waters. "Chi non ha la forza di uccidere la realtà non ha la forza di
crearla." But Proust is too much of an affectivist to be satisfied by the
intellectual symbolism of a Baudelaire, abstract and discursive. The
Baudelairean unity is a unity "post rem," a unity abstracted from plurality.
His "correspondence" is determined by a concept, therefore strictly limited
and exhausted by its own definition. Proust does not deal in concepts, he
pursues the Idea, the concrete. He admires the frescoes of the Paduan
Arena because their symbolism is handled as a reality, special, literal and
concrete, and is not merely the pictorial transmission of a notion. Dante, if
he can ever be said to have failed, fails with his purely allegorical figures,
Lucifer, the Griffin of the Purgatory and the Eagle of the Paradise, whose
significance is purely conventional and extrinsic. Here allegory fails as it
must always fail in the hands of a poet. Spenser's allegory collapses after a
few cantos. Dante, because he was an artist and not a minor prophet,
could not prevent his allegory from becoming heated and electrified into
anagogy. The *Vision of Mirza* is good allegory because it is flat writing.
For Proust the object may be a living symbol, but a symbol of itself. The
symbolism of Baudelaire has become the *autosymbolism* of Proust. Proust's

point of departure might be situated in Symbolism, or on its outskirts. But he does not proceed pari passu with France, towards an elegant scepticism and the marmorean modes, nor, as we have seen, with Daudet and the Goncourts to the "notes d'après nature," nor, of course, with the Parnassians to the ineffable gutter-snippets of François Coppée. He solicits no facts, and he chisels no Cellinesque pommels. He reacts, but in a different direction. He recedes from the Symbolists—back towards Hugo. And for that reason he is a solitary and independent figure. The only contemporary in whom I can discern something of the same retrogressive tendency is Joris Karl Huysmans. But he loathed it in himself and repressed it. He speaks bitterly of the "ineluctable gangrene of Romanticism," and yet his des Esseintes is a fabulous creature, an Alfred Lord Baudelaire.

We are frequently reminded of this romantic strain in Proust. He is romantic in his substitution of affectivity for intelligence, in his opposition of the particular affective evidential state to all the subtleties of rational cross-reference, in his rejection of the Concept in favour of the Idea, in his scepticism before causality. Thus his purely logical—as opposed to his intuitive—explanations of a certain effect invariably bristle with alternatives. He is a Romantic in his anxiety to accomplish his mission, to be a good and faithful servant. He does not seek to evade the implications of his art such as it has been revealed to him. He will write as he has lived—in Time. The classical artist assumes omniscience and omnipotence. He raises himself artificially out of Time in order to give relief to his chronology and causality to his development. Proust's chronology is extremely difficult to follow, the succession of events spasmodic, and his characters and themes, although they seem to obey an almost insane inward necessity, are presented and developed with a fine Dostoyevskian contempt for the vulgarity of a plausible concatenation. (Proust's impressionism will bring us back to Dostoyevski.) Generally speaking, the romantic artist is very much concerned with Time and aware of the importance of memory in inspiration,

> ("c'est toi qui dors dans l'ombre,
> ô sacré souvenir ! . . .)

but is inclined to sensationalise what is treated by Proust with pathological power and sobriety. With Musset, for example, the interest is more in a vague extratemporal identification, without any real cohesion or simultaneity, between the me and not-me than in the functional evocations of a specialised memory. But the analogy is too blurred and would lead nowhere, although Proust quotes Chateaubriand and Amiel as his spiritual

ancestors. It is difficult to connect Proust with this pair of melancholy
Pantheists dancing a fandango of death in the twilight. But Proust admired
the poetry of the Comtesse de Noailles. Saperlipopette!

The narrator had ascribed his "lack of talent" to a lack of observation,
or rather to what he supposed was a non-artistic habit of observation. He
was incapable of recording surface. So that when he reads such brilliant
crowded reporting as the Goncourts' Journal, the only alternative to the
conclusion that he is entirely wanting in the precious journalistic talent is
the supposition that between the banality of life and the magic of literature
there is a great gulf fixed. Either he is devoid of talent or art of reality.
And he describes the radiographical quality of his observation. The copiable
he does not see. He searches for a relation, a common factor, substrata.
Thus he is less interested in what is said than in the way in which it is said.
Similarly his faculties are more violently activated by intermediate than by
terminal—capital—stimuli. We find countless examples of these secondary
reflexes. Withdrawn in his cool dark room at Combray he extracts the
total essence of a scorching midday from the scarlet stellar blows of a
hammer in the street and the chamber music of flies in the gloom. Lying in
bed at dawn, the exact quality of the weather, temperature and visibility, is
transmitted to him in terms of sound, in the chimes and the calls of the
hawkers. Thus can be explained the primacy of instinctive perception—
intuition—in the Proustian world. Because instinct, when not vitiated by
Habit, is also a reflex, from the Proustian point of view ideally remote and
indirect, a chain reflex. Now he sees his regretted failure to observe
artistically as a series of "inspired omissions" and the work of art as
neither created nor chosen, but discovered, uncovered, excavated, pre-
existing within the artist, a law of his nature. The only reality is provided
by the hieroglyphics traced by inspired perception (identification of subject
and object). The conclusions of the intelligence are merely of arbitrary
value, potentially valid. "An impression is for the writer what an experiment is for the scientist—with this difference, that in the case of the
scientist the action of the intelligence precedes the event and in the case of
the writer follows it." Consequently for the artist, the only possible hierarchy in the world of objective phenomena is represented by a table of their
respective coefficients of penetration, that is to say, in terms of the subject.
(Another sneer at the realists.) The artist has acquired his text: the artisan
translates it. "The duty and the task of a writer (not an artist, a writer) are
those of a translator." The reality of a cloud reflected in the Vivonne is
not expressed by "Zut alors" but by the interpretation of that inspired

criticism. The verbal oblique must be restored to the upright: thus "you are charming" equals "it gives me pleasure to embrace you."

Proust's relativism and impressionism are adjuncts of this same anti-intellectual attitude. Curtius speaks of Proust's "perspectivism" and "positive relativism" as opposed to the negative relativism of the late nineteenth century, the scepticism of Renan and France. I think the phrase "positive relativism" is an oxymoron, I am almost sure that it does not apply to Proust, and I know that it came out of the Heidelberg laboratory. We have seen how in the case of Albertine (and Proust extends his experience to all human relations) the multiple aspects (read Blickpunkt for this miserable word) did not bind into any positive synthesis. The object evolves, and by the time the conclusion—if any—is reached, it is already out of date. In a sense Proust is a positivist, but his positivism has nothing to do with his relativism, which is as pessimistic and as negative as that of France, and employed as an element of comedy. The "book," for Proust a literary statement, is for the housekeeper a book of accounts and for Her Highness the visitors's register. Rachel Quand du Seigneur represents for the narrator thirty francs and a bored satisfaction, for Saint-Loup a fortune and unending misery. Similarly when Saint-Loup sees Albertine's photograph he cannot conceal his astonishment that such a vulgar nonentity should have attracted his brilliant and popular friend. The Comte de Crécy carves a turkey and establishes a calendar as surely as the death of Christ or the departure out of Egypt. For the Baron Musset's "infidèle" must be a buttons or a bus-conductor. This relativism is negative and comic. He owes his exaltation on hearing Vinteuil's music to the actress Léa, who alone could decipher the composer's posthumous manuscripts, and to the relations of Charlus with Charlie Morel, the violinist. Proust is positive only in so far as he affirms the value of intuition.

By his impressionism I mean his nonlogical statement of phenomena in the order and exactitude of their perception, before they have been distorted into intelligibility in order to be forced into a chain of cause and effect, [Examples: a napkin in the dust taken for a pencil of light, the sound of water in the pipes for a dog barking or the hooting of a siren, the noise of a spring-door closing for the orchestration of the Pilgrims' Chorus.] The painter Elstir is the type of the impressionist, stating what he sees and not what he knows he ought to see: for example, applying urban terms to the sea and marine terms to the town, so as to transmit his intuition of their homogeneity. And we are reminded of Schopenhauer's definition of the artistic procedure as "the contemplation of the world independently of the principle of reason." In this connection Proust can be related to

Dostoyevski, who states his characters without explaining them. It may be objected that Proust does little else but explain his characters. But his explanations are experimental and not demonstrative. He explains them in order that they may appear as they are—inexplicable. He explains them away.

Proust's style was generally resented in French literary circles. But now that he is no longer read, it is generously conceded that he might have written an even worse prose than he did. At the same time, it is difficult to estimate with justice a style of which one can only take cognisance by a process of deduction, in an edition that cannot be said to have transmitted the writings of Proust, but to have betrayed a tendency in that direction. For Proust, as for the painter, style is more a question of vision than of technique. Proust does not share the superstition that form is nothing and content everything, nor that the ideal literary masterpiece could only be communicated in a series of absolute and monosyllabic propositions. For Proust the quality of language is more important than any system of ethics or aesthetics. Indeed he makes no attempt to dissociate form from content. The one is a concretion of the other, the revelation of a world. The Proustian world is expressed metaphorically by the artisan because it is apprehended metaphorically by the artist: the indirect and comparative expression of indirect and comparative perception. The rhetorical equivalent of the Proustian real is the chain figure of the metaphor. It is a tiring style, but it does not tire the mind. The clarity of the phrase is cumulative and explosive. One's fatigue is a fatigue of the heart, a blood fatigue. One is exhausted and angry after an hour, submerged, dominated by the crest and break of metaphor after metaphor: but never stupefied. The complaint that it is an involved style, full of periphrasis, obscure and impossible to follow, has no foundation whatsoever.

It is significant that the majority of his images are botanical. He assimilates the human to the vegetal. He is conscious of humanity as flora, never as fauna. (There are no black cats and faithful hounds in Proust.) He deplores "the time one wastes in upholstering one's life with a human and parasitic vegetation." The wife and son of the Sidaner amateur appear to him on the shore at Balbec as two flowering ranunculi. Albertine's laugh has the colour and smell of a geranium. Gilberte and Odette are lilacs, white and violet. He speaks of a scene in *Pelléas et Mélisande* that exasperates his rose fever and makes him sneeze. This preoccupation accompanies very naturally his complete indifference to moral values and human justices. Flower and plant have no conscious will. They are shameless, exposing their genitals. And so in a sense are Proust's men and women, whose will is blind and hard, but never self-conscious, never abolished in the pure perception of a pure subject. They are victims of their volition, active with a grotesque predetermined activity, within the narrow limits of an impure world. But shameless. There is no question of right and wrong. Homosexuality is never called a vice: it is as devoid of moral implications as the mode of fecundation of the *Primula veris* or the *Lythrum salicoria*. And, like members of the vegetable world, they seem to solicit a pure subject, so that they may pass from a state of blind will to a state of representation. Proust is that pure subject. He is almost exempt from the impurity of will. He deplores his lack of will until he understands that will, being utilitarian, a servant of intelligence and habit, is not a condition of the artistic experience. When the subject is exempt from will the object is exempt from causality (Time and Space taken together). And this human vegetation is purified in the transcendental aperception that can capture the Model, the Idea, the Thing in itself.

So that there is no collapse of the will in Proust, as there is for example in Spenser and Keats and Giorgione. He sits up all night in Paris, with a branch of apple blossom laid beside his lamp, staring at the foam of the white corollae until the dawn comes to redden them. But this is not the terrible panic-stricken stasis of Keats, crouched in a mossy thicket, annulled, like a bee, in sweetness, "drowsed with the fume of poppies" and watching "the last oozings, hours by hours"; nor yet the remote, still, almost breathless passion of a Giorgione youth, the spirit shattered in corruption, damp and rotting, so finely suggested by d'Annunzio in his description of the Concerto ("ma se io penso alle sue mani nascoste, le immagino nell'atto di frangere le foglie del lauro per profumarsene le dita") and so grossly misinterpreted by the same writer when he sees in the rapt doomed figure of the Tempesta a vulgar Leander resting between orgasms; nor yet the horrible pomegranates of "Il Fuoco," bursting and bleeding, dripping the red ooze of their seed, putrid on the putrid water. The Proustian stasis is contemplative, a pure act of understanding, will-less, the "amabilis insania" and the "hölder Wahnsinn."

A book could be written on the significance of music in the work of Proust, in particular of the music of Vinteuil: the Sonata and the Septuor. The influence of Schopenhauer on this aspect of the Proustian demonstration is unquestionable. Schopenhauer rejects the Leibnitzian view of music as "occult arithmetic," and in his aesthetics separates it from the other arts, which can only produce the Idea with its concomitant phenomena, whereas music is the Idea itself, unaware of the world of phenomena, existing ideally outside the universe, apprehended not in Space but in Time only, and consequently untouched by the teleological hypothesis. This essential quality of music is distorted by the listener who, being an impure subject, insists on giving a figure to that which is ideal and invisible, on incarnating the Idea in what he conceives to be an appropriate paradigm. Thus, by definition, opera is a hideous corruption of this most immaterial of all the arts: the words of a libretto are to the musical phrase that they particularise what the Vendôme Column, for example, is to the ideal perpendicular. From this point of view opera is less complete than vaude-ville, which at least inaugurates the comedy of an exhaustive enumeration. These considerations explain the beautiful convention of the "da capo" as a testimony to the intimate and ineffable nature of an art that is perfectly intelligible and perfectly inexplicable. Music is the catalytic element in the work of Proust. It asserts to his unbelief the permanence of personality and the reality of art. It synthesises the moments of privilege and runs parallel to them. In one passage he describes the recurrent mystical experience as "a purely musical impression, nonextensive, entirely original, irreducible to any other order of impression, . . . sine materia." The narrator—unlike Swann who identifies the "little phrase" of the Sonata with Odette, spatialises what is extraspatial, establishes it as the national anthem of his love—sees in the red phrase of the Septuor, trumpeting its victory in the last move-ment like a Mantegna archangel clothed in scarlet, the ideal and immate-rial statement of the essence of a unique beauty, a unique world, the invariable world and beauty of Vinteuil, expressed timidly, as a prayer, in the Sonata, imploringly, as an aspiration, in the Septuor, the "invisible reality" that damns the life of the body on earth as a pensum and reveals the meaning of the word: "defunctus."

GERMAINE BRÉE

The Closed Door

When we pass from *Sodome et Gomorrhe* to *La Prisonnière* we leave
one world and enter another. The Combray cycle does not reappear until
the end of *Albertine disparue*. Albertine is dead by then, and with time the
memory of her has died too. "My mother," writes the narrator, "had
taken me to spend a few days in Venice, and there I delighted in impressions much like those I have so often felt in Combray, but transposed into
an entirely different and richer dimension." Combray then reappears in
Venice:

> When at ten o'clock in the morning my shutters were thrown
> open, I saw ablaze in the sunlight, not the black marble into
> which the slates of St-Hilaire used to turn, but the Golden
> Angel on the Campanile of St-Mark's ... I was reminded of
> the shops of Combray ... But on the second morning what I
> saw when I woke up were the impressions of my first morning
> stroll in Venice, Venice whose daily life was no less real than
> that of Combray, where as in Combray on Sunday mornings
> one had the delight of emerging upon a festive street.

Sundays in Venice, in the spring, are superimposed upon the Sundays in
Combray and carry along in their wake Mme Sazerat, Mme de Villeparisis,
M. de Norpois; and then two letters received by the narrator recall all the
people belonging to Swann's way and the Guermantes. Gilberte has mar-

From *Marcel Proust and Deliverance from Time*, translated by Catherine Jandine
Richards and Anne D. Truitt. © 1955, 1969 by Trustees of Rutgers College in New
Jersey. Rutgers University Press, 1969.

37

ried Saint-Loup and, on Charlus's side, Jupien's niece has married the
young Marquis de Cambremer. Tansonville has joined Guermantes and
Balbec has met Paris. The social cycles which began in Combray are
closed, the Swann cycle as well as the Charlus cycle. Everything in *Sodome
et Gomorrhe* had already forecast this meeting. When M. de Charlus
appears at La Raspelière after his "conjunction" with Jupien, we see the
social spheres draw near each other; the slow rising of Odette's salon
paves the way for the Saint-Loup-Gilberte union, and "that crossing of
two generations and two societies" which the narrator witnesses.

In Venice an amusing and distressing scene takes place between the
narrator and his mother; it recalls the bedtime scene in Combray:

> When I heard, on the very day upon which we were to start for
> Paris, that Mme Putbus, and consequently her maid, had just
> arrived in Venice, I asked my mother to put off our departure
> for a few days; her air of not taking my request into consider-
> ation, of not even listening to it seriously, reawakened in my
> nerves, excited by the Venetian springtime, that old desire
> to rebel against an imaginary plot woven against me by my
> parents ... that fighting spirit, that desire which drove me in
> the past to enforce my wishes upon the people whom I loved
> best in the world, though I was prepared to conform to their
> wishes after I had succeeded in making them yield.

This time the narrator does not win out as he had in Combray. He tries at
first to impose upon his mother the decision to remain in Venice. She
refuses and he decides to remain there alone: "And when the hour came at
which, accompanied by all my luggage, she set off for the station, I
ordered a drink to be brought out to me on the terrace overlooking the
canal, and settled down there, watching the sunset, while from a boat that
had stopped in front of the hotel a musician sang 'O Sole Mio.' "

In Combray the decision to disobey his mother had stilled the child's
anguish. In Venice, this decision is followed by an anxiety that mounts in
crescendo as the hour of the train's departure approaches. To the accom-
paniment of "O Sole Mio," his unhappiness strips Venice of its poetry; it
becomes commonplace, cramped, unfriendly, and distant. Suddenly the
young man jumps up and rushes to rejoin his mother just before the train
leaves. The moral cycle begun in Combray, it seems, is also closed. Instead
of forcing his mother to give in to his whims, this time he gives way to her.
The virtues of Combray at last begin to exert an influence on him.

It is toward Combray, to Tansonville, where he stays with Gilberte, that the narrator "returns." The world he had sought to know is now explored; he knows its limits, for he has reached them. His childhood dream is spent. The two "extra-terrestrial" directions of Méséglise and Guermantes, united socially, close in geographically one upon the other:

> I repeated every evening, in the opposite direction, the walks which we used to take in Combray, in the afternoon when we went toward Méséglise . . . The walks that we took thus together were very often those that I used to take as a child . . . And it distressed me to find how little I relived my early years. I thought the Vivonne a meager ugly rivulet beneath its towpath.

The source of the Vivonne is only "a kind of square washbasin in which bubbles rose," and it is now "easy to go to Guermantes by way of Méséglise." Combray has lost its dimension of mystery and beauty. The door to the past is closed.

However, other perspectives have opened for the narrator. Complex and mobile depths now appear behind the flat magic-lantern images that once were the inhabitants of Tansonville or Guermantes. Instead of an image, each name evokes a network of actions and reactions, of causes and consequences, of relationships in perpetual flux. The simple categories according to which the intellectual and moral world of Combray was organized are irremediably confused; the people one knows are also those whom "one does not know." All the narrator's experiences and all his meditations have only brought him into collision with the unknowable. He discerns a certain permanence in the mechanisms of human behavior, which are always the same. What are Saint-Loup, Gilberte, and Morel if not a variation of the Charlus, Swann, and Odette combination? But the narrator discerns nothing beyond that; on the intellectual side too the world is closed and offers nothing further to his investigation.

Nor does there seem to remain anything to discover in himself. He knows so well the rules of his own sensitivity that he can automatically create love in himself. He knows by heart the only lesson he has learned from his repeated experiences: that love is merely a mirror one holds out to a woman without ever seeing in it anything but one's own image; and, too, that human destiny condemns everything to disappear with time into oblivion and into death, the final obliteration.

The horizon is closed on all sides. There remains nothing for the narrator to do but to wait behind the walls of a sanatorium for death to put an end to a "lost" life. He feels as though he has outlived himself, for living merely means prolonging his existence without opening up any new horizons. The setting for the final dramatic moment of his life is now complete; he is ready for the return to Combray, this time through memory and the magic words *François le Champi*.

Yet between *Sodome et Gomorrhe* and the trip to Venice at the end of *Albertine disparue* which leads to the narrator's return to Combray, stretch the two strange and often arid volumes which trace the evolution of the narrator's troubled love for Albertine. His plan for a trip to Venice, constantly put off, reappears at more or less regular intervals in *La Prisonnière* and *Albertine disparue*, as if to bridge the gap between *Sodome* and the Venice episode. But in Balbec a sudden change of tone introduces the episode which adumbrates *La Prisonnière;* and we move from *Albertine disparue* on to Venice through a break in the story, but with no transition.

There are three distinct cycles in *A la recherche du temps perdu:* the Swann cycle, the Charlus cycle, and the Albertine cycle. It is true that Proust, through his narrator, links Albertine to Swann: "It was he who had made me want to go to Balbec . . . without which I shouldn't have known Albertine." Throughout his story he introduces markers which connect Albertine to everything that has gone before; through Mlle Vinteuil and the theme of homosexuality, she is even connected with Combray. But, as the proofs of the 1913 edition reveal, Proust added this cycle to his book after the publication of *Du Côté de chez Swann* and had not originally planned for it. Swann is, as the narrator says, the "pedestal" which supports the novel. He introduces us to all the groups whom the narrator explores and to most of the themes of the novel: the Guermantes, the Verdurins, and indirectly through his friendship with Charlus, the homosexual set. It is he who speaks to the narrator of Balbec and Venice, of Bergotte and La Berma; he knows Elstir and is moved by Vinteuil's Sonata. His love for Odette is a prelude to the narrator's loves. But although Swann does indeed announce all the themes of *A la recherche du temps perdu,* he does not prepare us at all for Albertine.

Albertine appears at about the same time as M. de Charlus, but her story never has any point of contact with the baron's. The young girl, silent and passive, merely accompanies the narrator during his visits to La Raspelière, whither Charlus follows Morel. Charlus's adventures are developed on an entirely different level. Albertine has no connection either with the Swanns or the Guermantes. For a while she appears in Balbec as one of the "jeunes filles en fleurs." Then she reappears in a minor rôle in the second part of the *Côté de Guermantes*. During the narrator's second stay in Balbec, the theme of Gomorrah begins to cast its shadow on her, but the narrator's love for her still develops along the normal lines of Proustian loves, through the fluctuations of jealousy toward habit and boredom.

As soon as the narrator decides he will never be separated from Albertine, we change worlds. If the Guermantes are still in the picture, it is only in a subordinate rôle. The Verdurins reappear but they too are only incidental to the story of Albertine. Never, after Balbec, do Albertine and the narrator appear together in a salon. Gradually they are surrounded by a shadowy world, hinted at rather than described, in which Andrée, the chauffeur, Bloch's cousin Léa, Aimé, the headwaiter of the Balbec hotel, play curious parts. This world has ramifications in the sphere of Charlus's hidden life and in the sordid squabbles between Morel and Jupien's niece; it is a world of shady servants and pimps, characterized by a certain depravity to which the rest of the novel has not accustomed us. It is through Morel that the cycle of Albertine touches the Charlus cycle.

Until *La Prisonnière*, love, as Proust evokes it, is surrounded with worldliness and poetry at its birth, and has a certain dignity in its sadness when the lover feels the being to whom he is attached elude him. Even in jealousy, love retains in some measure an atmosphere of courtesy. Swann's jealousy, however painful and unpleasant, is shrouded in melancholy and is dignified by the unreal and leisurely atmosphere in which his story takes place. His very suffering is imbued with the charm which emanates from the first picture we have of Swann in Combray, elegant, mysterious, and peacefully married to Odette. The narrator's love for Gilberte, with its exchanges of childish fetishes, marbles, books, letters, its chocolate cakes, its games of prisoner's base, its joys and sorrows, is all imbued with the innocence of childhood, with solid family security and with the glamour emanating from Odette Swann. The sunlight of Balbec and all the joys of life on the beach set the tone of the narrator's first love for Albertine, while his slow accession to the Guermantes's world dominates its second phase.

The world of *La Prisonnière* and of *Albertine disparue*, after a few pages of prelude, is completely lacking in such graces, in any poetic background; nothing redeems its harshness. The beautiful poetic passages which *La Prisonnière* contains, and there are many, seem like separate selections which fit in rather badly with the remainder of the story. Proust seems not to have had sufficient time in this part of his work to make the transformations which might have blended it into a harmonious whole. A moralizing tone, which is not in keeping with the situation presented, sometimes dominates the narrative, creating a strange atmosphere of un-easiness. The narrator, in Venice, has forgotten this period of his life. The reader has not, and this part of the book never quite gives the impression of complete mastery which makes a character like Charlus come to life and gives him a sane reality.

The story told by Proust in this last part of his work seems to be related to a particular incident in his own life, the love he had for his secretary, young Agostinelli, and his grief at the young man's death in an airplane accident. In any event, it has its roots in a somewhat dark side of Proust's personality, revealed by his habit of actually having "prisoners" in his house, jealously guarded, and hidden from his friends. The episode does not seem to have benefited from the filtering of memories in time, which Proust himself considers necessary to art. The tale is still laden with all the raw material of life and the artistic transposition remains imperfect. In any case, the life described is very curious.

The narrator is cloistered in a room from which he rarely emerges; Albertine lives in the same apartment and goes out all the time, accompanied by a chauffeur, a friend of Morel and of Andrée. The narrator authorizes these outings and receives reports from the chauffeur and from Andrée on any meetings which Albertine may have had. Albertine is never alone. On these terms, the narrator showers expensive presents upon her, and at the same time acts the rôle of accuser, avidly questioning her about her slightest gestures and words, present or past. He seems to have only one object, to catch her in the wrong. Through the slow development of these two parts of the novel, what breaks through at times and gives a new dimension to the story, is neither dream nor memory, nor love, nor even homosexual love, but the shadow of impending madness. It threatens to shut upon the narrator a door too heavy to be easily reopened. The narrator escapes from his creator, and betrays him. At no time does Proust seem to take measure of all the strangeness of the world into which he thrusts us, and which at times is more reminiscent of a psychiatric case history than of literature.

After Swann, after Charlus, the narrator now moves into the foreground. He occupies it almost alone from his bed in the bedroom which he seldom leaves. Until now he has played the apparently modest but all-powerful rôle of the magician who comments on the shadows he evokes, his own as well as others. He has revealed himself primarily through the states of mind which gave their own color to each part of his story: the quiet luminous reveries of Combray, the lively sunlit dreams of Balbec, the amused detachment mingled with curiosity of Guermantes, the Cervantes-like vision of Sodome. He has communicated his states of mind to the reader, who always adopts his point of view. This is no longer true in *La*

Prisonnière and *Albertine disparue*. The reader's point of view diverges from the narrator's. The reader must make an effort which the previous part of the novel does not demand in order to accept the bizarre situation as a real premise, even within the framework of fiction. Perhaps one should say especially within the framework of fiction. The strange and far too peculiar reality which gleams through the story challenges even literature. The reader cannot easily enter Albertine's world.

The story unfolds against a background of rather curious facts. A young woman, of her own free will, goes to live with the narrator and is thereby condemned to his ugly accusations. She is surrounded by a network of spies and subjected to incessant interrogation. Her slightest words are used against her, her slightest plans crossed. Her relations with the narrator are those of suspect and inquisitor. But no trial ever takes place; the spies are counteragents and all the plots made by the narrator are turned against him to betray him in fictitious trips, mythical outings, spurious explanations, lying servants. The narrator is a victim of his own inquisition and in this double rôle becomes odious. The masochism he caters to in preparing the setting for his own suffering and the latent sadism which drives him to pursue and track down Albertine, even beyond death, make the reader uneasy and doubtful as to the purpose of such a game.

A rather obscure psychological drama serves as background for these facts. The themes of homosexuality, of jealousy, of guilt and expiation, are strangely and apparently arbitrarily mingled. A direct and unexpected moral concern appears and throws a sinister light even upon the moving story of Swann. The narrator tells us that when he listened to Swann's story, he "had dangerously allowed to widen in him the noxious path, destined to be painful, of knowledge." The very tone tends, at times, to become solemn and oratorical, vibrating with an emotion which has slipped into the story from the outside and which is not created by it. The last pages of *Sodome et Gomorrhe* are heavily charged with such an emotion. The words torture, fatal, terrible, punishment, grief, suffering, pile up for ten or more pages. The "deluge of reality" which, according to the narrator, "submerges" him, is "enormous" compared with the "timid and insignificant suppositions that had foreshadowed it." The intensity of the tone is surprising and seems out of proportion to the cause—the suspicion that Albertine is a lesbian—even if we take into account the explosive force of the memory of Montjouvain. It is this memory surging from the past which sets off the drama. Proust clearly indicates his intention to explore the jealousy connected with homosexuality.

The narrator wants to break off with Albertine because a word which she says by chance about Mlle Vinteuil brings to his memory the image of Montjouvain: "kept alive deep within me . . . to torture me, to punish me, who knows, perhaps for having let my grandmother die." Nothing in the story which precedes explains by what "crossroad" the image of Montjouvain is connected in the narrator's world with the idea of punishment. This association of ideas is all the more surprising because it is linked with a feeling of guilt about his dead grandmother, a "victim," it would seem, of her grandson. However, the association is sustained. The narrator sees the image of Montjouvain springing up "like Orestes from the depths of the night where it had seemed forever buried, striking like an avenger in order to cast him into a life deservedly terrible and new." Deservedly? Nothing in the narrator's life explains this qualification. His laziness seems a negligible shortcoming to cause such a "rain of brimstone and fire." Nothing explains his punishment, unless it be the intimate drama that Proust himself lived, and into which he did not want to drag his narrator but which here escapes his control.

In Proust there is always a connection between the idea of carnal love and sacrilege. The sacrilege relates to his beloved mother. He often uses the words "pleasure" and "vice" interchangeably. The connection may be attributed to his own position as a homosexual, the adored son of an austere mother of strict morality whom he loved and to whom he was very close in thought and feeling. This theme of culpability appears in one of Proust's first stories in *Les Plaisirs et les jours,* "The Confession of a Young Girl." Coming unexpectedly upon her daughter in the throes of sexual pleasure in the arms of a young man, the mother falls and dies; there remains nothing for the stricken girl to do but to commit suicide. The Montjouvain situation follows a similar pattern, but adds to it the theme of homosexuality. Mlle Vinteuil's sapphism slowly kills her father. After his death, before she gives herself up to the pleasure which makes her feel guilty, Mlle Vinteuil persuades her friend to spit on the photograph of her father whom, nonetheless, she loves. Her feelings of guilt are disclosed by this sadistic gesture. The narrator himself follows this pattern. If his mother, he tells us, had discovered Albertine's friendship for Mlle Vinteuil "It would have been an unsurmountable obstacle . . . not only to a marriage . . . but even to her spending a few days in the house." Why, then, since it is Albertine who is suspected of sapphism, and since it is Mlle Vinteuil who practices it, this curious retrospective self-accusation of the narrator when he accuses himself of having killed his grandmother? Why this offer to expiate a grave sin precisely by the compensating suffering which Albertine's special vice causes him?

The relationship between Albertine and the narrator is not only that between a lover and the woman of whom he is jealous. In order to preserve his narrator from the too special tendency of Sodom, perhaps to put him at a greater distance from himself, Proust has until now, though not without some difficulty, kept him outside the realm of homosexuality. That he should once, through an open window, come upon a scene of sapphism, is acceptable to us; that once, hidden under a stairway, he should by chance witness from beginning to end the consummation of the Charlus-Jupien union we are also willing to accept; that still by chance he should discover Jupien's house of ill-fame adds up to a lot of chances; but when he obstinately sets about to make love to a little bourgeoise and by chance again she evokes the maze of homosexuality which he himself has never explored, credulity falters. If we see behind Albertine the silhouette of Agostinelli or other prisoners, we also seem to see a part of Proust himself which he can, through the narrator, harshly rebuke.

The shadow of the narrator's mother also plays its part in this portion of the novel. She and Albertine are never together in the apartment; their simultaneous presence seems to be incompatible. The narrator's mother vainly opposes the young couple's intimacy. Yet the narrator, with a lack of filial respect reminiscent of Mlle Vinteuil's, constantly compares the peace induced by his erotic games with Albertine with the peace which his mother's presence used to bestow upon him at night. On the other hand, when he speaks to Albertine about her "vice" and the "wrong" she does, he uses, he tells us, the same high moral tone his mother uses when she upbraids him. The problem which Albertine's way of life poses for the narrator is, indeed, exactly the same as that posed for Mme Proust by the son who loved her deeply, yet concealed from her a whole portion of his existence which she must, however, have suspected.

There are moments in *La Prisonnière* when the feverish agitations of the narrator's mind do not apparently concern jealousy but rather what could easily be the state of perpetual moral struggle in which Proust found himself caught. This is the only explanation for the high moral tone of certain conversations which the narrator has with his companion, and the judgments he passes on her. It also explains why he is so quick to point out Albertine as the guilty one, condemned in advance and pilloried with such righteous indignation. Besides her use as a pretext for jealousy, Albertine seems also useful as a scapegoat.

"I preferred," the narrator says, "to have life remain at the high level of my intuitions, in particular the intuition which I had had that first day on the beach, when I thought that those girls *embodied the frenzy of pleasure, were vice incarnate,* and again on the evening when I had seen Albertine's teacher leading the passionate girl home to the little villa, as one thrusts into its cage a wild animal which nothing in the future, despite appearances, will ever succeed in taming, even if my intuitions did not agree with what Bloch had told me when he had made the world seem so fair to me, making me thrill at every encounter during my walks by showing me the universality of desire."

Albertine disappears in death, laden with all the sins of the flesh. "Perhaps," says the narrator about Bergotte, "it is only in really vicious lives that the problem of morality can be posed with all the force of indignation." There is much indignation in *La Prisonnière*. Homosexuality appears there as a heavy moral responsibility which makes any chance of happiness quite problematical.

The very title, *La Prisonnière*, is ambiguous. The narrator explains: he learns by chance from Albertine, that the friend who brought her up is Mlle Vinteuil; "But the words: 'That friend is Mlle Vinteuil' had been the 'Open Sesame' which I myself would have been unable to find and which had let Albertine into the depths of my broken heart. And I could have searched a hundred years without finding the means of opening the door that had closed on her."

So Albertine is a prisoner in the narrator's heart. She is also prisoner of an image, that of Montjouvain, and of a story, Swann's. A prisoner also, according to the narrator, of her taste for pleasure and her weakness for women. She is an actual prisoner too, since she lives with a man who sets spies on her and subjects her to his slightest whim. "She was startled to learn," when she settled down in Paris at the narrator's, "that she was in a strange world that had customs unknown to her, regulated by a code that could not be infringed."

But is it not rather the narrator who is prisoner? Prisoner of his temperament which keeps him locked up in a room; prisoner of the images which obsess him; prisoner of roving desires for passersby—milkmaids and others—which his imagination forces Albertine to satisfy for him; prisoner of the network of spying and lies which he builds up; and, finally, prisoner of all that phantasmagoria which keeps him furthest from what he wants to be—an author. Albertine, is, after all, only the instrument he uses to build an imaginary life which diverts his thoughts from work. It is not Albertine, but the narrator's mind—his will, his very life—that is imprisoned; it will be set free only by Albertine's death. The whole relation between Albertine and the narrator has the same ambivalence as their tormentor-victim relationship.

In that sense, *La Prisonnière* and *Albertine disparue* have a very special importance in the novel. The narrator has until now moved toward life, toward joys outside himself which tempted him like veritable Armida's gardens. Nothing has led him to expect the dark dungeon he is now in; he has had only the faintest intimations that it might exist. And his unexpected captivity sometimes seems all too lengthy to the reader.

However, once these reservations have been made, once we have accepted the conventions which Proust imposes, we gradually succumb to the tone peculiar to this part of the novel. It is marked by a long meditative soliloquy which connects it with the opening pages of the novel in which Combray is first evoked. The theme of the room, of sleep and awakening, re-emerges. The narrator leaves the realm of the imaginary in order to "climb once more the abrupt slope of introspection" in an effort to understand the test he is undergoing. Except for the long "interpolated" passages in which Morel, Charlus, and the Verdurins are discussed, the narrator's attention is focussed almost entirely on the "changing moods" of his "inner climate." What prevails over his shifting moods and the febrility of his analyses is the muted tone of meditation; everything appears to be subdued by its passage from an inner distance. The "game of hide-and-seek" which the narrator and Albertine play is symbolic rather than real and, although described at length, it is only the means whereby Proust throws light upon a more general underlying drama: that of solitude and of loneliness.

The fluctuations and chronic fits of jealousy develop in slow motion, but they only repeat, amplify, and clarify the rhythm of the malady that Swann knew so well. While jealousy seems always to trample the same threshing floor, beating blindly over the same ground, the narrator progresses toward a knowledge of a different kind. He is torn between two opposite poles, for he begins to realize the two-sided nature of his solitude. At the same time, he seeks to be rid of his loneliness, at any price:

> The bonds which unite another person with ourselves exist only
> in our youth. As memory grows fainter they become flaccid;
> notwithstanding the illusion by which we would fain be cheated
> and with which we would cheat other people because of love,

friendship, politeness, deference, or duty, *we exist alone.* Man
is a creature who cannot emerge from himself; and when he
asserts otherwise, he lies.

This is the truth toward which, in spite of himself, the narrator progresses.
It remains when the particular experience which made it his is completely
forgotten.

Every man is a prisoner, shut up in himself as the narrator is shut up
in his room; but it is not a state he accepts any more readily than the
narrator, who, it becomes apparent, uses jealousy to struggle every inch of
the way against whatever separates him from Albertine:

> It was just as well, I told myself, that by incessantly asking
> myself what she could be doing, thinking, wanting, at every
> moment . . . I should keep that door open, that communicating
> door which love had opened in me, and that I should feel
> another person's life flood through open sluices into the reser-
> voir which must not become stagnant.

The story henceforth assumes its general import, which far surpasses the
narrator's particular and somewhat bizarre story. Furthermore, it takes its
place in the body of the novel, for what the author discovers during his
liaison with Albertine is that she is only the human pretext for an intellectual activity experienced in relation to her. Instead of being simply a
creature from whom some tenderness may be expected, Albertine is the
enigma that any human being presents to the intellect. Through her the
narrator realizes his own limitations, realizes that he cannot break through
them, and at the same time learns that the life of any other creature is
impenetrable. In thus defining the problem of solitude, though without
clarifying it, *La Prisonnière* and *Albertine disparue* give the novel its moral
dimension. The "communicating door" opened by love is closed to the
narrator; nothing remains for him but to turn toward another door, the
door Vinteuil's Septet opens in him and which the Sonata had for an
instant opened in Swann.

The two themes, solitude and the uneasy obsession about Albertine,
alternate quite regularly in *La Prisonnière.* The calm opening pages of this
volume are in striking contrast with the harassed tone of the last pages of
Sodome et Gomorrhe, a contrast which is characteristic of the whole story,
although the theme of anxiety gradually predominates over that of calm:

> At daybreak, my face still turned to the wall, and before I had
> seen above the big inner curtains the shade of the first streaks

of light, I could already tell what sort of day it was. The first sounds from the street had given me the information—whether they came to my ears dulled and distorted by the moisture of the atmosphere or quivering like arrows in the resonant and empty area of a spacious, crisply frozen, pure morning; as soon as I heard the clatter of the first streetcar, I could tell whether it was sodden with rain or setting forth into the blue. And perhaps these sounds had themselves been forestalled by some swifter and more pervasive emanation which, stealing into my slumber, diffused it in a melancholy that seemed to forecast snow, or gave utterance (through the lips of a little person who occasionally reappeared there) to so many hymns to the glory of the sun that, having first of all begun to smile in my sleep, having prepared my eyes, behind their shut lids to be dazzled, I awoke finally amid deafening peals of music.

In this peaceful description the narrator creates the atmosphere of a daily life which seems at first anchored in "domestic peace" because of the presence of Albertine in an adjacent room. His waking up, Albertine's visit, her outing, her return, her presence in the evening, and the peace of the night are brought bit by bit into the harmony.

But two opposing elements soon stand out. The morning awakenings, the street cries, the atmospheric changes bring with them happy peace; Albertine's presence destroys it. "It was especially from my room that I was aware, during this period, of life outside of me." But the narrator perceives this outside life only when Albertine is not around him; "as soon as she had left for her outing I was revived, if only for a few moments, by the virtues of solitude." As soon as Albertine appears, either in person or in the narrator's thought, this atmosphere is dispelled. The exchange, peaceful as breathing, that had been made in solitude between the narrator's inner and outer worlds gives way to an uneasy restlessness. His attention is scattered; his thoughts rush around in a series of abrupt, blind sallies. "She was capable," he tells us of Albertine, "of causing me suffering, but not joy." What he expects from her above all is peace of mind, a peace which will free his spirit so that nothing will interfere with his perceptions. In a singular contradiction, he asks Albertine to make solitude possible for him by assuring him complete peace of mind. But in order to achieve this peace of mind he cannot countenance the slightest mystery about her, he must know everything about her:

The image that I sought . . . was no longer that of an Albertine who led a life about which I knew nothing, it was that of an

> Albertine who was not the reflection of a far-away world, but
> who wanted nothing except to be with me, to be just like me,
> an Albertine who was the reflection of what was mine and not
> of the unknown.

The narrator conceives his own life as being at the center of Albertine's
universe, and everything in her life as depending upon it. What he wants
from her is perfect unison with himself. The narrator's jealousy is focussed
on what remains unknown in Albertine—all the people she knows, all her
actions, all her desires beyond himself. He tells us that "we feel love for a
person of whose actions we are jealous." Because of his jealousy he plans
to scrutinize Albertine's actions; he starts an investigation, the results of
which pose problems that go beyond jealousy and are of another nature.
From this point of view, *La Prisonnière* and *Albertine disparue* could be
entitled "In Search of the Unknown Albertine."

In *La Prisonnière,* the investigation is made through Albertine herself,
and secondarily through the testimonies of the chauffeur or Andrée.
Albertine's death changes the nature of the investigation but not that of
the results obtained. The narrator discovers that Albertine's life is dispersed in space, goes back in time, is tied to countless people. It is
impossible to encompass her life. Before disappearing, Albertine, like the
Jacques Godeau in Jules Romain's *Mort de Quelqu'un,* had filled an
indefinable space which has depth in the memories of other people and
also exists on the surface of time. Gradually the narrator realizes that there
is an unsuspected permanence and a continuity in Albertine that cannot be
grasped—in the very Albertine whom he had wanted to reduce to the
proportions of what he himself saw of her when he watched her sleeping.
Their relations, as he had understood them, are transformed; he realizes
that

> that long complaint of the soul which thinks that it is living
> shut up within itself is a monologue in appearance only, since
> the echoes of reality alter its course; such a life is apparently
> like a spontaneous essay in subjective psychology, which from a
> distance furnishes its "action" to a purely realistic novel of
> another reality, another existence, the vicissitudes of which in
> their turn inflect the curve and change the direction of the
> psychological essay.

All the information that the narrator obtains about Albertine's life is
fragmentary, contradictory, and enigmatic; it resists any coherent recon-

struction. He also gives it different interpretations, depending upon his mood. If, in order to satisfy his love, Albertine must not be a lesbian, the information he finds supports this hypothesis; if, when he has become indifferent, Albertine's guilt is no longer of great importance to him, the information he comes upon seems to reveal her guilt. We are reminded of his outings in Balbec with Mme de Villeparisis: "Before getting into the carriage," he says, "I had already composed the seascape which I was going to look for." Furthermore, the nature of the information which reaches him matters little; it actually has no intrinsic interest. What slowly becomes apparent as the information on Albertine accumulates is the complete absurdity of such an enterprise. The results of the narrator's quest for information seem dubious to the reader because never, as long as Albertine is alive, does he attempt to obtain her cooperation and confidence; after she is dead it is too late. Besides, Albertine is in some ways deception personified. However, what Albertine's confidence could have contributed he eventually discovers in his meditations about himself and about his own life; deception seems to him inherent in the life of even the most highly ethical human being. "I ought to have reflected" he thinks "that there are two worlds, one covering the other, one consisting of the things that the best, the most sincere people say, and behind it the world of the same people's actions." So, in the last analysis, Albertine is in that respect like anyone and everyone.

The narrator's investigation of Albertine constantly brings to light surprising and unexpected fragments of life which disconcert him. Albertine's present life, which he tries carefully to circumvent, escapes him on all sides—in outer space, in inner space and in time—dragging along the past and overflowing into the future. "Behind each of her words" he feels "a lie; behind each house to which she says she is going, another house; behind each action, each person, another action, another person." As for the past, "her admissions, insofar as they concerned the past, left large blanks which I had to try to fill in completely, but before I could fill them in I had to learn about her life." His attempt "to learn about her life" from the outside, and to reconstruct it on the basis of evidence, only succeeds in increasing his confusion and in accumulating a mass of tangled contradictions which seem to the narrator to hide what he considers most important. His quest accomplishes nothing but the total destruction of his peace of mind; he is sure that only a life lived in complete blindness is possible with Albertine. "The only result of my exploration of one sector of the great zone that extended round me had been to banish further from me that unknowable entity which another person's life, when we seek to form a definite idea of it, invariably is to us.''

In order to imagine effectively the "real life" of a person we must break through our habits, or through the indifference which our superb egocentricity creates in our relation to that person. Love accepts mystery and thrives on the unknown: ordinary jealousy is for the narrator a less powerful instigator of anxious curiosity than homosexuality. The image of Montjouvain suddenly places Albertine in a world which is by definition closed to the young man; he will never be able to enter it, reduce it to a known quantity. And so his anxiety can never be stilled, nor his struggle with the unknown come to an end, except in oblivion. Only Albertine's absence and her death bring forgetfulness. Her objective reality is the core of his obsession; it is because Albertine is "another" that their relationship incurs so much drama. There is a real, logical link connecting the image of Montjouvain with the pitiless investigation which it occasions; but it takes the narrator much further than he expected. The obscure world Albertine contains within her is unknowable at any given moment, even to herself; and this is true too of the whole movement of her life in the past, a movement which no one, including herself, could adequately retrace.

Her death poses another problem for the narrator. It confirms her disappearance, but changes nothing in the hypothetical character of everything that the narrator, and with him the reader, can learn about her. From the moment of her death she follows, though more slowly, the road of the narrator's grandmother, the road which leads to forgetfulness. And so Albertine, who despite all the narrator's efforts has remained a stranger to him, disappears completely from his memory. Her death is a fact, final and absolute, from which nothing can be learned. It is only her life, transitory and relative, but in which she was a unique individual, that is of any importance. It is this unique quality of her life which all the narrator's jealous concentration cannot penetrate. Albertine, alive and irreducible, with "her dark and unrelenting will," alone has value in the young man's eyes. Her death again brings up the problem of the value of transitory life—a problem already raised by the grandmother's death. Proust places beside it Bergotte's death and the survival of the work which he leaves, and also the survival of Vinteuil in his Septet. The elements are all gathered here, ready for the discovery and the synthesis that the narrator will make at the Guermantes matinée, when he will at last realize that death is not accidental, and that it is drawing near for him too. The theme of solitude leads straight to that of death.

The narrator's impassioned investigation of Albertine alternates with moments of private communion with himself. Shut up in his room, he gradually becomes more conscious of the inner reaches of time; he is made aware of them by certain moments of the past which spring to life and impinge upon the present. For the first time he notices "correspondences" which certain sensations awaken between his inner and outer worlds:

> Françoise came in to light the fire, and to make it draw, threw upon it a handful of twigs, the scent of which, forgotten for a year, traced round the fireplace a magic circle within which, perceiving myself poring over a book, now in Combray, now in Doncières, I was as joyful, while remaining in my bedroom in Paris, as if I had been on the point of starting for a walk toward Méséglise, or of going to join Saint-Loup and his friends on the training-ground ... The scent in the frosty air of the twigs of brushwood was like a fragment of the past, an invisible floe broken off from the ice of a winter of long ago that stole into my room, often variegated moreover with this perfume or that light, as though with a sequence of different years, in which I found myself plunged, overwhelmed, even before I had identified them, by the eagerness of hopes long since abandoned.

He discovers an "inner violin" which certain sensations, born of solitude, cause to vibrate; they open up a whole world within him:

> By themselves these modifications (which though they came from without, were internal) refashioned for me the world outside. Communicating doors, long barred, swung open in my brain. The life of certain towns, the gaiety of certain expeditions resumed their place in my consciousness. All athrob in harmony with the vibrating string, I would have sacrificed my dull life in the past, and all my life to come, erased with the india rubber of habit, for one of these special, unique moments.

Immobile, the narrator discovers within himself gradations of the "I" superimposed one upon another, starting with the basic one, a "small inarticulate sun worshipper," and moving toward "the philosopher." He is quite content to contemplate them passively. When Albertine has disappeared, he thinks back over the period of their life together:

> So, then, my life was entirely altered. What had made it ... attractive when I was alone was precisely the perpetual resur-

gence, at the bidding of identical moments, of moments from the past. From the sound of the rain I recaptured the scent of the lilacs in Combray, from the shifting of the sun's rays on the balcony, the pigeons in the Champs-Elysées, from the muffling of all noise in the heat of the morning hours, the cool taste of cherries, the longing for Brittany or Venice from the sound of the wind and the return of Easter.

But he draws no conclusion from these impressions. At first his thoughts are all absorbed in the pursuit of the enigma of Albertine, then he is torn by the anguish her death causes him until he finally forgets her. The objective reality which Albertine represented once more makes the narrator turn away from himself and the contemplative life which he has been leading from his bed. The slow process of forgetfulness brings him the counterpart of these experiences and brings them to him in perfect symmetry. The narrator sees Gilberte, whom he does not recognize, and feels a sensual desire for her:

> Under the action of desire, and consequently of the desire for happiness, which Gilberte had aroused in me during these hours in which I had supposed her to be someone else, a certain number of miseries, of painful preoccupations, which only a little while earlier had obsessed my mind, had been released, *carrying with them a whole block of memories,* probably long since crumbled and become precarious, about Albertine.

The narrator never makes the connection between this "suppression" of "a whole part of his association of ideas" with the slow progress of that "invisible floe set loose from a winter of long ago" which a fire had brought back to his mind.

Under the influence of his suffering, his mind lingers over the problem of his various past identities and the moments "lost" in forgetfulness rather than over the complementary problem of his identity in the moments "regained" in solitude:

> The memory of all the events that had followed one another in my life ... in the course of those last months of Albertine's existence had made these months seem to me much longer than a year; and now this oblivion of so many things separated me by gulfs of empty space from quite recent events which they made me think remote because I had had what is called "the time" to forget them. This oblivion, by its fragmentary, irregu-

lar interpolation in my memory—like a thick fog at sea which obliterates all the landmarks—confused, destroyed my sense of distances in time, contracted in one place, extended in another, and made me suppose myself now farther away from things, now far closer to them than I really was. And as in the fresh spaces, as yet unexplored, which extended before me, there would be no more trace of my love for Albertine than there had been in the time past which I had just traversed of my love for my grandmother, my life appeared to me to offer a succession of periods in which, after a certain interval, nothing of what had sustained the previous period survived in that which followed; my life appeared as something so devoid of the support of an individual, identical and permanent self, something so useless in the future and so protracted in the past, that death might just as well put an end to its course here or there, without *in the least concluding it.*

The processes of memory, which he has not yet completely understood, make life seem insignificant and absurd, without meaning or direction. This attitude is more important than the suffering from which it springs, for it marks a change in the relationship of the narrator with his life. He has reached the threshold of indifference. Art alone seems still to escape the triteness of life. The resurrection of past "I's" in his moments of solitude, and the apparently unconnected "I's" which succeed one another in time are contradictory elements which he does not attempt to reconcile; they are the two facets of the experience which will open for him the vistas of *Le Temps retrouvé.* In his exploration of solitude the narrator again approaches the mystery of time, but he fails to understand its double aspect. The door closes on the search which had been motivated by his jealousy, leaving him only the conviction of failure. "Truth and life are hard taskmasters; although I did not really know them, all they left me was an impression of sadness which gave way to weariness." With the end of the Albertine episode, the narrator enters the realm of despair. His life turns from the future toward the past, from imagination to recollection, from the world outside to the world within him. In this part of his work, Proust restates, not without some repetition, all the psychological and moral "truths" scattered throughout the whole novel, and bestows upon them the weight of definitive truths; he gives so abstract a character to this analysis that it seems at times almost a treatise on psychology. The narrator puts these concepts in a new perspective, orienting them around

memory and its lapses, and explains in this way all the other "intermit-
tences" in his inner life; but the overall impression is one of monotony, in
the experiences he describes as well as in the "truths" he formulates.

These truths are not without their aesthetic counterpart. The narrator
never succeeds in reconstructing Albertine's life, in really knowing her. He
never succeeds in seeing this young woman in all her aspects, or in
unravelling the tangle of her complex relations in time and space. Albertine
breaks up into a thousand fragments because the narrator has no key to
the "inner soul which gave cohesion" to "this ephemeral and active
whole." What was Albertine's story during her stay at the narrator's, and
consequently what was the real story of the narrator's life with her? And
the real story of Swann and Odette? This question arises about all the
characters in the Proustian world, and in all kinds of ways about the
narrator himself.

Proustian characters are unknown quantities and the narrator is obliged
finally to accept this fact, which the whole novel illustrates. People enter
his field of vision, group themselves as in tableaux vivants, play their parts,
then disappear only to reappear later, just as untouched and impenetrable
as before. It is curious to see how each character "makes his entrance"
before the narrator, either in a series of candid camera shots or in slow
motion. The narrator may ponder at length their successive appearances,
but even his closest scrutiny never succeeds in explaining their various
aspects, or in finding a connection between the different "snapshots"
which could define their character: Miss Sacripant, Odette de Crécy,
Odette, friend of the Verdurins, the Botticelli-like Odette beloved of Swann,
Mme Swann, the mistress of the Duc de Guermantes. How many other
Odettes are there between each of these "photographic proofs" of Odette?
And how many others in that part of her life which never coincides with
the narrator's? Even the narrator's life is neither reconstructed nor explained in all its continuity. Nothing ever explains his vocation, for example, which is simply given as a fact, like a place, Combray, or a person, the
Duchesse. There are great stretches of shadow behind everyone in *A la
recherche du temps perdu*—shadow which Proust suggests in the narrator's analysis of character. But the analysis is limited to those aspects of
them which are visible to the narrator. They remain in great part as
unknown to us as Albertine.

The narration in the first person has a definite function in this respect.
In *La Prisonnière* and *Albertine disparue* the narrator realizes that his
investigation always reflects his own frame of mind, the lapses of his
attention, his alternate anxiety and calm. The same holds true for the rest

of the novel. Proust relates the analysis of his characters to the narrator's particular point of view rather than to the character being analyzed. He does not impose it upon the character observed, or even upon the reader: actions, bodies, and words present a surface which analysis never succeeds in disturbing. The relationship between what the narrator sees and what he thinks is quite subtle; all his thoughts are tinged with its uncertainty. If he is to "decipher" the symbols that people are, he must first clearly read the hieroglyphs in himself. As he discovers in the case of Albertine, it is futile to try to reconstruct the world of others according to his own emotions. The whole complex rationale which accumulates around Proustian characters becomes, after a certain stage, speculation and hypothesis just as it does in the case of Albertine. The narrator "formulates truths" which are really simple observations of fact, drawn from what he sees of the world and generalized in reference to that world.

There would be a real contradiction in Proust's work if we could logically reconstruct any of his characters and explain their evolution. For his whole novel is proof of his own assertion that what gives men their individuality can only be translated by art, which transcends the intellect. Proustian analysis, with all its keen attention to exact detail, is the means Proust uses to isolate what is unique in an individual; analysis allows him to strip his characters of everything which is explicable, and therefore not particular to them. What remains is their essential being, mysterious and inexplicable. The narrator could perhaps more fully understand and explain the people around him if he were in constant contact with them; but because they appear intermittently, they preserve their autonomy. Despite their continual appearances and disappearances, they give the impression of continuity and, up to a certain point, they can be explained. But what the narrator analyzes is the outward person; no amount of analysis can explain the essence of the inner person. It is simply a matter of vision.

Proust presents his characters as his narrartor sees them—when their paths cross his and a fragment of their lives is spotlighted. We are left with the impression that they are moving independently along their own trajectories, which at intervals automatically cross the narrator's path. Each follows his isolated course, distinct from the narrator's and from that of any other character. All the characters seem "distant" from each other, strangers, though they move in the same world. We catch innumerable glimpses of them; a Proustian character is primarily a series of diverse images which we know are connected and animate, but it is never possible to distinguish exactly how. The same is also true of minor characters like Jupien, Aimé, or even Princesse Sherbatoff.

Proust is infinitely greater as a creator of characters than as a psychologist, simply because his characters resist all psychological theories—even his own. They are remarkable for their resistance to logic, for their sheer impact upon the imagination. Because each character is a complete, closed world in himself, his world determines for him his values, his joys, and his suffering. But only the narrator is able to force open the door to his own world, and then only for himself.

WALTER BENJAMIN

The Image of Proust

The thirteen volumes of Marcel Proust's *A la recherche du temps perdu* are the result of an unconstruable synthesis in which the absorption of a mystic, the art of a prose writer, the verve of a satirist, the erudition of a scholar, and the self-consciousness of a monomaniac have combined in an autobiographical work. It has rightly been said that all great works of literature found a genre or dissolve one—that they are, in other words, special cases. Among these cases this is one of the most unfathomable. From its structure, which is fiction, autobiography, and commentary in one, to the syntax of endless sentences (the Nile of language, which here overflows and fructifies the regions of truth), everything transcends the norm. The first revealing observation that strikes one is that this great special case of literature at the same time constitutes its greatest achievement of recent decades. The conditions under which it was created were extremely unhealthy: an unusual malady, extraordinary wealth, and an abnormal disposition. This is not a model life in every respect, but everything about it is exemplary. The outstanding literary achievement of our time is assigned a place in the heart of the impossible, at the center—and also at the point of indifference—of all dangers, and it marks this great realization of a "lifework" as the last for a long time. The image of Proust is the highest physiognomic expression which the irresistibly growing discrepancy between literature and life was able to assume. This is the lesson which justifies the attempt to evoke this image.

From *Illuminations,* edited by Hannah Arendt and translated by Harry Zohn. ©1955 by Suhrkamp Verlag, ©1968 by Harcourt, Brace Jovanovich, Inc. Schocken Books, 1978.

We know that in his work Proust did not describe a life as it actually was, but a life as it was remembered by the one who had lived it. And yet even this statement is imprecise and far too crude. For the important thing for the remembering author is not what he experienced, but the weaving of his memory, the Penelope work of recollection. Or should one call it, rather, a Penelope work of forgetting? Is not the involuntary recollection, Proust's *mémoire involontaire,* much closer to forgetting than what is usually called memory? And is not this work of spontaneous recollection, in which remembrance is the woof and forgetting the warp, a counterpart to Penelope's work rather than its likeness? For here the day unravels what the night has woven. When we awake each morning, we hold in our hands, usually weakly and loosely, but a few fringes of the tapestry of lived life, as loomed for us by forgetting. However, with our purposeful activity and, even more, our purposive remembering each day unravels the web and the ornaments of forgetting. This is why Proust finally turned his days into nights, devoting all his hours to undisturbed work in his darkened room with artificial illumination, so that none of those intricate arabesques might escape him.

The Latin word *textum* means "web." No one's text is more tightly woven than Marcel Proust's; to him nothing was tight or durable enough. From his publisher Gallimard we know that Proust's proofreading habits were the despair of the typesetters. The galleys always went back covered with marginal notes, but not a single misprint had been corrected; all available space had been used for fresh text. Thus the laws of remembrance were operative even within the confines of the work. For an experienced event is finite—at any rate, confined to one sphere of experience; a remembered event is infinite, because it is only a key to everything that happened before it and after it. There is yet another sense in which memory issues strict weaving regulations. Only the *actus purus* of recollection itself, not the author or the plot, constitutes the unity of the text. One may even say that the intermittence of author and plot is only the reverse of the continuum of memory, the pattern on the back side of the tapestry. This is what Proust meant, and this is how he must be understood, when he said that he would prefer to see his entire work printed in one volume in two columns and without any paragraphs.

What was it that Proust sought so frenetically? What was at the bottom of these infinite efforts? Can we say that all lives, works, and deeds that matter were never anything but the undisturbed unfolding of the most banal, most fleeting, most sentimental, weakest hour in the life of the one to whom they pertain? When Proust in a well-known passage described the hour that was most his own, he did it in such a way that everyone can find it in his own existence. We might almost call it an everyday hour; it comes with the night, a lost twittering of birds, or a breath drawn at the sill of an open window. And there is no telling what encounters would be in store for us if we were less inclined to give in to sleep. Proust did not give in to sleep. And yet—or, rather, precisely for this reason—Jean Cocteau was able to say in a beautiful essay that the intonation of Proust's voice obeyed the laws of night and honey. By submitting to these laws he conquered the hopeless sadness within him (what he once called *"l'imperfection incurable dans l'essence même du présent* [the incurable imperfection in the very essence of the present moment]") and from the honeycombs of memory he built a house for the swarm of his thoughts. Cocteau recognized what really should have been the major concern of all readers of Proust and yet has served no one as the pivotal point of his reflections or his affection. He recognized Proust's blind, senseless, frenzied quest for happiness. It shone from his eyes; they were not happy, but in them there lay fortune as it lies in gambling or in love. Nor is it hard to say why this paralyzing, explosive will to happiness which pervades Proust's writings is so seldom comprehended by his readers. In many places Proust himself made it easy for them to view this *œuvre,* too, from the time tested, comfortable perspective of resignation, heroism, asceticism. After all, nothing makes more sense to the model pupils of life than the notion that a great achievement is the fruit of toil, misery, and disappointment. The idea that happiness could have a share in beauty would be too much of a good thing, something that their *ressentiment* would never get over.

There is a dual will to happiness, a dialectics of happiness: a hymnic and an elegiac form. The one is the unheard-of, the unprecedented, the height of bliss; the other, the eternal repetition, the eternal restoration of the original, the first happiness. It is this elegiac idea of happiness—it could also be called Eleatic—which for Proust transforms existence into a preserve of memory. To it he sacrificed in his life friends and companionship, in his works plot, unity of characters, the flow of the narration, the play of the imagination. Max Unold, one of Proust's more discerning readers, fastened on the "boredom" thus created in Proust's writings and likened it to "pointless stories." "Proust managed to make the pointless story interesting. He says: 'Imagine, dear reader, yesterday I was dunking a cookie in my tea when it occurred to me that as a child I spent some time in the country.' For this he uses eighty pages, and it is so fascinating that you think you are no longer the listener but the daydreamer himself." In such stories—"all ordinary dreams turn into pointless stories as soon as

one tells them to someone"—Unold has discovered the bridge to the
dream. No synthetic interpretation of Proust can disregard it. Enough
inconspicuous gates lead into it—Proust's frenetically studying resemblances,
his impassioned cult of similarity. The true signs of its hegemony do not
become obvious where he suddenly and startlingly uncovers similarities in
actions, physiognomies, or speech mannerisms. The similarity of one thing
to another which we are used to, which occupies us in a wakeful state,
reflects only vaguely the deeper resemblance of the dream world in which
everything that happens appears not in identical but in similar guise,
opaquely similar one to another. Children know a symbol of this world:
the stocking which has the structure of this dream world when, rolled up
in the laundry hamper, it is a "bag" and a "present" at the same time. And
just as children do not tire of quickly changing the bag and its contents
into a third thing—namely, a stocking—Proust could not get his fill of
emptying the dummy, his self, at one stroke in order to keep garnering that
third thing, the image which satisfied his curiosity—indeed, assuaged his
homesickness. He lay on his bed racked with homesickness, homesick for
the world distorted in the state of resemblance, a world in which the true
surrealist face of existence breaks through. To this world belongs what
happens in Proust, and the deliberate and fastidious way in which it
appears. It is never isolated, rhetorical, or visionary; carefully heralded and
securely supported, it bears a fragile, precious reality: the image. It detaches
itself from the structure of Proust's sentences as that summer day at
Balbec—old, immemorial, mummified—emerged from the lace curtains
under Françoise's hands.

II

We do not always proclaim loudly the most important thing we have
to say. Nor do we always privately share it with those closest to us, our
intimate friends, those who have been most devotedly ready to receive our
confession. If it is true that not only people but also ages have such a
chaste—that is, such a devious and frivolous—way of communicating
what is most their own to a passing acquaintance, then the nineteenth
century did not reveal itself to Zola or Anatole France, but to the young
Proust, the insignificant snob, the playboy and socialite who snatched in
passing the most astounding confidences from a declining age as from
another, bone-weary Swann. It took Proust to make the nineteenth century
ripe for memoirs. What before him had been a period devoid of tension
now became a field of force in which later writers aroused multifarious

currents. Nor is it accidental that the two most significant works of this kind were written by authors who were personally close to Proust as admirers and friends: the memoirs of Princess Clermont-Tonnerre and the autobiographical work of Léon Daudet; the first volumes of both works were published recently. An eminently Proustian inspiration led Léon Daudet, whose political folly is too gross and too obtuse to do much harm to his admirable talent, to turn his life into a city. *Paris vécu,* the projection of a biography onto the city map, in more than one place is touched by the shadows of Proustian characters. And the very title of Princess Clermont-Tonnerre's book, *Au temps des équipages,* would have been unthinkable prior to Proust. This book is the echo which softly answers Proust's ambiguous, loving, challenging call from the Faubourg Saint-Germain. In addition, this melodious performance is shot through with direct and indirect references to Proust in its tenor and its characters, which include him and some of his favorite objects of study from the Ritz. There is no denying, of course, that this puts us in a very aristocratic milieu, and, with figures like Robert de Montesquiou, whom Princess Clermont-Tonnerre depicts masterfully, in a very special one at that. But this is true of Proust as well, and in his writings Montesquiou has a counterpart. All this would not be worth discussing, especially since the question of models would be secondary and unimportant for Germany, if German criticism were not so fond of taking the easy way out. Above all, it could not resist the opportunity to descend to the level of the lending-library crowd. Hack critics were tempted to draw conclusions about the author from the snobbish milieu of his writings, to characterize Proust's works as an internal affair of the French, a literary supplement to the *Almanach de gotha.* It is obvious that the problems of Proust's characters are those of a satiated society. But there is not one which would be identical with those of the author, which are subversive. To reduce this to a formula, it was to be Proust's aim to design the entire inner structure of society as a physiology of chatter. In the treasury of its prejudices and maxims there is not one that is not annihilated by a dangerous comic element. Pierre-Quint was the first to draw attention to it. "When humorous works are mentioned," he wrote, "one usually thinks of short, amusing books in illustrated jackets. One forgets about *Don Quixote, Pantagruel,* and *Gil Blas*—fat, ungainly tomes in small print." These comparisons, of course, do not do full justice to the explosive power of Proust's critique of society. His style is comedy, not humor; his laughter does not toss the world up but flings it down—at the risk that it will be smashed to pieces, which will then make him burst into tears. And unity of family and personality, of sexual morality and professional honor, are indeed smashed to bits. The pretensions of the bourgeoisie are shattered by laughter. Their return and reassimilation by the aristocracy is the sociological theme of the work.

Proust did not tire of the training which moving in aristocratic circles required. Assiduously and without much constraint, he conditioned his personality, making it as impenetrable and resourceful, as submissive and difficult, as it had to be for the sake of his mission. Later on this mystification and ceremoniousness became so much part of him that his letters sometimes constitute whole systems of parentheses, and not just in the grammatical sense—letters which despite their infinitely ingenious, flexible composition occasionally call to mind the specimen of a letter writer's handbook: "My dear Madam, I just noticed that I forgot my cane at your house yesterday; please be good enough to give it to the bearer of this letter. P.S. Kindly pardon me for disturbing you; I just found my cane." Proust was most resourceful in creating complications. Once, late at night, he dropped in on Princess Clermont-Tonnerre and made his staying dependent on someone bringing him his medicine from his house. He sent a valet for it, giving him a lengthy description of the neighborhood and of the house. Finally he said: "You cannot miss it. It is the only window on the Boulevard Haussmann in which there still is a light burning!" Everything but the house number! Anyone who has tried to get the address of a brothel in a strange city and has received the most long-winded directions, everything but the name of the street and the house number, will understand what is meant here and what the connection is with Proust's love of ceremony, his admiration of the Duc de Saint-Simon, and, last but not least, his intransigent French spirit. Is it not the quintessence of experience to find out how very difficult it is to learn many things which apparently could be told in very few words? It is simply that such words are part of a language established along lines of caste and class and unintelligible to outsiders. No wonder that the secret language of the salons excited Proust. When he later embarked on his merciless depiction of the *petit clan,* the Courvoisiers, the "esprit d'Oriane," he had through his association with the Bibescos become conversant with the improvisations of a code language to which we too have recently been introduced.

In his years of life in the salons Proust developed not only the vice of flattery to an eminent—one is tempted to say, to a theological—degree, but the vice of curiosity as well. We detect in him the reflection of the laughter which like a flash fire curls the lips of the Foolish Virgins represented on the intrados of many of the cathedrals which Proust loved.

It is the smile of curiosity. Was it curiosity that made him such a great parodist? If so, we would know how to evaluate the term "parodist" in this context. Not very highly. For though it does justice to his abysmal malice, it skirts the bitterness, savagery, and grimness of the magnificent pieces which he wrote in the style of Balzac, Flaubert, Sainte-Beuve, Henri de Régnier, the Goncourts, Michelet, Renan, and his favorite Saint-Simon, and which are collected in the volume *Pastiches et mélanges*. The mimicry of a man of curiosity is the brilliant device of this series, as it is also a feature of his entire creativity in which his passion for vegetative life cannot be taken seriously enough. Ortega y Gasset was the first to draw attention to the vegetative existence of Proust's characters, which are planted so firmly in their social habitat, influenced by the position of the sun of aristocratic favor, stirred by the wind that blows from Guermantes or Méséglise, and inextricably intertwined in the thicket of their fate. This is the environment that gave rise to the poet's mimicry. Proust's most accurate, most convincing insights fasten on their objects as insects fasten on leaves, blossoms, branches, betraying nothing of their existence until a leap, a beating of wings, a vault, show the startled observer that some incalculable individual life has imperceptibly crept into an alien world. The true reader of Proust is constantly jarred by small shocks. In the parodies he finds again, in the guise of a play with "styles," what affected him in an altogether different way as this spirit's struggle for survival under the leafy canopy of society. At this point we must say something about the close and fructifying interpenetration of these two vices, curiosity and flattery. There is a revealing passage in the writings of Princess Clermont-Tonnerre. "And finally we cannot suppress the fact that Proust became enraptured with the study of domestic servants—whether it be that an element which he encountered nowhere else intrigued his investigative faculties or that he envied servants their greater opportunities for observing the intimate details of things that aroused his interest. In any case, domestic servants in their various embodiments and types were his passion." In the exotic shadings of a Jupien, a Monsieur Aimé, a Célestine Albalat, their ranks extend from Françoise, a figure with the coarse, angular features of St. Martha that seems to be straight out of a Book of Hours, to those grooms and *chasseurs* who are paid for loafing rather than working. And perhaps the greatest concentration of this connoisseur of ceremonies was reserved for the depiction of these lower ranks. Who can tell how much servant curiosity became part of Proust's flattery, how much servant flattery became mixed with his curiosity, and where this artful copy of the role of the servant on the heights of the social scale had its limits? Proust presented such a copy, and he could not help doing so, for, as he once admitted, *"voir"* and *"désirer imiter"* were one and the same thing to him. This attitude, which was both sovereign and obsequious, has been preserved by Maurice Barrès in the most apposite words that have ever been written about Proust: *"Un poète persan dans une loge de portière* [a Persian poet in a porter's lodge]."

There was something of the detective in Proust's curiosity. The upper ten thousand were to him a clan of criminals, a band of conspirators beyond compare: the Camorra of consumers. It excludes from its world everything that has a part in production, or at least demands that this part be gracefully and bashfully concealed behind the kind of manner that is sported by the polished professionals of consumption. Proust's analysis of snobbery, which is far more important than his apotheosis of art, constitutes the apogee of his criticism of society. For the attitude of the snob is nothing but the consistent, organized, steely view of life from the chemically pure standpoint of the consumer. And because even the remotest as well as the most primitive memory of nature's productive forces was to be banished from this satanic magic world, Proust found a perverted relationship more serviceable than a normal one even in love. But the pure consumer is the pure exploiter—logically and theoretically—and in Proust he is that in the full concreteness of his actual historical existence. He is concrete because he is impenetrable and elusive. Proust describes a class which is everywhere pleged to camouflage its material basis and for this very reason is attached to a feudalism which has no intrinsic economic significance but is all the more serviceable as a mask of the upper middle class. This disillusioned, merciless deglamorizer of the ego, of love, of morals—for this is how Proust liked to view himself—turns his whole limitless art into a veil for this one most vital mystery of his class: the economic aspect. He did not mean to do it a service. Here speaks Marcel Proust, the hardness of his work, the intransigence of a man who is ahead of his class. What he accomplishes he accomplishes as its master. And much of the greatness of this work will remain inaccessible or undiscovered until this class has revealed its most pronounced features in the final struggle.

III

In the last century there was an inn by the name of "Au Temps Perdu" at Grenoble; I do not know whether it still exists. In Proust, too, we are guests who enter through a door underneath a suspended sign that sways in the breeze, a door underneath a suspended sign that sways in the breeze, a door behind which eternity and rapture await us. Fernandez rightly distinguished between a *thème de l'éternité* and a *thème du temps* in Proust. But his eternity is by no means a platonic or a utopian one; it is rapturous. Therefore, if "time reveals a new and hitherto unknown kind of eternity to anyone who becomes engrossed in its passing," this certainly does not enable an individual to approach "the higher regions which a Plato or Spinoza reached with one beat of the wings." It is true that in Proust we find rudiments of an enduring idealism, but it would be a mistake to make these the basis of an interpretation, as Benoist-Méchin has done most glaringly. The eternity which Proust opens to view is convoluted time, not boundless time. His true interest is in the passage of time in its most real—that is, space-bound—form, and this passage no-where holds sway more openly than in remembrance within and aging without. To observe the interaction of aging and remembering means to penetrate to the heart of Proust's world, to the universe of convolution. It is the world in a state of resemblances, the domain of the *correspondances;* the Romanticists were the first to comprehend them and Baudelaire embraced them most fervently, but Proust was the only one who managed to reveal them in our lived life. This is the work of the *mémoire involontaire*, the rejuvenating force which is a match for the inexorable process of aging. When the past is reflected in the dewy fresh "instant," a painful shock of rejuvenation pulls it together once more as irresistibly as the Guermantes way and Swann's way become intertwined for Proust when, in the thirteenth volume, he roams about the Combray area for the last time and discovers the intertwining of the roads. In a trice the landscape jumps about like a child. *"Ah! que le monde est grand à la clarté des lampes! Aux yeux du souvenir que le monde est petit!* [Oh, how large the world is in the brightness of the lamps. How small the world is in the eyes of recollection]." Proust has brought off the tremendous feat of letting the whole world age by a lifetime in an instant. But this very concentration in which things that normally just fade and slumber consume themselves in a flash is called rejuvenation. *A la recherche du temps perdu* is the constant attempt to charge an entire lifetime with the utmost awareness. Proust's method is actualization, not reflection. He is filled with the insight that none of us has time to live the true dramas of the life that we are destined for. This is what ages us—this and nothing else. The wrinkles and creases on our faces are the registration of the great passions, vices, insights that called on us; but we, the masters, were not home.

Since the spiritual exercises of Loyola there has hardly been a more

radical attempt at self-absorption. Proust's, too, has as its center a loneliness which pulls the world down into its vortex with the force of a
maelstrom. And the overloud and inconceivably hollow chatter which
comes roaring out of Proust's novels is the sound of society plunging down
into the abyss of this loneliness. This is the location of Proust's invectives
against friendship. It was a matter of perceiving the silence at the bottom
of this crater, whose eyes are the quietest and most absorbing. Something
that is manifested irritatingly and capriciously in so many anecdotes is the
combination of an unparalleled intensity of conversation with an unsur-
passable aloofness from his partner. There has never been anyone else with
Proust's ability to show us things; Proust's pointing finger is unequaled.
But there is another gesture in amicable togetherness, in conversation:
physical contact. To no one is this gesture more alien than to Proust. He
cannot touch his reader either; he could not do so for anything in the
world. If one wanted to group literature around these poles, dividing it
into the directive and the touching kind, the core of the former would be
the work of Proust, the core of the latter, the work of Péguy. This is
basically what Fernandez has formulated so well: "Depth, or, rather,
intensity, is always on his side, never on that of his partner." This is
demonstrated brilliantly and with a touch of cynicism in Proust's literary
criticism, the most significant document of which is an essay that came
into being on the high level of his fame and the low level of his deathbed:
"A Propos de Baudelaire." The essay is Jesuitic in its acquiescence in his
own maladies, immoderate in the garrulousness of a man who is resting,
frightening in the indifference of a man marked by death who wants to
speak out once more, no matter on what subject. What inspired Proust
here in the face of death also shaped him in his intercourse with his
contemporaries: so spasmodic and harsh an alternation of sarcasm and
tenderness that its recipients threatened to break down in exhaustion.

The provocative, unsteady quality of the man affects even the reader
of his works. Suffice it to recall the endless succession of *"soit que . . . ,"*
by means of which an action is shown in an exhaustive, depressing way in
the light of the countless motives upon which it may have been based. And
yet these paratactic sequences reveal the point at which weakness and
genius coincide in Proust: the intellectual renunciation, the tested skepticism with which he approached things. After the self-satisfied inwardness
of Romanticism Proust came along, determined, as Jacques Rivière puts it,
not to give the least credence to the *"Sirènes intérieures."* "Proust approaches experience without the slightest metaphysical interest, without
the slightest penchant for construction, without the slightest tendency to

console." Nothing is truer than that. And thus the basic feature of this work, too, which Proust kept proclaiming as being planned, is anything but the result of construction. But it is as planned as the lines on the palm of our hand or the arrangement of the stamen in a calyx. Completely worn out, Proust, that aged child, fell back on the bosom of nature—not to drink from it, but to dream to its heartbeat. One must picture him in this state of weakness to understand how felicitously Jacques Rivière interpreted the weakness when he wrote: "Marcel Proust died of the same inexperience which permitted him to write his works. He died of ignorance of the world and because he did not know how to change the conditions of his life which had begun to crush him. He died because he did not know how to make a fire or open a window." And, to be sure, of his psychogenic asthma.

The doctors were powerless in the face of this malady; not so the writer, who very systematically placed it in his service. To begin with the most external aspect, he was a perfect stage director of his sickness. For months he connected, with devastating irony, the image of an admirer who had sent him flowers with their odor, which he found unbearable. Depending on the ups and downs of his malady he alarmed his friends, who dreaded and longed for the moment when the writer would suddenly appear in their drawing rooms long after midnight—*brisé de fatigue* and for just five minutes, as he said—only to stay till the gray of dawn, too tired to get out of his chair or interrupt his conversation. Even as a writer of letters he extracted the most singular effects from his malady. "The wheezing of my breath is drowning out the sounds of my pen and of a bath which is being drawn on the floor below." But that is not all, nor is it the fact that his sickness removed him from fashionable living. This asthma became part of his art—if indeed his art did not create it. Proust's syntax rhythmically and step by step reproduces his fear of suffocating. And his ironic, philosophical, didactic reflections invariably are the deep breath with which he shakes off the weight of memories. On a larger scale, however, the threatening, suffocating crisis was death, which he was constantly aware of, most of all while he was writing. This is how death confronted Proust, and long before his malady assumed critical dimensions— not as a hypochondriacal whim, but as a *"réalité nouvelle,"* that new reality whose reflections on things and people are the marks of aging. A physiology of style would take us into the innermost core of this creativeness. No one who knows with what great tenacity memories are preserved by the sense of smell, and smells not at all in the memory, will be able to call Proust's sensitivity to smells accidental. To be sure, most memories that we search for come to us as visual images. Even the free-floating forms of the *mémoire involontaire* are still in large part isolated, though enigmatically present, visual images. For this very reason, anyone who wishes to surrender knowingly to the innermost overtones in this work must place himself in a special stratum—the bottommost—of this involuntary memory, one in which the materials of memory no longer appear singly, as images, but tell us about a whole, amorphously and formlessly, indefinitely and weightily, in the same way as the weight of his net tells a fisherman about his catch. Smell—that is the sense of weight of someone who casts his nets into the sea of the *temps perdu*. And his sentences are the entire muscular activity of the intelligible body; they contain the whole enormous effort to raise this catch.

For the rest, the closeness of the symbiosis between this particular creativity and this particular malady is demonstrated most clearly by the fact that in Proust there never was a breakthrough of that heroic defiance with which other creative people have risen up against their infirmities. And therefore one can say, from another point of view, that so close a complicity with life and the course of the world as Proust's would inevitably have led to ordinary, indolent contentment on any basis but that of such great and constant suffering. As it was, however, this malady was destined to have its place in the great work process assigned to it by a furor devoid of desires or regrets. For the second time there rose a scaffold like Michelangelo's on which the artist, his head thrown back, painted the Creation on the ceiling of the Sistine Chapel: the sickbed on which Marcel Proust consecrates the countless pages which he covered with his handwriting, holding them up in the air, to the creation of his microcosm.

RENÉ GIRARD

The Worlds of Proust

Combray is a closed universe. In it the child lives in the shadow of his parents and the family idols with the same happy intimacy as the medieval village in the shadow of the belfry. Combray's unity is primarily spiritual rather than physical. Combray is the vision shared by all the members of the family. A certain order is superimposed on reality and becomes indistinguishable from it. The first symbol of Combray is the magic lantern whose images take on the shape of the objects on which they are projected and are returned in the same way to us by the wall of the room, the lamp shades, and the doorknobs.

Combray is a closed culture, in the ethnological sense of the word, a *Welt* as the Germans would say, "a little closed world" the novelist calls it. The gulf between Combray and the rest of the world is on the level of perception. Between the perception of Combray and that of the "barbarians" there is a specific difference which it is the essential task of the novelist to reveal. The two bells at the entrance provide us with only a symbol, rather than an illustration of that difference. The bell which "any person of the household ... put ... out of action by coming in 'without ringing' " and "the double peal—timid, oval, gilded—of the visitors' bell" evoke two totally incommensurable universes.

At a very superficial level Combray is still capable of making out the difference in perceptions. Combray notices the difference between the two bells; Combray is not unaware that *its* Saturday has a color, a tonality all its own. Lunch is moved up an hour on that day.

From *Deceit, Desire and the Novel,* translated by Yvonne Freccero. © 1961 by Editions Bernard Grasset, © 1965 by Johns Hopkins University Press.

The return of this asymmetrical Saturday was one of those petty
occurrences, intra-mural, localised, almost civic, which, in un-
eventful lives and stable orders of society, create a kind of
national unity, and become the favourite theme for conversation, for pleasantries, for anecdotes which can be embroidered
as the narrator pleases; it would have provided a nucleus,
ready-made, for a legendary cycle, if any of us had had the epic
mind.

The members of Combray feel a certain solidarity and brotherliness when
they discover something which distinguishes them from the outside world.
Françoise, the maid, particularly enjoys this feeling of unity. Nothing
causes her more amusement than the little misunderstandings occasioned
by the family's forgetting, not that Saturdays are different, but that outsiders are not aware of that fact. The "barbarian" amazed at the change in
schedule of which he was not forewarned appears slightly ridiculous. He is
not *initiated* into the truth of Combray.

"Patriotic" rites spring up in that intermediate zone where the differences between ourselves and others become perceptible without being
completely effaced. The misunderstanding is still half voluntary. On a
more profound level it is not voluntary at all, and only the author-narrator
can bridge the abyss between the divergent perceptions of a *single* object.
Combray is incapable, for example, of understanding that apart from the
bourgeois, domestic Swann to whom it is accustomed, there exists another
aristocratic and elegant Swann, perceived only by high society.

And so, no doubt, from the Swann they had built up for their
own purposes my family had left out, in their ignorance, a
whole crowd of the details of his daily life in the world of
fashion, details by means of which other people, when they met
him, saw all the Graces enthroned in his face and stopping at
the line of his arched nose as at a natural frontier; but they
contrived also to put into a face from which its distinction had
been evicted, a face vacant and roomy as an untenanted house,
to plant in the depths of its unvalued eyes a lingering sense,
uncertain but not unpleasing, half-memory and half-oblivion,
of idle hours spent together.

The novelist is trying to make us see, touch, and feel what men by
definition never see, touch, or feel: two perceptive events which are as
imperative as they are contradictory. Between Combray and the outside

world there is only an appearance of communication. The misapprehension is total but its results are more comic than tragic. We are provided with another example of comic misunderstanding in the imperceptible thanks which Aunt Céline and Aunt Flora give Swann for a present he sent them. The allusions are so vague and distant that no one notices them, but the two old ladies do not for a moment suspect that they may not have been understood.

What is the origin of this inability to communicate? In the case of the "two Swanns" it would seem that it can all be traced to intellectual causes, to a simple lack of information. Certain of the novelist's expressions seem to confirm this hypothesis. The family's *ignorance* creates the Swann of Combray. The narrator sees in this familiar Swann one of the charming *errors* of his youth.

The error is usually accidental. It disappears as soon as the attention of the person involved is drawn to it, as soon as the means of correcting it are provided. But, in the case of Swann the evidence piles up, the truth about him comes in from all sides without the opinion of the family, and especially that of the great-aunt, being in the least affected. It is learned that Swann frequents the aristocracy; *Le Figaro* mentions paintings in "the collection of Charles Swann." But the great-aunt never swerves in her belief. Finally it is discovered that Swann is the friend of Mme de Villeparisis; far from causing the great-aunt to think more highly of Swann, however, this bit of news has the effect of lowering her opinion of Mme de Villeparisis: "How should she know Swann?" says the great-aunt to the grandmother, "A lady who, you always made out, was related to Marshal MacMahon!" The truth, like a bothersome fly, keeps settling on the great-aunt's nose only to be flicked away.

Thus the Proustian error cannot be reduced to its intellectual causes. We must take care not to judge Proust on the basis of one isolated expression, and especially of the particular meaning to which a particular philosopher might limit that expression. We must go beyond the words to the substance of the novel. The truth about Swann does not penetrate Combray because it contradicts the family's social beliefs and its sense of bourgeois hierarchies. Proust tells us that facts do not penetrate the world where our beliefs reign supreme. They neither gave rise to them nor can they destroy them. Eyes and ears are closed when the well-being and integrity of the personal universe are involved. His mother observes his father, but not too closely, for she does not want to understand "the secret of his superiorities." The aunts Céline and Flora possess to an even higher degree the precious ability of not perceiving; they stop listening the moment the conversation changes in their presence to something which does not interest them.

> Their sense of hearing ... would leave its receptive channels unemployed, so effectively that they were actually becoming atrophied. So that if my grandfather wished to attract the attention of the two sisters, he would have to make use of some such alarm signals as mad doctors adopt in dealing with their distracted patients; as by beating several times on a glass with the blade of a knife, fixing them at the same time with a sharp word and a compelling glance.

These defense mechanisms are obviously the result of mediation. When the mediator is as distant as in the case of Combray, they cannot be considered Sartrean "bad faith," but rather what Max Scheler in *Ressentiment* calls "organic falsehood." The falsification of experience is not carried out consciously, as in a simple lie; rather the process begins in advance of any conscious experience at the point at which representations and feelings about value are first elaborated. The "organic falsehood" functions every time someone wishes to *see* only that which serves his "interest" or some other disposition of his instinctive attention, whose object is thus modified even in memory. The man who deludes himself in this way no longer needs to lie.

Combray shies away from dangerous truths as a healthy organism refuses to digest something which would harm it. Combray is an eye which blinks out the particles of dust which might irritate. Everyone at Combray is therefore his own censor; but this self-censorship, far from being painful, blends with the peace of Combray, with the happiness of being a part of Combray. And in its original essence, it is identical with the pious watchfulness with which Aunt Léonie is surrounded. Everyone makes an effort to keep from her anything which might disturb her tranquillity. Marcel earns a reprimand for his lack of consideration when he tells her that during the course of a walk they had met "someone they didn't know."

In the child's eyes, Aunt Léonie's room is the spiritual center, the holy of holies of the family house. The night table crowded with *eau de Vichy*, medicines, and religious pamphlets is an altar at which the high priestess of Combray officiates with the aid of Françoise.

The aunt seems not to be active but it is she who is responsible for the metamorphosis of the heterogeneous data; she transforms it into "Combray lore." Out of it she makes a rich, tasty, and digestible food. She identifies passers-by and strange dogs; she reduces the unknown to the known. Combray owes all its knowledge and truth to her. Combray, "which a fragment of its medieval ramparts enclosed, here and there, in an outline as scrupulously circular as that of a little town in a primitive painting," is a perfect sphere and Aunt Léonie, immobile in her bed, is the center of the sphere. She does not join in the family activities but it is she who gives them their meaning. It is her daily *routine* which makes the sphere revolve harmoniously. The family crowds around the aunt like houses of the village around the church.

There are striking analogies between the organic structure of Combray and the structure of the fashionable salons. There is the same circular vision, the same internal cohesion sanctioned by a system of ritual gestures and words. The Verdurin salon is not simply a meeting place, it is a way of seeing, feeling, judging. The salon is also a "closed culture." Thus the salon will reject anything which threatens its spirtual unity. It possesses an "eliminative function" similar to that of Combray.

The parallel between Combray and the Verdurin salon can be followed all the more easily since the "foreign body" in both cases is the unfortunate Swann. His love for Odette draws him to the Verdurins. His crossing of social lines, his cosmopolitanism, and his aristocratic relations appear even more subversive at the Verdurins than at Combray. The "eliminative function" is exercised with great violence. The great-aunt is satisfied with a few relatively inoffensive sarcasms in reaction to the general feeling of uneasiness caused by Swann. There is no threat to good-neighborly relations; Swann remains *persona grata*. The situation evolves differently in the Verdurin salon. When the "patroness" realizes that Swann cannot be assimilated, the smiles turn to grimaces of hatred. Absolute excommunication is pronounced, the doors of the salon are closed with a bang. Swann is banished to the outer darkness.

There is something strained and rigid about the spiritual unity of the salon which is not present at Combray. This difference is particularly finely drawn at the level of the religious images expressing that unity. The images used to describe Combray are generally borrowed from the primitive religions, from the Old Testament, and from medieval Christianity. The atmosphere is that of young societies in which epic literature flourishes, faith is naïve and vigorous, and foreigners are always "barbarians" but are never hated.

The imagery of the Verdurin salon is completely different. The dominant themes belong to the Inquisition and the witch-hunts. Its unity seems constantly threatened. The patroness is always standing in the breach ready to repulse the attack of the infidels; she nips schisms in the bud; she keeps constant watch over her friends; she disparages distractions which are found beyond her influence; she demands an absolute loyalty; she roots out any sectarian and heretical spirit which compromises the ortho- doxy of her "little clan."

How can we account for the difference between the two different types of the sacred which give unity, the one to the Verdurin salon, the other to Combray? Where are the gods of Combray? Marcel's gods, as we have already seen, are his parents and the great writer Bergotte. They are "distant" gods with whom any metaphysical rivalry is completely out of the question. If we look around the narrator, we find this *external mediation* everywhere. Françoise's gods are the family and especially Aunt Léonie; god for Marcel's mother is his father whom she does not examine too closely in order not to cross the barrier of respect and adoration between him and her; the father's god is the friendly but Olympian M. de Norpois. These gods are always accessible, always ready to answer the call of their faithful, always ready to satisfy reasonable demands, but they are sepa- rated from mortals by an insuperable spiritual distance, a distance which prohibits any metaphysical rivalry. In one of the passages of *Jean Santeuil* which present a sketch of Combray can be found a veritable allegory of this collective external mediation. A swan symbolizes the mediator in the almost feudal universe of middle-class childhood. In this closed and pro- tected universe the prevailing impression is one of joy:

> Nor from that general rapture was the swan [excepted], moving slowly on the river bearing, he too, the gleam of light and happiness on his resplendent body . . . never, for a moment, disturbing the happiness about him, but showing by his joyful mien that he, too, felt it though not by a jot changing his slow, majestic progress, as a noble lady may watch with pleasure her servants' happiness, and pass near to them, not despising their gaiety, not disturbing it, but taking it in no part herself save by a show of gracious kindliness and by the presence of a charm shed by her dignity on all around.

Where, then, are the gods of the Verdurin salon to be found? The answer seems easy. In the first place there are the lesser divinities, painters, musicians, and poets, who frequent the salon: more or less ephemeral incarnations of the supreme divinity—ART—whose slightest emanations are enough to throw Mme Verdurin into ecstasies. There is no danger of the official cult going unnoticed. In its name the "Boetians" and the "bores" are banished. Sacrilege is punished more severely than at Combray; the slightest heresy can provoke a scandal. The temptation is to draw the conclusion that faith is more vigorous at the Verdurins than at Combray.

The difference between the two "closed worlds," the more rigid restriction of the salon, would therefore seem to be explained by a strengthening of *external* mediation; at any rate this is the conclusion suggested by appearances. But appearances are deceptive and the novelist rejects this conclusion. Behind the gods of external mediation who no longer have any real power at the Verdurins, there are the true, hidden gods of *internal* mediation, no longer gods of love, but of hate. Swann is expelled in the name of the official gods but in reality we must see here a reprisal against the implacable mediator, against the disdainful Guermantes who close their doors to Mme Verdurin and to whose world Swann suddenly reveals that he belongs. The real gods of the patroness are enthroned in the salon of the Guermantes. But she would rather die than openly or even secretly worship them as they demand. This is why she carries out the rites of her false aesthetic religion with a passion as frenetic as it is mendacious.

From Combray to the Verdurin salon the structure of the "closed little world" does not seem to have changed. The most obvious traits of this structure are merely strengthened and emphasized; the appearances are, if we might be permitted such an expression, more apparent than ever. The salon is a caricature of the organic unity of Combray, just as a mummified face is a caricature of a living face and accentuates its traits. On closer examination it is seen that the elements of the structure, identical in both cases, have a different hierarchy. At Combray the rejection of the barbarians is subordinate to the affirmation of the gods. At the Verdurins it is the reverse. The rites of union are camouflaged rites of separation. They are no longer observed as a means of communion with those who observe similar rites but as a means of distinction from those who do not observe them. Hatred of the omnipotent mediator supersedes love of the faithful. The disproportionate place the manifestations of this hatred hold in the existence of the salon provides the single but irrefutable indication of metaphysical truth: the hatred outsiders are the true gods.

The almost identical appearances conceal two very different types of mediation. We are now observing the transition from external to internal mediation not on the level of the individual but on that of the "closed little world." The childhood love of Combray yields to the adult rivalry in hatred, the metaphysical rivalry of snobs and lovers.

Collective internal mediation faithfully reproduces the trait of individual mediation. The happiness of being "among one's friends" is as unreal as the happiness of being oneself. The aggressive unity presented by the Verdurin salon to the outside world is simply a façade; the salon has only contempt for itself. This contempt is revealed in the persecution of the unfortunate Saniette. This character is the faithful of the faithful, the pure soul of the Verdurin salon. He plays, or would play if the salon were really all that it pretends to be, a role somewhat similar to Aunt Léonie's at Combray. But instead of being honored and respected, Saniette is buried under insults; he is the butt of the Verdurins. The salon is unaware that it despises itself in the person of Saniette.

The distance between Combray and the life of the salon is not the distance separating "true" from "false" gods. Nor is it the distance that separates a pious and useful lie from the cold truth. Nor can we agree with Heidegger that the gods have "withdrawn." The gods are nearer than ever. Here the divergence between neoromantic thought and novelistic genius becomes absolutely clear. Neoromantic thinkers loudly denounce the artificial character of a cult confined to accepted values and faded idols in the bourgeois universe. Proud of their perceptiveness, these thinkers never go beyond their first observations. They believe that the source of the sacred has simply dried up. They never stop to wonder what might be hidden behind middle-class *hypocrisy*. Only the novelist looks behind the deceptive mask of the official cult and finds the hidden gods of internal mediation. Proust and Dostoyevski do not define our universe by an absence of the sacred, as do the philosophers, but by the perversion and corruption of the sacred, which gradually poisons the sources of life. As one goes further from Combray the positive unity of love develops into the negative unity of hate, into the false unity which hides duplicity and multiplicity.

That is why only one Combray is necessary while there must be several rival salons. At first there are the Verdurin and Guermantes salons. The salons exist only as functions of each other. Among the collectivities that are simultaneously separated and united by double mediation we find a dialectic of master and slave similar to that which controls the relations of individuals. The Verdurin salon and the Guermantes salon carry on an underground struggle for mastery of the world of fashionable society. For most of the novel the Duchess of Guermantes retains her mastery. Haughty, indifferent, and contemptuous, the hawkfaced Duchess is so dominant that she almost seems the universal mediator of the salons. But like all mastery it proves empty and abstract. Naturally Mme de Guermantes does not see her salon with the eyes of those who long for admittance. If the bourgeois Mme Verdurin, who is supposed to be such an art lover, secretly longs only for aristocracy, the aristocratic Mme de Guermantes dreams only of literary and artistic glories.

For a long time Mme Verdurin is the underdog in the struggle with the Guermantes salon. But she refuses to humble herself and obstinately conceals her desire. Here as elsewhere the "heroic" lie finally wins its reward. The working of internal mediation demands Mme Verdurin's ultimate arrival in the residence of the Prince de Guermantes. As for the Duchess, whose *mastery* has been too blasé, she abuses her power and squanders her prestige. In the end she loses her position in society. The laws of the novel necessitate this double reversal.

Combray is always described as a patriarchal regime; it is impossible to say whether it is authoritarian or liberal since it functions all by itself. The Verdurin salon, on the other hand, is a frenzied dictatorship; the patroness is a totalitarian head of state who rules by a skillful mixture of demagoguery and ferocity. When Proust evokes the loyalist sentiments inspired by Combray, he speaks of *patriotism;* when he turns to the Verdurin salon he speaks of *chauvinism.* The distinction between patriotism and chauvinism is an accurate expression of the subtle yet radical difference between Combray and the salons. Patriotism is the result of external mediation while chauvinism is rooted in internal mediation. Patriotism already contains elements of self-love and therefore self-contempt but it is still a sincere cult of heroes and saints. Its fervor is not dependent upon rivalry with other countries. Chauvinism, on the contrary, is the fruit of such rivalry. It is a negative sentiment based on hatred, that is to say, on the secret adoration of the Other.

Proust's remarks on the First World War, despite their extreme caution, betray a profound disgust. Rose colored chauvinism is the product of a mediation similar to that of snobbism. The chauvinist hates a powerful, belligerent, and well-disciplined Germany because he himself is dreaming of war, power, and discipline. The revengeful nationalist feeds on Barrès and praises "the earth and the dead" but the earth and the dead are not important to him. He thinks that his roots go deep but he is floating in an abstraction.

At the end of *Remembrance of Things Past* war breaks out. The Verdurin salon becomes the center of the "fight to the bitter end" attitude in society. All the faithful fall in with the patroness's martial step. Brichot writes a belligerent column in a big Paris newspaper. Everyone, even the violinist Morel, wants to "do his duty." Society's chauvinism finds its complement in civic and national chauvinism. The appearance of chauvinism is thus much more than just appearance. Between the microcosm of

the salon and the macrocosm of the nation at war there is only a difference
of scale. The desire is the same. The metaphors which continually trans-
port us from one dimension to the other draw our attention to this identity
of structure.

France is to Germany what the Verdurin salon is to the Guermantes
salon. Now Mme Verdurin, the sworn enemy of the "bores," ends by
marrying the Prince of Guermantes and removing her arms and baggage
into the enemy camp. The rigorous parallelism between social and national
chauvinism suggests that we should seek in the order of the macrocosm a
parallel to the dramatic reversal in the microcosm, a reversal which can
without exaggeration be considered to touch on "treachery." If the novel
does not provide this parallel it is simply because it ends too soon. Twenty
more years and a second world war are needed to produce the event which
would have allowed Proust to round out his metaphor. In 1940 a certain
kind of abstract chauvinism embraced the cause of triumphant Germany
after years of fulminating against those who timidly suggested a *modus
vivendi* with an "hereditary" enemy not yet gone mad and still confined
within his own frontiers. Similarly, Mme Verdurin inspires terror in her
"little clan" and excommunicates the "faithful" at the slightest sign of
weakness toward the "bores," right up to the day when she marries the
Prince of Guermantes, closes the doors of her salon to the "faithful," and
opens them wide to the worst snobs of the Faubourg Saint-Germain.

Naturally some critics see in the social about-face of Mme Verdurin
proof of her "freedom." We are lucky if they do not make use of this
so-called freedom to "rehabilitate" Proust in the eyes of current thinkers
and to cleanse the novelist of the terrible suspicion of "psychologism."
"Look," they say, "Mme Verdurin is capable of abandoning her principles; this character therefore is certainly worthy of participating in an
existential novel and Proust, too, is a novelist of *freedom!*"

Obviously these critics are making the same mistake as Jean Prévost
when he mistook the political conversion of M. de Rênal for a spontaneous gesture. If Mme Verdurin is "spontaneous" then the enthusiastic
"collaborators" are also, since they were fanatical nationalists only a short
time before. In reality no one is spontaneous: the laws of double mediation
are at work in both cases. The spectacular reprisals against the persecuting
divinity always give way to an attempt at "fusion" when circumstances
appear favorable. Thus the underground man interrupts his plans of ven-
geance to write a passionate, raving letter to the officer who insulted him.
None of these apparent "conversions" contributes anything new. Here we
have no freedom asserting its omnipotence by an authentic break with the

past. The convert has not even changed his mediator. We have the illusion of change because we had not recognized a mediation whose only fruits were "envy, jealousy, and impotent hatred." The bitterness of these fruits concealed from us the presence of the god.

The structural identity of the two chauvinisms is again revealed in the expulsion of Baron de Charlus. The affair is a more violent version of Swann's misadventure. Charlus is drawn to the Verdurins by Morel; Swann was attracted by Odette. Swann was the friend of the Duchess of Guermantes; Charlus is her brother-in-law. Thus the Baron is eminently a "bore" and subversive. The "eliminative function" of the salon is exerted against him with particular savagery. The oppositions and contradictions aroused by metaphysical desire are even more obvious and painful than in *Swann in Love* for the mediator has come much nearer.

War has been declared; the account of the themes which accompany the execution of the sentence is colored by the atmosphere of the time. To the traditional terms describing a "bore" is added "German spy." Microcosmic and macrocosmic aspects of "chauvinism" are almost indistinguishable and Mme Verdurin is soon to blend them. She announces to all her visitors that Charlus has been "spying continuously" on her salon for two years.

The sentence reveals very clearly the systematic distortion of the real by metaphysical desire and hatred. This distortion provides the subjective unity of perception. Our immediate thought is that the sentence fits the patroness too well to fit her object too: the Baron de Charlus. If we have to find the individual essence in an irreducible difference, the sentence cannot reveal the essence of Mme Verdurin without falsifying the essence of the Baron de Charlus. It cannot contain the mutually incompatible essences of both.

Yet this is the miracle it accomplishes. When she declares that Charlus has for two years been a spy in her salon, Mme Verdurin depicts herself, but she also depicts the Baron. Charlus is not, of course, a spy. The patroness exaggerates wildly but she is very well aware of what she is doing; the barb pierces Charlus in the most vulnerable part of his being. Charlus is a terrible defeatist. He is not content to despise Allied propaganda in silence. He launches into subversive suggestions even in the streets. His Germanism chokes him.

Proust analyzes at length Charlus's defeatism. He gives many explanations but the most important of them is homosexuality. Charlus feels a hopeless desire for the handsome soldiers swarming all over Paris. These unattainable soldiers are "exquisite tormentors" for him. They are auto-

matically associated with Evil. The war which divides the universe into
two enemy camps provides nourishment for the instinctive dualism of the
masochist. The Allied cause being that of the wicked persecutors, Germany
must of necessity be associated with the persecuted Good. Charlus confuses his own cause with that of the enemy nation all the more easily that
the Germans inspire in him real physical revulsion; he makes no distinction between their ugliness and his own, their military defeats and his own
amorous defeats. Charlus is justifying himself when he justifies a crushed
Germany.

These feelings are essentially negative. His love for Germany is not
nearly as strong as his hatred of the Allies. The frenzied attention he pays
to chauvinism is that of the subject to the mediator. Charlus's Weltan-
schauung is a perfect illustration of the masochistic scheme we described in
the preceding chapter. The unity of Charlus's existence becomes even more
obvious if we explore his social life, an intermediary zone between his
sexual life and his defeatist opinions.

Charlus is a Guermantes. He is the object of an idolatrous cult in the
salon of his sister-in-law, the Duchess of Guermantes. He never misses an
opportunity, especially in front of his plebeian friends, of proclaiming the
superiority of his background, but for him the Faubourg Saint-German has
none of the fascination it holds for the bourgeois snobs. By definition,
metaphysical desire is never aimed at an accessible object. Thus the baron's desires are not drawn by the noble Faubourg but by the lower
"riff-raff." This "descending" snobbism explains his passion for the de-
bauched character Morel. The prestige of baseness with which Charlus
endows him extends to the whole Verdurin salon. The nobleman can
scarcely distinguish this bourgeois hue from the more garish colors which
are the normal background of his clandestine pleasures.

Chauvinist, immoral, and bourgeois, the Verdurin salon is a fascinat-
ingly wicked place at the heart of that greater and equally chauvinist,
immoral, and bourgeois place, France. The Verdurin salon offers a refuge
for the seductive Morel; France at war is full of proud officers. The Baron
feels no more "at home" in the Verdurin salon than he does in chauvinist
France. But he lives in France and his desire draws him to the Verdurin
salon. The Guermantes salon, aristocratic and insipidly virtuous, plays in
the Baron's social system a role similar to that of the beloved but distant
Germany in his political system. Love, social life, and war are the three
circles of this existence which is perfectly unified, or rather perfectly
double in its contradiction. All levels correspond and verify the obsessive
logic of the Baron.

Thus the counterpart of Mme Verdurin's "chauvinist" obsession is the "antichauvinist" obsession of Charlus. The two obsessions do not isolate the two victims as common sense would expect. They do not close them into two incommensurable worlds; they bring them together in a communion of hatred.

These two existences combine the same elements but organize them inversely. Mme Verdurin claims to be loyal to her salon but her heart is with the Guermantes. Charlus claims to be loyal to the Guermantes but his heart is with the Verdurins. Mme Verdurin praises her "little clan" and scorns the "bores." Charlus praises the Guermantes salon and scorns the "nobodies." We need only reverse the signs to pass from one universe to the other. The disagreement of the two characters is a perfect negative agreement.

This symmetry enables Mme Verdurin to give grotesque but striking expression to the truth about herself and about the Baron in a single sentence. To accuse Charlus of being a spy is Mme Verdurin's secret protest against the scorn of the Guermantes. Common sense cannot see what good it would serve the German High Command to have "detailed reports of the organisation of the little clan." Thus common sense sees through the folly of Mme Verdurin but the more one fixes his attention on her folly the greater the risk that it will fail to see the corresponding folly of Charlus. It is precisely to the extent that she slips into the irrational that Mme Verdurin resembles the Baron. The madness of one joins the madness of the other in an insane unity, disregarding completely the barriers that common sense would presume to exist between society, life, and the war. Mme Verdurin's chauvinism is aimed at the Guermantes salon and Charlus's defeatism is aimed at the Verdurin salon. Each has only to yield to his madness to understand the other with an acute but incomplete knowledge—acute because passion triumphs over the object-fetishism which paralyzes common sense; incomplete because passion does not perceive the triangle of desire, it fails to recognize the anguish behind the other's pride and apparent mastery.

In a one-sentence reference of Mme Verdurin to Charlus's "spying" Proust lets us glimpse the complexity of the bonds hatred can weave between two individuals. Mme Verdurin's words reveal both understanding and blindness, a subtle truth and a glaring lie; they are as rich in associations and implications of all kinds as a line of Mallarmé but the novelist is not inventing anything. His genius draws directly on an intersubjective truth which is almost completely unknown to the psychological and philosophical systems of our time.

These words indicate that relationships on the level of the salons and of internal mediation are very different from those established, or rather which cannot be established, at the level of external mediation. As we have seen, Combray is the kingdom of misunderstanding. Since the autonomy is real, relationships with the outside world must of necessity be superficial; no lasting intrigue can be formed. The brief scenes of Combray, like Don Quixote's adventures, are independent of each other. The order in which they succeed each other is almost a matter of indifference for each adventure constitutes a significant totality whose essence is misunderstanding.

Communication would seem to be even more impossible on the level of internal mediation since individuals and salons clash with each other even more violently. As the differences become more acute, any relationship would seem to become impossible in the small worlds which are more and more closed to each other. The aim of all romantic writers is to convince us of precisely this. Romanticism seeks that which is irreducibly ours in that which opposes us most violently to others. It distinguishes two parts in an individual, that which is superficial and permits agreement with others and a more essential part in which agreement is impossible. But this distinction is false and the novelist proves it. The heightening of ontological sickness does not throw the individual out of gear. Mme Verdurin's chauvinism and Charlus's antichauvinism fit each other perfectly for one is hollow where the other projects. The *differences* displayed by the romantic are the teeth of the gears; they and they alone cause the machine to turn, and they give birth to a *novelistic world* which did not exist before.

Combray was truly autonomous but the salons are not. They are only the less autonomous for their shrill claims to autonomy. At the level of internal mediation, the collectivity, like the individual, ceases to be an absolute reference point. The salons can now be understood only by contrasting them with rival salons, by fitting them into the totality of which each of them is no more than an element.

On the level of external mediation there are only "closed little worlds." The bonds are so loose that there is not as yet any real *novelistic world*, any more than there is a "concert of Europe" before the seventeenth century. That "concert" is a result of rivalry on the national scale. Nations are obsessed with each other. Every day their relationships become closer but they often assume a negative aspect. Just as individual fascination gives birth to individualism, so collective fascination spawns a "collective individualism" which is called nationalism and chauvinism. Individualist and collectivist myths are brothers for they always mask the opposition of the same to the same. The desire to be "among one's friends" just as much as the desire to be oneself hides a desire to be the other.

The "small closed worlds" are neutral particles which have no action on each other. The salons are positive and negative particles which both attract and repel each other, like atomic particles. There are no more monads but semblances of monads which form one vast closed world. The unity of this world, as coherent as that of Combray, is based on an inverse principle. At Combray love still has the upper hand, but hatred generates the world of the salons.

In the hell of *Cities of the Plain* the triumph of hate is absolute. Slaves gravitate around their masters and the masters themselves are slaves. Individuals and collectivities are at once inseparable and completely isolated. Satellites gravitate around planets and planets around stars. This image of the world of the novel as a cosmic system recurs frequently in Proust and brings with it the image of the novelist astronomer who measures the orbits and derives the laws that govern them.

The world of the novel obtains its cohesion from these laws of internal mediation. Only knowledge of these laws makes it possible to answer the question of Vyacheslav Ivanov in his work on Dostoyevski: "How," the Russian critic asks, "can separation become a principle of union, how can hatred keep the very ones who hate bound together?"

The movement from Combray to the universe of the salons is continuous, with no perceptible transitions. The opposition between *external* and *internal* mediation is not an opposition between Good and Evil, it is not an absolute separation. A closer examination of Combray will reveal, in a nascent state, all the features of the worldly salons.

The great-aunt's ridicule at Swann's expense is an early and faint sketch of the thunderbolts Mme Verdurin and Mme de Guermantes will unleash. The petty persecutions endured by the innocent grandmother prefigure the cruelty of the Verdurins toward Saniette and the frightful coldness of Mme de Guermantes toward her great friend Swann. Marcel's mother refuses, in true bourgeois fashion, to receive Mme Swann. Even the narrator profanes the sacred in the person of Françoise, whom he tries to "demystify." He continually tries to destroy her naïve faith in Aunt Léonie. Aunt Léonie herself abuses her supernatural prestige; she foments sterile rivalries between Françoise and Eulalie; she turns into a cruel tyrant.

The negative element is already present at Combray; thanks to it the closed little world is shut up in itself. It secures the elimination of dangerous truths. This negative element grows gradually larger and ends by devouring everything in the worldly salons. And, as usual, this negative element is rooted in pride and its mediated desire. Pride prevents the great-aunt from perceiving Swann's social position, pride prevents Marcel's mother from receiving Mme Swann. This is but a nascent pride but its essence will not change from one end of the novel to the other. It has scarcely started on its destructive work, but the decisive choice has already been made. The seed of *Cities of the Plain* can already be found in Combray. All that is necessary to move from one universe to the other is to give in to the incline of the slope, to that movement which increases steadily and takes us ever further from the mystic center. This movement is almost imperceptible in Aunt Léonie stretched out in her bed; it becomes more rapid in the child who gazes too hard at the gods of Combray and prepares to succumb to every kind of exoticism.

What is this center which is never reached, which is left further and further behind? Proust gives no direct answer but the symbolism of his work speaks for him and sometimes against him. Combray's center is the church, "epitomising the town, representing it, speaking of it and for it to the horizon." At the center of the church is the steeple of Saint-Hilary, which is for the town what Léonie's room is for the household. The steeple "shaped and crowned and consecrated every occupation, every hour of the day, every point of view in the town." All the gods of Combray are assembled at the foot of this steeple:

> It was always to the steeple that one must return, always it which dominated everything else, summing up the houses with an unexpected pinnacle, raised before me like the Finger of God, Whose Body might have been concealed below among the crowd of human bodies without fear of my confounding It, for that reason, with them.

The steeple is visible everywhere but the church is always empty. The human and earthly gods of external mediation have already become idols; they do not fall in line vertically with the steeple. But they always remain near enough to it so that one glance can encompass Combray and its church. The nearer the mediator comes to the desiring subject the more remote transcendency becomes from that vertical. It is deviated transcendency at work. It drags the narrator and his novelistic universe further and further from the steeple, in a series of concentric circles entitled *Within a Budding Grove, The Guermantes Way, Cities of the Plain, The Captive* and *The Sweet Cheat Gone*. The greater the distance from the mystic center, the more painful, frenzied, and futile becomes the agitation, until we arrive at *The Past Recaptured,* which reverses this movement. This double movement of flight and return is prefigured in the evening pursuits of the crows of Saint-Hilary:

> From the tower windows, it [the steeple] released, it let fall at regular intervals flights of jackdaws which for a little while would wheel and caw, as though the ancient stones which allowed them to sport thus and never seemed to see them, becoming of a sudden uninhabitable and discharging some infinitely disturbing element, had struck them and driven them forth. Then after patterning everywhere the violet velvet of the evening air, abruptly soothed, they would return and be absorbed in the tower, deadly no longer but benignant.

Does Proust's work have a sociological value? It is frequently said that *Remembrance of Things Past* is inferior in this respect to *The Human Comedy* or *The Rougon-Macquart*. We are told that Proust is interested only in the old nobility. His work therefore lacks "breadth and objectivity." Beneath these unfavorable comments we recognize the old realist and positivist conception of the art of the novel. Novelistic genius draws up a detailed inventory of men and things; it should present us with a panorama as complete as possible of economic and social reality.

If this idea were taken seriously, then Proust would be an even more mediocre novelist than they supposed. He is reproached with having "limited his inquiry to the Faubourg Saint-Germain," but that would be giving him credit for more than he attempts. Proust does not embark on any systematic exploration, even in the narrow area which the critics are willing to grant him. He tells us vaguely that the Guermantes are very rich, and that others have been ruined. Where the conscientious novelist would bury us under a heap of records, wills, inventories, accounts, bailiffs' procedures, portfolios of shares and bonds, Proust merely reports a few scraps of conversation over a cup of tea. And he never introduces them for their own sake but simply in relation to something else. There is nothing in all this which warrants the pompous title of *research*. Proust does not even try to suggest, by a definitive tone or an enumeration of unusual objects, that he has "exhausted the documentation."

None of the questions that interest the sociologist seem to attract Proust's attention. We conclude that this novelist is not interested in the problems of society. This indifference, whether it is blamed or praised, is always conceived as a negative element, a kind of mutilation in the service of a particular aesthetic, something similar to the proscription of plebeian words in classical tragedy.

We have learned enough to reject this narrow concept of the art of the novel. The novelist's truth is total. It embraces all aspects of individual and collective existence. Even if the novel neglects some of these aspects it is sure to indicate a perspective. Sociologists can recognize nothing in Proust which reminds them of their own approach because there is a fundamental opposition between the sociology of the novel and the sociology of sociologists. This opposition involves not only the solution and methods but also the data of the problem to be resolved.

In the eyes of the sociologist the Faubourg Saint-Germain is a very tiny but real sector of the social landscape. The frontiers seem to be so clearly fixed that no one questions them. But these frontiers become increasingly blurred the further one reads in Proust's novel. The narrator suffers a terrible letdown when he eventually gains admittance to the Guermantes'! He discovers that the conversation and thought in their salon does not differ from that to which he is accustomed. The essence of the Faubourg seems to vanish. The Guermantes salon loses its individuality and blends into the vague grey of already known milieux.

The Faubourg cannot be defined by tradition since that tradition is no longer understood by so considerable and vulgar a character as the Duke of Guermantes. The Faubourg cannot be defined by heredity since a member of the middle class like Mme Leroi can enjoy a more brilliant social position in it than a Mme de Villeparisis. Since the end of the nineteenth century the Faubourg has not really been a center of political or financial power despite the fact that wealth abounds there and men of influence frequent it in great numbers. Nor is the Faubourg distinguished by a peculiar mentality. It is reactionary in politics, snobbish and superficial in art and literature. There is nothing in all of this to distinguish the milieu of the Guermantes from those of the other idle rich of the early twentieth century.

The sociologist interested in the Faubourg Saint-Germain should not turn to *Remembrance of Things Past*. This novel is not only useless, it can be dangerous. The sociologist thinks he has hold of the object of his research and suddenly he finds it slipping between his fingers. The Faubourg is neither a class, nor a group, nor a milieu; none of the categories currently used by sociologists is applicable to it. Like certain atomic particles, the Faubourg vanishes when scientific instruments are brought to bear on it. This object cannot be isolated. The Faubourg ceased to exist a hundred years ago. And yet it exists because it excites the most violent desires. Where does the Faubourg begin, and where does it end? We do not know. But the snob knows; he never hesitates. It is as if the snob possessed a sixth sense which determined the exact social standing of a salon.

The Faubourg exists for the snob and does not exist for the nonsnob. We should say, rather, that it would not exist for the nonsnob were it not that the latter agrees to accept the snob's testimony in order to settle the question once and for all. Obviously the Faubourg exists only for the snob.

Proust is accused of confining himself to too narrow a milieu but no one recognizes and denounces that narrowness better than Proust. Proust shows us the insignificance of "high society" not only from the intellectual and human angle but also from the *social* point of view: "The members of the fashionable set delude themselves as to the social importance of their names." Proust pushes the demystification of the Faubourg Saint-Germain much further than his democratic critics. The latter, in fact, believe in the objective existence of the magic object. Proust constantly repeats that the object does not exist. "Society is the kingdom of nothingness." We must take this affirmation literally. The novelist constantly emphasizes the contrast between the objective nothingness of the Faubourg and the enormous reality it acquires in the eyes of the snob.

The novelist is interested neither in the petty reality of the object nor in that same object transfigured by desire; he is interested in the process of transfiguration. This has always been the fundamental concern of the great novelists. Cervantes is not interested in either the barber's basin or Mambrino's helmet. What fascinates him is that Don Quixote can confuse a simple barber's basin with Mambrino's helmet. What fascinates Proust is that the snob can mistake the Faubourg Saint-Germain for that fabled kingdom everyone dreams of entering.

The sociologist and the naturalistic novelist want only *one* truth. They impose this truth on all perceiving subjects. What they call *object* is an insipid compromise between the incompatible perceptions of desire and nondesire. This object's credibility comes from its intermediate position, which weakens all the contradictions. Instead of taking the edge off these contradictions the great novelist sharpens them as much as possible. He underscores the metamorphoses brought about by desire. The naturalistic writer does not perceive this metamorphosis because he is incapable of criticizing his own desire. The novelist who reveals triangular desire cannot be a snob but he must have been one. He must have known desire but must now be beyond it.

The Faubourg is an enchanted helmet to the snob and a barber's basin to the nonsnob. Every day we are told that the world is controlled by "concrete" desires: wealth, well-being, power, oil, etc. The novelist asks an apparently harmless question: "What is snobbism?"

In his probe of snobbism the novelist is asking himself in his own way just what might be the hidden springs that make the social mechanism tick. But the scientists shrug their shoulders. The question is too frivolous for them. If they are urged to give an answer they become evasive. They will suggest that the novelist is interested in snobbism for the wrong reasons. He himself is a snob. Let us say rather he was one. That is true; but the question remains. What is snobbism?

The snob seeks no concrete advantage; his pleasures and sufferings are purely *metaphysical*. Neither the realist, the idealist, nor the Marxist can answer the novelist's question. Snobbism is the grain of dust that finds its way into the gears of "science" and throws it out of kilter.

The snob desires nothingness. When the concrete differences among men disappear or recede into the background, in any sector whatever of society, abstract rivalry makes its appearance, but for a long time it is confused with the earlier conflicts whose shape it assumes. The snob's abstract anguish should not be confused with class oppression. Snobbism does not belong to the hierarchies of the past as is generally thought, but to the present and still more to the democratic future. The Faubourg Saint-Germain in Proust's time is in the vanguard of an evolution that changes more or less rapidly all the layers of society. The novelist turns to the snobs because their desire is closer to being completely void of content than ordinary desires. Snobbism is the caricature of these desires. Like every caricature, snobbism exaggerates a feature and makes us see what we would never have noticed in the original.

The Faubourg Saint-Germain is a pseudo-object and thus plays a privileged role in novelistic revelation. This role can be compared to that of radium in modern physics. Radium occupies a position in nature as limited as the Faubourg Saint-Germain in French society. But this extremely rare compound possesses exceptional properties which contradict certain principles of the old physics and gradually overthrows all the perspectives of an earlier "science." Similarly, snobbism gives the lie to certain principles of standard sociology; it shows us motives for action never suspected by scientific thought.

The genius of Proust's novel derives from snobbism transcended. His snobbism takes the author to the most abstract place in an abstract society, toward the most outrageously empty pseudo-object—in other words, to the place most suited to novelistic revelation. In retrospect, snobbism must be identified with the first steps of genius; an infallible judgment is already at work, as well as an irresistible impetus. The snob must have been excited by a great hope and have suffered tremendous letdowns, so that the gap between the object of desire and the object of nondesire imposes itself on his consciousness, and that his consciousness may triumph over the barriers erected each time by a new desire.

After serving the author, the caricatural force of snobbism should now serve the reader. In reading we relive the spiritual experience whose form is that of the novel itself. After conquering his truth, the novelist can descend from the Faubourg Saint-Germain to the less rarefied regions of social existence, like the physicist who extends to "ordinary" compounds the facts he has learned from that "extraordinary" compound, radium. In most circles of middle- and even lower-class existence Proust discovers the same triangular structure of desire, the sterile opposition of contraries, hatred of the hidden god, the excommunications and destructive taboos of internal mediation.

This progressive broadening of novelistic truth entails the extension of the term snobbism to the most diverse professions and environments. In *Remembrance of Things Past*, we find a snobbism of professors, doctors, lawyers, and even servants. Proust's uses of the word snobbism define an "abstract" sociology, universal in its application, but whose principles are most active among the very rich and idle.

Thus Proust is far from indifferent to social reality. In a sense this is all he talks of, for to the novelist of triangular desire interior life is already social and social life is always the reflection of individual desire. But Proust stands in radical opposition to the old positivism of Auguste Comte. He is equally opposed to Marxism. Marx's *alienation* is analogous to metaphysical desire. But alienation has little correspondence with anything but external mediation and the upper stages of internal mediation. The Marxist analyses of bourgeois society are more penetrating than most but they are vitiated at the outset by yet another illusion. The Marxist thinks he can do away with all alienation by destroying bourgeois society. He makes no allowance for the extreme forms of metaphysical desire, those described by Proust and Dostoyevski. The Marxist is taken in by the object; his materialism is only a relative progress beyond middle-class idealism.

Proust's work describes new forms of alienation that succeed the old forms when "needs" have been satisfied and when concrete differences no longer control relationships among men. We have seen how snobbism raises abstract barriers between individuals who enjoy the same income, who belong to the same class and to the same tradition. Some of the intuitions of American sociology help us appreciate the fertility of Proust's point of view. Thorstein Veblen's idea of "conspicuous consumption" is already triangular. It deals a fatal blow to materialist theories. The value of the article consumed is based solely on how it is regarded by the other. Only another's desire can produce desire. More recently, David Riesman and Vance Packard have shown that even the vast American middle class, which is as free from want and even more uniform than the circles described by Proust, is also divided into abstract compartments. It produces more and more taboos and excommunications among absolutely similar but opposed units. Insignificant distinctions appear immense and produce incalculable effects. The individual's existence is still dominated by the other but this other is no longer a class oppressor as in Marxist alienation; he is the neighbor on the other side of the fence, the school friend, the professional rival. The other becomes more and more fascinating the nearer he is to the self.

The Marxists explain that these are "residual" phenomena connected with the bourgeois structure of society. Their reasoning would be more convincing if analogous phenomena were not observed in Soviet society. Bourgeois sociologists are only shuffling the cards when they claim, observing these phenomena, that "classes are forming again in the U.S.S.R." Classes are not forming again: new alienations are appearing where the old ones have disappeared.

Even in their boldest intuitions the sociologists do not succeed in completely throwing off the tyranny of the object. None of them has gone as far as novelistic reflection. They tend to confuse the old class distinctions, distinctions imposed externally, with the inner distinctions created by metaphysical desire. It is easy to make this confusion since the transition from one alienation to another covers a long period during which double mediation is proceeding underground without ever coming to the surface. The sociologists never get as far as the laws of metaphysical desire because they do not realize that even material values are finally swallowed up by double mediation. The snob desires nothing concrete. The novelist observes this and traces the symmetrical and empty oppositions of snobbism on all levels of individual and collective life. He shows us how the abstract triumphs in private, professional, national, and even international life. He shows that the First World War, far from being the last of the national conflicts, is the first of the great abstract conflicts of the twentieth century. In short, Proust takes up the history of metaphysical desire at the very point where Stendhal left it. He shows us double mediation crossing national frontiers and acquiring the planetary dimensions which we find that it has today.

After describing social rivalries in terms of military operations, Proust describes military operations in terms of social rivalries. What we considered a moment ago as an image now becomes an object and the object becomes an image. As in contemporary poetry, the two terms of the image are interchangeable. The same desire triumphs in both microcosm and macrocosm. The structure is the same, only the pretext changes. Proust's metaphors deflect our attention from the object and direct it to the mediator; they help us turn from linear desire to triangular desire.

Charlus and Mme Verdurin confuse social life with the First World War; the novelist goes beyond this madness as it in turn had outgrown "common sense." He no longer confuses the two areas, he methodically assimilates them to one another. The novelist for this reason runs the risk of appearing superficial in the eyes of *specialists*. He is accused of explaining big events by "little causes." Historians want history to be taken seriously and they will never forgive Saint-Simon for having interpreted some of Louis XIV's wars in terms of court rivalries. They forget that nothing which concerned Louis XIV's favor could be considered unimportant during his reign.

The distance between pure and simple futility and cataclysmic futility is imperceptible. Saint-Simon is aware of this and so are the novelists. There are, in any case, no "causes" great or small, there is only the infinitely active void of metaphysical desire. The First World War, like the war of the salons, is the fruit of this desire. To be convinced of this, we have only to consider the antagonists. We see the same indignation, the same theatrical gestures, on both sides. The speeches are all the same: to make them admirable or atrocious, depending on the listener, all that is necessary is to reverse the proper names. Germans and French slavishly copy each other. A comparison of certain texts gives Charlus an opportunity for some very bitter laughter.

Some years ago we could still smile at this universal snobbism. A prisoner of his own obsession with society, the novelist seemed to us far removed from contemporary horrors and anguish. But Proust should be reread in the light of recent historical development. Everywhere there are symmetrical *blocs* opposing each other. Gog and Magog imitate and hate each other passionately. Ideology is merely a pretext for ferocious oppositions which are secretly in agreement. The *Internationale* of nationalism and the nationalism of the *Internationale* blend and intersect in inextricable confusion.

In his book, *1984*, the English novelist George Orwell portrays directly certain aspects of this historical structure. Orwell clearly understands that the totalitarian structure is always *double*. But he does not show the connection between individual desire and the collective structure. We sometimes get the impression from his books that the "system" has been imposed from the outside on the innocent masses. De Rougemont in *Love in the Western World* goes still further; he is even closer to novelistic insight when he traces the source of collective wills to power and totalitarian structures to that individual pride which originally gave birth to the mystics of passion. "Unmistakably, when rival wills to power confront one another—and there were already *several* Totalitarian States!—they are bound to clash passionately. Each becomes for some other an *obstruction*. The real, tacit, and inevitable aim of the totalitarian elevation was therefore war, and war means *death*."

We are told that Proust has neglected the most important aspects of modern social life, that he does no more than describe a relic of former times, a survival destined to disappear, and which at best is only slightly picturesque. In a way this is true. Proust's little world is rapidly receding from our life. But the great world in which we are beginning to live grows more like it every day. The setting is different, the scale is different, but the structure is the same.

A quarter of a century of this ambiguous historical evolution has made a relatively obscure and difficult work crystal clear. Critics have noticed the growing clarity of this masterpiece and they see in it the result of its own radiance. The novel itself is supposed to be training its own readers and shedding more and more light on the understanding of itself. This optimistic point of view is linked to the romantic idea of the artist as a creator of new values, another Prometheus refining the celestial fire in order to give it to a grateful human race. This theory certainly cannot be applied to the novel. The novel does not contribute new values; with great effort, it reconquers the values of previous novels.

Remembrance of Things Past no longer seems obscure but it is not necessarily better *understood*. The spiritual influence of great novels is weak, as we know, and it is very seldom exerted in the direction anticipated by the author. The reader projects into the work the same meanings he already projects into the world. With the passing of time this projection becomes easier since the work is "ahead" of society, which gradually catches up with it. The secret of this advance is in no way mysterious. In the first place, it is the novelist who feels desire the most intensely. His desire leads him into the most abstract regions and to the most meaningless objects. Thus his desire almost automatically leads him to the summit of the social edifice. As we have already remarked in connection with Flaubert, this is where the ontological sickness is most acute. The symptoms observed by the novelist will gradually spread to the lower layers of that society. The metaphysical situations portrayed in the novel will become familiar to a great number of readers; the oppositions in the novel will find their exact replicas in day-to-day existence.

The novelist who reveals the desire of the social elite is almost always *prophetic*. He is describing intersubjective structures that will gradually become banal. What is true of Proust is also true of other novelists. Almost all the great novelists yield to the temptation of an aristocratic background. In all of Stendhal's novels there is a double movement from the provinces to the capital and from middle-class life to fashionable life. Don Quixote's adventures gradually lead him toward the aristocracy. Stavrogin, the universal mediator of *The Possessed,* is an aristocrat. *The Idiot, The Possessed, The Raw Youth*, and *The Brothers Karamazov* are "aristocratic" novels. Dostoyevski often explains the role of the Russian aristocracy in his novels. Its degeneracy and moral corruption act as a magnifying glass on Russian life, excluding the life of the peasant. If allowance is made for the differences of language and ethical outlook, that is precisely the role played by the aristocracy in the novels of Cervantes, Stendhal, and Proust.

The great novels end in the sterile abstraction of high society because the whole society gradually tends toward that abstraction. Such diverse minds as Paul Valéry and Jean-Paul Sartre have criticized Proust for the frivolity of his book. Everyone says that he does not understand France, that he confuses it with the Faubourg Saint-Germain. We must agree with the critics, but in this brilliant confusion lies one of the great secrets of Proust's creation. Those who portray the social elite are either very superficial or very profound depending on whether they reflect metaphysical desire or whether on the contrary they succeed in revealing it.

HOWARD MOSS

The Windows

My curiosity emboldening me by degrees, I went down to the
groundfloor window, which also stood open with its shutters ajar.
                                                    —*Cities of the Plain*

While Marcel waits for his mother to come up and kiss him good night, he peers down into the garden through his bedroom window. That window is to become a point of view, a transparency more viable than that which ordinarily separates the spectator from the visible while it makes vision possible. In Proust, the window is, psychologically, the voyeur's picture. Accidental images of other people's pleasure fulfill a painful need in the viewer. Contributing a power within himself to what he sees, Marcel is the victim of what is to be seen.

We are introduced to the window device in a subtle way. In Marcel's room at Combray, he looks at the lantern slides of Golo and Geneviève de Brabant, that ancestress of the Duchesse de Guermantes who first stirs the sediment that is to coalesce around the Duchesse's name and person. Marcel is able, by manipulating the projector, to focus the magic lantern slides on any part of his room. Their images are both deeded and willed.

There is a finespun association between the colors of the lantern slides and the colors Proust uses in the scene in which Marcel first sees the Duchesse in church. In the slides, Geneviève de Brabant wears a blue girdle, the castle and the moor are yellow, and the body of Golo, overcoming material obstacles, floats on the walls, on the door handle, wearing his red cloak. His face is described as pale. Here, in part, is the church scene:

From *The Magic Lantern of Marcel Proust*. © 1963 by Howard Moss. Macmillan, 1962.

> Suddenly, during the nuptial mass, the beadle, by moving to
> one side, enabled me to see, sitting in a chapel, a lady with fair
> hair and a large nose, piercing blue eyes, a billowy scarf of
> mauve silk, glossy and new and brilliant, and a little spot at the
> corner of her nose. And because the surface of her face, which
> was red. . . .

This passage is followed by this interesting connecting link to the lantern
slides:

> we were uncertain, till then, whether we were not looking
> merely at a projection of limelight from a lantern.

And ends thus:

> Her eyes waxed blue as a periwinkle flower, wholly beyond my
> reach, yet dedicated by her to me; and the sun, bursting out
> again from behind a threatening cloud and darting the full
> force of its rays on to the Square and into the sacristy, shed a
> geranium glow over the red carpet laid down for the wedding,
> along which Mme. de Guermantes smilingly advanced, and
> covered its woolen texture with a nap of rosy velvet, a bloom
> of light.

The colors of the lantern slides and the stained-glass windows, both
illuminating figures pertinent to the Duchesse's geneology—Gilbert le
Mauvais in stained glass, Geneviève de Brabant in the lantern's hues—
shine down and through the Duchesse de Guermantes. They suggest, too,
the fluidity of the apparently stable, the immateriality of what appears to
be real. Just as Golo and Geneviève de Brabant can be focused on a
doorknob in Marcel's room, so the light of the Duchesse's stained-glass
ancestors focus their past illuminations on her, transcending her physical
body, making her—as Marcel sees her—something more than mortal. The
affinity between the lantern slides and the stained-glass windows is one of
the finer shades on Proust's palette, for it is to be through the "lenses" of
windows that Marcel is to observe certain secrets of life, each one enlight-
ening a mysterious past he did not understand, or projecting a significant
image into the future.

At Montjouvain, on one of Marcel's solitary walks along the Méséglise
way, he falls asleep outside Vinteuil's house. When he wakes, he sees the
first horror scene of *Remembrance of Things Past*, Mlle. Vinteuil's seduction by a woman friend, preceded by the sadistic ritual of spitting on

Vinteuil's photograph. This scene follows one in which Marcel yearns to seduce a peasant girl—one who will be an extension of the countryside itself, a female avatar of the local ground, a precursor to the spectral landscapes locked up in the bodies of Gilberte, the Duchesse, and Albertine. What is the point of this scene?

A serious relation between sex and art is being established, for it is through his love for his daughter, and the misery her Lesbian attachment causes him, that Vinteuil, a country tunesmith—our first impression of him—is transformed into a great composer. And it will be, ironically, this very same friend of his daughter's who will save Vinteuil's septet for posterity by meticulously collating various manuscripts of the score that Vinteuil left behind him when he died. Like Aunt Léonie's delusions, this woman is both a "cause" and a "cure"; ruining Vinteuil's life, she redeems herself by preserving his art, part of whose greatness is attributable to her very existence. It is also the first introduction of the homosexual theme in *Remembrance of Things Past.* Significantly, it will be through a window again that Marcel sees the meeting of Charlus and Jupien, their recognition and ritual pattern of seduction. This second revelation sheds a further light on the meaning of the first.

These two scenes—Montjouvain and the courtyard scene that opens *Cities of the Plain*—are linked in many fashions, aside from being two explicit visions of sexual perversion. The pollenization of a rare orchid by a bee, the only insect that can fertilize it, picks up the biological motif with its flower metaphor, a motif implicit in the earlier scene in Marcel's desire to possess a human fragment of the Méséglise soil. Both scenes are seen through windows, and both scenes require the presence of a passive viewer whose existence is unknown to the participants. To Marcel, the helpless witness of both, they are more than prurient visions; they are *happenings* that are to have the profoundest effect on the future of his life.

Homosexuals play a particular biological role in *Remembrance of Things Past.* Acting behind windows through which their secrets can be observed—windows that often overlook gardens—they illustrate both the irrationality of human emotions and the capriciousness of nature. Like the rare orchid that waits to be fertilized by a bee in the Duchesse de Guermantes's courtyard, Charlus and Jupien exemplify a rare form of existence. Created from, but not creating life, they are a form, neverthe-less, that has existed always. If instinct has become insidious in Swann's choice of Odette and Marcel's of Albertine—choices that go counter to probability and reason—Charlus's choice of Morel goes counter to biology itself, if one assumes the purpose of biology to be reproduction. The impossibility of homosexual relationships in Proust is vitiated by two facts: the pervasive maternal fog through which he sees *all* sexual relations, and the lack of a noncompulsive heterosexual relationship that might form a standard of comparison. If love itself is a disease psychic in origin, but as predictable in its ultimate effects as pneumonia or cholera, it matters little how diseased any particular version of it is. In Proust, the homosexuals are just as unhappy as the heterosexuals.

Homosexuals cannot be distinguished by any biological peculiarities observable to the scientist. They cannot necessarily be detected socially by any overt behavior. Being secret, they represent the qualities of secrecy. To the heterosexual made aware of their existence, as Marcel is at Montjouvain and in the Duchesse's courtyard, the homosexual becomes a permanent reminder of the unconscious nature of sexuality per se, of the irrationality and power of all sexual attraction.

Convincing as Proust may be, there is one peculiarly illogical drawback to the biological and psychological function homosexuals serve in his novel: Chosen as exceptions to illustrate a general theory of love, the more they illustrate it the less exceptional they become.

In society, homosexuals form a tenacious underground. At the Princesse de Guermantes's party in *Cities of the Plain,* the usher announcing the Duc de Chattellerault has slept with him a few days earlier, under the impression he was an "Englishman." A footman, unaware of Charlus's identity, offers to introduce him to the Prince de Guermantes, a relative to whom Charlus hardly needs an introduction. And Charlus himself, one of the great arbiters of French society, a man who sets the tone for a whole civilization, winds up in a male brothel being beaten by a male prostitute. (The inefficacy of the paid-for beating is not merely one irony gilding another, it is the final, rotted core of the disease of the ideal. Even here—chosen, arranged for, paid for, in a house Charlus has helped set up for just such an occasion—the experience is unsatisfactory. The prostitute, a good sort, is not able convincingly to simulate hostility.) The freemasonry of homosexuality is a red thread binding the beggar to the king, the ambassador to the footman. The secrecy of the homosexual, the hypocrisy of society are twin mirrors. Each must pretend something; disguise is the necessary catalyst to both.

Homosexuals, a society within a society, are rooted in a biological incongruity, perpetually subject to social judgment, just as society, in a larger sense, springs from a false conception of human relationships, and is perpetually at the mercy of individual criticism. The mysteries of genetics produce a secret sect; the arbitrariness of genealogy (and, later, money, for the Duchesse de Guermantes's "breeding" is no more fortuitous than Mme. Verdurin's "millions") produces its social equivalent—the world of the Faubourg Saint-Germain.

A minority group, driven by guilt and producing it, homosexuals are, according to Proust, outcasts of society only because society casts them out for its own special purposes: the survival of any social group depends on the ability to exclude. At the Verdurin musicale at Quai Conti, Charlus first excludes Mme. Verdurin, isolating her, through rudeness, from what he considers her social superiors. Then she excludes him by turning Morel against him, who publicly denounces Charlus. In each case, the weapons are social: status and prejudice. It is the Queen of Naples who rescues Charlus, taking him by the arm and leading him out of the room. We are back where we started: the Queen is putting Mme. Verdurin in her place.

Because the homosexual is forced to assume a false social role, he is, paradoxically, a microcosm of society itself. The homosexual generates the condition that precedes social grouping, exclusion; as a member of society, he is a travesty, therefore, of its mechanics. The social grouping of the homosexual is of particular interest to Proust because only a single arbitrary area of connection among individuals is necessary for the formation of the group. Thus, in the Dreyfus case, the social equivalent of this psychological process occurs. The Faubourg Saint-German and the anti-Semitic elements of the bourgeosie, ordinarily without any interests in common, find themselves in a forced but mutually profitable alliance. Similarly, it requires only Swann's passion for Odette to make him fall in love with the Verdurins—at first—when, in actuality, they are the very sort of people he detests. Homosexuality is most illustrative here because it produces the condition of least choice: psychological compulsion. Homosexuals cannot help excluding what they cannot include, heterosexual love. Society must pretend to be equally helpless. The Duchesse chooses whom she is to see in only a very limited sense; that is why it is important both for her prestige and self-esteem to assume an enormous range of possibilities: She will go to this party, but not that, receive this particular person, but not the other. Actually, like the homosexual, her choices are precircumscribed.

Charlus shares with Swann a distinction accorded only these two characters: they are observed, but they are also extensions of the observer: Swann is the heterosexual version of the Marcel who is observed, Charlus the homosexual one. They each occupy roughly similar positions, Swann dominating the first half of the book, Charlus the second. We infer this splitting up of character from the following facts:

Swann's love affair with Odette, though it occurs many years before Marcel's birth, is a similar relationship to that of Marcel and Albertine. In spite of the difference in time, both relationships revolve at their beginnings around the closed circle of the Verdurin "little clan" and both have Vinteuil's "theme" as their leit-motif. Vinteuil's sonata belongs to Swann, his septet to Marcel. More significantly, the psychological patterns are similar: it is the enigmatic nature of the woman, the torture of her absence rather than the pleasure of her presence, that constitutes the clue to passion. The emotional exchange occurs within the lover, not between the lover and the beloved. It is jealousy that primes the heart rather than mutual satisfaction. Swann's jealousy is felt most keenly at a point where he becomes aware of Odette's having had lesbian contacts as well as heterosexual ones—this fear of Odette's inversion becomes more credible if we connect Swann-Marcel with Odette-Albertine than it would be as an isolated fact. For there is nothing in the rest of Odette's life or Swann's history of jealousy to explain this rather unexpected phenomenon. By the time Swann marries Odette, he is no longer in love with her: she has freed him from jealousy, she who was both its object and its cure, and she has detached him from the social world of the Faubourg to which he had belonged. Only one Faubourg daydream remains: Swann's fantasy of having Odette and Gilberte received by the Duchesse de Guermantes (the Princesse de Laumes at the time of Swann's marriage) as part of her intimate circle, a daydream denied Swann all his life and accomplished only after his death. Jealousy of a more specific sort drives Marcel into the labyrinth of Albertine's personality—his suspicions of her lesbian tendencies. But when Marcel returns from that labyrinth, he does not return empty-handed; he has been forced to explore the labyrinth of himself, at the end of which is the book we are reading. Albertine, too, detaches Marcel from the social world—more completely than Odette does Swann, for Odette at least substitutes the society of the petty bourgeois for the Faubourg. Albertine, kept prisoner secretly, disguised as Marcel's cousin on the few occasions when they go out, absorbs all of Marcel, his will drained by obsession. For Marcel, all social life becomes meaningless.

In both cases, impossibility is the great propulsion to love. Odette is domesticated, Albertine imprisoned. Under surveillance, they do not give up their secrets.

Swann marries Odette in the relief of liberation; Marcel lives with Albertine in the despair of imprisonment. But Swann's liberation is only delusive. Swann and Marcel follow the same path; Swann goes part of the way but not all of the way toward the truth. Swann fails by succeeding; he marries Odette. Marcel succeeds by failing, he loses Albertine, and writes his book. The fineness of Swann's mind, the delicacy of his perceptions remain those of an extraordinary dilettante, but a dilettante all the same. Death strangles him with cancer among the nonentities of his life, who never have really loved him. Marcel trades life for the secret of time regained, the triumph of art. He does not create a dilettante's work, like the book on Vermeer that Swann never finishes—or live a life Vermeer might have approved of, which is Swann's pathetic justification of his own life—but a work of art worthy of Vermeer himself.

If Swann and Marcel are the victims of a form of love that creates its objects out of itself, making a genuine union impossible, Charlus's relationship to Morel exemplifies the same general proposition. Love is completely symbolic; the lover is half of a metaphor constantly searching for its relevant image. The metaphor is never completed because the relevant image is always itself. In homosexuality, where both terms of the metaphor are more nearly the same, where there is an actual duplication in the physical bodies of the lovers, this version of love is given its most credible demonstration.

In Marcel's love for Albertine, we re-explore the development of Swann's love for Odette, then step over a boundary on the other side of which lies the country of Charlus and Morel. The exploration is deeper, the nuances finer, the depths more horrifying. But essentially Albertine seems to be in part Odette, in part Morel; Marcel in part Swann, in part Charlus.

If a window is a transparency necessary to the voyeur, the ability to project images is necessary to the masturbator. The fact that crucial sexual scenes are witnessed in Proust through windows takes us back to the magic lantern of Marcel's boyhood. Like the window, it is a lens; unlike the window, it is held in the hand, it projects images, and it is manipulable. The lantern slides shed further light once we realize that Geneviève de Brabant was falsely accused by Golo of committing adultery. Even these seemingly innocent childhood images contained a sexual secret. Proust includes a masturbation scene in which the images of a window, a flower, and a tower are used:

> Alas, it was in vain that I implored the dungeon-keep of Roussainville ... when, from the top floor of our house at Combray, from the little room that smelt of orris-root, I had peered out and seen nothing but its tower, framed in the square of the half-opened window, while, with the heroic scruples of a

traveller setting forth for unknown climes, or of a desperate
wretch hesitating on the verge of self-destruction, faint with
emotion, I explored, across the bounds of my own experience,
an untrodden path, which, I believed, might lead me to my
death, even—until passion spent itself and left me shuddering
among the sprays of flowering currant which, creeping in through
the window, tumbled about my body.

The sexual meaning of the window is not confined to Marcel. When
Swann goes to visit Odette during the early months of their courtship, he
taps upon her window as a signal for her to come to the door to let him in.
And, on two separate occasions when Swann suspects Odette of deceiving
him with Forcheville, the window image is invoked. Odette asks Swann to
mail some letters for her, one of which is addressed to Forcheville. Swann
reads the letter through the envelope, and confirms the suspicion that
Odette has betrayed him:

> For a time Swann stood still there, heartbroken, bewildered,
> and yet happy; gazing at this envelope which Odette had handed
> to him without a scruple, so absolute was her trust in his
> honour; through its transparent window there had been dis-
> closed to him, with the secret history of an incident which he
> had despaired of ever being able to learn, a fragment of the life
> of Odette, seen as through a narrow, luminous incision, cut
> into its surface without her knowledge. Then his jealousy re-
> joiced at the discovery, as though that jealousy had had an
> independent existence, fiercely egotistical, gluttonous of every-
> thing that would feed its vitality, even at the expense of Swann
> himself.

Later, he tries to peer through Odette's window to substantiate his
fears. It is the wrong window and he wakens two sleeping old gentlemen.
If the picture Swann sees framed in the window is not charged with the
sexual meaning he expected, or the sexual intensity of the two homosexual
scenes witnessed by Marcel, the scene is at least unconsciously consistent,
for what Swann sees, no matter how comic or ludicrous at the moment,
are two people of the same sex.

The image of two people of the same sex, a relief to Swann, is to
become a torture to Marcel. When Albertine's friendship with Mlle. Vinteuil's
anonymous lesbian partner is revealed, the scene he had witnessed in his
boyhood behind the window at Montjouvain is set in motion; the dor-

mant, still picture becomes animated. It is Albertine's capacity to make Marcel suffer that defines the nature of his love, and it is her invisible lesbianism that forms the substance of the long, analytical inquisition their relationship is to become. It is maternalness that Marcel seeks in his mother, and it is girlhood he seeks in Albertine ("my love for Albertine had been but a transitory form of my devotion to girlhood"). The particular horror of Albertine for Marcel is that she is not only the chosen deity who springs to life out of a general desire, but that she is his very competitor in that desire ("all my desires helped me to understand, to a certain degree, what hers had been"). She betrays him not only as a lover but as a man, just as his mother betrayed him earlier, in a more complicated sense, not only as a child but as a son. It is the emotional relationship Marcel has with his mother *combined* with the homosexual content of the Montjouvain scene that gives Albertine her special power. What Marcel feels and sees as a child comes true to haunt him as a fact—a fact he wants and does not want to know, since his pleasure consists primarily in his ability to feel pain—a direct association with Charlus who is explicitly masochistic and needs, finally, to be beaten with chains to feel sexual pleasure. What does pain-pleasure consist in for Marcel? Helplessness— the watching of the performance of others, either childishly, as in the bedroom scene; sexually and literally, as in the two window scenes; or figuratively, as in his obsessive jealousy of Albertine.

Marcel looks in at Mme. Swann's winter garden through a window, and out of the dining-room window of the Balbec hotel at the sea—against whose blue he draws the first portrait of Saint-Loup, and out of whose depths the goddess, Albertine, is to rise. He stares out the corridor window of the Grand Hotel at the countryside whose distant greenery encloses La Raspelière, the Verdurins's estate, and those small, provincial towns where Albertine goes on her "sketching expeditions," which, in retrospect, become the stations of the cross on the itinerary of the sexual prowler. Through the windows of the restaurant of Rivebelle he sees an intoxicated reality; and it is through a window of Elstir's studio that he sees Albertine racing by. Looking out of the window of Saint-Loup's room, he sees the reflected shape of a hill that is to color all his memories of his stay at Doncières. Window images proliferate in Proust and are dramatically pulled together by a final association of three windows.

The linking of the "mother" window at Combray, and the two "homosexual" windows—the one at Montjouvain, and the one overlooking the Duchesse's courtyard—provides a tension between two subjects, establishes a bond between two emotions that is reenforced again in a further association. In Venice, Marcel describes a particular window at the hotel:

> On the piazza, the shadow that would have been cast at Combray by the linen-draper's awning and the barber's pole, turned into the tiny blue flowers scattered at its feet upon the desert of sun-scorched tiles by the silhouette of a Renaissance façade, which is not to say that, when the sun was hot, we were not obliged, in Venice as at Combray, to pull down the blinds between ourselves and the Canal, but they hung behind the quatrefoils and foliage of gothic windows. Of this sort was the window in our hotel behind the pillars of which my mother sat waiting for me, gazing at the Canal with a patience which she should not have displayed in the old days at Combray, at that time when, reposing in myself hopes which had never been realized, she was unwilling to let me see how much she loved me. Nowadays she was well aware that an apparent coldness on her part would alter nothing, and the affection she lavished upon me was like those forbidden foods which are no longer withheld from invalids, when it is certain that they are past recovery. To be sure, the humble details which gave an individuality to the window of my aunt Léonie's bedroom, seen from the Rue de l'Oiseau ... the equivalent of all these things existed in this hotel in Venice ... she [his mother] sent out to me, from the bottom of her heart, a love which stopped only where there was no longer any material substance to support it on the surface of her impassioned gaze which she brought as close to me as possible, which she tried to thrust forward to the advanced post of her lips, in a smile which seemed to be kissing me, in the framework and beneath the canopy of the more discreet smile of the arched window illuminated by the midday sun; for these reasons ... ever since then, whenever I see a cast of that window in a museum, I feel the tears starting to my eyes, it is simply because the window says to me the thing that touches me more than anything else in the world: "I remember your mother so well."
>
> (*Sweet Cheat Gone*)

The correspondence between the Combray bedroom window and the window in Venice, both maternal shrines, is here made explicit.

In the ultimate horror scene of *Remembrance of Things Past*, a scene whose implications project backward through four transparencies—the Venetian window, the window overlooking the Duchesse de Guermantes's courtyard, the Montjouvain window, and the window of Marcel's bedroom at Combray—we come upon the following passage:

> And I heard the cracking of a whip, probably made still more cutting with nails, for I heard cries of pain. Then I noticed that this room had a small, round window opening on the hallway, over which they had neglected to draw the curtain; tip toeing in the darkness, I made my way softly to this window and there, chained to a bed like Prometheus to his rock, and being beaten by Maurice with a cat-o'-nine-tails which was, as a matter of fact, studded with nails, I saw before me M. de Charlus, bleeding all over and covered with welts which showed that this was not the first time the torture had taken place.
>
> (*The Past Recaptured*)

The "ultimate horror scene" for specific reasons. For, if, earlier "My Hell was all that Balbec . . .", this further vision of Hell peculiarly transcends the personal and fuses the sexual and social motifs of the novel. During a blackout, Marcel has taken refuge in a building that turns out to be a male brothel run by Jupien and supported by Charlus. He is first made aware in this scene of Saint-Loup's homosexuality—a suspicion confirmed when Saint-Loup carelessly leaves behind his *croix de guerre* at Jupien's. The brothel scene is immediately followed by the bombing of Paris. The Paradise of Aunt Léonie's garden has led, by inevitable stages, to a vision of Hell that is, psychologically, the product of inversion (the brothel), and, socially, the *coup de grâce* of Europe's ruling classes (the bombing). Stupidity, corruption, malevolence, selfishness, disease—they are combined in two acts of aggression: the beating of Charlus, the end product of centuries of civilization, and the attempted destruction of Paris, the historical and material center of the same civilization.

It is no accident that three out of the four major male representatives of the French aristocracy in Proust's novel—Prince Gilbert de Guermantes (who spends a night with Morel at a house of prostitution at Maineville), Saint-Loup, and Baron Charlus—are all depicted at one point or another as patrons of male prostitutes. The one male Guermantes who eludes this category, the Duc, substitutes for it a lifelong obsession with adultery.

In *The Captive*, at a moment of great anxiety, Marcel experiences the following:

> Suddenly, in the silence of the night, I was startled by a sound
> apparently insignificant which, however, filled me with terror,
> the sound of Albertine's window being violently opened.

The sound, apparently insignificant, is of the utmost importance. It
signals the departure of Albertine—an action suspected, dismissed, then
actual, like Marcel's vision of the Persian church at Balbec, which is
oriental in imagination, prosaic in reality, and, then, partly Persian in fact.
But between the opening of this window, when Albertine makes the
preparations for her departure, and her actual escape, she and Marcel take
a trip to Versailles. Hearing a sound they cannot at first identify, Albertine
says, "Why ... there is an aeroplane ... high up in the sky" (*The
Captive*).

It is at the violent opening of a window in his own house that Marcel
suffers in anticipation the departure of Albertine. Like the other windows,
this one sets the scene for a future surprise; Albertine not only parts from
Marcel, she departs from life itself. This image of a window being violently
opened, which fills Marcel "with terror," is thematically linked to the
earlier brothel scene. Each one—for Marcel and Albertine have quarreled
about her relationship to Andrée—involves the rediscovery of inversion, a
real or symbolic reference to the French aristocracy (Guermantes, *croix de
guerre,* Versailles) and the presence of an aeroplane (the bombing of Paris,
Albertine's remark about the plane "high in the sky").

Like the ringing of the garden gate bell—a sound heard both at the
beginning and the end of Proust's novel—the bedroom window at Combray
becomes a repetitive motif. It narrows into a "peephole" behind which a
once unimagined, and now desired and detested action takes place, transforming the childhood pictures of legend and history projected by Marcel's
magic lantern into a horrifying vision of sexual love.

ROGER SHATTUCK

Proust's Binoculars

Proust's sensitivity to time and tense must not draw our attention permanently away from other aspects of his work that give it body and variety. Particularly I want to insist on how fully he assimilated into his universe of vision two perspectives often treated as merely decorative or even out of place. The first is Proust's sense of the comic. His masterful handling of realistic detail gives us an insight into every social level, be it Françoise's *cuirs* or the Guermantes's so-called wit. The slow motion scene of Marcel "kissing" Albertine is as right and as ridiculous as Mme. Cottard falling helplessly asleep after dinner. A form of the comic more basic to the book appears in the recurring pattern of mistaken identities. More than any comedy by Plautus with two sets of identical twins as its principal characters, *A la Recherche* advances through an arsenal of disguises which, before they serve as the means of revealing partial truths, provide us with sustained comic diversion. But the largest dimension of comic meaning in Proust's novel concerns the very progression of the action in a manner only too easy to overlook. The whole first portion of Combray concerning his *tante* Léonie, is embroidered around a minor matter of local interest: Did Mme. Goupil arrive at mass before the elevation? Léonie, from her ringside seat on village life, becomes obsessed by the question and then forgets completely to find out the answer from her only sure source of information, Eulalie. This trivial yet imperious question, from which hangs a whole day of her existence (and fifty pages of the novel along with

From *Proust's Binoculars: A Study of Memory, Time and Recognition in* A la recherche du temps perdu. © 1963 by Roger Shattuck. Random House, 1963.

it, leads us into the churning of Léonie's subjective processes. And exactly this process of tumor-like growth lodges at the base of Swann's prolonged jealousy over Odette: Had Forcheville been with her the day she had not answered the door? Two whole volumes of the novel spin themselves out over Marcel's self-torture about the possibility of Albertine's having indulged her lesbian inclinations. The ludicrous resides next door to the serious. The most crucial and passionate concerns of our existence, after having produced a condition of elephantiasis in our inner thoughts, dwindle to nothing, like a comic shadow. Throughout the book many of the most serious moments and the most earnest theoretical discussions push our sense of the incongruity of events to the point where laughter is the only possible reaction. At the opening of the last scene in the prince's salon, the scene which is going to bring him the final grasp of truth, Marcel says gaily of M. d'Argencourt, fallen into senile decay: "I had a crazy laugh at this sublime dotard [*gaga*]." The remark spans the entire comic perspective of magnified realism, mistaken identity, and obsession; it is not plastered over the surface of the book as decoration but penetrates to its basic structure and composition.

Alongside this deep-running comedy, another powerful perspective lends coherence to the immensity of Proust's work. In the uniqueness and inconsistency of the particular, Proust's intelligence perpetually seeks a hidden order. He speaks without hesitation of "psychological laws" and uses numerous scientific metaphors such as "moral chemistry" to suggest that men as much as things obey the workings of universal law. The entire apparatus of optical figures applied to our conscious and unconscious faculties as well as to social history implies that a set of laws forming a coherent science can describe these human processes. For the most part Proust avoids classifications that delimit individual behavior in favor of generalizations that discover a regularity and coherence within a state of perpetual change. He had the scientist's and moralist's sense of law as something exciting and alive, and many times his patient, probing intelligence seems to partake of the genius of Fabre and La Rochefoucauld and Poincaré.

Encouraged by Proust's own remarks in many texts on the comparative importance of "sensibility" and "intelligence" in his work, critics have hotly debated the role of laws and generalizations as a form of knowledge and as an element of art in *A la recherche*. Some critics maintain that Proust's highest accomplishment lay in his capacity to shape highly original generalizations about human conduct into a work of fiction that brings them to life. A more numerous group object to the undeniable rational

strain in Proust's writing and confine their admiration to his highly developed poetic sensibility before nature, before his own subjective processes,
and before the illusory nature of our relations with others. Proust himself
can be quoted at length and tellingly in support of both attitudes and in
opposition to them. In the closing pages of "Combray," when Marcel is
losing hope of ever becoming a writer, he speaks of the "particular
pleasure" of certain sensations and of his ignorance of their significance.
With heavy irony he depicts his youthful ignorance in equating literature
with intelligence: "It was not impressions of that sort, surely, that were able
to restore my lost hope of one day being a writer and a poet, for they were
all linked to a particular object of no intellectual value and led to no
abstract truth." The remarks surrounding most of the *moments bienheureux*
include a comparable disparagement of rational processes; *Contre Sainte-
Beuve* opens with the uncompromising sentence, "Every day I attach less
value to the intelligence." Nevertheless, Proust has to admit in the same
volume that Nerval, though "there is a little too much intelligence in what
he writes," embodied into the "masterpiece" *Sylvie* the same six or seven
"laws of thought" that Proust had counted up. Certain passages in *A la
recherche* sound more like the pronouncements of a nineteenth-century
determinist than of a twentieth-century poet. "Thus it is useless to observe
social behavior, for one can deduce it all from psychological laws." "Anything really important for a man can happen only in spite of him, by the
action of some great natural law." And in the end, viewed with just a little
objectivity, even the highly particularized and seemingly exceptional world
Proust-Marcel has been describing dwindles into a pattern very close to
typical.

> Mais si je sortais de moi et du milieu qui m'entourait immédiate-
> ment, je voyais que ce phénomène social n'était pas aussi isolé
> qu'il m'avait paru d'abord et que du bassin de Combray où
> j'étais né, assez nombreux en somme étaient les jets d'eau qui
> symétriquement à moi s'étaient élevés au-dessus de la même
> masse liquide qui les avait alimentés.

> But if I looked beyond myself and my immediate environment,
> I saw that this social phenomenon was not as isolated as it had
> at first appeared to me and that, from the Combray basin
> where I was born, quite numerous after all were the fountains
> that had risen symmetrically with myself above the liquid mass
> which had fed them all.

Chosen for the purpose, one's quotes can prove pretty much what one wants about the role of law and intelligence in *A la recherche*—a fact which usually reduces any discussion of the question to confusion. Furthermore, many of Proust's "laws" appear far more the fruit of an intuitive process than of systematic observation and induction. But Proust's work shows that he was not unaware of his ambivalent attitude toward human rational powers and he made it one of the themes of his work. Marcel vacillates in his feelings toward his own intelligence very much as he vacillates in his affection for Gilberte and Mme. de Guermantes and Albertine. The early portions of the book generally favor sentiment; increasingly toward the end, reason is admitted to an important place alongside sentiment and complementing it. A highly "reasonable" passage toward the end of the novel—probably added late in its composition yet now a part of its texture provides a full description of the perspective of intelligence of generalization within the larger optic of memory or recognition.

> ... de ce que l'intelligence n'est pas l'instrument le plus subtil, le plus puissant, le plus approprié pour saisir le vrai, ce n'est qu'une raison de plus pour commencer par l'intelligence et non par un intuitivisme de l'inconscient, par une foi aux pressentiments toute faite. C'est la vie qui, peu à peu, cas par cas, nous permet de remarquer que ce qui est le plus imporant pour notre coeur, ou pour notre esprit, ne nous est pas appris par le raisonnement mais par des puissances autres. Et alors, c'est l'intelligence elle-même qui, se rendant compte de leur supériorité, abdique, par raisonnement, devant elles, et accepte de devenir leur collaboratrice et leur servante. Foi expérimentale.

> [the fact that our intellect is not the most subtle, the most powerful, the most appropriate instrument for grasping the truth, is only a reason the more for beginning with the intellect, and not with a subconscious intuition, a ready-made faith in presentiments. It is life that, little by little, case by case, enables us to observe that what is most important to our heart, or to our mind, is learned not by reasoning but by other powers. And then it is the intellect itself which, taking note of their superiority, abdicates its sway to them upon reasoned grounds and consents to become their collaborator and their servant. It is faith confirmed by experiment.]

The intelligence with its capacity to discriminate and to generalize can be a faithful guide along the path to discovery; or, as Proust writes in *Contre Sainte-Beuve*, "For if intelligence does not merit the supreme crown, still only intelligence is capable of bestowing it." Without an "experimental faith" in this faculty, we shall not work up to the subtler and higher faculties which combine images without recourse to laws. This passage defines the fullness of Proust-Marcel's attitude. toward human faculties more clearly than the better-known page which states that the truths of the intelligence "enchase" the higher truths of certain sensations recreated out of time. The role of the intelligence is not to decorate, but point out the route along which one can find the higher vision. Thus I take exception to Albert Feuillerat's conclusion about the word *enchâsser*: "this word defines precisely the kind of work Proust devoted himself to in revising his first draft" (*Comment Proust a composé son roman,*). Quite the contrary: insofar as Proust did add pages of analysis and generalization to the earlier "poetic" version of his novel (and Feuillerat quite understandably overstates his thesis) he was not just drawing in useless arabesques, but filling in the stages by which a mature person as contrasted to a child or adolescent reaches the "Proustian vision."

The relation of intelligence to intuition, of law to consciousness and "free will" becomes one of the most crucial questions in all the great novelists whose ambition drove them to portray both the life of an era and an individual attitude toward life. Stendhal and Tolstoy display deeply divided loyalties similar to Proust's, and this circumstance seems to have something to do with the novel as a form, as an order of magnitude for experience. In *De l'amour*, Stendhal affirms at the start that he is going to give us "an exact and scientific description of a kind of madness very rare in France." Naturally the book becomes less and less systematic until it devolves into a series of fragments and appendices. Stendhal's point of view in his novels and even his journals alternates between passionate abandonment to his characters and detachment from them in order to reduce them to a pattern of behavior. Tolstoy is driven by a comparable alternating current. He sets up and defends inflexible laws of history and morality, yet the individuality of his greatest characters from Kutuzov to Ivan Ilych lies in their grasp of these laws not by reason but by feeling, by intuition. Both Stendhal and Tolstoy show a strong inclination to cinch a demonstration by putting it into military terms—or better yet, mathematical terms, as if this latter form were truly irrefutable. (Tolstoy gives us equations for measuring military morale. In *Henri Brulard* Stendhal justifies his love for mathematics because it "does not admit hypocrisy and vagueness, my two pet aversions.") But the point is that both, like Proust, erect an extensive edifice of law and intelligence in order to abandon it when the occasion arises. The secret is to know when to abdicate the categories of reason for a higher, more mysterious, and more hazardous faculty. Or— and the question must finally be asked—do the two commonly separated sets of terms for intelligence and sensibility stand for different settings and yields of a single mental process rather than for two opposed processes? I pass, as Proust passed; the question remains.

I wonder, in fact, if Proust's searching and cryptic term in the last quotation, "experimental faith," does not refer to a process related to Keats's "negative capability." Keats wished to dwell "in uncertainties, Mysteries, doubts, without any irritable reaching after fact and reason." But whereas Keats as a poet sought to maintain a pure state of selfless response to the world around him without being bound by the categories of personality and intelligence, the three novelists accept such a state as exceptional, the rare moment of elevation we may experience, if we are able, under proper circumstances, to break free from habits of thought. By which I do not mean to suggest that Proust and Stendhal and Tolstoy were disappointed poets unable to keep the spirit in flight. They observed an essentially human mode of existence: the intermittent rhythm of awareness they depict swings between laws of behavior and moments of pure uninhibited freedom and insight. This double mode of existence arises from the most fundamental condition of man, his dual nature—or at least his dual grasp of his nature. Stendhal's obsession with love, Tolstoy's with history, and Proust's with memory allow them to investigate along converging paths the very beat of life. The soaring of a poem by Keats represents a single unsullied act. The novel in the hands of these three epic authors records a long series of moments on different levels of intensity. This order of magnitude encompasses many moods, many mansions.

Both the perspective of comedy (alternating with seriousness) and the perspective of law (alternating with pure sensibility) tell us a great deal about Proust's mind and about the unity of his novel. But I should contend that they do not reveal quite so much as the handful of optical principles that describe how Proust's vision influenced the nature of his art, the form of his fiction. How, specifically, does the combination of slightly dissimilar images, the essential role of interval and forgetting, bear on the form of *A la recherche?* The answer, though lengthy, is revealing.

The opening reverie of the book gradually focuses on the one vivid scene Marcel can recall from his childhood: being deprived of his mother's goodnight kiss. The unexpected spell of the *madeleine* experience suddenly enlarges the narrow aperture of his memory to reveal the whole of Combray—the place and the era. Marcel's secure and almost unstained vision of the world as something whose existence he could believe in as it appears to him, begins to waver only when he tries to fix it at the end in a fragmentary work of art—the description he writes of seeing the *clochers de Martinville* from the carriage. After these two hundred pages of overture, the aperture of Marcel's memory enlarges even further to include the story of his older friend and alter ego, Swann, and then opens so wide as to disappear in the total recall of his own past. But these twenty-six hundred pages pick up every whisper and shadow of perverseness and corruption in the overture and pursue them relentlessly, until we have been plunged into a universe characterized by total disorder, unintelligibility, and disintegration of all values. Only in the last two hundred pages will the pieces be fitted together again: but not exactly as in the beginning. For what intervenes has not been a mere diversion. The body of the novel consists in a prolonged series of false answers which Marcel follows with pathetic enthusiasm: sentimental love, the allurement of aristocratic society, the desire for fame, friendship. They all turn out to be "inevitable disappointments." The action of the novel reproduces on a large scale the "deceptive" presentation Proust pointed out in Dostoyevski's treatment of character. After the opening, we venture out into the wide world in Marcel's company on a long series of false scents, each of which is followed into an impasse. In the bulk of the incidents of the novel he comes up against false answers to the basic questions of life.

Love is selfish and self-deluding. Elegant society is a sham and dupes no one so completely as its own initiates. Celebrity corrupts a man until he becomes an unbearable travesty of himself. Friendship too is suspect. The only thing Marcel sees clearly once he has lost his pristine vision, is the perverse incapacity of men to experience life directly, face to face. Our "moral perspective" prevents us from enjoying pleasure when we attain it and sets us yearning after any mysterious absent being that tantalizes our desire. The surest thing about people is their perverseness and the instability of their desires. Conversely, "Time passes, and little by little every falsehood spoken becomes true." And thus it happens that any partial interpretation of Proust's work, based primarily on the beginning and middle sections, falls into irretrievable error. So intelligent a critic as Denis Saurat has tried to show Proust's world as one of sensuous pleasure and illness, a picture as incomplete as an attempt to interpret the Christian religion without taking into account the resurrection.

Most of *A la recherche* moves negatively along false scents, backwards into the future as I have suggested earlier. I can say the same thing now in an optical figure and thus relate this aspect of the book to much of what has been said so far. Marcel and the reader, after the opening glimpse of paradise in Combray, move on into the world with only one eye open. Relief in time, binocular vision of reality, come only in moments of mysterious pleasure provoked by an unfamiliar setting (carriage, train, hotel) or by music. Then suddenly at the end, the other eye opens when we are sure it has atrophied, and Marcel attains both the wholeness of vision to recognize himself and his world, and the final certainty of his vocation. Snobbery, physical desire, egotistical perverseness—all these are aspects of an incomplete vision of the world seen with one eye open. And Proust obliges us to see in that limited fashion for a long time. The novel, in retrospect, begins to take on the appearance of a game of twenty questions, all but the last of which elicit a negative answer; or a detective story, in which every clue leads to a blind alley until an unforeseeable insight recombines them all into the solution.

And we now confront a perfectly legitimate yet rarely asked question, which applies not only to Proust but to every tale of quest and long-delayed discovery. Why take twenty-six hundred pages to narrate in great detail and vividness all Marcel's missteps and false conclusions? Why present us with so magnificent a construction of the erroneous universe from which the true time dimension is missing? The answer delves toward the very foundations of the novel as a form of art, the novel, which is always to some degree—though usually less massively than *A la recherche*—a tissue of errors. The kind of loose narrative we have come to call the novel rests on error both as to its esthetics and the source of its moral tone. Because we are what we are, habit-ridden and perverse, the false scent or the one-eyed vision of things will at first lead us closer to true knowledge and insight than will full divulgence. We remain immobilized until we confront and fully comprehend our mistakes. Swann cannot at first believe that the Vinteuil he knew in Combray could possibly be the composer with the same name who wrote the sonata. Later this association reinforces his admiration for the music. In the famous scene relating Marcel's discovery of Charlus's true biological identity, Proust forces us to relate the recognition of truth to error. After mentioning that "Ulysses himself did not recognize Athena at first," the paragraph concludes: "An error, when dissipated, gives us an additional sense." And later we read, "This perpetual error which is precisely 'life,' does not bestow its thousand forms merely upon the visible and the audible universe but upon the social universe, the sentimental universe, the historical universe, and so forth."

Error, optical illusion, provides the material out of which truth must emerge, as evolution must emerge out of the regression and elimination of many species.

But *emerge* is as vague a word as the language possesses for so crucial a process, biological, moral, or esthetic. Emerge how? The biologist can give us a fairly convincing description of natural selection. In his ambitious work *Space, Time, and Deity* the philosopher S. Alexander offers a somewhat less convincing description of "emergent" deity, the next evolutionary step for man. What happens in the novel is much closer to us than either of these, a process Proust carried to the extreme of length and intensity. Throughout the central portion of *A la recherche*, the dominant attitude of Marcel before the world is summed up in the deceptively simple phrase, "cet immense désir de connaître la vie." But matched in an apparently losing struggle against this curiosity, which ranges from the innocent to the morbid, Marcel shows a deeply ingrained idealism: "I preferred that life should be on a level with my intuitions." Both these remarks are made in connection with Marcel's obsessive desire to learn the "truth" about Albertine's life and character; he discovers no truth, only a cryptic sequence of falsehoods. Truth and reality in Proust have no objective, verifiable existence. They are the esthetic creations of our intuitions, of our minds, fixed in a work of art. Therefore it is by an act of creation that truth "emerges" from deception and illusion. Marcel's vision of truth and his sense of vocation occur as one "recognition" in the novel, for they are merely different aspects of the same process of creating our world. We must ourselves create the truth of existence insofar as we can recognize its pattern and relief in time; and in the same way we truly create ourselves, our character, by a long and often delayed act of self-recognition. The moral and esthetic meanings are thus fused in a concept of self-creation very close to what we have become familiar with in statements of existentialist conviction. In *L'Etre et le néant* and later works, Sartre assembles a whole battery of special terms (*imagination, assomption, transcendance, être-pour-soi*) to describe this mysterious emergence out of ourselves. We are what we turn ourselves into. In order to make anything of ourselves, we first follow a long path of error, our own particularized error. For Proust-Marcel there are twenty-six hundred pages of it.

Thus Proust's literary and moral construction in *A la recherche*, which approaches truth obliquely along the false scent of error, has brought us inexorably to the question of the length of the novel. Proust wrote voluminously—so much so, some readers feel, that he suffocates us in his brilliant portrait of the iniquity of man. We come close to losing any sense of uprightness or integrity in human beings. But having once grasped the basic structure of his novel around 1909 or 1910, Proust never shrank from the enormous dimensions such a concept demanded. In 1919 he wrote to Paul Souday, "My composition is veiled and its outline only gradually perceptible because it unfolds on so vast a scale" (*Correspondance générale*). In his article on Flaubert, he extends the figure when he refers to the "rigorous composition" of the first volume of his own novel as "difficult to discern because drawn with the compass legs wide apart and because the section that corresponds to an earlier section, cause and effect, are located at a great distance from one another" (*Chroniques*). Sheer mass was an essential element of his art and he resolved not to sacrifice it. "The writer may embark upon a long work without apprehension." In a letter to the editor of *Les Annales* in 1921, defending himself against charges of writing a purely analytical novel, he states he wants to subject reality "to the least possible shrinkage."

There is another important consideration, closely related to the esthetic of the false scent, that explains this resoluteness before the task of composing a novel of vast dimensions. Proust wrote at length in order to create within the frame of his novel an interval of *oubli*, the forgetting which would allow the reader a true experience of remembering and recognizing. This contention runs a great critical risk, for it appears equivalent to saying that to describe anger or boredom one should write in an angry or boring fashion, and so on. But Proust's style is in no way forgetful, nor is he describing *oubli*; he is reproducing it as a speech in a play reproduces anger. He dramatizes forgetting and memory and recognition in a prolonged monologue which need not stop to describe what it most simply *is*. Proust recreates his compound vision of the world in a metaphor so extended we forget the first term and then recall it. Just as in "Combray" we forget the narrative thread of Mme. Goupil being late to Mass, in the full work we, like Marcel himself, have forgotten many of the characters by the time they reappear in the last scene. So much wealth of experience cannot be carried along perpetually on the surface of our minds.

Twice, Proust hints at the relations between the length of his narrative and the importance he attributes to *oubli*. Just at the end of his meditations, before entering the prince's salon, Marcel mentions having recently leafed through several novels of Bergotte, first read long ago, in order to see how they end.

> Car je ne me rappelais plus bien ce qui était arrivé à ces personnages, ce qui ne les différenciait d'ailleurs pas des personnes

qui se trouvaient cet après-midi chez Mme. de Guermantes et
dont, pour plusieurs au moins, la vie passée était aussi vague
pour moi que si je l'eusse lue dans un roman à demi oublié.

[For I no longer remembered just what happened to these
characters—in which, moreover, they resembled the persons
who were at Mme. de Guermantes' this afternoon and whose
past life, in several cases at least, was as vague in my mind as if
I had read it in some half-forgotten novel.]

The "half-forgotten novel" is no mere figure: it lies under our eyes
and is approaching its climax, a novel which shades off into a misty past
like our own lives and our own experience. This existence in depth begins
to reveal the very essence of Proust, a multi-dimensionality that could
never be conveyed by an epigram or even a short story. And a few pages
later Marcel realizes his attainment to a "new life" no longer depends on a
condition of solitude:

(comme j'avais cru autrefois, comme cela avait peut-être été
pour moi autrefois, comme cela aurait peut-être dû être encore
si je m'étais harmonieusement développé, au lieu de ce long
arrêt qui semblait seulement prendre fin).

[as I had formerly believed and as had perhaps formerly been
true in my case and might, perhaps, have still been true if I had
developed in a uniform manner, without that long suspension
of activity which seemed to be only just coming to an end.]

The long "arrest" in his development between the opening and the
close of the novel, his years of wandering in the labyrinth of delusion,
again turn out to be the very force which bring him face to face with the
true life. That wandering in the desert, to have its full effect in a work of
literature as Proust conceived it, must be reproduced and re-created in the
body of the narrative. Only after establishing this life-sized scale of events
did Proust allow himself to state flatly that "many years passed" before
Marcel left the sanatorium; he has earned the right to that abbreviation of
narrative.

The dimensions of Proust's novel, however, though grandiose in their
original conception and execution as offered for publication in 1912,
almost tripled in length during the ten years which followed. There is a
famous culinary legend about the head chef of Louis XIV, who discovered
he had put his potatoes into deep fat too soon for the king's arrival.

Anxiously he took them out, gambling his reputation in the process, and plunged them back in at the last moment to complete the cooking. In so doing, and to his everlasting glory, he discovered *pommes soufflées*, one of the greatest delicacies the humble potato can yield. After the not very successful publication of the first volume in 1913, the serving up of Proust's novel was similarly delayed by the circumstance of war. What began appearing again seven years later bears a certain relation to a literary *pomme soufflée*. The size and scope of the novel had been blown up enormously, even though the basic ingredients and structure had not changed. And it is my contention that for the reasons just given concerning scale of narration, Proust thus improved his novel and produced a work of art more forceful and original in its significance than the first version.

This conviction brings me once again up against the critic Feuillerat, who takes an opposite position. After stating that the opening and, for the most part, the conclusion of *A la recherche* stayed in place through all modifications, he concludes: "But everything in between has been violently and irretrievably dislocated, and without our being able to discover the tiniest constructive intent in the way the additions were inserted" (*Comment Marcel Proust a composé son roman*). A few pages later he takes Proust to task both for abandoning the clarity of his original chronology and for adding generalizations which "déchirerent à tout instant l'atmosphère de rève éveillé." Feuillerat's sense of loss over the lineaments of the original that have been buried or mutilated in the new prevents him from perceiving what has been gained, indeed what *adds* to the atmosphere of a waking dream. For dislocation is exactly the word to describe the mood and "logic" of dream. The original tripartite structure of the book, with its two ends anchored in involuntary memory and self-recognition, was sturdy enough to bear a great deal more length and weight in the middle. And its progression, which rests not on an unbroken chronological sequence as Feuillerat mistakenly thought but on an interruption (*arrêt*) and transposition of time onto a higher level, could tolerate the interposition of great chunks of narrative—even some of inferior literary quality. But these additions allow us a deeper perspective on the story because of the wider spacing of the images finally combined. The sheer length creates *oubli*, materializes into a long literary excursion the postponement of Marcel's vocation, and heightens the effect of revelation and reversal at the end. Proust's additions, the product in part of intelligent generalization as well of youthful revery, combine to expand the time or space (both apply) of the novel in which his "psychology in time" can unfold. Moreover, the twisting of many asides and subordinate incidents into a single though sometimes tangled strand of text, gives the book the texture of something that has aged as a person or a tree ages, suggesting a past as well as a present and recording in its appearance the stress of experience in many weathers. It is the result of an author's unflagging dedication to a single work—the gnarled, sturdy, and cross-grained sense of reality we discover in Montaigne's *Essays*, in Baudelaire's *Les Fleurs du mal*, and in Whitman's *Leaves of Grass*. More than any of these others, Proust followed an all-encompassing structure, often referred to in musical composition as ABA. He extended it to the utmost by prolonging the B section to the point where we forget A. But in that temporary masking or camouflaging of the structure without destroying it lies a remarkable achievement of the book. The second A, *Le Temps retrouvé*, rises up suddenly like the genie from his bottle, when we least expect him.

The dimensions of the novel, then, the aspect which makes it difficult to grasp it in its entirety and to approach it with conventional critical concepts of unity or the transitoriness of poetic inspiration, work a transformation upon our experience which could not be fully conveyed in any other fashion. When in the closing pages, Proust seeks to bring this vastness closer to the individual reader, to make him feel more at home with its immensity, he turns us back to look not at the novel but *through* it at the world and ourselves.

> En réalité, chaque lecteur est, quand il lit, le propre lecteur de soi-même. L'ouvrage de l'écrivain n'est qu'une espèce d'instrument optique qu'il offre au lecteur afin de lui permettre de discerner ce que, sans ce livre, il n'eût peut-être pas vu en soi-même.

> [In reality, each reader reads only what is already within himself. The book is only a sort of optical instrument which the writer offers to the reader to enable the latter to discover in himself what he would not have found but for the aid of the book.]

> mon livre n'étant qu'une sorte de ces verres grossissants comme ceux que tendait à un acheteur l'opticien de Combray; mon livre, grâce auquel je leur fournirais le moyen de lire en eux-mêmes.

> [my book serving merely as a sort of magnifying glass, such as the optician of Combray used to offer to a customer, so that through my book I would give them the means of reading in their own selves.]

Bientôt je pus montrer quelques esquisses [de mon oeuvre]. Personne n'y comprit rien. Même ceux qui furent favorables à ma perception des vérités que je voulais ensuite graver dans le temple, me félicitèrent de les avoir découvertes au "microscope," quand je m'étais au contraire servi d'un téléscope pour apercevoir des choses, très petites an effet, mais paree qu'elles étaient situées à une grande distance, et qui étaient chacune un monde.

[Soon I was able to show a few sketches. No one understood a word. Even those who were favorable to my conception of the truths which I intended later to carve within the temple congratulated me on having discovered them with a microscope when I had, on the contrary, used a telescope to perceive things which, it is true, were very small but situated afar off and each of them a world in itself.]

Telescopes, yes, but bi- or multi-ocular: on this I insist over and above Proust's apt images. For *A la recherche* provides us with an image combined out of many images, a stereoscopic re-creation of the world in depth.

Usually when we look at a novel, we see a set of characters enacting a series of events and gradually achieving reality as personalities. Proust, having accomplished this in greater relief than had ever been attempted before, proceeded to turn his machinery back toward life, toward himself. He created a transparent novel, a set of characters who, once created, disappear and leave us the limpidity of an optical glass. The earliest remarks on the novel in *A la recherche* center around the "opaque" quality of real people contrasted with the "immateriality" of a novelist's imaginary creations, permitting us to see into the latter. Marcel carries this immateriality even further by simply vanishing from the scene after meeting Mlle. de Saint-Loup. The action moves abruptly to another level, and the sentiments of respect or indulgence or spite toward Marcel felt by the characters resurrected in the last scene are left behind. Marcel withdraws into pure consciousness for the last fifteen pages, becomes a transparent subjectivity addressing itself to a work of art. This concluding self-effacement of Marcel as a person in any realistic or novelistic sense gives the book its quality of being less an object of our vision than an optical medium or instrument that modifies and directs our vision. As a novel, *A la recherche* finally jettisons any story and changes into a device for beholding and transmuting life, Proust's, our own, everyone's. The most recent, painstaking, and literal minded of Proust's biographers, George D. Painter, calls *A la recherche* "a creative autobiography" in which, "though he invented nothing, he altered everything." But such a point of view can be taken only after reading the book through *as fiction* and following its own interior transformation into a reflection back on life and truth.

Just what do we see, looking back at life through the lens of Proust's novel? Many things, that are in the end one thing. First of all it is worth insisting—particularly in view of the bowdlerized English translation of the title, *Remembrance of Things Past,* to which Proust himself objected strongly—that the novel does not simply relate a pleasant stroll down memory lane to find the redolent memoirs of an era. After its complicated chronological preliminaries, the novel *moves forward* in time even though the action in its psychological and social preoccupations *faces the past.* The narrative tone that results, composed of sudden apparitions and gradual disappearances, hauntingly recalls the view from the rear platform of an old-fashioned observation car. There one always felt a faint wistful vertigo produced by this backward advance into the future out of a diminishing past. Thus in Proust we travel through the age of names and of places, and on across the wider expanses of the age of loves and the age of laws. Only at the end do we gain release from this restricted outlook in which life appears to be a perpetual dwindling of experience, and reach a higher view, the "special sense" whose "application" Proust considered the origin of his book (*Correspondance générale*).

We have been carefully prepared for this special sense from the beginning. The opening pages of "Combray" contain it implicitly in the wavering state of mind which characterizes Marcel's *drame du coucher.* His only consolation on going to bed is his mother's coming to kiss him good night.

> Mais ce bonsoir durait si peu de temps, elle redescendait si vite, que le moment où je l'entendais monter . . . était pour moi un moment douloureux. Il *announçait* celui qui allait le suivre, où elle m'aurait quitté, où elle serait redescendue. De sorte que ce bonsoir que j'aimais tant, j'en arrivais à souhaiter qu'il vînt le plus tard possible, à ce que se *prolongeât* le temps de répit où maman n'était pas encore venue.
>
> [But this good night lasted for so short a time: she went down again so soon that the moment in which I heard her climb the stairs . . . was for me a moment of keenest sorrow. It *announced* the moment to follow, when she would have left me and gone

back downstairs. So much did I love that good night that I
reached the stage of hoping that it would come as late as
possible, so as to *prolong* the time of respite during which
Mamma would not yet have appeared.]

The two verbs in italics designate the two complementary aspects of
time: its action of forever replacing one moment with another which
extinguishes the last, the destructive apsect; and its action of sustaining
certain moments by anticipation or prolongation or recollection, its creative aspect. Marcel remains pinioned between these two effects of time
until the closing pages. Then, in the middle of the Prince de Guermantes's
reception, he grasps his dilemma as man and artist.

Mais une raison plus grave expliquait mon angoisse; je découvrais
cette action destructrice du Temps au moment même où je voulais
entreprendre de rendre claires, d'intellectualiser dans une oeuvre
d'art, des réalités extratemporelles.

[But a still graver reason explained my distress; I was discovering this destructive action of Time at the very moment when I
was about to undertake to make clear and to intellectualise in a
literary work certain extratemporal realities.]

What Marcel has watched but never recognized in the blurred, de-
flected experiences of many years, now becomes the most naked and
importunate presence in that crowded salon. Time, which will soon destroy him, affords him the only opportunity to apply his "special sense" of
life to a work that will express the "extretemporal realities" of memory
and recognition. Marcel, lying in bed as a child, could prolong his mother's good night for a short time by his imaginative resourcefulness. But
Marcel, the writer, working desperately *against* time, must strive to deliver
these experiences from destruction into art.

What we find first then, looking back through the novel at life, is this
special sense that I have dwelt on in terms of the optics of time. Particularly we see it in Proust's stereopticon views of personality, what he
referred to in his interview with Elie-Joseph Bois in *Le Temps* (12 Novembre,
1913) as "not plane psychology, but psychology in time." But (as
Joseph Frank has suggested in a brilliant essay, "Spatial Form in Modern
Literature," *The Sewanee Review*, 1945) when the principal characters are
reassembled and displayed in an elaborate overlay of all the ages and
actions at the end of the book, *time has become space*: we see it from a

distance all at once. Proust himself now changes terms and describes his composition as "psychology in space," a juxtaposition of all the contradictions and false scents of psychology in time.

Because of the aptness of his terminology, Mr. Frank succeeds in describing succinctly the nature of Proust's esthetic as it is generally understood in reference to the *moments bienheureux*. "Proust's purpose is only achieved, therefore, when these units of meaning are referred to each other reflexively in a moment of time." Following a remark by Ramon Fernandez, he affirms that the essence of these momentary experiences is a "spatialization of time." The metaphor is instructive and relates to the stereoscopic principle already discussed: Proust arrests the flow of time by grasping it in certain related units, in [snapshots]. The first and doubtless best known example, is the enumeration in the opening pages of the rooms Marcel has lived in. These different places clearly represent different times as well, now held simultaneously in the mind. But quite apart from having overlooked the more fundamental experience of recognition, Mr. Frank, like most critics, has grievously missed the point. If we look back through the novel as a whole, and not just at the anthology pieces, we see something far different and more significant.

Except for a few fleeting revelations in the beginning, Marcel comes into full possession of this special sense of time only at the end of a long and almost abandoned quest. He has to penetrate a sequence of historical events along the false scents of temporal order before attaining the vision of pure time. It is not given but earned, achieved. *A la recherche* relates a journey, a progress which cannot be discounted just because it reaches its destination against all expectations. *There is no substitute for living, for the thickness of human time traversed.* Just here, Proust's prolonged narrative and oblique, flickering presentation of character resolve into a courageous personal morality rarely discerned: we must create our own character by living, by surviving the succession of errors which is our lot. When he comes to declare himself directly on life and art in one of the capital passages of the book, Proust significantly frames it by attributing it to the painter Elstir.

> "Il n'y a pas d'homme si sage qu'il soit, me dit-il, qui n'ait à telle époque de sa jeunesse prononcé des paroles, ou même mené une vie, dont le souvenir lui soit désagréable et qu'il souhaiterait être aboli. Mais il ne doit pas absolument le regretter, parce qu'il ne peut être assuré d'être devenu un sage, dans la mesure où cela est possible, que s'il a passé par toutes les

incarnations ridicules ou odieuses qui doivent précéder cette
dernière incarnation-là. Je sais qu'il y a des jeunes gens, fils et
petits-fils d'hommes distingués, à qui leurs précepteurs ont
enseigné la noblesse de l'esprit et l'élégance morale dès le collège.
Ils n'ont peut-être rien à retrancher de leur vie, ils pourraient
publier et signer tout ce qu'ils ont dit, mais ce sont de pauvres
esprits, descendants sans force de doctrinaires, et de qui la
sagesse est négative et stérile. On ne reçoit pas le sagesse, il faut
la découvrir soi-même après un trajet que personne ne peut
faire pour nous, ne peut nous épargner, car elle est un point de
vue sur les choses. Les vies que vous admirez, les attitudes que
vous trouvez nobles n'ont pas été disposées par le père de
famille ou par le précepteur, elles ont été précédées de débuts
bien différents, ayant été influencées par ce qui régnait autour
d'elles de mal ou de banalité. Elles représentent un combat et
une victoire. Je comprends que l'image de ce que nous avons été
dans une période première ne soit plus reconnaissable et soit en
tous cas déplaisante. Elle ne doit pas être reniée pourtant, car
elle est un témoignage que nous avons vraiment vécu, que c'est
selon les lois de la vie et de l'esprit que nous avons, des éléments
communs de la vie, de la vie des ateliers, des coteries artistiques
s'il s'agit d'un peintre, extrait quelque chose qui les dépasse."

["There is no man," he began, "however wise, who has not at
some period of his youth said things, or lived in a way the
consciousness of which is so unpleasant to him in later life that
he would gladly, if he could, expunge it from his memory. And
yet he ought not entirely to regret it, because he cannot be
certain that he has indeed become a wise man—so far as it is
possible for any of us to be wise—unless he has passed through
all the fatuous or unwholesome incarnations by which that
ultimate stage must be preceded. I know that there are young
fellows, the sons and grandsons of famous men, whose masters
have instilled into them nobility of mind and moral refinement
in their schooldays. They have, perhaps, when they look back
upon their past lives, nothing to retract; they can, if they
choose, publish a signed account of everything they have ever
said or done; but they are poor creatures, feeble descendants of
doctrinaires, and their wisdom is negative and sterile. We are
not provided with wisdom, we must discover it for ourselves,
after a journey through the wilderness which no one else can

take for us, an effort which no one can spare us, for our
wisdom is the point of view from which we come at last to
regard the world. The lives that you admire, the attitudes that
seem noble to you are not the result of training at home, by a
father, or by masters at school, they have sprung from beginnings of a very different order, by reaction from the influence
of everything evil or commonplace that prevailed round about
them. They represent a struggle and a victory. I can see that the
picture of what we once were, in early youth, may not be
recognisable and cannot, certainly, be pleasing to contemplate
in later life. But we must not deny the truth of it, for it is
evidence that we have really lived, that it is in accordance with
the laws of life and of the mind that we have, from the common elements of life, of the life of studios, of artistic groups—
assuming that one is a painter—extracted something that goes
beyond them."]

Read attentively in the light of the entire novel, this page needs little
comment. It is as personal and as universal an affirmation of individual
experience as Montaigne's superb essays, "Du repentir" and "De l'ex-
périence." Elstir tells Marcel (to whom it all means very little until much
later, when he has learned for himself) that life cannot be dispensed with
and cannot be taught; it must be lived. One has to find out for oneself, and
what one comes to is a "point of view" on one's own experience. Here lies
true wisdom. The victory may belong to an instant, but it cannot be
attained without lengthy combat. In this code of self-reliance the novel
reaches beyond any particular ethic or morality to assert a faith in the
process of life as discovery. We can now better understand Proust-Marcel's
profound preoccupation with and reverence for age. A genuine prestige
attaches to the mere fact of a person's having passed through a certain
segment of time. This attitude forms one of many biblical elements in *A la
recherche.*

I consider it significant that Tolstoy takes the same blunt attitude
toward the irreducible, irreplaceable process of living. In the magnificent
story, *Family Happiness*, Sergey finally explains to his wayward wife why
he did not use his authority or persuasion to keep her from the temptation
of worldly society.

"Yes," he began, as if continuing his thoughts aloud, "all of us,
and especially you women, must have personal experience of all

the nonsense of life, in order to get back to life itself; the evidence of other people is no good."

And the reason why Pierre occupies the center of interest in *War and Peace*, gradually displacing Andrew and Natasha for all their allure, is that he pursues so many false scents. We feel the full force of his experience, his restlessness, and his impatience with shoddy answers. No one answers Pierre's mighty questions; he simply takes time to discover his being and assume himself.

Now, for all the rugged strength of this attitude toward life, it confronts us with a great dilemma regarding literature. Does it not seem that these two masters of the novel confound themselves by denying any final value to their own work? If we must learn through personal experience, following a progress of self-realization that cannot be hastened or influenced without some kind of damage to what we really are, what is the purpose of literature? Why read a book which, according to the deepest convictions of its author, we cannot substitute for life truly lived? The question is not specious. On the contrary, it probes toward the essential nature of literary experience and artistic experience in general. But I shall defer any attempt to answer the question, both because the appropriate terms will emerge later and because merely ruminating over the question a while may induce better understanding of it.

What Marcel achieves or earns through living in Proust's novel, the art found after a lifetime of disappointments and missteps, comes clear to us as readers but cannot serve us as it serves him. Proust-Marcel's aestheticism, or what some would call his mysticism, grows in this world where we must fend for ourselves. No matter how refined and tenuous Proust's fabric may become, he never swerves from a sense of "life as worthy of being lived"

> cette réalité que nous risquerions fort de mourir sans avoir connue, et qui est tout simplement notre vie. La vraie vie, la vie enfin découverte et éclaircie, la seule vie par conséquent réellement vécue, c'est la littérature; cette vie qui, en un sens, habite à chaque instant chez tous les hommes aussi bien que chez l'artiste.

> [the reality which there is grave danger we might die without ever having known and yet which is simply our life. Life as it really is, life disclosed at last and made clear, consequently the only life that is really lived, is literature; that life which in one sense is to be found at every moment in every man, as well as in the artist.]

We hear the strength of conviction that lodges in the word, "literature," as Proust closes in on it. But what follows, the little phrase, "in one sense," concedes that this value cannot mean to all of us (in spite of the statement) what it means to the author-narrator.

It might be possible now to define *A la recherche* as the dramatization of a set of moral and epistemological truths; but the weakest part of that description is the word "dramatization." Marcel's drama is so slow-paced, so extended and even attenuated between beginning and end, that we can use the word only in a restricted, nearly Oriental sense of an inward drama expressed in a few highly ritualized gestures. And the Oriental aspect of *A la recherche* goes very deep. A multiplicity of images, laws, and fleeting illuminations lie along the course of our existence, but only a sustained and disciplined pursuit of ourselves inwardly, only life truly lived leads to wisdom. One of the greatest achievements in the Western tradition of the novel, *A la recherche* also joins the Oriental tradition of works of meditation and initiation into the mysteries of life. We can read as far into it as our age and understanding allow. A dedicated *mondain* in Paris for half his life, Proust went on to probe far beyond the culture that reared him, and far beyond Catholicism, Judaism, and idealist philosophy. The poet and Orientalist René Daumal provides a frame in which to see this achievement.

> The Modern Man believes himself adult, a finished product, with nothing to do for the rest of his life but alternately earn and spend material things (money, vital forces, skills), without these exchanges having the slightest effect on the thing called "I." The Hindu regards himself as something still to be formed, a false vision to be corrected, a composite of substances to be transmuted, a multitude to be unified. . . .
>
> Among us, men are considered equal in what they *are*, and different by what they *have*: innate qualities and acquired skills. The Hindu recognizes a hierarchy in men's degree of being. The master is not just more knowing or more clever than the student; the former *is*, in substance, more than the latter. This is what makes possible the unbroken transmission of the truth. (*Chaque fois que l'aube paraît*)

In his intricate weaving of figures around the optics of time and in his emphasis on creating our own deliverance from time in the inwardness of life at every moment, Proust reveals his close kinship to Oriental thought and the traditional Oriental mood of life. Amid the bravura activism and possessiveness of the West—political, commercial, social, and sentimental—his novel assumes the proportions of a gospel. Proust had no use for "the poor in spirit," confident in their upbringing and inheritance. He wrote for those, including himself, who feel that the full meaning and value of life is ours to discover.

Signs and Thought

What constitutes the unity of *In Search of Lost Time?* We know, at least, what does not. It is not recollection, memory, even involuntary memory. What is essential to the Search is not in the madeleine or the cobblestones. On the one hand, the Search is not simply an effort of recall, an exploration of memory: search, *recherche*, is to be taken in the strong sense of the term, as we say "the search for truth." On the other hand, Lost Time is not simply "time past"; it is also time wasted, lost track of. It follows that memory intervenes as a means of search, of investigation, but not the most profound means; and time past intervenes as a structure of time, but not the most profound structure. In Proust, the steeples of Martinville and Vinteuil's little phrase, which cause no memory, no resurrection of the past to intervene, will always prevail over the madeleine and the cobblestones of Venice, which depend on memory and thereby still refer to a "material explanation."

What is involved is not an exposition of involuntary memory, but the narrative of an apprenticeship: more precisely, the apprenticeship of a man of letters. The Méséglise way and the Guermantes way are not so much the sources of memory as the raw materials, the lines of an apprenticeship. They are the two ways of a "formation." Proust constantly insists on this: at one moment or another, the hero does not yet know this or that; he will learn it later on. He is under a certain illusion, which he will ultimately discard. Whence the movement of disappointments and revelations, which imparts its rhythm to the Search as a whole. One might invoke Proust's

---

From *Proust and Signs,* translated by Richard Howard. © 1972 by George Braziller, Inc.

Platonism: to learn is still to remember. But however important its role, memory intervenes only as the means of an apprenticeship which transcends recollection both by its goals and by its principles. The Search is oriented to the future, not to the past.

Learning is essentially concerned with *signs*. Signs are the object of a temporal apprenticeship, not of an abstract knowledge. To learn is first of all to consider a substance, an object, a being as if they emitted signs to be deciphered, interpreted. There is no apprentice who is not "the Egyptologist" of something. One becomes a carpenter only by becoming sensitive to the signs of wood, a physician by becoming sensitive to the signs of disease. Vocation is always predestination with regard to signs. Everything which teaches us something emits signs, every act of learning is an interpretation of signs or hieroglyphs. Proust's work is based not on the exposition of memory, but on the apprenticeship to signs.

From them it derives its unity and also its astonishing pluralism. The word sign, *signe*, is one of the most frequent in the work, notably in the final systematization which constitutes Time Regained (*Le Temps Retrouvé*). The Search is presented as the exploration of different worlds of signs which are organized in circles and intersect at certain points, for the signs are specific and constitute the substance of one world or another. We see this at once in the secondary characters: Norpois and the diplomatic code, Saint-Loup and the signs of strategy, Cottard and medical symptoms. A man can be skillful at deciphering the signs of one realm but remain a fool in every other case: thus Cottard, a great clinician. Further, in a shared realm, the worlds are partitioned off: the Verdurin signs have no currency among the Guermantes; conversely Swann's style or Charlus's hieroglyphs do not pass among the Verdurins. The worlds are unified by their formation of sign systems emitted by persons, objects, substances; we discover no truth, we learn nothing except by deciphering and interpreting. But the plurality of worlds is such that these signs are not of the same kind, do not have the same way of appearing, do not allow themselves to be deciphered in the same manner, do not have an identical relation with their meaning. The hypothesis that the signs form both the unity and the plurality of the Search must be verified by considering the worlds in which the hero participates directly.

The first world of the Search is the world of, precisely, worldliness. There is no milieu which emits and concentrates so many signs, in such reduced space, at so great a rate. It is true that these signs themselves are not homogeneous. At one and the same moment they are differentiated, not only according to classes but according to even more fundamental "families of mind." From one moment to the next, they evolve, crystallize, or give way to other signs. Thus the apprentice's task is to understand why someone is "received" in a certain world, why someone ceases to be so; what signs do the worlds obey, which signs are legislators, and which high priests. In Proust's work, Charlus is the most prodigious emitter of signs, by his worldly power, his pride, his sense of theater, his face and his voice. But Charlus, driven by love, is nothing at the Verdurins; and even in his own world he will end by being nothing when its implicit laws have changed. What then is the unity of the worldly signs? A greeting from the Duc de Guermantes is to be interpreted, and the risks of error are as great in such an interpretation as in a diagnosis. The same is true of a gesture of Mme. Verdurin.

The worldly sign appears as the replacement of an action or a thought. It stands for action and for thought. It is therefore a sign which does not refer to something else, to a transcendent signification or to an ideal content, but which has usurped the supposed value of its meaning. This is why worldliness, judged from the viewpoint of actions, appears to be disappointing and cruel; and from the viewpoint of thought, it appears stupid. One does not think and one does not act, but one makes signs. Nothing funny is said at the Verdurins, and Mme. Verdurin does not laugh; but Cottard makes a sign that he is saying something funny, Mme. Verdurin makes a sign that she is laughing, and her sign is so perfectly emitted that M. Verdurin, not to be outdone, seeks in his turn for an appropriate mimicry. Mme. de Guermantes has a heart which is often hard, a mind which is often weak, but she always has charming signs. She does not act for her friends, she does not think with them, she makes signs to them. The worldly sign does not refer to something, it "stands for" it, claims to be equivalent to its meaning. It anticipates action as it does thought, annuls thought as it does action, and declares itself adequate: whence its stereotyped aspect, and its vacuity. We must not thereby conclude that such signs are negligible. The apprenticeship would be imperfect, and even impossible, if it did not pass through them. These signs are empty, but this emptiness confers upon them a ritual perfection, a kind of formalism we do not encounter elsewhere. The worldly signs are the only ones capable of causing a kind of nervous exaltation, expressing the effect upon us of the persons who are capable of producing them.

The second circle is that of love. The Charlus-Jupien encounter makes the reader a party to the most prodigious exchange of signs. To fall in love is to individualize someone by the signs he bears or emits. It is to become sensitive to these signs, to undergo an apprenticeship to them (thus the slow individualization of Albertine in the group of young girls). It may be that friendship is nourished on observation and conversation, but love is born from and nourished on silent interpretation. The beloved appears as a sign, a "soul": the beloved expresses a possible world unknown to us, implying, enveloping, imprisoning a world which must be deciphered, that is, interpreted. What is involved, here, is a plurality of worlds; the pluralism of love does not concern only the multiplicity of loved beings, but the multiplicity of souls or worlds in each of them. To love is to try to *explicate*, to *develop* these unknown worlds which remain enveloped within the beloved. This is why it is so easy for us to fall in love with women who are not of our "world," nor even our type. It is also why the loved women are often linked to landscapes which we know sufficiently to long for their reflection in a woman's eyes, but which are then reflected from a viewpoint so mysterious that they become virtually inaccessible, unknown landscapes: Albertine envelops, incorporates, amalgamates "the beach and the breaking waves." How can we gain access to a landscape which is no longer the one we see, but on the contrary the one in which we are seen? "If she had seen me, what could I have meant to her? From what universe did she select me?"

There is, then, a contradiction of love. We cannot interpret the signs of a loved person without proceeding into worlds which have not waited for us in order to take form, which formed themselves with other persons, and in which we are at first only an object among the rest. The lover wants his beloved to devote to him her preferences, her gestures, her caresses. But the beloved's gestures, at the very moment they are addressed to us, still express that unknown world which excludes us. The beloved gives us signs of preference; but since these signs are the same as those which express worlds to which we do not belong, each preference by which we profit draws the image of the *possible world* in which others might be or are preferred. "All at once his jealousy, as if it were the shadow of his love, was completed by the double of this new smile which she had given him that very evening, and which, conversely now, mocked Swann and was filled with love for someone else. . . . So that he came to regret each pleasure he enjoyed with her, each caress they devised whose delight he had been so indiscreet as to reveal to her, each grace he discerned in her, for he knew that a moment later they would constitute new instruments of his torment." The contradiction of love consists of this: the means we count on to preserve us from jealousy are the very means which develop that jealousy, giving it a kind of autonomy, of independence with regard to our love.

The first law of love is subjective: subjectively, jealousy is deeper than love, it contains love's truth. This is because jealousy goes further in the apprehension and interpretation of signs. It is the destination of love, its finality. Indeed, it is inevitable that the signs of a loved person, once we "explicate" them, should be revealed as deceptive: addressed to us, applied to us, they nonetheless express worlds which exclude us and which the beloved will not and cannot make us know. Not by virtue of any particular ill will on the beloved's part, but of a deeper contradiction, which inheres in the nature of love and in the general situation of the beloved. Love's signs are not like the signs of worldliness; they are not empty signs, standing for thought and action. They are deceptive signs which can be addressed to us only by concealing what they express: the origin of unknown worlds, of unknown actions and thoughts which give them a meaning. They do not excite a superficial, nervous exaltation, but the suffering of a deeper exploration. The beloved's lies are the hieroglyphics of love. The interpreter of love's signs is necessarily the interpreter of lies. His fate is expressed in the motto: to love without being loved.

What does the lie conceal in love's signs? All the deceptive signs emitted by a loved woman converge upon the same secret world: the world of Gomorrah, which itself no longer depends on this or that woman (though one woman can incarnate it better than another), but is the feminine possibility *par excellence*, a kind of *a priori* which jealousy discovers. This is because the world expressed by the loved woman is always a world which excludes us, even when she gives us a mark of preference. But, of all the worlds, which one is the most excluding, the most exclusive? "It was a terrible *terra incognita* on which I had just landed, a new phase of unsuspected sufferings which was beginning. And yet this deluge of reality which submerges us, if it is real in relation to our timid presuppositions, was nonetheless anticipated by them. . . . The rival was not like me, the rival's weapons were different, I could not join battle on the same terrain, give Albertine the same pleasures, nor even conceive just what they might be." We interpret all the signs of the loved woman; but at the end of this painful decipherment, we come up against the sign of Gomorrah as though against the deepest expression of an original feminine reality.

The second law of Proustian love is linked with the first: objectively, heterosexual loves are less profound than homosexual ones; they find their truth in homosexuality. For if it is true that the loved woman's secret is the secret of Gomorrah, the lover's secret is that of Sodom. In analogous circumstances, the hero of the Search surprises Mlle. Vinteuil, and surprises Charlus. But Mlle. Vinteuil explicates all loved women, as Charlus implicates all lovers. At the infinity of our loves, there is the original Hermaphrodite. But the Hermaphrodite is not a being capable of reproducing itself. Far from uniting the sexes, it separates them, it is the source from which there continually proceed the two divergent homosexual series, that of Sodom and that of Gomorrah. It is the Hermaphrodite which possesses the key to Samson's prophecy: "The two sexes shall die, each in a place apart." To the point where heterosexual loves are merely the appearance which covers the destination of each sex, concealing the accursed depth where everything is elaborated. And if the two homosexual series are the most profound, it is still in terms of signs. The characters of Sodom, the characters of Gomorrah compensate by the intensity of the sign for the secret to which they are bound. Of a woman looking at Albertine, Proust writes: "One would have said that she was making signs to her as though with a beacon." The entire world of love extends from the signs revealing deception to the concealed signs of Sodom and of Gomorrah.

The third world is that of sensuous impressions or qualities. It may happen that a sensuous quality gives us a strange joy at the same time that it transmits a kind of imperative. Thus experienced, the quality no longer appears as a property of the object which now possesses it, but as the sign of an *altogether different* object which we must try to decipher, at the cost of an effort which always risks failure. It is as if the quality enveloped, imprisoned the soul of an object other than the one it now designates. We "develop" this quality, this sensuous impression, like a tiny Japanese paper which opens under water and releases the captive form. Examples of this kind are the most famous in the Search, and accelerate at its end (the final revelation of "time regained" is announced by a multiplication of signs). But whatever the examples—madeleine, steeples, trees, cobblestones, napkin, noise of a spoon or a pipe—we witness the same procedure. First a prodigious joy, so that these signs are already distinguished from the preceding ones by their immediate effect. Further, a kind of obligation is felt, the necessity of a mental effort: to seek the sign's meaning (yet we may evade this imperative, out of laziness, or else our investigations may fail out of impotence or bad luck, as in the case of the trees). Then, the sign's meaning appears, yielding to us the concealed object—Combray for the madeleine, young girls for the steeples, Venice for the cobblestones. . . .

It is doubtful that the effort of interpretation ends there. For it remains to be explained why, by the solicitation of the madeleine, Combray is not content to rise up again as it was once present (simple association of ideas), but rises up absolutely, in a form which was never experienced, in its "essence" or its eternity. Or, what amounts to the same thing, it remains to be explained why we experience so intense and so particular a joy. In an important text, Proust cites the madeleine as a case of failure: "I had then postponed seeking the profound causes." Yet, the madeleine looked like a real success, from a certain viewpoint: the interpreter had found its meaning, not without difficulty, in the unconscious memory of Combray. The three trees, on the contrary, are a real failure, since their meaning is not elucidated. We must then assume that in choosing the madeleine as an example of inadequacy, Proust is aiming at a new stage of interpretation, an ultimate stage.

This is because the sensuous qualities or impressions, even properly interpreted, are not yet in themselves adequate signs. But they are no longer empty signs, giving us a factitious exaltation like the worldly signs. They are no longer deceptive signs which make us suffer, like the signs of love whose real meaning prepares an ever greater pain. These are true signs which immediately give us an extraordinary joy, signs which are fulfilled, affirmative and joyous. *But they are material signs.* Not simply by their sensuous origin. But their meaning, as it is developed, signifies Combray, young girls, Venice, or Balbec. It is not only their origin, it is their explanation, their development which remains material. We feel that this Balbec, that this Venice . . . do not rise up as the product of an association of ideas, but in person and in their essence. Yet we are not ready to understand what this ideal essence is, nor why we feel so much joy. "The taste of the little madeleine had reminded me of Combray. But why had the images of Combray and of Venice, at the one moment and at the other, given such a certainty of joy, adequate, with no further proofs, to make death itself a matter of indifference to me?"

At the end of the Search, the interpreter understands what had escaped him in the case of the madeleine or even of the steeples: that the material meaning is nothing without an ideal essence which it incarnates. The mistake is to suppose that the hieroglyphs represent "only material objects." But what now permits the interpreter to go further is that meanwhile the problem of art has been raised, and has received a solution. Now the world of art is the ultimate world of signs, and these signs, as though *dematerialized,* find their meaning in an ideal essence. Henceforth, the world revealed by art reacts on all the others, and notably on the sensuous signs; it integrates them, colors them with an esthetic meaning and imbues what was still opaque about them. Then we understand that the sensuous signs *already* referred to an ideal essence which was incarnated in their material meaning. But without art we should not have understood this, nor transcended the law of interpretation which corresponded to the analysis of the madeleine. This is why all the signs converge upon art; all apprenticeships, by the most diverse paths, are already unconscious apprenticeships to art itself. At the deepest level, the essential is in the signs of art.

We have not yet defined them. We ask only the reader's concurrence that Proust's problem is the problem of signs in general; and that the signs constitute different worlds, worldly signs, empty signs, deceptive signs of love, sensuous material signs, and lastly the essential signs of art (which transform all the others).

THE IMAGE OF THOUGHT

If time has great importance in the Search, it is because every truth is a truth of time. But the Search is first of all a search for truth. Thereby is manifested the "philosophical" bearing of Proust's work: it vies with philosophy. Proust sets up an image of thought in opposition to that of philosophy. He attacks what is most essential in a classical philosophy of the rationalist type: the presuppositions of this philosophy. The philosopher readily presupposes that the mind as mind, the thinker as thinker, wants the truth, loves or desires the truth, naturally seeks the truth. He assumes in advance the good will of thinking; all his investigation is based on a "premeditated decision." From this comes the method of philosophy: from a certain viewpoint, the search for truth would be the most natural and the easiest; it would suffice to make the decision to undertake it, and to possess a method capable of overcoming the external influences which distract the mind from its vocation and cause it to take the false for the true. It would be a matter of discovering and organizing ideas according to an order which would be that of thought, as so many explicit significations or formulated truths which would then fulfill the search and assure agreement between minds.

In the "philosopher" there is the "friend." It is important that Proust offers the same critique of philosophy as of friendship. Friends are, in relation to one another, like minds of good will who are in agreement as to the signification of things and words: they communicate under the effect of a mutual good will. Philosophy is like the expression of a Universal Mind which is in agreement with itself in order to determine explicit and communicable significations. Proust's critique touches the essential point: truths remain arbitrary and abstract, so long as they are based on the good will of thinking. Only the conventional is explicit. This is because philosophy, like friendship, is ignorant of the dark regions in which are elaborated the effective forces which act on thought, the determinations which *force* us to think; a friend is not enough for us to approach the truth. Minds communicate to each other only the conventional; the mind engenders only the possible. The truths of philosophy are lacking in necessity, and the mark of necessity. As a matter of face, the truth is not revealed, it is betrayed; it is not communicated, it is interpreted; it is not willed, it is involuntary.

The great theme of Time regained is that the search for truth is the characteristic adventure of the involuntary. Thought is nothing without something which forces and does violence to it. More important than thought, there is "what leads to thought"; more important than the philosopher, is the poet. Victor Hugo writes philosophy in his first poems because he "still thinks, instead of being content, like nature, to lead to thought." But the poet learns that what is essential is outside of thought, in what forces us to think. The *leitmotif* of Time regained is the word *force*: impressions which force us to look, encounters which force us to interpret, expressions which force us to think.

> The truths which intelligence grasps directly in the open light of day have something less profound, less *necessary* about them than those which life has communicated to us *in spite of ourselves* in an impression, a material impression because it has reached us through our senses, but whose spirit we can extract. . . . I would have to try to interpret the sensations as the *signs* of so many laws and ideas, by attempting to think, that is, to bring out of the darkness what I had felt, and convert it into a spiritual equivalent. . . . Whether this was a matter of reminiscences of the kind which included the noise of the fork or the taste of the madeleine, or of those truths written with the help of figures whose meaning I was trying to discover in my mind, where like steeples or weeds, they composed a complicated and elaborate *herbal*, their first character was that *I was not free* to choose them, that they were given to me as they were. And I felt that this must be the mark of their authenticity. *I had not gone looking* for the two cobblestones of the courtyard where I had stumbled. But precisely the *fortuitous, inevitable* way in which the sensation had been *encountered* governed the truth of a past which it resuscitated, of the images which it

released, since we feel its effort to rise toward the light, since
we feel the joy of reality regained.... In order to read the
inner book of these unknown *signs* (*signs* in relief, it seemed,
which my attention would seek out, would bump into, would
pass by, like a diver exploring the depths), no one could help
me by any rules, such reading consisting in an act of creation in
which nothing can take our place or even collaborate with
us.... The ideas formed by pure intelligence have only a
logical truth, a possible truth, their choice is arbitrary. The
book whose characters are figured, *not traced by us*, is our only
book. Not that the ideas we form cannot be logically exact, but
we do not know whether they are true. Only the impression,
however paltry their substance seems, however unlikely their
traces, is a criterion of truths and on this account alone merits
being apprehended by the mind, for only the impression is
capable, if the mind can disengage this truth from it, of leading
the mind to a greater perfection and of giving it a pure joy.

What forces us to think is the sign. The sign is the object of an
encounter; but it is precisely the contingency of the encounter which
guarantees the necessity of what it leads us to think. The act of thinking
does not proceed from a simple natural possibility; on the contrary, it is
the only true creation. Creation is the genesis of the act of thinking within
thought itself. This genesis implicates something which does violence to
thought, which wrests it from its natural stupor, and its merely abstract
possibilities. To think is always to interpret—to explicate, to develop, to
decipher, to translate a sign. Translating, deciphering, developing are the
form of pure creation. There is no more an explicit signification than a
clear idea. There are only meanings implicated in signs; and if thought has
the power to explicate the sign, to develop it in an Idea, this is because the
Idea is already there in the sign, in the enveloped and involuted state, in
the obscure state of what forces us to think. We seek the truth only within
time, constrained and forced. The truthseeker is the jealous man who
catches a lying sign on the beloved's face. He is the sensitive man, in that
he encounters the violence of an impression. He is the reader, the auditor, in
that the work of art emits signs which will perhaps force him to create,
like the call of genius to other geniuses. The comunications of garrulous
friendship are nothing, compared with a lover's silent interpretations.
Philosophy, with all its method and its good will, is nothing compared with
the secret pressures of the work of art. Creation, like the genesis of the act

of thinking, always starts from signs. The work of art is born from signs as much as it generates them; the creator is like the jealous man, interpreter of the god, who scrutinizes the signs in which the truth *betrays itself*.

The adventure of the involuntary recurs on the level of each faculty. In two different ways, the worldly signs and the signs of love are intepreted by the intelligence. But this is no longer that abstract and voluntary intelligence, which claims to find logical truths by itself, to have its own order and to anticipate pressures from the outside world. This is an involuntary intelligence, the intelligence which undergoes the pressure of signs and comes to life only in order to interpret them, in order thus to exorcise the void in which it chokes, the suffering which submerges it. In science and in philosophy, the intelligence always "comes before"; but characteristic of signs is their appeal to the intelligence insofar as it comes after, insofar as it must come after. The same is true of memory: the sensuous signs force us to seek the truth, but thereby mobilize an involuntary memory (or an involuntary imagination born of desire). Finally the signs of art force us to think: they mobilize pure thought as a faculty of essences. They release within thought what depends least on its good will: the act of thinking itself. The signs mobilize, constrain a faculty: intelligence, memory, or imagination. This faculty, in its turn, mobilizes thought, forces it to conceive essences. Under the signs of art, we learn what pure thought is as a faculty of essences, and how the intelligence, the memory, or the imagination diversify it in relation to the other kinds of signs.

Voluntary and involuntary do not designate different faculties, but rather a different exercise of the same faculties. Perception, memory, imagination, intelligence, and thought itself have only a contingent exercise as long as they are exercised voluntarily: so that what we perceive, we could just as well remember, imagine, or conceive, and conversely. Neither perception, nor voluntary memory, nor voluntary thought gives us profound truth, but only possible truths. Here, nothing forces us to interpret something, to decipher the nature of a sign, or to dive deep like "the diver who explores the depths." All the faculties are harmoniously exercised, but one in place of the other, in the arbitrary and in the abstract. On the contrary, each time that a faculty assumes its involuntary form, it discovers and attains its own limit, it rises to a transcendent exercise, it understands its own necessity as well as its irreplaceable power. It ceases to be interchangeable. Instead of an indifferent perception, a sensibility which apprehends and receives signs: the sign is the limit of this sensibility, its vocation, its extreme exercise. Instead of a voluntary intelligence, a voluntary memory, a voluntary imagination, all these faculties appear in their

involuntary and transcendent form: then each one discovers that it alone
can interpret, each explicates a type of sign which does it particular
violence. Involuntary exercise is the transcendent limit or the vocation of
each faculty. Instead of voluntary thought, it is all that forces us to think,
all that is forced to think, all of involuntary thought which can conceive
only essences. Only the sensibility grasps the sign as such; only intelligence, memory, or imagination explicate the meaning, each according to a
certain kind of sign; only pure thought discovers essence, is forced to
conceive essence as the sufficient reason of the sign and its meaning.

It may be that Proust's critique of Philosophy is eminently philosophical. What philosopher would not hope to set up an image of thought
which no longer depends on the good will of the thinker and on a
premeditated decision? Each time we propose a concrete and dangerous
thought, we know that it does not depend on an explicit decision or
method, but on an encountered, refracted violence which leads us in spite
of ourselves to Essences. For the essences dwell in dark regions, not in the
temperate zones of the clear and the distinct. They are involved in what
forces us to think; they do not answer to our voluntary effort; they let
themselves be conceived only if we are forced to do so.

Proust is a Platonist, but not in the vague sense, not because he
invokes essences or Ideas apropos of Vinteuil's little phrase. Plato offers us
an image of thought under the sign of encounters and violences. In a
passage of the *Republic*, Plato distinguishes two kinds of things in the
world: those which leave the mind inactive, or give it only the pretext of
an appearance of activity; and those which lead it to think, which force us
to think. The first are the objects of recognition; all the faculties are
exercised upon these objects, but in a contingent exercise, which makes us
say "that is a finger," that is an apple, that is a house, and so on. On the
contrary, there are other things which force us to think: no longer
recognizable objects, but things which do violence, *encountered* signs.
These are "simultaneously contrary perceptions," Plato states. (Proust will
say: sensations common to two places, to two moments.) The sensuous
sign does us violence: it mobilizes the memory, it sets the soul in motion;
but the soul in its turn excites thought, transmits to it the constraint of the
sensibility, forces it to conceive essence, as the only thing which must be
conceived. Thus the faculties enter into a transcendent exercise, in which
each confronts and joins its own limit: the sensibility which apprehends
the sign; the soul, the memory, which interprets it; the mind which is
forced to conceive essence. Socrates can rightly say: I am Love more than
the friend, I am the lover; I am art more than philosophy; I am constraint

and violence, rather than good will. *The Symposium,* the *Phaedrus,* and the *Phaedo* are the three great studies of signs.

But the Socratic demon, irony, consists in anticipating the encounters. In Socrates, the intelligence still comes before the encounters; it provokes them, it instigates and organizes them. Prout's humor is of another nature: Jewish humor as opposed to Greek irony. One must be endowed for the signs, ready to encounter them, one must open oneself to their violence. The intelligence always comes after, it is good when it comes after, it is good only when it comes after. We have seen how this difference from Platonism involved many more. *There is no Logos, there are only hieroglyphs.* To think is therefore to interpret, is therefore to translate. The essences are at once the thing to be translated and the translation itself, the sign and the meaning. They are involved in the sign in order to force us to think, they develop in the meaning in order to be necessarily conceived. Everywhere is the hieroglyph, whose double symbol is the accident of the encounter and the necessity of thought: "fortuitous and inevitable."

GÉRARD GENETTE

Time and Narrative
in A la recherche du temps perdu

I suggest a study of *narrative discourse* or, in a slightly different formulation, of *narrative (récit) as discourse (discours)*. As a point of departure, let us accept the hypothesis that all narratives, regardless of their complexity or degree of elaboration—and Proust's *A la Recherche du temps perdu*, the text I shall be using as an example, reaches of course a very high degree of elaboration—can always be considered to be the development of a verbal statement such as "I am walking," or "He will come," or "Marcel becomes a writer." On the strength of this rudimentary analogy, the problems of narrative discourse can be classified under three main headings: the categories of *time* (temporal relationships between the narrative [story] and the "actual" events that are being told [history]); of *mode* (relationships determined by the distance and perspective of the narrative with respect to the history); and of *voice* (relationships between the narrative and the narrating agency itself: narrative situation, level of narration, status of the narrator and of the recipient, etc.). I shall deal only, and very sketchily, with the first category.

The time-category can itself be divided into three sections: the first concerned with the relationships between the temporal *order* of the events that are being told and the pseudotemporal order of the narrative; the second concerned with the relationships between the *duration* of the events and the duration of the narrative; the third dealing with relationships of

From *Aspects of Narrative: Selected Papers from the English Institute,* edited by J. Hillis Miller and translated by Paul de Man. © 1971 by Columbia University Press.

frequency of repetition between the events and the narrative, between history and story.

ORDER

It is well known that the folktale generally keeps a one-to-one correspondence between the "real" order of events that are being told and the order of the narrative, whereas literary narrative, from its earliest beginnings in Western literature, that is, in the Homeric epic, prefers to use the beginning *in medias res*, generally followed by an explanatory flashback. This chronological reversal has become one of the formal *topoi* of the epic genre. The style of the novel has remained remarkably close to its distant origin in this respect: certain beginnings in Balzac, as in the *Duchesse de Langeais* or *César Birotteau*, immediately come to mind as typical examples.

From this point of view, the *Recherche*—especially the earlier sections of the book—indicates that Proust made a much more extensive use than any of his predecessors of his freedom to reorder the temporality of events.

The first "time," dealt with in the six opening pages of the book, refers to a moment that cannot be dated with precision but that must take place quite late in the life of the protagonist: the time at which Marcel, during a period when, as he says, "he often used to go to bed early," suffered from spells of insomnia during which he relived his own past. The first moment in the organization of the narrative is thus far from being the first in the order of the reported history, which deals with the life of the hero.

The second moment refers to the memory relived by the protagonist during his sleepless night. It deals with his childhood at Combray, or, more accurately, with a specific but particularly important moment of this childhood: the famous scene that Marcel calls "the drama of his going to bed," when his mother, at first prevented by Swann's visit from giving him his ritualistic good-night kiss, finally gives in and consents to spend the night in his room.

The third moment again moves far ahead, probably to well within the period of insomnia referred to at the start, or a little after the end of this period: it is the episode of the *madeleine*, during which Marcel recovers an entire fragment of his childhood that had up till then remained hidden in oblivion.

This very brief third episode is followed at once by a fourth: a second return to Combray, this time much more extensive than the first in temporal terms since it covers the entire span of the Combray childhood. Time segment (4) is thus contemporary with time segment (2) but has a much more extensive duration.

The fifth moment is a very brief return to the initial state of sleeplessness and leads to a new retrospective section that takes us even further back into the past, since it deals with a love experience of Swann that took place well before the narrator was born.

There follows a seventh episode that occurs some time after the last events told in the fourth section (childhood at Combray): the story of Marcel's adolescence in Paris and of his love for Gilberte. From then on, the story will proceed in more closely chronological order, at least in its main articulations.

A la recherche du temps perdu thus begins with a zigzagging movement that could easily be represented by a graph and in which the relationship between the time of events and the time of the narrative could be summarized as follows: N(arrative) 1 = H(istory) 4; N2 = H2; N3 = H4; N4 = H2; N5 = H4; N6 = H1 (Swann's love); N7 = H3. We are clearly dealing with a highly complex and deliberate transgression of chronological order. I have said that the rest of the book follows a more continuous chronology in its main patterns, but this large-scale linearity does not exclude the presence of a great number of anachronisms in the details: *retrospections*, as when the story of Marcel's stay in Paris during the year 1914 is told in the middle of his later visit to Paris during 1916; or *anticipations*, as when, in the last pages of *Du Côté de chez Swann*, Marcel describes what has become of the Bois de Boulogne at a much later date, the very year he is actually engaged in writing his book. The transition from the *Côté de Guermantes* to *Sodome et Gomorrhe* is based on an interplay of ananchronisms: the last scene of *Guermantes* (announcing the death of Swann) in fact takes place later than the subsequent first scene of *Sodome* (the meeting between Charlus and Jupien).

I do not intend to analyze the narrative anachronisms in detail but will point out in passing that one should distinguish between *external* and *internal* anachronisms, according to whether they are located without or within the limits of the temporal field defined by the main narrative. The external anachronisms raise no difficulty, since there is no danger that they will interfere with the main narrative. The internal anachronisms, on the contrary, create a problem of interference. So we must subdivise them into two groups, according to the nature of this relation. Some function to fill in a previous or later blank (ellipsis) in the narrative and can be called *completive* anachronisms, such as the retrospective story of Swann's death. Others return to a moment that has already been covered in the narrative: they are *repetitive* or apparently redundant anachronisms but fulfill in fact a very important function in the organization of the novel. They function as *announcements* (in the case of prospective anticipations) or as *recalls* (when they are retrospective). Announcements can, for example, alert the reader to the meaning of a certain event that will only later be fully revealed (as with the lesbian scene at Montjouvain that will later determine Marcel's jealous passion for Albertine). Recalls serve to give a subsequent meaning to an event first reported as without particular significance (as when we find that Albertine's belated response to a knock on the door was caused by the fact that she had locked herself in with Andrée), or serve even more often to alter the original meaning—as when Marcel discovers after more than thirty years' time that Gilberte was in love with him at Combray and that what he took to be a gesture of insolent disdain was actually meant to be an advance.

Next to these relatively simple and unambiguous retrospections and anticipations, one finds more complex and ambivalent forms of anachronisms: anticipations within retrospections, as when Marcel remembers what used to be his projects with regard to the moment that he is now experiencing; retrospections within anticipations, as when the narrator indicates how he will later find out about the episode he is now in the process of telling; "announcements" of events that have already been told anticipatively or "recalls" of events that took place earlier in the story but that have not yet been told; retrospections that merge seamlessly with the main narrative and make it impossible to identify the exact status of a given section, etc. Finally, I should mention what is perhaps the rarest but most specific of all instances: structures that could properly be called *achronisms*, that is to say, episodes entirely cut loose from any chronological situation whatsoever. These occurrences were pointed out by J. P. Houston in a very interesting study published in *French Studies*, January 1962, entitled "Temporal Patterns in *A la recherche du temps perdu*." Near the end of *Sodome et Gomorrhe*, as Marcel's second stay at Balbec draws to a close, Proust tells a sequence of episodes not in the order in which they took place but by following the succession of roadside-stops made by the little train on its journey from Balbec to La Raspelière. Events here follow a geographical rather than a chronological pattern. It is true that the sequence of places still depends on a temporal event (the journey of the train), but this temporality is not that of the "real" succession of events. A similar effect is achieved in the composition of the end of *Combray*, when the narrator successively describes a number of events that took place on the Méséglise way, at different moments, by following the order of their increasing distance from Combray. He follows the temporal succession of a walk from Combray to Méséglise and then, after returning to his spatial and temporal point of departure, tells a sequence of events that took place on the Guermantes way using exactly the same principle. The temporal order of the narrative is not that of the actual succession of events, unless it happens to coincide by chance with the sequence of places encountered in the course of the walk.

I have given some instances of the freedom that Proust's narrative takes with the chronological order of events, but such a description is necessarily sketchy and even misleading if other elements of narrative temporality such as duration and frequency are not also taken into account.

DURATION

Generally speaking, the idea of an isochrony between narrative and "history" is highly ambiguous, for the narrative unit which, in literature, is almost always a narrative text cannot really be said to possess a definite duration. One could equate the duration of a narrative with the time it takes to read it, but reading-times vary considerably from reader to reader, and an ideal average speed can only be determined by fictional means. It may be better to start out from a definition in the form of a relative quantity, and define isochrony as a uniform projection of historical time on narrative extension, that is, number of pages per duration of event. In this way, one can record variations in the speed of the narrative in relation to itself and measure effects of acceleration, deceleration, stasis, and ellipsis (blank spaces within the narrative while the flow of events keeps unfolding).

I have made some rather primitive calculations of the relative speed of the main narrative articulations, measuring on the one hand the narrative of the *Recherche* by number of pages and on the other hand the events by quantity of time. Here are the results.

The first large section, *Combray* or Marcel's childhood, numbers approximately 180 pages of the Pléiade edition and covers about ten years (let me say once and for all that I am defining the duration of events by general consensus, knowing that it is open to question on several points). The next episode, Swann's love affair with Odette, uses approximately 200 pages to cover about two years. The Gilberte episode (end of *Swann*, beginning of *Jeunes filles en fleurs*) devotes 160 pages to a duration that can be evaluated at two or three years. Here we encounter an ellipsis involving two years of the protagonist's life and mentioned in passing in a few words at the beginning of a sentence. The Balbec episode numbers 300 pages for a three-month-long time-span; then the lengthy section dealing with life in Paris society (*Côté de Guermantes* and beginning of *Sodome et Gomorrhe*) takes up 750 pages for two and a half years. It should be added that considerable variations occur within this section: 110 pages are devoted to the afternoon party at Mme de Villeparisis's that lasts for about two hours, 150 pages to the dinner of nearly equal length at the Duchesse de Guermantes's, and 100 pages to the evening at the Princesse de Guermantes's. In this vast episode of 750 pages for two and a half years, 360 pages—nearly one half—are taken up by less than ten hours of social life.

The second stay at Balbec (end of *Sodome*) covers approximately six months in 380 pages. Then the Albertine sequence, reporting the hero's involvement with Albertine in Paris (*La Prisonnière* and the beginning of *La Fugitive*), requires 630 pages for an eighteen-month period, of which 300 deal with only two days. The stay in Venice uses 35 pages for a few weeks, followed by a section of 40 pages (astride *La Fugitive* and *Le Temps retrouvé*) for the stay in Tansonville, the return to the country of Marcel's childhood. The first extended ellipsis of the *Recherche* occurs here; the time-span cannot be determined with precision, but it encompasses approximately ten years of the hero's life spent in a rest home. The subsequent episode, situated during the war, devotes 130 pages to a few weeks, followed by another ellipsis of ten years again spent in a rest home. Finally, the concluding scene, the party at the Princesse de Guermantes's, devotes 190 pages to a two- or three-hour-long reception.

What conclusions can be derived from this barren and apparently useless enumeration? First of all, we should note the extensive shifts in relative duration, ranging from one line of text for ten years to 190 pages for two or three hours, or from approximately one page per century to one page per minute. The second observation refers to the internal evolution of the *Recherche* as a whole. It could be roughly summarized by stressing, on the one hand, the gradual slowing down of the narrative achieved by the insertion of longer and longer scenes for events of shorter and shorter duration. This is compensated for, on the other hand, by the presence of more and more extensive ellipses. The two trends can be easily united in one formula: increasing discontinuity of the narrative. As the Proustian narrative moves toward its conclusion, it becomes increasingly discontinuous, consisting of gigantic scenes separated from each other by enormous gaps. It deviates more and more from the ideal "norm" of an isochronic narrative.

We should also stress how Proust selects among the traditional literary forms of narrative duration. Among the nearly infinite range of possible combinations of historical and narrative duration, the literary tradition has made a rather limited choice that can be reduced to the following fundamental forms: (1) the *summary*, when the narrative duration is greatly reduced with respect to the historical duration; it is well known that the summary constitutes the main connective tissue in the classical *récit*; (2) the dramatic *scene*, especially the dialogue, when narrative and historical time are supposed to be nearly equal; (3) the narrative *stasis*, when the narrative discourse continues while historical time is at a standstill, usually in order to take care of a description; and (4)*ellipsis*, consisting of a certain amount of historical time covered in a zero amount of narrative. If we consider the *Recherche* from this point of view, we are struck by the total absence of summarizing narrative, which tends to be absorbed in the ellipses, and by the near-total absence of descriptive stasis: the Proustian descriptions always correspond to an actual observation-time on the part of the character; the time-lapse is sometimes mentioned in the text and is obviously longer than the time it takes to read the description (three-quarters of an hour for the contemplation of the Elstir paintings owned by the Duc de Guermantes, when the description takes only four or five pages of the text). The narrative duration is not interrupted—as is so often the case with Balzac—for, rather than *describing*, Proust *narrates* how his hero perceives, contemplates, and experiences a given sight; the description is incorporated within the narrative and constitutes no autonomous narrative form. Except for another effect with which I shall deal at some length in a moment, Proust makes use of only two of the traditional forms of narrative duration: scene and ellipsis. And since ellipsis is a zero point of the text, we have in fact only one single form: the scene. I should add, however, without taking time to develop a rather obvious observation, that the narrative function of this traditional form is rather strongly subverted in Proust. The main number of his major scenes do not have the purely dramatic function usually associated with the classical "scene." The traditional economy of the novel, consisting of summarizing and nondramatic narrative alternating with dramatic scenes, is entirely discarded. Instead, we find another form of alternating movement toward which we must now direct our attention.

FREQUENCY

The third kind of narrative temporality, which has in general received much less critical and theoretical attention than the two previous ones, deals with the relative frequency of the narrated events and of the narrative sections that report them. Speaking once more very schematically, the most obvious form of narration will tell once what happens once, as in a narrative statement such as: "Yesterday, I went to bed early." This type of narrative is so current and presumably normal that it bears no special name. In order to emphasize that it is merely one possibility among many, I propose to give it a name and call it the *singulative* narrative (*récit singulatif*). It is equally possible to tell several times what happened several times, as when I say: "Monday I went to bed early, Tuesday I went to bed early, Wednesday I went to bed early," etc. This type of anaphoric narrative remains singulative and can be equated with the first, since the repetitions of the story correspond one-to-one to the repetitions of the events. A narrative can also tell several times, with or without variations, an event that happened only once, as in a statement of this kind: "Yesterday I went to bed early, yesterday I went to bed early, yesterday I tried to go to sleep well before dark," etc. This last hypothesis may seem *a priori* to be a gratuitous one, or even to exhibit a slight trace of senility. One should remember, however, that most texts by Alain Robbe-Grillet, among others, are founded on the repetitive potential of the narrative: the recurrent episode of the killing of the centipede, in *La Jalousie*, would be ample proof of this. I shall call *repetitive* narrative this type of narration, in which the story-repetitions exceed in number the repetitions of events. There remains a last possibility. Let us return to our second example: "Monday, Tuesday, Wednesday," etc. When such a pattern of events occurs, the narrative is obviously not reduced to the necessity of reproducing it as if its discourse were incapable of abstraction or synthesis. Unless a deliberate stylistic effect is aimed for, even the simplest narration will choose a formulation such as "every day" or "every day of the week" or "all week long." We all know which of these devices Proust chose for the opening sentence of the *Recherche*. The type of narrative in which a single narrative assertion covers several recurrences of the same event or, to be more precise, of several analogical events considered only with respect to what they have in common, I propose to call by the obvious name of *iterative* narrative (*récit itératif*).

My heavy-handed insistence on this notion may well seem out of place, since it designates a purely grammatical concept without literary relevance. Yet the quantitative amount and the qualitative function of the iterative mode are particularly important in Proust and have seldom, to my knowledge, received the critical attention they deserve. It can be said without exaggeration that the entire Combray episode is essentially an iterative narrative, interspersed here and there with some "singulative" scenes of salient importance such as the motherly good-night kiss, the meeting with the Lady in the pink dress (a retrospective scene), or the profanation of Vinteuil's portrait at Montjouvain. Except for five or six such scenes referring to a single action and told in the historical past (*passé défini*), all the rest, told in the imperfect, deals with what used to happen at Combray regularly, ritualistically, every night or every Sunday, or every Saturday, or whenever the weather was good or the weather was bad, etc. The narrative of Swann's love for Odette will still be conducted, for the most part, in the mode of habit and repetition; the same is true of the story of Marcel's love for Swann's daughter Gilberte. Only when we reach the stay at Balbec in the *Jeunes filles en fleurs* do the singulative episodes begin to predominate, although they remain interspersed with numerous iterative passages: the Balbec outings with Mme de Villeparisis and later with Albertine, the hero's stratagems at the beginning of *Guermantes* when he tries to meet the Duchess every morning, the journeys in the little train of the Raspelière (*Sodome*, II), life with Albertine in Paris (the first eighty pages of *La Prisonnière*), the walks in Venice (*La Fugitive*), not to mention the iterative treatment of certain moments within the singulative scenes, such as the conversations about genealogy during the dinner at the Duchess's, or the description of the aging guests at the last Guermantes party. The narrative synthesizes these moments by reducing several distinct occurrences to their common elements: "the *women* were like this . . . the *men* acted like that; *some* did this, *others* that," etc. I shall call these sections *internal iterations*, in contrast with other, more common passages, in which a descriptive-iterative parenthesis begins in the middle of a singulative scene to convey additional information needed for the reader's understanding and which I shall call *external iterations*. An example would be the long passage devoted, in the middle of the first Guermantes dinner, to the more general and therefore necessarily iterative description of the Guermantes wit.

The use of iterative narrative is by no means Proust's invention; it is one of the most classical devices of fictional narrative. But the frequency of the mode is distinctively Proustian, a fact still underscored by the relatively massive presence of what could be called *pseudo-iterations*, scenes presented (mostly by the use of the imperfect tense) as if they were iterative, but with such a wealth of precise detail that no reader can seriously believe that they could have taken place repeatedly in this way, without variations. One thinks for example of some of the conversations between Aunt Léonie and her maid Françoise that go on for page after page, or of conversations in Mme Verdurin's or Mme Swann's salon in Paris. In each of these cases, a singular scene has arbitrarily, and without any but grammatical change, been converted into an iterative scene, thus clearly revealing the trend of the Proustian narrative toward a kind of inflation of the iterative.

It would be tempting to interpret this tendency as symptomatic of a dominant psychological trait: Proust's highly developed sense of habit and repetition, his feeling for the *analogy* between different moments in life. This is all the more striking since the iterative mode of the narrative is not always, as in the Combray part, based on the repetitive, ritualistic pattern of a bourgeois existence in the provinces. Contrary to general belief, Proust is less aware of the specificity of moments than he is aware of the specificity of places; the latter is one of the governing laws of his sensibility. His moments have a strong tendency to blend into each other, a possibility which is at the root of the experience of spontaneous recollection. The opposition between the "singularity" of his spatial imagination and, if I dare say so, the "iterativity" of his temporal imagination is nicely illustrated in the following sentence from *Swann*. Speaking of the Guermantes landscape, Proust writes: "[Its] specificity would *at times*, in my dreams, seize upon me with almost fantastical power" ["le paysage dont *parfois*, la nuit dans mes rêves, l'individualité m'étreint avec une puissance presque fantastique"]. Hence the highly developed sense of *ritual* (see, for example, the scene of the Saturday luncheons at Combray) and, on the other hand, the panic felt in the presence of irregularities of behavior, as when Marcel, at Balbec, wonders about the complex and secret law that may govern the unpredictable absences of the young girls on certain days.

But we must now abandon these psychological extrapolations and turn our attention to the technical questions raised by the iterative narration.

Every iterative sequence can be characterized by what may be called its *delimitation* and its *specification*. The delimitation determines the confines within the flow of external duration between which the iterative sequence, which generally has a beginning and an end, takes place. The delimitation can be vague, as when we are told that "from a certain year on, Mlle Vinteuil could never be seen alone," or precise, defined—a very rare occurrence in Proust—by a specific date, or by reference to a particular event, as when the break between Swann and the Verdurins puts an end to an iterative sequence telling of Swann's encounters with Odette and starts off a new sequence. The specification, on the other hand, points out the recurring periodicity of the iterative unit. It can be indefinite (as is frequently the case in Proust who introduces an iterative statement by such adverbs of time as "sometimes," "often," "on certain days," etc.) or definite, when it follows an absolute and regular pattern such as: "every day," "every Sunday," etc. The pattern can also be more irregular and relative, as when the walks toward Méséglise are said to take place in bad or uncertain weather, or the walks toward Guermantes whenever the weather is good. Two or more specifications can of course be juxtaposed. "Every summer" and "every Sunday" combine to give "every Sunday in the summer," which is the iterative specification of much of the Combray section.

The interplay between these two dimensions of the iterative narrative varies and enriches a temporal mode threatened, by its very nature, by a degree of abstraction. Provided it has a certain length, an iterative section can very closely resemble an ordinary narrative, except for some grammatical traits. Yet it goes without saying that a narrative such as "Sunday at Combray" that would retain only events that *all* Sundays have in common would run the risk of becoming as dryly schematic as a stereotyped time-schedule. The monotony can be avoided by playing on the internal delimitations and specifications.

Internal delimitations: for instance, the diachronic caesura brought about by the story of the encounter with the "Lady in the pink dress" in the narration of Marcel's Sunday afternoon readings: this encounter will bring about a change of locale, after the quarrel between Marcel's parents and Uncle Adolphe has put the latter's room out of bounds. Another instance would be the change of direction in the hero's dreams of literary glory after his first encounter with the Duchess in the church of Combray. The single scene, in those instances, divides the iterative sequence into a *before* and an *after*, and so diversifies it into two subsequences which function as two *variants*.

Internal specifications: I mentioned the good weather/bad weather pattern which introduces a definite specification in the iterative series of the Sunday walks and determines the choice between Guermantes and Méséglise. Most of the time, however, the iterative narrative is diversified in indefinite specifications introduced by "sometimes . . ." or "one time . . . some other time . . . ," etc. These devices allow for a very flexible system of variations and for a high degree of particularization, without leaving the iterative mode. A characteristic example of this technique occurs toward the end of the *Jeunes filles en fleurs* in a description of Albertine's face. The iterative mode, indeed, applies just as well to the descriptive as to the narrative passages; half of Proust's descriptions make use of this mode:

> *Certains jours*, mince, le teint gris, l'air maussade, une transparence violette descendant obliquement au fond de ses yeux comme il arrive quelquefois pour la mer, elle semblait éprouver une tristesse d'exilée. *D'autres jours*, sa figure plus lisse engluait les désirs à sa surface vernie et les empêchait d'aller au delà; *à moins que* je ne la visse tout à coup de côté, car ses joues mates comme une blanche cire à la surface étaient roses par transparence, ce qui donnait tellement envie de les embrasser, d'atteindre ce teint différent qui se dérobait. *D'autres fois*, le bonheur baignait ces joues d'une clarté si mobile que la peau, devenue fluide et vague, laissait passer comme des regards sous-jacents qui la faisaient paraître d'une autre couleur, mais non d'une autre matière, que les yeux; *quelquefois*, sans y penser, quand on regardait sa figure ponctuée de petits points bruns et où flottaient seulement deux taches plus bleues; C'était comme on eût fait d'un oeuf de chardonneret, *souvent* comme d'une agate opaline travaillée et polie à deux places seulement où, au milieu de la pierre brune, luisaient, comme les ailes transparentes d'un papillon d'azur, les yeux où la chair devient miroir et nous donne l'illusion de nous laisser, plus qu'en les autres parties du corps, approcher de l'âme. Mais *le plus souvent* aussi elle était plus colorée, et alors plus animée: *quelquefois* seul était rose, dans sa figure blanche, le bout de son nez, fin comme celui d'une petite chatte sournoise avec qui l'on aurait eu envie de jouer; *quelquefois* ses joues étaient si lisses que le regard glissait comme sur celui d'une miniature sur leur émail rose, que faisait encore paraître plus délicat, plus intérieur, le couvercle entr'ouvert et superposé (de ses cheveux noirs; *il arrivait que* le teint de ses

joues atteingnît) le rose violacé du cyclamen, et *parfois* même,
quand elle était congestionnée ou fiévreuse, et donnant alors
l'idée d'une complexion maladive qui rabaissait mon désir à
quelque chose de plus sensuel et faisait exprimer à son regard
quelque chose de plus pervers et de plus malsain, la sombre
pourpre de certaines roses d'un rouge presque noir; et chacune
de ces Albertine était différente, comme est différente chacune
des apparitions de la danseuse dont sont transmutées les couleurs,
la forme, le caractère, selon les jeux innombrablement variés
d'un projecteur lumineux.

[*On certain days*, slim, with grey cheeks, a sullen air, a violet
transparency falling obliquely from her such as we notice sometimes on the sea, she seemed to be feeling the sorrows of exile.
On other days her face, more sleek, caught and glued my
desires to its varnished surface and prevented them from going
any farther; *unless* I caught a sudden glimpse of her from the
side, for her dull cheeks, like white wax on the surface, were
visibly pink beneath, which made me anxious to kiss them, to
reach that different tint, which thus avoided my touch. *At other
times* happiness bathed her cheeks with a clarity so mobile that
the skin, grown fluid and vague, gave passage to a sort of
stealthy and subcutaneous gaze, which made it appear to be of
another colour but not of another substance than her eyes;
sometimes, instinctively, when one looked at her face punctuated with tiny brown marks among which floated what were
simply two larger, bluer stains, it was like looking at the egg of
a goldfinch—or *often* like an opalescent agate cut and polished
in two places only, where, from the heart of the brown stone,
shone like the transparent wings of a sky-blue butterfly her
eyes, those features in which the flesh becomes a mirror and
gives us the illusion that it allows us, more than through the
other parts of the body, to approach the soul. But *most often of
all* she showed more colour, and was then more animated;
sometimes the only pink thing in her white face was the tip of
her nose, as finely pointed as that of a mischievous kitten with
which one would have liked to stop and play; *sometimes* her
cheeks were so glossy that one's glance slipped, as over the
surface of a miniature, over their pink enamel, which was made
to appear still more delicate, more private, by the enclosing

though half-opened case of her black hair; *or it might happen that* the tint of her cheeks had deepened to the violet shade of the red cyclamen, and, *at times, even,* when she was flushed or feverish, with a suggestion of unhealthiness which lowered my desire to something more sensual and made her glance expressive of something more perverse and unwholesome, to the deep purple of certain roses, a red that was almost black; and each of these Albertines was different, as in every fresh appearance of the dancer whose colours, form, character, are transmuted according to the innumerably varied play of a projected limelight.]

The two devices (internal delimitation and internal specification) can be used together in the same passage, as in this scene from *Combray* that deals in a general way with returns from walks. The general statement is then diversified by a delimitation (itself iterative, since it recurs every year) that distinguishes between the beginning and the end of the season. This second sequence is then again diversified by a single indefinite specification: "certains soirs. . . ." The following passage is built on such a system; very simple but very productive:

Nous rentrions *toujours* de bonne heure de nos promenades, pour pouvoir faire une visite à ma tante Léonie avant le dîner. *Au commencement de la saison,* où le jour finit tôt, quand nous arrivions rue du Saint-Esprit, il y avait encore un reflet du couchant sur les vitres de la maison et un bandeau de pourpre au fond des bois du Calvaire, qui se reflétait plus loin dans l'étang, rougeur qui, accompagnée souvent d'un froid assez vif, s'associait, dans mon esprit, à la rougeur du feu au-dessus duquel rôtissait le poulet qui ferait succéder pour moi au plaisir poétique donné par la promenade, le plaisir de la gourmandise, de la chaleur et du repos. *Dans l'été, au contraire,* quand nous rentrions le soleil ne se couchait pas encore; et pendant la visite que nous faisions chez ma tante Léonie, sa lumière qui s'abaissait et touchait la fenêtre, était arrêtée entre les grands rideaux et les embrasses, divisée, ramifiée, filtrée, et, incrustant de petits morceaux d'or le bois de citronnier de la commode, illuminait obliquement la chambre avec la délicatesse qu'elle prend dans les sous-bois. Mais, *certains jours forts rares,* quand nous rentrions, il y avait bien longtemps que la commode avait perdu ses incrustations momentanées, il n'y avait plus, quand nous arrivions rue du Saint-Esprit, nul reflet de couchant étendu sur les vitres, et l'étang au pied du calvaire avait perdu sa rougeur, quelquefois il était déjà couleur d'opale, et un long rayon de lune, qui allait en s'élargissant et se fendillait de toutes les rides de l'eau, le traversait tout entier.

[We used *always* to return from our walks in good time to pay aunt Léonie a visit before dinner. *In the first weeks of our Combray holidays*, when the days ended early, we would still be able to see, as we turned into the Rue du Saint-Esprit, a reflection of the western sky from the windows of the house and a band of purple at the foot of the Calvary, which was mirrored further on in the pond; a fiery glow which, accompanied often by a cold that burned and stung, would associate itself in my mind with the glow of the fire over which, at that very moment, was roasting the chicken that was to furnish me, in place of the poetic pleasure I had found in my walk, with the sensual pleasures of good feeding, warmth and rest. *But in summer*, when we came back to the house, the sun would not have set; and while we were upstairs paying our visit to aunt Léonie its rays, sinking until they touched and lay along her windowsill, would there be caught and held by the large inner curtains and the bands which tied them back to the wall, and split and scattered and filtered; and then, at last, would fall upon and inlay with tiny flakes of gold the lemonwood of her chest-of-drawers, illuminating the room in their passage with the same delicate, slanting, shadowed beams that fall among the boles of forest trees. *But on some days, though very rarely*, the chest-of-drawers would long since have shed its momentary adornments, there would no longer, as we turned into the Rue du Saint-Esprit, be any reflection from the western sky burning along the line of windowpanes; the pond beneath the Calvary would have lost its fiery glow, sometimes indeed had changed already to an opalescent pallor, while a long ribbon of moonlight, bent and broken and broadened by every ripple upon the water's surface, would be lying across it, from end to end.]

Finally, when all the resources of iterative particularization have been exhausted, two devices remain. I have already mentioned pseudo-iteration (as in the conversations between Françoise and Aunt Léonie); this is admittedly a way of cheating or, at the very least, of stretching the reader's benevolence to the limit. The second device is more honest—if such ethical terminology can have any sense in the world of art—but it represents an extreme case leading out of the actually iterative mode: in the midst of an iterative section the narrator mentions a particular, singular occurrence, either as illustration, or example, or, on the contrary, as an exception to the law of repetition that has just been established. Such moments can be introduced by an expression such as "thus it happened that . . ." ["c'est ainsi que . . ."] or, in the case of an exception, "this time however . . ." ["une fois pourtant . . ."]. The following passage from the *Jeunes filles* is an example of the first possibility: "*At times*, a kind gesture of one [of the girls] would awaken within me an expansive sympathy that replaced, for a while, my desire for the others. *Thus it happened that* Albertine, one day . . ." etc. The famous passage of the Martinville clock towers is an example of the second possibility. It is explicitly introduced as an exception to the habitual pattern: generally, when Marcel returns from walks, he forgets his impressions and does not try to interpret their meaning. "This time, however" (the expression is in the text), he goes further and composes the descriptive piece that constitutes his first literary work. The exceptional nature of an event is perhaps even more explicitly stressed in a passage from *La Prisonnière* that begins as follows: "*I will put aside*, among the days during which I lingered at Mme de Guermantes's, one day that was marked by a small incident . . . ," after which the iterative narrative resumes: "*Except for this single incident*, everything went *as usual* when I returned from the Duchess's."

By means of such devices, the singulative mode merges, so to speak, with the iterative section and is made to serve it by positive or negative illustrations, either by adhering to the code or by transgressing it—which is another way of recognizing its existence.

The final problem associated with iterative temporality concerns the relationship between the duration or, rather, the internal diachrony of the iterative unit under consideration, and the external diachrony, that is, the flow of "real" and necessarily singulative time between the beginning and the end of the iterative sequence. A unit such as "sleepless night," made up of a sequence that stretches over several years, may very well be told in terms of its own duration from night to morning, without reference to the external passage of years. The typical night remains constant, except for internal specifications, from the beginning to the end of the sequence, without being influenced by the passage of time outside the particular iterative unit. This is, in fact, what happens in the first pages of the *Recherche*. However, by means of internal delimitations, the narrative of an iterative unit may just as readily encompass the external diachrony and narrate, for example, "a Sunday at Combray" by drawing attention to changes in the dominical ritual brought about by the passage of years: greater maturity of the protagonist, new acquaintances, new interests, etc. In the Combray episodes, Proust very skillfully plays upon these possibilities. J. P. Houston claimed that the narrative progresses simultaneously on three levels: with the duration of the day, of the season, and of the years. Things are perhaps not quite as clear and systematic as Houston makes them out to be, but it is true that, in the Sunday scenes, events taking place in the afternoon are of a later date than those taking place in the morning and that, in the narration of the walks, the most recent episodes are assigned to the longest itineraries. For the reader, this creates the illusion of a double temporal progression, as if the hero were a naïve little boy in the morning and a sophisticated adolescent at night, aging several years in the course of a single day or a single walk. We are touching here upon the outer limits of the iterative narrative mode.

Thus Proust appears to substitute for the *summary*, which typifies the classical novel, another form of synthesis, the iterative narrative. The synthesis is no longer achieved by acceleration, but by analogy and abstraction. The rhythm of Proust's narrative is no longer founded, as in the classical *récit*, on the alternating movement of dramatic and summarizing sections, but on the alternating movement of iterative and singular scenes. Most of the time, these alternating sections overlay a system of hierarchical subordinations that can be revealed by analysis. We already encountered two types of such systems: an iterative-explanatory section that is functionally dependent on an autonomous singular episode: the Guermantes wit (iterative) in the midst of a dinner at the Duchess's (singular): and a singular-illustrative section dependent on an autonomous iterative sequence (in the scenes used as illustrations or exceptions). The hierarchical systems of interdependence can be more complex, as when a singular scene illustrates an iterative section that is itself inserted within another singulative scene: this happens, for example, when a particular anecdote (such as Oriane's wordplay on Taquin le Superbe) is used to illustrate the famous Guermantes wit: here we have a singulative element (Taquin le Superbe) within an iterative sequence (Guermantes wit) itself included in a singulative scene (dinner at Oriane de Guermantes's). The description of these structural relationships is one of the tasks of narrative analysis.

It often happens that the relationships are less clear and that the Proustian narrative fluctuates between the two modes without visible concern for their respective functions, without even seeming to be aware of the differences. Some time ago, Marcel Vigneron pointed out confusions of this sort in the section dealing with Marcel's love for Gilberte at the Champs-Elysées: an episode would start off in the historical past (*passé défini*), continue in the imperfect, and return to the historical past, without any possibility for the reader to determine whether he was reading a singular or an iterative scene. Vigneron attributed these anomalies to last-minute changes in the manuscript made necessary by publication. The explanation may be correct, but it is not exhaustive, for similar discrepancies occur at other moments in the *Recherche* when no such considerations of expediency can be invoked. Proust probably at times forgets what type of narrative he is using; hence, for example, the very revealing sudden appearance of a historical past within a pseudo-iterative scene (I, 104, 722). He was certainly also guided by a secret wish to set the narrative forms free from their hierarchical function, letting them play and "make music" for themselves, as Proust himself said of Flaubert's ellipses. Hence the most subtle and admirable passages of all, of which J. P. Houston has mentioned a few, in which Proust passes from an iterative to a singular passage or uses an almost imperceptible modulation—such as an ambiguous imperfect of which it is impossible to know whether it functions iteratively or singularly, or the interposition of directly reported dialogue without declarative verb and, consequently, without determined mode, or a page of commentary by the narrator, in the present tense—to achieve the opposite effect; such a modulation, lengthily developed and to all appearances carefully controlled, serves as a transition between the first eighty pages of *La Prisonnière* that are in an iterative mode, and the singulative scenes that follow.

I have particularly stressed the question of narrative frequency because it has often been neglected by critics and by theoreticians of narrative technique, and because it occupies a particularly prominent place in the work of Marcel Proust. A paper that deals so sketchily and provisionally with a single category of narrative discourse cannot hope to reach a conclusion. Let me therefore end by pointing out that, together with the daring manipulations of chronology I have mentioned in the first part of my paper and the large-sized distortions of duration described in the second, Proust's predilection for an iterative narrative mode and the complex and subtle manner in which he exploits the contrasts and relations of this mode with a singulative discourse combine to free his narrative forever from the constraints and limitations of traditional narration. For it goes without saying that, in an iterative temporality, the order of succession and the relationships of duration that make up classical temporality are from the very beginning subverted or, more subtly and effectively, *perverted*. Proust's novel is not only what it claims to be, a novel of time lost and recaptured, but also, perhaps more implicitly, a novel of controlled, imprisoned, and bewitched time, a part of what Proust called, with reference to dreams, "the formidable game it plays with Time [le jeu formidable qu'il fait avec le Temps]."

LEO BERSANI

Proust and the Art of Incompletion

For Flaubert, the success of art depends on its ability to provide a definitive image of a reality anterior to art. Although the end of *Madame Bovary* gives to the novel a dimension it cannot explore but merely points to—that of a social order best characterized by the place it allows for the apothecary, M. Homais—this open-endedness is more apparent than real within the structure of the work. In its references to social history, *Madame Bovary* is deliberately incomplete, but formally its ending authentically concludes the work by helping, like the beginning, to enclose Emma's life within a larger and less analytically detailed picture of French provincial life. The intended finality of the work is indirectly reflected in Flaubert's awkward transitions from paragraph to paragraph and from chapter to chapter. His notion of style imprisons him in isolated, drawn-out battles with each narrative unit. And between the perfect and perfectly self-contained sentences and paragraphs, there is—ideally, we might also say—nothing but the creative void in which the novelist's work (his novel and his struggle) has simply ceased to exist.

When Proust's narrator praises, in *La Prisonnière*, the "marvelously incomplete" nature of nineteenth-century masterpieces, he is suggesting—hesitantly and ambivalently, it is true—that the most interesting fact about artistic creation may be the very *im*possibility of writing definitive sentences and definitive works. The passage I am thinking of (in which Marcel refers to Wagner, Hugo, Michelet, and Balzac) has several shifts of tone and

From *Aspects of Narrative: Selected Papers from the English Institute,* edited by J. Hillis Miller and translated by Paul de Man. © 1971 by Columbia University Press.

position, for two very different things appeal to the Proustian narrator: the fragmentary nature of major artistic productions in the nineteenth century, and the notion that great art, by definition, has a "vital" unity and completeness which critical recognition can make explicit but does not create. I think that the latter expresses a nostalgic view of the relation of art to the world and to the self which the narrator's experience tends most profoundly to undermine. And we can easily see the possibly radical consequences of Marcel's admiration for what he calls the "literary miscarriages" of the nineteenth century's "greatest writers." If the quality of completeness is recognized as a cultural imperative rather than an attribute inherent to art, art runs the risk of losing the privileged status it has always been granted among life's activities. If, like other processes in life, it can never be thought of as "completed," it no longer stands as a kind of epistemological monument in relation to the rest of our experience. Art ceases to reassure us about reality as intrinsically meaningful and conclusively shaped. The real is no longer the *object* of art any more than it is the object of any other activity—like making love or playing chess—which simply coexists with all the other activities we call reality. It then naturally becomes much more difficult than ever before to define what is specifically "artistic" about the activity of art, and the attempt to do so has, in the modern period, given us works which have become more and more open-ended and purely interrogative. Is art *about* anything? Is there a subject "behind" the work? Do we have to discard an aesthetic of imitation of expressiveness?

At the extreme limit of this problematic self-reflection in contemporary literature, we have, in Maurice Blanchot and in Samuel Beckett, a literature about the necessity of its own failure. The narrator of *A la recherche du temps perdu* is, of course, far from maintaining that the most interesting nineteenth-century artists are great *because* they failed. But his remarks in *La Prisonnière* correspond to the most original aspects of his own literary achievement. It is the lifelike incompleteness of that achievement which I want to examine. The Proustian art of incompletion has helped to subvert an aesthetic of art as the lifeless if instructive museum where we enter, in the "pauses" of experience, to replenish ourselves with the dead significance of safely immutable trophies of life.

The correspondences which Proust's narrator will establish between art and the rest of his life appear to have, as their point of departure, questions raised by Flaubert in order to assert the separation between art and life. A Flaubertian preoccupation with the correspondences between language and reality would seem also to characterize Marcel in *A la recherche du temps perdu.* But the problem is posed in a way which brings Proust's work, in spite of its bleak analyses of human possibilities, closer to the most optimistic Stendhalian assertions of human freedom than to the nihilistic conclusions of *Madame Bovary* and *L'Education sentimentale.* For Flaubert, the experience of dealing novelistically with the question of how expressive words are of reality does nothing to change the way in which he asks the question. Emma's tragedy is the result of what we might call her uncritical dependence on Flaubert's formulation of the novelistic dilemma. Apparently, nothing that happened in the writing of *Madame Bovary* led Flaubert to suspect that he had perhaps created an unnecessary dead-end in thinking that art must be a perfect fit between expression and a preexistent reality. And Emma does nothing but reenact the same assumptions from, as it were, the other direction. Flaubert dreams of a style adequate to the independent reality of his subjects; Emma searches for the reality adequate to the vocabulary of romantic clichés.

Because Flaubert immediately equates having experience with a problem of verbal designation, language blocks Flaubert's interest in discriminating among the choices by which we experiment with different ways of defining the self and the world. The very fact that language has to be used in making such choices leads Flaubert to a tortured weighing of the instruments available to describe them. He is indifferent to the commitments which a *use* of language creates, and because he thus isolates language from the activities it inspires and accompanies, words naturally appear to have a frighteningly impersonal life of their own. In one sense, Flaubert's disgust with life could be explained by his never having *reached* life in his epistemological investigations. And his choice of art as an alternative to life is, as the progress of his fiction from *Madame Bovary* to *Bouvard et Pécuchet* suggests, just as much a rejection of art as it is of life. His activity in both is paralyzed by his reluctance to examine the consequences of different uses of language and his obsession with its supposed essence.

Superficially, Proust's narrator is as concerned as Flaubert and Emma with the problem of what words designate. Marcel's life, like Emma's, appears to be structured by a series of hopeful fantasies and "falls": Mme de Guermantes does not provide the reality needed to make the notion of Merovingian mysteries come alive, Balbec does not embody the idea of nature's glamorously violent life, and Berma's acting, at first, cannot be fitted to the notion of dramatic talent. During his adolescence, Marcel, a little like Emma, waits for life to bring what he vaguely but passionately expects from it. Fascinated by words—the names of people and of places, and moral abstractions—he strains anxiously to receive "the secret of Truth and Beauty, things half-felt by me, half-incomprehensible, the full understanding of which was the vague but permanent object of my thoughts." The disappointments Marcel suffers are of course important, but, interestingly enough, they do not provoke an obsessive mistrust of thought and language. And this, I think, is because his sense of self is so dependent on the shape of his expectations that their destruction literally *empties* his imagination. As a result, the Flaubertian rhythm of illusion and disillusion is redefined by Proust as a discordance between the self and the world rather than as an imbalance between inexhaustible, impersonal fictions and a reality which is always either hypothetical and beyond language (Flaubert's Platonic subject) or flatly material and inferior to language (Tostes and Yonville).

The fragility of Marcel's sense of self will of course be recognized by readers of Proust as the principal "theme" of Marcel's life. It is the source of an anguish from which there seemed no escape at Combray and which only literature can provide a way of circumventing or, more exactly, of transforming into a creative exhilaration. *A la recherche* is punctuated by crucial episodes which dramatize a spectacular loss of being: the description at the beginning of *Combray* of the narrator's dizzying flights from one bedroom to another—and from one identity to another—when he awakes at night not knowing where, and therefore who, he is; the child's panic when he is separated from his mother at night; Marcel's horror at being surrounded, in the Balbec hotel room, by "enemies," by "things which did not know me"; and the emptiness of personality ("I was nothing more than a heart that throbbed") which prevents Marcel from recognizing the city of Venice when his mother angrily leaves without him for the railway station. In none of these cases is it a question of the Flaubertian excess of designation which removes the individual from the world and imprisons him in a rich but objectless imagination. Rather, the failure to recognize a place is experienced as a failure of all designation—most painfully, as a failure of self-recognition.

Such incidents could, I think, be traced to Marcel's sense of the sinfully individualizing nature of desire. Marcel's desires—sexual, social, and aesthetic—define his self; they express his designs on the world and give to his history its personal shape. But he feels a guilt about individuality which seems to be passed from his mother to Marcel: she herself attempts to erase all signs of her own personality after her mother's death, for anything purely self-expressive might be a blasphemous violation of Marcel's grandmother's memory. It is as if Marcel came to feel that *any* desires directed somewhere else (the loved one's sexual interest in someone else is the most dramatic version of this) express a sinister project for independence. They threaten the fantasy of a tranquil, really deathlike coincidence of being between two people in which each one merely receives, is wholly contained within, and sends back the image of the other. This is the security Marcel yearns for between himself and his mother and grandmother, and the two women seem to encourage this cult of love as self-sacrificial and yet all-devouring. To desire a peasant girl from Méséglise or the baronne de Putbus's chambermaid is to be someone different from *maman*; thus desire is felt—with guilt—as dangerously aggressive because Marcel knows that in fact it is an aggression against those who would fix and limit his own being in their love. To immolate desire is to immolate the self; it is the payment he has to make in order not to escape from his mother's attention, in order to continue "receiving himself" from her.

And yet the temptation to be—which is the temptation of freedom—is painfully strong. Because Marcel seems to condemn his own passionate projects and desires as a betrayal of his mother, and because the resulting conflict over them increases their potency while limiting their frequency of expression, he comes to fear them, without, however, renouncing the independent identity they create. If the loss of self is the punishment for desire—that is, for energetic designs on the world—some new form of self-assertion becomes necessary in order to protect Marcel from the consequences of self-assertion. The very extremity to which he is reduced—his emptiness, his loss of memory, the discontinuity of being from which he suffers—authorizes the most thoroughgoing investigation of ways to construct and possess a self which could no longer be lost. The punishment, we might say, legitimizes the crime. Literature in *A la recherche du temps perdu* is Marcel's indulgence in the "crime" of his own individuality as well as his subtle strategy for imprisoning others within the designs of his own desires. But in the enactment of what can easily be seen in Proust, as an ungenerous solution to this problem of being, the project of imprisoning the self and the world in a document of ontological security is transformed into the courageous exercise of making the self as indefinite and indefinable as possible, and even of protecting the freedom of others.

We can easily see the continuity between the drastic self-depletions from which Marcel suffers and the narrator's ambivalent attitude toward "incomplete" art. The dream of art as a way of achieving a deathlike fixity of self in life, for example, has the appeal of promising a kind of sculptural organization of the self and the world into immutably intelligible patterns. To salvage the self from the dissipation it suffers at moments of passionate desire, Marcel, while he never really considers the renunciation of desire, is tempted by the possibility of satisfying desires by de-energizing them. A certain self-petrification would seem to be the compromise between an uninhibited appetitive attack on the world and the probably expiatory victimizing of a "throbbing heart" by a world hostilely different from the self. And the perspective of memory allows for just this sort of passionless reenactment of desires, although, as we shall presently see, it also can permit a manipulating of the past for the sake of a richer future. In part, Proust's novel illustrates the truth of Sartre's claim that only in reflection can we posit affectivity for itself, that is, in terms of mental *states* which make for a psychology of the inert. Cut off from the objects which inspired and defined them, Marcel's desires, so to speak, no longer have anywhere to go. They do not "move" toward the world, but only around one another, creating those peculiar inner constellations which encourage the narrator to speak of mental life as if it were organized into clearly delimited conflicting states, and enacted as allegorical confrontations. Thus the narrator can at last live according to his desires, or, more exactly, *within* his desires. The retrospective expression of desire coincides with self-possession. Indeed, it belatedly constructs a self shaped by projects now transformed into abstractions. The psychology of states in *A la recherche du temps perdu*, like the general laws about human behavior, allows Marcel to think of literature as the reassuring completion of life. Both are maneuvers for placing art in the privileged position of giving permanent forms and significance to experience; as the place in which psychological truths are distilled, the narrator's work defines and closes his life.

But Marcel discovers another possibility of self-identification (as well as of contact with the world), a possibility which allows for a richly incomplete life and a richly incomplete work. Marcel's jealousy can provide a first illustration of how this discovery is made. In *La Fugitive*, the narrator speaks of a certain "compensation" in the suffering which the lies of "insensitive and inferior women" inflict on sensitive and intellectual men. Behind each of the loved one's words, the narrator writes, such men "feel that a lie is lurking, behind each house to which she says that she has gone, another house, behind each action, each person, another action, another person." And, he concludes, "all this creates, in front of the sensitive and intelligent man, a universe [in depths] which his jealousy would fain plumb and which is not without interest to his intelligence." Any statement felt or recognized as a lie evokes the possibly truthful statements to which it could be compared. But if the lover cannot fix on any one house or action or person as the reality behind the lie, the lie itself can never be eliminated from the attempt to know the truth. The fictive version of their behavior proposed by Albertine or Odette becomes the center on which Marcel and Swann organize a group of conjectures. The pain of not being able to eliminate that center—it is necessary to inspire the different conjectures whose lesser or greater probability it also helps to determine—is somewhat compensated for by the variety and depth which the lover's searching and unsatisfied imagination gives to the world. The need for truth stimulates the novelistic impulse, and the impossibility of truth makes of experience an infinitely expandable novel.

Involuntary memories provide a similar variety of points of view, and this time we can see more explicitly how expandable versions of experience in A la recherche are equivalent to expansive self-definitions. Numerous commentators have rightly emphasized the importance of involuntary memories in the novel, but it seems to me that the crucial role they play in Proust's work derives from what most of his readers have been unwilling to admit: their extremely modest significance. Involuntary memory is a brief coincidence between a present moment and a past one: a sensation now (such as the taste of the *madeleine*) accidentally awakens the full sensory memory of a past experience, and, "for the duration of a lightning flash," Marcel appears to exist "between" the present and the past, that is, in the similarity between the two—a similarity which is actually an abstraction from experience but which the senses fleetingly live. Now these memories *create* nothing; the extratemporal essence which the narrator claims they disengage from a present sensation and a past sensation may not have been previously felt as such, but it is nonetheless a truth about Marcel's *history* of sensations and in itself it contains nothing to inspire a future.

The interest of the so-called essences which involuntary memories reveal is that they make impossible any definitive self-formulations. The towel with which Marcel wipes his mouth in the Guermantes library, having "precisely the same sort of starchy stiffness as the towel with which I had so much trouble drying myself before the window the first day of my stay at Balbec," evokes a vision of "azure blue," spreads out, "in its various folds and creases, like a peacock's tail, the plumage of a green and blue ocean. And I drew enjoyment, not only from those colours, but from a whole moment of my life which had brought them into being and had no doubt been an aspiration toward them, but which perhaps some feeling of fatigue or sadness had prevented me from enjoying at Balbec and which now, pure and disembodied, freed from all the imperfections of objective perception, filled me with joy." This remark from *Le Temps retrouvé* implies nothing less than a reorganization of the hierarchy of interests and projects by which we rationally, and most habitually, recognize and define ourselves. It would be banal merely to point out that we are never completely aware of all our interests in any given situation. But, first of all, involuntary memory is a particularly powerful proof of this. Furthermore, Marcel's "return" to Balbec in the Guermantes library undermines the anxiety he felt at the time. It suggests that at least as strong as his fears was an aspiration toward certain colors, a thirst for sensations which complicates the episode of his arrival at Balbec by making it impossible for us— and for him—to settle on any one characterization of his feelings. Involuntary memory, while it appears to offer evidence of "an individual, identical, and permanent self," and thus appeases Marcel's fear of psychological discontinuity, also *dislocates* self-definitions by illustrating how incomplete they always are.

The importance of this is somewhat obscured by the narrator's emphatic distinctions between loss of self and self-possession; but the strategies for self-possession are by no means strategies for permanent self-immobilizations. And involuntary memory "returns" Marcel to himself at the same time that it demolishes the coherent views of his past which, in spite of the crises in which he seems to lose his past, he of course possesses all the time in his intellectual or voluntary memory. The taste of the *madeleine* and the sensations in the Guermantes library are trivial and tentative self-possessions, and this is exactly why they point the way to a literature of inventive autobiography. The essence liberated by an involuntary memory is, therefore, first of all personal: it is not in things, but in the particular analogies or identities which Marcel's sensory apparatus establishes among sensations. And it is in no sense the essence of his personality; it is, instead, just the essence of a particular relation in his history. Finally, by relocating or at least raising doubts about what was most important to him at a past moment, Marcel's involuntary memories legitimize an open-ended view of personality which informs the psychologically re-creative activity of writing *A la recherche du temps perdu*.

"Informs" in what way, exactly? How is the view of the self which I find implicit in Marcel's involuntary memories expressed and confirmed by style and novelistic structure in *A la recherche*? If what the narrator calls the "fundamental notes" of personality is inadequately rendered in the language we ordinarily use in our attempts to be recognized by others as belonging to a life already familiar to them, he must find a language which contains his most personal accent without, however, sacrificing the signs by which that accent may be communicated to others. The solution to this problem depends on the literary exploitation of what we might call experimental knowledge through self-disguises. Now the disguises of personality have both a positive and a negative value in *A la recherche*. The narrator insists so often on the pain caused by such disguises that we may not see at once the extent of his own indulgence in a liberating art of disguise. Sexuality—especially homosexuality—is presented in the novel as the field in which the Proustian "creatures of flight" can most effectively conceal their personalities by "dressing" them in desires inconceivable to the pursuing and possessive lover. Marcel cannot understand the "play" of Albertine's lesbianism because he cannot imagine what "role" she plays in it. Her love of women is an impenetrable disguise of his own love of women; she has his desires, but since she is a woman, he cannot recognize himself in them.

The connection between complicated sexual roles and the willful elusiveness of personality is most strikingly dramatized in the scene at Rachel's theater in *Le Côté de Guermantes*. Rachel's flirtation with a young male dancer who reminds her of another woman and to whom she speaks of having "a wonderful time" with him "and a girl I know" plunges Saint-Loup's jealous imagination into a labyrinth of psychological disguises. Images of desire become inextricably embroiled in a costume play in which the man would presumably be playing the role of a woman for Rachel or her friend, or for both, and they might be taking the role of a man with a man looking like a woman. Finally, the most baroque costumes of sexual desire are evoked in the letter Charlus accidentally reads from the lesbian actress Léa to Morel. In it Léa uses an expression about Morel which Charlus has always associated with homosexuality ("toi tu en es au moins"), but homosexuality here seems to mean that Morel has "the same taste as certain women for other women." Poor Charlus finds himself confronted with "the sudden inadequacy of a definition," and the letter sets up an unsolvable problem for the baron's imagination: by what images and identifications can the homosexual man calm his jealousy of another homosexual man who finds his pleasure with lesbians? "Where" is Morel in such pleasures? What is it like to be a man being treated like a woman who desires women acting like men?

Such are the disguises of escape from others, disguises which, as we see in Rachel's case, can be sadistically adopted in order to make the lover suffer from a spectacularly mysterious assertion of otherness. But in the literary work which devotes so much space to the anguished documenta-

tion of this sinister art of self-concealment, the narrator discovers other
techniques of self-diffusion, techniques which transform the accidental and
infrequent "airing" of personality which involuntary memories provide
into a willed and continuous process of self-renewal. I am thinking mainly
of the therapeutical diffusiveness of metaphorical representation in art.
Analogy in *A la recherche* is often humorous. This is especially evident
when the narrator compares some prosaic aspect of his past to an illustrious historical event. Françoise's passionate and fearful commentary of
Léonie's slightest change of mood, of the way she gets up in the morning
or has a meal, reminds the narrator of the nobility's anxious attentiveness
to almost imperceptible signs of favor or disfavor in Louis XIV. And the
cruelty with which Françoise strangles the chickens she serves to Marcel's
family at Combray changes the boy's view of her moral merits and makes
him think of all the brutality hidden behind the official piety with which
royal figures from the past are represented to us in religious art. Finally,
the water lily ceaselessly carried from one bank of the Vivonne to the
other by the river's currents fascinates Marcel, who watches it thinking of
the "strange, ineluctable, fatal daily round" in the habits of "certain
victims of neurasthenia," and then expands his anology to include an
illustrious literary precedent which, by a final humorous twist, brings him
back to his own staring at the "possessed" plant:

> Such as these [the victims of neurasthenia] was the water lily,
> and also like one of those wretches whose peculiar torments,
> repeated indefinitely throughout eternity, aroused the curiosity
> of Dante, who would have inquired of them at greater length
> and in fuller detail from the victims themselves, had not Virgil,
> striding on ahead, obliged him to hasten after him at full speed,
> as I must hasten after my parents.

On the one hand, such analogies make fun of Françoise, Léonie, and
Marcel; they give a mock-heroic importance to the most unremarkable
events or habits in their lives. But they also trivialize life at Versailles and
Dante's trip through hell. From both points of view the uniqueness of each
element in the metaphor is undermined by its availability for an unexpected comparison. The analogies clarify, but they are also reductive, and
they easily serve intentions of mockery. Historical repetition may be
instructive, but it also parodies individuality; or, perhaps more precisely, it
makes us skeptical about or indifferent to individuality since the quality
which two incidents have in common is detached from the historical
existence of each incident. Life at Versailles is an episodic illustration of a

type of life reincarnated in a scene from French provincial life at the end of the nineteenth century. Now such historical continuities are exactly what the narrator finds, or invents, as he writes the story of his own life. But the repetitions of autobiography are of course *self*-repetitions. And in the purely verbal organization of a literary work, the chronological sequence of events can be thought of as spatialized in constellations of literary metaphors. From his perspective of re-creative memories, the narrator constantly anticipates future events by "trying them out" metaphorically before they happen. Georges Poulet has spoken of a "reciprocal intelligibility" among originally distinct episodes in Marcel's life; analogies establish patterns that bring together apparently isolated moments, and they both evoke what has already been written and point to what is yet to be written.

This network of metaphorical correspondences does give to the work what at first appears to be a self-contained unity. But, more originally, such correspondences are also psychologically disintegrating. They have the effect of drawing us away from any fixed *center* of the self from which all its images might proceed. It has often been said that the narrator has very little personality compared to the other characters of *A la recherche*. And this is usually meant as an adverse judgment of the novel: as B. G. Rogers puts it, "the absence of a real hero in Marcel is hard to reconcile with the massive emotional and spiritual emphasis placed upon him in *Le Temps retrouvé*." This impression is particularly interesting in view of the fact that no reader can be unaware of the psychological repetitiveness in *A la recherche du temps perdu*. And the narrator does tell us enough about himself so that we easily recognize the psychological patterns repeated throughout the novel as belonging to *his* personality. It is nonetheless true that he tends to disappear as the visible and sharply defined source of those patterns. But I take this to be the sign of the narrator's most impressive achievement. The vagueness of Marcel as the center of his world can be the basis of a reproach only if we impose on the work notions of what it means "to have personality" which the work is engaged in discarding. What we might call the narrator's scattering of self is the technique of an often humorous and always liberating displacement of his most crippling fantasies. There is no one version of those fantasies more authoritative than other versions, and the self therefore has the freedom of *being* the variety of its disguises.

The various uses of metaphor in *A la recherche* have, fundamentally, the function of entertaining as many interpretive extensions of experience as possible. There is, for example, a certain type of social life which we recognize as the narrator's particular sense of society. And the continuities among different social images in the novel are often astonishingly transparent. The Verdurin receptions repeat details from the Guermantes receptions. La Patronne, like Oriane, boasts about the paintings Elstir did for her. An annoyance with illness and death because they spoil dinner parties and dances is repeated in progressively more shocking (and more improbable) versions: in the Duc de Guermantes's refusal to be told that his cousin is dead at the end of *Le Côté de Guermantes*; in M. Verdurin's insisting, one day at la Raspelière, that no one speak of Dechambre's death to Mme Verdurin; and in the latter's nervy denial—during the party at the quai Conti in *La Prisonnière*—that she feels any sorrow over the Princess Sherbatoff's death. We might say either that the narrator describes three different social events in a surprisingly similar manner, or that he finds impressively different disguises for a rather simple and bitter view of social life. But the various disguises of that view make it difficult to fix the exact quality of the pessimism. There is a greater tolerance of emotional callousness in the presentation of Oriane's inability to decide if she should give up her parties after Swann tells her he is going to die than in the image of Mme Verdurin's defiant advertising of her indifference to the princess's death. The second incident enacts a pessimistic view of social life in a manner more likely to shock the narrator out of social life. Each repetition of a radical skepticism about human feeling allows for different consequences, broadens or narrows the range of possible response to an essentially unchanged but nonetheless flexible conviction.

Furthermore, the world Marcel is presumably remembering strikes us in many respects as a projection of his own psychology and history. In the process of remembering an impenetrable world, and while documenting with somber lucidity the hopelessness of seeking to know the lives of others, Marcel has both illustrated his thesis and partially refuted it by now drawing the world of his past into the orbit of a single, recognizably continuous personality: his own. What might be called the creative space between the narrator and the world he describes—the actual work of self-dramatization which Balzac and Stendhal hide by suggesting that the decisions of writing are decisions of point of view toward a world already there—becomes a principal object of our attention in *A la recherche du temps perdu*. The novel provokes the drama of our own unsettled feelings about the exact sense in which these people and events belong to Marcel's past. And they seem to "belong" to *him* in an allegorical sense. The narrator thus seems to be illustrating, more or less transparently and in spite of his explicit claims that he is reporting on the real world of his past, the processes by which a novelist invents a world of fiction, and, more specifically, the degree of differentiation possible within a group of self-projective images.

Every incident and every character in *A la recherche* could be placed on a range of self-projection, a range extending from the most transparent versions of Marcel's psychology to those complexly particularized images in which allegory and observation appear to coincide. The inability to differentiate others from the self is dramatized within the novel as the anguish of love, at the same time that it defines the limits of characterization in a novel about love. Thus Albertine, by being so embroiled in Marcel's tortured doubts about her real personality, is an occasion for demonstrating an abortive attempt to disguise novelistic conjecture as a clear and fixed image of the external world. Saint-Loup and Mme de Guermantes, on the other hand, are so sharply individualized that they do seem to exist, so to speak, independently of the narrator's inventiveness, although Saint-Loup's love for Rachel parallels Marcel's possessively jealous love for Albertine, and Oriane's anxious reluctance (common to all the Guermantes) to let her guests leave at the end of a party reminds us of Marcel's terror at being separated from his mother. The psychology which we find so idiosyncratic and even pathological in Combray takes into account enough variety of experience so that its social "disguises" impress us as intelligent conclusions about life rather than the given limitations with which the narrator approaches life. If the world of Marcel's past becomes, in the process of writing, a fiction dramatizing Marcel himself, the very self-dramatization is such a liberal and inclusive one that it strikes us as a viable or livable framework in which to place the world.

Viable and therefore capable of development. What Marcel gives us is by no means a final, limiting version of experience. The fact that in describing the world he shapes it into an almost allegorical reflection of his own imagination diminishes the constraints of reality on his life. Superficially, this psychological repetitiousness in his work would seem to testify to the narrowness of his responses; more profoundly, by illustrating the power of his self-projections, it subverts the impoverishing authority of reality in whatever he says. No fact is strong enough to expel Marcel's fantasies from his report of it, which means that nothing in his life, short of death, can prevent him from using fact for a continuous revision of fantasy. He is as free as his imagination can make him precisely because, when he is most faithful to his experience, he has no illusion of being able to make statements about reality from which his imagination would be absent. The inconclusiveness of "knowledge" allows for the theoretically limitless use of the world as a testing-ground for fictions.

Flaubert's superstition of the real naturally led him to a process of constant deletion in his writing: how could he ever be sure that each sentence or each metaphor was not saying too much about reality, and therefore violating it? Proust, on the other hand, can add endlessly to his work, for it is as if he discovered, through his narrator's self-recreative memory, that even the most oppressively narrow experience can be interpreted into a constantly open-ended view of the world. And there is nothing naïve in this. Objects and other people are present; they impinge on Marcel's consciousness and they make him suffer. But in the process of admitting his inability to possess and control them, he finds that the barrier of his subjectivity gives him another kind of power: the power to invent and revise the significance of events and, by the excesses of experimental revision, to coerce reality into the field of his desires.

We could even say that *because* everything that happens in *A la recherche* is in Marcel's past, he has never in his life enjoyed more freedom than now. The final, definitive quality of events is felt at the moment we live them. It is then that we experience most concretely the impoverishing limitations and exclusions implicit in each emotion we have, each spectacle we see, each decision we make. It is only in memory that the future of each moment appears promisingly uncertain and therefore open to possibility. For in memory we can profit from a larger notion of consequences than we can afford to use at the "first" or present version of each experience. Retrospectively, the immediate effects of events can be subverted by an interpretive will; at the actual time, of those events, we were too busily engaged in their first consequences to see those consequences as anything but necessary and final. Proust's novel constantly illustrates this distinction; it is a literary dramatization of the psychoanalytic assumption that in certain conditions a restatement of the past creates new possibilities for the future. For all its apparent looking backward, *A la recherche du temps perdu* is a more projective novel than, say, *La Chartreuse de Parme*. Fabrice only rushes forward in time, and the pathos of his life is that his experience creates an irreversible destiny. Life narrows the range of his projects until, with unattackable logic, he has nothing more to do but die. When he returns to his past it is to rest, not to re-create. Proust's narrator, in a characteristic gesture of false surrender, turns his back on life in order to make some extraordinary claims for the future of his life. Aggressively active and self-revising, he remakes a once disappointing past into the field of an extravagant exercise in self-expansion.

Repetition in *A la recherche* is therefore a mode of freedom. But while the freedom which the narrator enjoys throughout his work is self-creative, it also coincides with a kind of impersonality. His metaphorical style allows him to repeat himself at the same time that it raises the contents of self-definitions above any one embodiment of them. "In anyone we love," the narrator writes in *Le Temps retrouvé*, "there is always present some dream that we cannot always discern but which we constantly seek to attain. It was my faith in Bergotte and Swann which had made me love Gilberte, just as it was my belief in Gilbert the Bad which had made me love Mme. de Guermantes. And what a wide expanse of unfathomable ocean was set apart in my love for Albertine, painful, jealous and individual though that love was? Moreover, just on account of this individual quality which we pursue with such eagerness, our love for someone else is already somewhat of an aberration." Our loves are most deeply characterized by a "persistent, unconscious dream" which seeks to incarnate itself in various persons. The dream is a specific type of desire; *it expresses an individuality more general than individuals.* And that individuality is what Proust's narrator calls an "essence"; it belongs to "the world of differences" which only art reveals.

The individuality of a point of view embodied in but not dependent on the existence of an individual person: as Gilles Deleuze has brilliantly defined it, this is what the narrator comes to recognize as the source of the pleasure he experiences in front of great art. And this identification of the absolutely individual with a region of Being transcending individuals saves the Proustian narrator from the despair of feeling that language can never communicate the "fundamental notes" of an artist's personality. By distinguishing between individuality and what we ordinarily think of as subjectivity, he can entrust the expression of individuality to a system of communication in which meanings are always *shared* meanings. Only an aesthetic of the ineffably personal rejects words because of their inescapably generalizing nature. Nothing could be further from the kind of personality which *A la recherche du temps perdu* seeks to express. Its austere drama consists in the narrator's effort to *abstract* an individual style from a life in which style is constantly threatened by the obsessions of a particular existence.

The narrative texture of *A la recherche* is open-endedly metaphorical, which is one of the ways in which it differs most strikingly from that of *Jean Santeuil*. Metaphor in *Jean Santeuil* is essentially ornamental and psychologically distracting. In a sense, that novel is a far more "literary" or "written" work than *A la recherche*; it has an uninteresting stylistic complexity which makes each of its sections a self-contained, carefully wrought—overwrought—"piece." Proust could not, I think, have changed the essential discontinuity of *Jean Santeuil* by providing more links from one episode to another; to make smoother transitions would not have changed the underlying conception of style as an exercise of verbally enshrining disconnected experiences. As a result of this conception, incidents in *Jean Santeuil* often have a kind of depth which is largely eliminated from the later work. In *A la recherche*, on the one hand, metaphors enrich specific incidents without completely "covering" them; on the other hand, the freedom of the metaphors themselves is protected by their extensions into other parts of the novel, by their being containers always larger than whatever they contain at any given moment. There is no network of multiple interpretations in *Jean Santeuil*, and, consequently, we frequently *see through* episodes to a single, definite, and limiting significance. We may, for example, feel that Jean's overwhelmed reaction at the discovery that Charlotte is willing to give him certain erotic satisfactions is intelligible only if we think of the scene as a mask for an unexpected homosexual encounter. There is nothing in Proust's treatment of the scene which lifts it above the peculiarity of its literal detail. As far as "content" goes, *A la recherche* has equally peculiar episodes; but the style now has a centrifugal energy which prevents us from considering such content as the transparent sign of something unsaid, of a hidden reality. Incidents no longer extend "behind" themselves into the author's veiled psychology; instead, they are now coerced by metaphor into extensions leading to other metaphorical inventions throughout the novel. They are, as it were, horizontally rather than vertically transcendent. The significance of each passage is limited only by the amount of novelistic space which the narrator will have the time to fill in the process of self-enlargement which is his literary vocation.

Literature in Proust's world does involve a certain moving away from life. The image of the writer sealed up in his cork-lined room is a dramatic enough metaphor for that removal. But the narrator in his hermetic seclusion reveals the mechanisms of self-removal as operative throughout his life; as a result, we see the establishment of aesthetic distances as the most creative and liberating activity within all life's occasions. To be the artist of one's life involves the possibility of living within styles rather than within obsessions—that is, the possibility of repeating ourselves in an entertaining variety of performances rather than in the stultifying monotony of fantasies which break through each play of the self to be revealed as the boring "truth" of the self. A profound commitment to disguise (to what might even be labeled duplicity in an ethos of sincerity) is therefore perhaps essential for an exuberantly expansive self. *A la recherche du temps perdu* is certainly a novel about art, but it is not—as *Madame Bovary* is—a novel about the impossible distance between art and life; it is rather an inventory of techniques which make for a highly artful life.

PAUL DE MAN

Reading (Proust)

Georges Poulet has taught us to consider, in *A la recherche du temps perdu*, the juxtaposition of different temporal layers rather than the unmediated experience of an identity, given or recovered by an act of consciousness (involuntary memory, proleptic projection, etc.). The specificity of Proust's novel would instead be grounded in the play between a prospective and a retrospective movement. This alternating motion resembles that of reading, or rather that of the rereading which the intricacy of every sentence as well as of the narrative network as a whole constantly forces upon us. Moreover, as Poulet describes it, the moment that marks the passage from "life" to writing corresponds to an act of reading that separates from the undifferentiated mass of facts and events, the distinctive elements susceptible of entering into the composition of a text. This occurs by means of a process of elision, transformation, and accentuation that bears a close resemblance to the practice of critical understanding. The intimate relationship between reading and criticism has become a commonplace of contemporary literary study.

What does *A la recherche du temps perdu* tell us about reading? I approach the question in the most literal and, in fact, naïve way possible by reading a passage that shows us Marcel engaged in the act of reading a novel. This procedure in fact begs the question, for we cannot *a priori* be certain to gain access to whatever Proust may have to say about reading by way of such a reading of a scene of reading. The question is precisely whether a literary text is *about* that which it describes, represents, or

From *Allegories of Reading*. © 1979 by Yale University. Yale University Press, 1979.

states. If, even at the infinite distance of an ideal reading, the meaning *read* is destined to coincide with the meaning *stated*, then there would in fact be no real problem. All that would be left to do would be to allow oneself to be brought nearer to this ideal perfection by taking Marcel for our model. But if reading is truly problematic, if a nonconvergence between the stated meaning and its understanding may be suspected, then the sections in the novel that literally represent reading are not to be privileged. We may well have to look elsewhere, in Marcel's erotic, political, medical, or wordly experiences, to discover the distinctive structures of reading, or we may have to go further afield still and use a principle of selection that is no longer thematic. This circular difficulty should not, however, prevent us from questioning the passage on actual reading, if only to find out whether or not it does make paradigmatic claims for itself. The uncertainty as to whether this is indeed the case creates a mood of distrust which, as the later story of Marcel's relationship with Albertine makes clear, produces rather than paralyzes interpretative discourse. Reading has to begin in this unstable commixture of literalism and suspicion.

The main text on reading occurs early in the novel, in the first volume of *Du côté de chez Swann*. It stands out as distinctly marked in the narrative of "Combray" where it follows immediately upon the young Marcel's visit to his uncle, the first explicit example of his ritualistic initiation to the ambivalences of good and evil. The scene is set within a thematic of closeted and hidden spaces, the "temple of Venus" of Françoise's bower, the "dark and fresh" smelling closet in which Uncle Adolphe retires, which will engender a chain of associations that will articulate the entire middle part of the book, the "dark freshness" of the room in which Marcel will hide in order to read, the "little sentry-box" where he finds refuge when his grandmother orders him to go outside. The symbolic significance of this setting is summarized in the interiorized image of the mind as a "cradle at the bottom of which I remained sheltered, even in order to observe what was happening outside." The first section of the passage does not deal with reading; it is three pages later when Marcel will climb to his room with a book, and only when he has been sent into the garden will the principal and very systematically structured discourse on reading be allowed to develop. But this preliminary section is solidly linked to the main body of the passage by a transitional scene centered on the characters of Françoise and the kitchen maid who was the main figure in the first section: "While the kitchen maid—unwittingly making Françoise's superiority shine at its brightest, just as Error, by contrast, makes the triumph of Truth more dazzling—served coffee which, in my mother's judgment, was mere hot water and then carried to our rooms hot water that was barely tepid, I had stretched out on my bed, with a book." The allegorical pair of Truth and Error crowns a passage that will be particularly rich in rotating polarities. But here, in this context of comedy, the chain of substitutions in no way preserves the integrity of the point of origin: the tepid liquid is a lowly version of genuine hot water, itself a degraded substitute for coffee. The kitchen maid is only a pale reflection of Françoise; in substituting for truth, error degrades and outwears it, causing a sequence of lapses that threatens to contaminate the entire section. All the later polarities will have to be on the defensive when placed under the aegis of the initial antithesis between truth and error.

Thus reading is staged, from the beginning of the text, as a defensive motion in a dramatic contest of threats and defenses: it is an inner, sheltered place (bower, closet, room, cradle) that has to protect itself against the invasion of an outside world, but that nevertheless has to borrow from this world some of its properties. The inside room "tremblingly shelters . . . its transparent and fragile coolness from the afternoon sun." The inner world is unambiguously valorized as preferable to the outside, and a consistent series of attractive attributes are associated with the well-being of the enclosed space: *coolness*, the most desirable of qualities in this novel of the "solar myth" in which the barometer so often indicates fine weather, itself linked to the restorative *darkness* of shaded light (Marcel being never so happy as when he dwells in the shade of the vegetal world), and finally *tranquility*, without which no time would be available for contemplation. But Marcel cannot rest satisfied with these positive aspects of a sedentary solitude. The truly seductive force of the passage is revealed only when the confinement to the obscure, private existence of inward retreat turns out to be a highly effective strategy for the retrieval of all that seemed to have been sacrificed. The text asserts the possibility of recuperating, by an act of reading, all that the inner contemplation had discarded, the opposites of all the virtues necessary to its well-being: the *warmth* of the sun, its *light*, and even the *activity* that the restful immobility seemed to have definitively eliminated. Miraculously enriched by its antithetical properties, the "dark coolness" of the room thus acquires the light without which no reading would be possible, "the unmediated, actual, and persistent presence" of the summer warmth and finally even "the shock and the animation of a flood of activity [*un torrent d'activité*]." The narrator is able to assert, without seeming to be preposterous, that by staying and reading in his room, Marcel's imagination finds access to "the total spectacle of Summer," including the attractions of direct physical action, and that he possesses it much more effectively than if he had been actually present in an outside world that he then could only have known by bits and pieces.

Two apparently incompatible chains of connotations have thus been set up: one, engendered by the idea of "inside" space and governed by "imagination," possesses the qualities of coolness, tranquility, darkness as well as totality, whereas the other, linked to the "outside" and dependent on the "senses," is marked by the opposite qualities of warmth, activity, light, and fragmentation. These initially static polarities are put in circulation by means of a more or less hidden system of relays which allows the properties to enter into substitutions, exchanges, and crossings that appear to reconcile the incompatibilities of the inner with the outer would. Proust can affect such confidence in the persuasive power of his metaphors that he pushes stylistic defiance to the point of stating the assumed synthesis of light and dark in the incontrovertible language of numerical ratio: "The dark cool of my warm room was to the full sunlight of the street what the shadow is to the sunray, that is to say equally luminous." In a logic dominated by truth and error the equation is absurd, since it is the difference of luminosity that distinguishes between shadow and light: "that is to say [c'est à dire]" in the quotation is precisely what cannot be said. Yet the logic of sensation and of the imagination easily remains convinced of the accuracy of the passage and has not the least difficulty in accepting it as legitimate. One should ask how a blindness comes into being that allows for a statement in which truth and falsehood are completely subverted to be accepted as true without resistance. There seems to be no limit to what tropes can get away with.

Structures and relays of this kind, in which properties are substituted and exchanged, characterize tropological systems as being, at least in part, paradigmatic or metaphorical systems. Not surprisingly, therefore, this introductory passage on reading that was placed, from the beginning, under the auspices of the epistemological couple of truth and error, also contains statements claiming the priority of metaphor in a binary system that opposes metaphor to metonymy. The passage reflects on the modality of the sun's presence in the room: it is first represented in visual terms by means of the metaphor of a "reflection of light which ... succeeded in making its yellow wings appear [behind the blinds], and remained motionless ... poised like a butterfly"; then in aural terms by the resonance of "blows struck ... against the dusty crates" in the street, and finally, still in aural terms, by the buzzing of the flies, generalized into "the chamber music of summer." The crossing of sensory attributes in synaesthesia is only a special case of a more general pattern of substitution that all tropes have in common. It is the result of an exchange of properties made possible by a proximity or an analogy so close and intimate that it allows the one to substitute for the other without revealing the difference necessarily introduced by the substitution. The relational link between the two entities involved in the exchange then becomes so strong that it can be called necessary: there could be no summer without flies, no flies without summer. The "necessary link" that unites flies and summer is natural, genetic, unbreakable; although the flies are only one minute part of the total event designated by "summer," they nevertheless partake of its most specific and total essence. The synecdoche that substitutes part for whole and whole for part is in fact a metaphor, powerful enough to transform a temporal contiguity into an infinite duration: "Born of the sunny days, resurrected only upon their return, containing some of their essence, [the buzzing of the flies] not only reawakens their image in our memory but certifies their return, their actual, persistent, unmediated presence." Compared to this compelling coherence, the contingency of a metonymy based only on the casual encounter of two entities that could very well exist in each other's absence would be entirely devoid of poetic power. "The tune of human music [as opposed to the "natural" flies] heard perchance during summertime" may be able to stimulate memory in a mechanical way, but fails to lead to the totalizing stability of metaphorical processes. If metonymy is distinguished from metaphor in terms of necessity and contingency (an interpretation of the term that is not illegitimate), then metonymy is per definition unable to create genuine links, whereas no one can doubt, thanks to the butterflies, the resonance of the crates, and especially the "chamber music" of the flies, of the presence of light and of warmth in the room. On the level of sensation, metaphor can reconcile night and day in a *chiaroscuro* that is entirely convincing. But the passage plays for higher stakes.

For it does not suffice for the sound of the flies to bring the outside light into the dark room; if it is to achieve totalization, the inwardness of the sheltered reader must also acquire the power of a concrete action. The mental process of reading extends the function of consciousness beyond that of mere passive perception; it must acquire a wider dimension and become an action. The light metaphors are powerless to achieve this: it will take the intervention of an analogical motion stemming from a different property, this time borrowed not from the warmth of the light but from the coolness of the water: "The dark coolness of my room . . . matched my repose which (thanks to the adventures narrated in my book, which stirred my tranquility) supported, like the quiet of a hand held motionless in the middle of a running brook, the shock and the animation of a flood of activity [mon repos . . . supportait, pareil au repos d'une main immobile au milieu d'une eau courante, le choc et l'animation d'un torrent d'activité]." The persuasive power of the passage depends on the play on the verb "supporter" which must be strong enough to be read not just as "tolerate" but as "support," suggesting that the repose is indeed the foundation, the ground that makes activity possible. Repose and action are to merge as intimately as the "necessary link" that ties the column to its pedestal.

The ethical investment in this seemingly innocent narrative description is in fact considerable enough to match the intricacy of the rhetorical strategy. For the burden of the text, among other things, is to reassure Marcel about his flight away from the "real" activity of the outer world. The guilty pleasures of solitude are made legitimate because they allow for a possession of the world at least as virile and complete as that of the hero whose adventures he is reading. Against the moral imperative speaking through the grandmother who "begs Marcel to go outside," Marcel must justify his refusal to give up his reading, together with all the more or less shameful pleasures that go with it. The passage on reading has to attempt the reconciliation between imagination and action and to resolve the ethical conflict that exists between them. If it were possible to transform the imaginary content of the fiction into actions performed by the reader, then the desire would be satisfied without leaving a residue of bad conscience. An ethical issue that is obviously involved in the success of the metaphor is connected to the central Proustian motive of guilt and betrayal that governs the narrator's relationship to himself and to those united to him by ties of love or affection. Guilt is always centered on reading and on writing, which the novel so often evokes in somber tones. This connection between metaphor and guilt is one of the recurrent themes of autobiographical fiction.

One should not conclude that the subjective feelings of guilt motivate the rhetorical strategies as causes determine effects. It is not more legitimate to say that the ethical interests of the subject determine the invention of figures than to say that the rhetorical potential of language engenders the choice of guilt as theme; no one can decide whether Proust invented metaphors because he felt guilty or whether he had to declare himself guilty in order to find a use for his metaphors. Since the only irreducible "intention" of a text is that of its constitution, the second hypothesis is in fact less unlikely than the first. The problem has to be left suspended in its own indecision. But by suggesting that the narrator, for whatever reason, may have a vested interest in the success of his metaphors, one stresses their operational effectiveness and maintains a certain critical vigilance with regard to the promises that are being made as one passes from reading to action by means of a mediating set of metaphors.

In this passage, the metaphorical relay occurs by way of the flowing water: repose supports action "like the quiet of a hand, held motionless in the middle of a running brook." In the sunny mood of the text, the image is convincing enough: nothing could be more attractive than this feeling of freshness rising from the clear water. But coolness, it will be remembered, is one of the attributes of the "inner" world, associated with shelter, bowers, and closed rooms. The analogical image of the hand is therefore not able to cross over, by its own power, towards a life of action. The water carries with it the property of coolness, but this quality, in the binary logic of the passage, belongs to the imaginary world of reading. To gain access to action, the trope should capture one of the properties that belongs to the antithetical chain such as, for example, warmth. The cool repose of the hand should be made compatible with the heat of action. This transfer occurs, still within the space of a single sentence, when it is said that repose supports *un torrent d'activité*. In French, this expression is not—or is no longer—a metaphor but a cliché, a dead or sleeping metaphor which has lost its literal connotations (in this case, the connotations associated with the word *torrent*) and has only kept a proper meaning. (Thus illustrating the tripartite structure of all metaphors, often stressed by theoreticians of rhetoric, but not clearly embodied in ordinary English language, which distinguishes only vaguely between literal and "proper" meaning. When Homer calls Achilles a lion, the literal meaning of the figure signifies an animal of a yellowish brown color, living in Africa, having a mane, etc. The figural meaning signifies Achilles and the proper meaning the attribute of courage or strength that Achilles and the lion have in common and can therefore exchange. In the cliché *torrent d'activité* [as when I say of a hyperactive Mr. X that he is *un torrent d'activité*] the literal meaning of torrent has been lost and only the shared attribute of "muchness" remains.) *Torrent d'activité* properly signifies a lot of activity, the quantity of activity likely to agitate someone to the point of making him feel hot. The proper meaning converges with the connotation supplied, on the level of the signifier, by the "torride" ("hot") that one can choose to hear in *torrent*. Heat is therefore inscribed in the text in an underhand, secretive manner, thus linking the two antithetical series in one single chain that permits the exchange of incompatible qualities: if repose can be hot and active without however losing its distinctive virtue of tranquility, then the "real" activity can lose its fragmentary and dispersed quality, and become whole without having to be any less real.

The transfer is made seductive and convincing by a double-faced play on the cliché *torrent d'activité*. The neighboring image of flowing water (the hand suspended "in a running brook") reawakens, so to speak, the dozing metaphor which, in the cliché, had become the mere contiguity of two words (*torrent and activité*) syntagmatically joined by repeated usage and no longer by the constraints of meaning. *Torrent* functions in at least a double semantic register: in its reawakened literal sense, it relays and "translates" the property of coolness actually present in the water that covers the hand, whereas in its figural meaning it designates an amplitude of action suggestive of the contrary quality of heat.

The rhetorical structure of this part of the sentence ("repose . . . supported . . . the shock and the animation of a flood of activity") is therefore not simply metaphorical. It is at least doubly metonymic: first because the coupling of two terms, in a cliché, is not governed by the "necessary link" of a resemblance (and potential identity) rooted in a shared property, but dictated by the mere habit of proximity (of which Proust, elsewhere, has much to say), but also because the reanimation of the numbed figure takes place by means of a statement ("running brook") which happens to be close to it, without however this proximity being determined by a necessity that would exist on the level of transcendental meaning. To the contrary, the property stressed by the neighboring passage is precisely not the property that served in the coinage of the original metaphor, now degraded and become a cliché: the figure *torrent d'activité* is based on amplitude and not on coolness. This property functions in fact against the quality that the text desires.

The structure is typical of Proust's language throughout the novel. In a passage that abounds in successful and seductive metaphors and which, moreover, explicitly asserts the superior efficacy of metaphor over that of metonymy, persuasion is achieved by a figural play in which contingent figures of chance masquerade deceptively as figures of necessity. A literal and thematic reading that takes the value assertions of the text at their word would have to favor metaphor over metonymy as a means to satisfy a desire all the more tempting since it is paradoxical: the desire for a secluded reading that satisfies the ethical demands of action more effectively than actual deeds. Such a reading is put in question if one takes the rhetorical structure of the text into account.

The central text on reading develops in the wake of this initial compli-

cation. It has all the appearances of a set piece, so firmly constructed that
it constantly attracts attention to its own system and invites representation
by means of synoptic diagrams. The text follows "from inside to outside
the layers simultaneously juxtaposed in [the] consciousness" of the reader.
It extends the complexity of a single moment in time upon an axis oriented
from maximum intimacy to the external world. This construct is not
temporal, for it involves no duration. The diachrony of the passage, as the
narrative moves from a center towards a periphery, is the spatial representation of a differential but complementary articulation within one single
moment. For a novel that claims to be the narrative extension of one single
moment of recollection, the passage undoubtedly has paradigmatic significance. The transposition of the present moment into a consecutive sequence would correspond to the act of fiction writing as the narration of
the moment. This act would then be coextensive with the act of self-
reading by means of which the narrator and the writer, now united in one,
fully understand their present situation (including all its negative aspects)
by means of the retrospective recapitulation of its genesis. Nor would it
differ from the response available to the reader of *A la recherche du temps
perdu* who, mediated by Proust's novel, understands the narrative voice as
the dispenser of a true knowledge that also includes him. ("In truth, each
reader is, when he reads, the actual [*propre*] reader of himself.") The
"moment" and the "narration" would be complementary and symmetrical, specular reflections of each other that could be substituted without
distortion. By an act of memory or of anticipation, the narrative can
retrieve the full experience of the moment. We are back in the totalizing
world of the metaphor. Narrative is the metaphor of the moment, as
reading is the metaphor of writing.

The passage is indeed ordered around a central, unifying metaphor, the
"single and unbending projection of all the forces of my life [même et
infléchissable jaillissement de toutes les forces de ma vie]" within which
the various levels of reading are said to constitute "sections at the different
levels of an iridescent fountain that appeared to be motionless." (In a
famous passage of *The Prelude*, Wordsworth speaks of "The stationary
blast of waterfalls." A more literal and less benevolent version of this same
waterspout appears in *Sodome et Gomorrhe*: the fountain designed by
Hubert Robert that splashes Mme. d'Arpajon to the great merriment of
the grand duke Wladimir.) The figure aims at the most demanding of
reconciliations, that of motion and stasis, a synthesis that is also at stake in
the model of narrative as the diachronic version of a single moment. The
continuous flow ("jaillissement") of the narrative represents an identity

that is beyond the senses and beyond time as something accessible to sight
and sensation and therefore comprehensible and articulated, just as the
unique and timeless fascination of reading can be divided into consecutive
layers shaped like the concentric rings of a tree trunk. Within a closed
system of part and whole, the complementarity of the vertical juxtaposition and the horizontal succession is firmly established. With regard to the
narrative, the proof of this complementarity will be the absence of inter-
ruptions, the lack of jagged edges which allows for the characterization of
the novel's narrative texture as a play of fragmentation and reunification
that can be called *fondu*, (i.e., smooth [Gérard Genette]) or *soudé*, (i.e.,
welded [Proust]). (For example, in a passage referring to Vinteuil's septuor: "two entirely different modes of questioning, the one breaking up a
pure and continuous line into brief requests, the other welding [*soudant*]
stray fragments into one single, sturdy frame," Gérard Genette ["Métonymie
chez Proust"] mentions a passage from Proust's correspondence which uses
the expression *espèce de fondu*.) The continuity is not only apparent in the
fluency of the transitions or in the numberless symmetries of the composition, but also in the strict coherence between meaning and structure. The
passage is a persuasive case in point: to the stated assertion that reading is
grounded in a firm relationship between inside and outside corresponds a
text that is structured in a particularly rigorous and systematic way. but if
the complementarity were to be an illusion, a very different story would
ensue, more like the loss of entropy that occurs as one moves from
Françoise's hot coffee to the kitchen maid's tepid shaving water.

The persuasive value of the passage depends on one's reading of the
fountain as an entity which is both immobile and iridescent. The irides-
cence is prefigured a few pages earlier in the description of consciousness
as a "shimmering screen [un écran diapré]." The miraculous interference of
water and light in the refracted rainbow of the color spectrum makes its
appearance throughout the novel, infallibly associated with the thematics
of metaphor as totalization. (Some examples among many others: Elstir's
workshop is compared to a "block of rock-crystal, of which one of the
facets, already cut and polished, shines like an iridescent mirror"; Françoise's
famous asparagus "reveal in their nascent colors of early dawn, in their
suggestions of rainbows . . . [their] costly essence"; "if I could have analyzed the prism [of the Duchess de Guermante's eyes] . . . the essence of
the unknown life that appeared in them might have been revealed to me";
"the art of Vinteuil, like that of Elstir, reveals [the ineffable character of
individuality] by expressing into the colors of the spectrum the intimate
being of the worlds we call individuals"; "just as the spectrum represents

for us the composition of light, the harmony of a Wagner or the color of an Elstir allows us to know the qualitative essence of another individual's sensations.") It is the perfect analogon for the figure of complementarity, the differences that make up the parts absorbed in the unity of the whole as the colors of the spectrum are absorbed in the original white light. The solar myth of *A la recherche du temps perdu* would then be condensed in the scarf of Iris, as when the flower metaphors associated with girls and women are said to "appear at once on their two sides, like complementary colors." The "necessary link" between the imagined figure and its sensory qualities make it more seductive than the empirical, "real" landscape of Combray. Unlike this real landscape, the symbolic one is "a true part of Nature itself, worthy of study and meditation."

The superiority of the "symbolic" metaphor over the "literal," prosaic, metonymy is reasserted in terms of chance and necessity. Within the confines of the fiction, the relationship between the figures is indeed governed by the complementarity of the literal and the figural meaning of the metaphor. Yet the passage seems oddly unable to remain sheltered within this intra-textual closure. The complementarity is first asserted with reference to the narrator's relationship to the landscape he inhabits, but it soon extends towards another binary set of themes, those of "love" and "voyage": "Therefore, if I always imagined, surrounding the woman I loved, the landscape I most keenly wished to see at that moment . . . it was not because my dreams of love and of travel were only moments—which I now artificially disentangle . . .—in the single and unbending projection of all the forces of my life." But what is here called "love" and "travel" are not, like the narrator and his natural setting, two intra-textual moments in a fiction, but rather the irresistible motion that forces any text beyond its limits and projects it towards an exterior referent. The movement coincides with the need for a meaning. Yet at the beginning of the passage Marcel has stated the impossibility for any consciousness to get outside itself, suggesting this very ideality, paradoxically enough, by means of an analogy derived from a physical phenomenon: "When I saw something external, my awareness of the fact that I was seeing it remained between the object and myself, bordering it as with a thin spiritual layer that prevented me from touching it directly; the object would evaporate, so to speak, before I could come into contact with it, just as a red-hot body that approaches a wet object is unable to touch its humidity, since it is always preceded by a zone of vapor." Three pages further on, it seems that the language of consciousness is unable to remain thus ensconced and that, like so many objects and so many moments in Proust's novel, it has to turn itself out and become the outer enveloping surface: (The metonymy by which the covered-up entity becomes its own cover [*enveloppé* becoming *enveloppant*] is much in evidence in the concluding section of this passage, where "the afternoons have gradually surrounded and enclosed" the hours: the spatial container becomes the temporally contained, and vice versa. The famous passage on the *carafes de la Vivonne* is the *locus classicus* of this figure. Gérard Genette quotes it, and it has since been much conmmented upon, without however exhausting the connotations of its context and of its tropological significance. Walter Benjamin well perceived the importance of this metonymy when he compared Proust's figures to a rolled-up sock which is its own outside and which, when unrolled, like the Möbius strip, is also its own inside.) "For if we have the impression of being constantly surrounded by our consciousness [*âme*], it is not as by an unmovable prison; much rather, we feel carried by it in a perpetual impulse to move beyond itself and to reach outside." The epistemological significance of this impulse is clearly stated when, a few paragraphs earlier, we heard of a "central belief ... that made ceaseless motions from inside outward, toward the discovery of truth." Like Albertine, consciousness refuses to be captive and has to take flight and move abroad. This reversal by which the intra-textual complementarity chooses to submit itself to the test of truth is caused by "the projection of all the forces of life."

Proust's novel leaves no doubt that this test must fail; numberless versions of this failure appear throughout the pages of the *Recherche*. In this section, it is stated without ambiguity: "We try to find again, in things that have thus become dear to us, the reflection that our consciousness [*âme*] has projected upon them; we are disappointed in discovering that, in their natural state, they lack the seduction that, in our imagination, they owed to the proximity of certain ideas." Banal when taken by itself, the observation acquires considerable negative power in context, when one notices that it occurs at the center of a passage whose thematic and rhetorical strategy it reduces to naught. For if the "proximity" between the thing and the idea of the thing fails to pass the test of truth, when it fails to acquire the complementary and totalizing power of metaphor and remains reduced to "the chance of a mere association of ideas." The co-presence of intra- and extra-textual movements never reaches a synthesis. The relationship between the literal and the figural senses of a metaphor is always, in this sense, metonymic, though motivated by a constitutive tendency to pretend the opposite.

The image of the iridescent fountain is a clear case in point. Everything orients the trope towards the seduction of metaphor: the sensory attractiveness, the context, the affective connotations, all cooperate to this aim. As soon however as one follows Proust's own injunction to submit the reading to the polarity of truth and error (a gesture that can be repressed but never prevented), statements or strategies that tended to remain unnoticed become apparent and undo what the figure seemed to have accomplished. The shimmering of the fountain then becomes a much more disturbing movement, a vibration between truth and error that keeps the two readings from converging. The disjunction between the aestheti-cally responsive and the rhetorically aware reading, both equally compel-ling, undoes the pseudo-synthesis of inside and outside, time and space, container and content, part and whole, motion and stasis, self and under-standing, writer and reader, metaphor and metonymy, that the text has constructed. It functions like an oxymoron, but since it signals a logical rather than a representational incompatibility, it is in fact an aporia. It designates the irrevocable occurrence of at least two mutually exclusive readings and asserts the impossibility of a true understanding, on the level of the figuration as well as of the themes.

The question remains whether by thus allowing the text to deconstruct its own metaphors one recaptures the actual movement of the novel and comes closer to the negative epistemology that would reveal its hidden meaning. Is this novel the allegorical narrative of its own deconstruction? Some of its most perceptive recent interpreters seem to think so when they assert, like Gilles Deleuze, the "powerful unity" of the *Recherche* despite its inherent fragmentation or, like Genette, stress the "solidity of the text" despite the perilous shuttle between metaphor and metonymy.

What is at stake is the possibility of including the contradictions of reading in a narrative that would be able to contain them. Such a narrative would have the universal significance of an allegory of reading. As the report of the contradictory interference of truth and error in the process of understanding, the allegory would no longer be subject to the destructive power of this complication. To the extent that it is not itself demonstrably false, the allegory of the play of truth and falsehood would ground the stability of the text.

One would have to untie the complex interlacing of truth and lie in *A la recherche du temps perdu* to decide whether or not the work corre-sponds to this model. But the passage on reading gives a first indication how such an analysis would have to proceed. It is preceded by an episode which deals, as by coincidence, with the question of allegory and which can serve as a warning for the difficulties that any attempt to reach an inclusive allegorical reading of the novel are bound to encounter. The passage consists of Marcel's meditation on the nickname "Giotto's Charity" by which Swann is accustomed to refer to the kitchen maid persecuted with such cruelty by Françoise, the cook.

Slave of a slave, pathetic emblem of servitude, the kitchen maid is first described as what one could call, with Goethe, *Dauer im Wechsel*, the element that remains permanent in the midst of change. She is characterized as "a permanent institution, whose unchanging attributes guaranteed an appearance of continuity and identity, beyond the succession of transitory forms in which she was incarnated." Swann, the personification of metaphor, is endowed with a particular knack for the discovery of resemblances, and he has observed the near-emblematic quality of this particular kitchen maid. She carries the "humble basket" of her pregnancy in a manner that, by its resemblance to the surcoat of the allegorical frescoes painted by Giotto in the Arena of Padua, reveals her universal essence. All the agonies and all the humiliations of the successive kitchen maids are concentrated in this particular trait of her physiognomy, thus raised to the level of an emblem. An allegory thus conceived is in no way distinguished from the structure of metaphor, of which it is in fact the most general version. In the same manner, metaphor warrants the identity of art as a "permanent institution" that transcends the singularity of its particular incarnations. What may appear surprising is that Proust selected servitude as the essence intended and reached by the figure. More surprising still, the allegorical figure that Swann's sagacity has singled out is Charity, a virtue whose relationship with servitude is not one of mere resemblance. By generalizing itself in its own allegory the metaphor seems to have displaced its proper meaning.

Marcel, who has a more literary (that is to say, rhetorically less naïve) mind than Swann, has observed that the kitchen maid and Giotto's Charity resemble each other in still another way than physical shape. Their resemblance also has a dimension linked to reading and understanding, and in this capacity it is a curiously negative one. The property shared by the maid and by Charity is that of a nonunderstanding: both distinguish themselves by features they display "without seeming to understand their meaning." Both seem to be condemned to the same dyslexia.

The passage describes with great precision this shared inability to read. The allegorical image or icon has, on the one hand, a representational value and power: Charity represents a shape whose physical attributes connote a certain meaning. Moreover, it makes gestures or (in the case of a verbal icon that would no longer be pictorial) it tells tales that are particularly conspicuous in their intent to convey meaning. The figures have to be endowed with a semantic intensity that confers upon them a particularly effective representational function. The allegorical icon must attract attention; its semantic importance must be dramatized. Marcel insists that the kitchen maid and the Giotto frescoes resemble each other by their common claim to focus our attention on an allegorical detail: "Envy's attention—and, by the same token, our own—[is] entirely concentrated on the action of her lips" just as "with the poor kitchen maid, [one's] attention is ceaselessly brought back to her belly by the load that weighs it down." In a metaphor, the substitution of a figural for a literal designation engenders, by synthesis, a proper meaning that can remain implicit since it is constituted by the figure itself. But in allegory, as here described, it seems that the author has lost confidence in the effectivness of the substitutive power generated by the resemblances: he states a proper meaning, directly or by way of an intra-textual code or tradition, by using a literal sign which bears no resemblance to that meaning and which conveys, in its turn, a meaning that is proper to it but does not coincide with the proper meaning of the allegory. The facial expression of the "heavy and mannish" matron painted by Giotto connotes nothing charitable and even when, as in the case of Envy, one could perhaps detect a resemblance between the idea and the face of Envy, the stress falls on an iconic detail that sidetracks our attention and hides the potential resemblance from our eyes.

The relationship between the proper and the literal meaning of the allegory, which can be called "allegoreme" and "allegoresis" respectively (as one distinguishes between "noeme" and "noesis"), is not merely a relationship of noncoincidence. The semantic dissonance goes further. By concentrating the attention of Envy's beholder on the picturesque details of the image, he has, says Marcel, "no time for envious thoughts." Hence the didactic effectiveness of allegory since it makes one forget the vices it sets out to represent—a little as when Rousseau pretends to justify the theater because it distracts, for a while, vile seducers from their evil pursuits. It actually turns out that, in the case of Envy, the mind is distracted towards something even more threatening than vice, namely death. From the structural and rhetorical point of view, however, all that matters is that the allegorical representation leads towards a meaning that diverges from the initial meaning to the point of foreclosing its manifestation.

In the case of the allegorical figuration of Charity, things are even more specific, especially if one takes the origins of the passage into account. Proust does not start out from a direct encounter with Giotto's frescoes, but from Ruskin's commentary on Giotto's Vices and Virtues of Padua. The commentary is of considerable interest in many respects but it is especially striking in this context because it deals with an error of reading and interpretation. Ruskin describes Charity brandishing, in her left hand, an object that looks like a heart; he first assumes that the scene represents God giving his own charitable heart to her, but he corrects himself in a later note. "There is no doubt that I misread this action: she *gives* her heart to God, while she makes offerings to mankind." Ruskin also discusses the painter's ambivalent rhetoric, which is, he says, "quite literal in [its] meaning as well as figurative." Describing the same gesture, Marcel follows Ruskin's rectified reading but displaces the meaning by adding a comparison which, at first sight, appears quite incongruous: "she stretches her incandescent heart towards God or, better, she hands it over to him (the French text says "elle le lui *passe* . . ." with "passe" italicized, which suggests various colloquial associations. For our purposes, one can confine oneself to the connotative field suggested by the "lowly" implications of the term), as a cook would hand a corkscrew through a window of her basement to someone who asks for it at street level." The comparison seems to be chosen merely to stress the homely quality of the gesture, but one of its other functions is to bring about the reentry into the text of "the cook," that is to say, Françoise. The kitchen maid resembles Giotto's Charity, but it appears that the latter's gesture also makes her resemble Françoise. The first resemblance is not entirely unlikely: the sufferings of the hapless girl are vividly enough evoked to inspire a feeling of pity that could easily be confused with charity. But the further resemblance, with Françoise, is harder to understand: if the image, as a representation, also connotes Françoise, it widely misses its mark, for nothing could be less charitable than Françoise, especially in her attitude toward the kitchen maid. The neighboring episode which narrates in great detail the refinements of Françoise's methods of torture, makes very clear that the literal sense of this allegory treats its proper sense in a most uncharitable manner. The rhetorical interest of the section, which culminates in the tragicomic scene where Françoise is seen weeping hot tears upon reading, in a book, a description of the very symptoms that prompt her most savage violence when she literally encounters them in her slave, is that a single icon engenders two meanings, the one representational and literal, the other allegorical and "proper," and that the two meanings fight each other with the blind power of stupidity. With the complicity of the writer, the literal meaning obliterates the allegorical meaning; just as Marcel is by no means inclined to deprive himself of Françoise's services, so the writer has no intention of doing without the thematic powers of literal representation and, moreover, would not be able to do so if he tried.

In the ethical realm of Virtue and Vice, the ambivalences of the allegorical figure thus lead to strange confusions of value. And if one bears in mind that, in Proust's allegory of reading, the couple Françoise/kitchen maid also enacts the polarity of truth and falsehood, then the epistemological consequences of the passage are equally troubling. Since any narrative is primarily the allegory of its own reading, it is caught in a difficult double bind. As long as it treats a theme (the discourse of a subject, the vocation of a writer, the constitution of a consciousness), it will always lead to the confrontation of incompatible meanings between which it is necessary but impossible to decide in terms of truth and error. If one of the readings is declared true, it will always be possible to undo it by means of the other; if it is decreed false, it will always be possible to demonstrate that it states the truth of its aberration. An interpretation of *A la Recherche du temps perdu* which would understand the book as being the narrative of its own deconstruction would still operate on this level. Such an interpretation (which is indispensable) accounts for the textual coherence postulated by Genette, Deleuze, and by Marcel's own critical theories and, at the far end of its successive negations, it will recover the adequation between structure and statement on which any thematic reading depends. But when it is no longer a matter of allegorizing the crossing, or chiasmus, of two modes of reading but Reading itself, the difficulty brought to light by the passage on Giotto's Charity is much greater. A literal reading of Giotto's fresco would never have discovered what it meant, since all the represented properties point in a different direction. We know the meaning of the allegory only because Giotto, substituting writing for representation, spelled it out on the upper frame of his painting: *KARITAS*. We accede to the proper meaning by a direct act of reading, not by the oblique reading of the allegory. This literal reading is possible because the notion of charity, on this level of illusion, is considered to be a referential and empirical experience that is not confined to an intra-textual system of relationships. The same does not apply to the allegorical representation of Reading which we now understand to be the irreducible component of any text. All that will be represented in such an allegory will deflect from the act of reading and block access to its understanding. The allegory of reading narrates the impossibility of reading. But this impossibility necessarily extends to the word "reading" which is thus deprived of any referential meaning whatsoever. Proust may well spell out all the letters of *LECTIO* on the frames of his stories (and the novel abounds in gestures aimed in that direction), but the word itself will never become clear, for according to the laws of Proust's own statement it is forever impossible to read Reading. Everything in this novel signifies something other than what it represents, be it love, consciousness, politics, art, sodomy, or gastronomy: it is always something else that is intended. It can be shown that the most adequate term to designate this "something else" is Reading. But one must at the same time "understand" that this word bars access, once and forever, to a meaning that yet can never cease to call out for its understanding.

The young Marcel is at first displeased by the discordance between the literal and the proper meaning of the allegory, but the maturity of his literary vocation is dated by his ability to come to admire it: "Later on, I understood that the uncanny attraction, the specific beauty of these frescoes was due to the prominent place taken up by the symbol, and that the fact that it was not represented symbolically (since the symbolized idea was not expressed) but as something real, actually experienced or materially handled, gave to the meaning of the work something more literal and more precise." This formulation, "plus tard, j'ai compris," is very familiar to readers of the *Recherche*, for it punctuates the entire novel like an incantation. Literary criticism has traditionally interpreted this "later on" as the moment of fulfillment of the literary and aesthetic vocation, the passage from experience to writing in the convergence of the narrator Marcel with the author Proust. In fact, the unbridgeable distance between the narrator, allegorical and therefore obliterating figure for the author, and Proust, is that the former can believe that this "later on" could ever be located in his own past. Marcel is never as far away from Proust as when the latter has him say: "Happy are those who have encountered truth before death and for whom, however close it may be, the hour of truth has rung before the hour of death." As a writer, Proust is the one who knows that the hour of truth, like the hour of death, never arrives on time, since what we call time is precisely truth's inability to coincide with itself. *A la recherche du temps perdu* narrates the flight of meaning, but this does not prevent its own meaning from being, incessantly, in flight.

WALTER KASELL

Writing and the Return to Innocence: Proust's "La Confession d'une jeune fille"

Among the stories in *Les Plaisirs et les jours*, "La Confession d'une jeune fille" most clearly anticipates, in its structure and theme, the strategies of Proust's mature novel, *A la Recherche du temps perdu*. It is a narrative whose end has caught up with its starting point, a confession told in the time between the narrator's suicide attempt and her death. Like the *Recherche*, "La Confession" describes a strategy of return to a moment of original innocence and plenitude through memory and writing. Perhaps even more clearly than the novel, however, this apparently sincere confession plays on the fundamental duplicity of writing. It claims to be the narrator's act of contrition for her mother's death, fulfilling that love by telling its story. In actuality, the confession replaces the figure of the mother in its most essential aspect, as a force of moral redemption.

The narrator, although obsessively attached to her mother, has caused her decline and death. In a final fit of remorse the daughter shoots herself, but failing to die instantly, writes this compensatory confession in her death agony. In dying, the narrator returns, through her imagination, to the summer park of her childhood, the scene of her fullest memories of her mother. Her mother would send her away each summer to "Les Oublis," in order to lessen her dependence and fortify her will, and visited her only rarely. The park is thus filled by continual anticipation of her return. Yet

From *The Art of the Proutsian Novel Reconsidered*, edited by Lawrence D. Joiner. © 1979 by Winthrop Studies in Major Modern Writers.

of the place from which her mother was most conspicuously absent, the narrator recalls, "Nul lieu n'est plus plein de ma mère [No other place is so full of my mother]." These visits were privileged moments, when her mother would reveal the true self, and the daughter was allowed to see clearly the gentleness behind the mask of *froideur:*

> Tant de doux moments recevaient une douceur de plus de ce que je sentais que c'était ceux-là où ma mère était véritablement elle-même et que son habituelle froideur devait lui coûter beaucoup.

> [Such sweet moments gained an added sweetness from my feeling that during them my mother was her true self and that her habitual reserve must cost her dearly.]

The fullness of these moments, however, also recalls the girl's first sexual transgression, for it ended in the kiss of forgiveness which her mother alone could offer. As a figure of nearly religious dimension, and a principle of purity, the mother can not only absolve the sinner, but transform her, and restore her innocence:

> Elle releva son voile pour m'embrasser . . . [et] allegéait le poids de ma conscience. Ce poids s'allégeait . . . j'étais tout âme. Une divine douceur émanait de ma mère et de mon innocence revenue.

> [She threw back her veil to kiss me . . . and lightened the weight of my conscience. That weight grew lighter . . . I was all soul. A divine fragrance emanated from my mother and from my recovered innocence.]

Nevertheless, the narrator's will fails, and she relapses into further sexual adventures, to the detriment of her mother's health. Her recuperation clearly depends on her daughter recovering her chastity. At last, only her mother's failing health can inspire repentance, and the daughter decides to marry. Yet on the eve of her marriage, and after a particularly touching embrace, when innocence seems at last to have been recaptured, the narrator allows herself to be seduced at a party, the sight of which lust kills her mother.

This is a story of repetition, of separation and return, where the kiss at the wedding party rediscovers the earlier moment of absolution. Its model is its earliest event, the mother's departure from "Les Oublis," for this is not a single event, but one repeated during the summer, like a "drame du coucher" filling the entire summer, and centering the girl's relationship to her mother around a crucial absence. In the passionate anticipation of return, these separations resemble the troubling goodnight kisses which her mother had ended earlier because the girl "y trouvai[t] trop de plaisir et trop de peine." Once kissed goodnight, the narrator recalls, "Je ne m'endormais plus à force de la rappeler pour me dire bonsoir encore ... n'en ressentant que davantage le besoin passionné." These moments are so much a product of the imagination that satisfaction fulfills less than it stimulates further desire.

Sometimes, if she were ill, her mother would visit unexpectedly, but in a similar fashion, the anticipated departure was so cruel that recuperation became a worse loss. As health implies separation, recovery must be postponed and convalescence extended as long as possible:

> Cette douceur, cette tendresse étaient tant pour moi que le charme des convalescences me fut toujours mortellement triste: le jour approchait où je serais assez guérie pour que ma mère pût repartir, et jusque-là je n'étais plus assez souffrante pour qu'elle ne reprît pas les sévérites.

> [That gentleness and tenderness meant so much to me that the charm of convalescence was always unbearably sad; the day was approaching when I should be sufficiently well again for my mother to leave me, and until then not sufficiently ill to keep her any longer from returning to her former severity.]

The goodnight kiss and convalescence lie at the center of the summers of visits and separations, fleeting events around which experience is created by imagination and memory.

Since departure is intolerable, the narrator's anticipation of her mother's return paradoxically turns "Les Oublis" into the place most filled with her presence. The emptiness of each day endows the park with the image of a perfect, but absent mother, for anticipation also assures her that upon return, her mother is most fully present and most genuinely herself. The project of returning to an imaginary or lost past by traveling to its apparent site is a motif central to Proust's later work: in his essays on Nerval, Proust focuses on the narrator's inability to separate the worlds of dream and memory from reality. However, here, as in *Sylvie*, the return seems to offer the narrator a way back to a landscape of innocence. For the repentant young girl, the park represents an enclave of untroubled happiness, free of corruption, and offering a perfect union with her mother. If her memories of the summers there recall her first transgression, the recollection is only a prelude to the glorious absolution that followed: "Les Oublis" is the place where it is possible to wipe clean the moral slate.

The sexual transgressions, which are seen as movements away from the mother, set off the recovery of purity, which is expressed as a return. Even in moments of sensuality, the remorse the girl feels in succumbing to temptation is focused on her mother, who alone can wash away the "poisoned joy" of lust. Her mother becomes a measure of the narrator's moral worth and a model of her aspirations. This lends moral dimension to any potential separation, for separation implies the disappearance of a center and the loss of her moral compass. In her mind, then, separation becomes tantamount to transgression, and permanent separation is simply unthinkable. The incident of the girl's sexual initiation shows the mother as a paragon of purity, apparently not even touched by the knowledge of sin. She hears and forgives her daughter's sins "without understanding them," and remains always "dans une ignorance de mes fautes," in a world where corruption has not yet occurred. Rather, the narrator recalls, "Ma mère baisait chaque jour mon front qu'elle n'avait jamais cessé de croire pur sans savoir qu'il était régénéré." Sensuality may again urge the girl into remorseful lust, but her mother offers a way out of the mixed and troubled feelings her conduct produces. Her mother's world is unmixed ("elle n'était que pure"), whereas the daughter always feels the lack of such unity. Her own actions are impulsive and unpredictable, and show no will.

All her actions seem confused and mixed in their nature, so that the impurity of her world expresses itself to her by its heterogeneity. She finds in her own conduct the same disparity she felt between surface appearance and underlying essence. Most disturbing to the narrator was the praise she received when her behavior least deserved it:

> [C'est] à ce moment où de tous les moments de ma vie j'ai le moins valu, que je fus le plus appréciée de tous. . . . Alors que je commettais envers ma mère le plus grand des crimes, on me trouvait, à cause de mes façons tendrement respectueuses avec elle, le modèle, des filles.

> [It was . . . at the very moment of my life when I was the most worthless that everyone esteemed me the most. . . . Just when I was committing the worst crime against my mother, everyone thought me, because of my tenderly respectful manner toward her, a model daughter.]

This disparity, which culminates when she sees herself in the mirror at the instant of her mother's death, is what actually leads her to suicide. It is not simply the reflection of lust that scandalizes her, but the inability of her appearance to express the remorse she feels—even as she indulges her lust:

> J'aimerais mieux que ma mère m'ait vue commettre d'autres crimes encore et celui-là même, mais qu'elle n'ait pas vu cette expression joyeuse qu'avait ma figure dans la glace.

> [I should rather my mother had seen me commit still other crimes, and even that one too, than that she should have seen that look of joy on my face in the mirror.]

She is more shamed by her image in the mirror than by her mother's direct view of her sin: she finds only brute sensuality in her reflection.

> Je me vis dans la glace. Toute cette vague angoisse de mon âme n'était pas peinte sur ma figure, mais toute elle respirait, des yeux brillants aux joues enflammées et à la bouche offerte, une joie sensuelle, stupide et brutale.

> [I saw myself in the mirror. None of the vague anguish of my soul was written on my face, but everything about it, from my shining eyes to my blazing cheeks, proclaimed sensual, stupid brutal joy.]

The narrator suddenly realizes that the remorse is missing from her face which would have redeemed her; in its absence she is implicated not only in sexual wrongdoing, but in deliberate duplicity. The tenderness which she has shown toward her mother just prior to this seduction becomes redefined as a cynical act of deception. No longer a mitigation of her sin, her solicitiousness seems to proclaim her *use* of appearance for vicious ends.

This concern with the ability of appearance to hide essence recalls Marcel's shock when he meets "la dame en rose," appalled to find that her appearance does not in the least manifest what he knows about actresses: "Je ne lui trouvais rien ... de l'expression diabolique qui eût été en rapport avec la vie qu'elle devait mener [I found nothing about her ... of the diabolical expression which would have been related to the life she must have led]." Marcel is most disturbed by her "ordinary" appearance, attesting to the lack of the essential "rapport" with her true life, as though it were doubly indecent for sin to appear so innocuous. Like the narrator of "La Confession," Marcel is troubled by vice's success masquerading as virtue: Odette's appearance transgresses the boundaries between the acceptable and the unacceptable. The ability of the diabolical to hide itself is the most troubling of its seductions: "Et pourtant, en pensant à ce que devait être sa vie, l'immoralité m'en troublait peut-être plus que si elle avait été concrétisée devant moi en une apparence spéciale [And yet, in thinking about what her life must have been, its immorality troubled me perhaps more than if it had been concretized in front of me in a special appearance]."

The triumph of appearance, acceptance of the outer mask as inner reality, disturbs both Marcel and the young girl because for them corruption *means* taking the sign at face value. For the narrator of "La Confession," her own moral degradation is expressed by her acceptance of surfaces, and documented by the successful use of appearance to disguise her actions. Thus, the most reprehensible aspect of her behavior is her enjoyment of this deception, and the delight she took in mocking those who were fooled by her act. To a large extent, the narrator's confession is her attempt to correct through writing the troubling disjunction of appearance and essence. It is part of a literary project to create a language which fully embodies its intention. If the primacy of appearance is the hallmark of corruption, then the recovery of innocence will be a return to an appearance fully and immediately itself: a transparent language, entirely free of deception.

In the final scene, however, when the narrator confronts herself in the mirror, the possibility of such return is called into question by the crucial failure of her reflection to show the redeeming regret at the heart of her immorality. She is betrayed by the inadequacy of her image, and condemned by the transparence of her reflection. The question is whether writing is not an equally duplicitous project, and whether the failure of the image does not already presage the hopelessness of the writing project. For even a "true" image would have been heterogeneous, showing the mixed nature of her feelings. The marks of duplicity would be inscribed even in the complexity of adequate appearance, while a simple image, ostensibly a sign of purity, is revealed as one-sided and inadequate. In a parable of discovering the inescapable duplicity of writing, the narrator in front of her reflection is forced to discover the essential role that remorse plays in the pleasure of her illicit sensuality;

> Je n'avais jamais pu lire sans des frémissements d'horreur le
> récit des tortures que des scélérats font subir à des animaux, à

leur propre femme, à leurs enfants; il m'apparaissait confusément maintenant que dans tout acte voluptueux et coupable il y a autant de férocité de la part du corps qui jouit, et qu'en nous autant de bonnes intentions, autant d'anges purs sont martyrisés et pleurent.

[I have never been able to read without shuddering with horror stories of those beasts who torture animals, their own wives, their own children; I now confusedly felt that in every sensual and sinful act there is just as much ferocity on the part of the body in the throes of pleasure, and that in us so many good intentions, so many pure angels are martyred, and weep.]

In much the same way, Marcel comes to this realization at Montjouvain, when he witnesses the "ritual profanations" by means of which Vinteuil's daughter tries to create the "appearance" of evil. In contrast to the narrator of "La Confession," however, Mlle Vinteuil is "so naturally virtuous" that she must enter into a strategy of theatrical gestures to invoke the pleasures that belong only to evil:

Dans le coeur de Mlle Vinteuil, le mal, au début du moins, ne fut sans doute pas sans mélange. Une sadique comme elle est l'artiste du mal, ce qu'une créature entièrement mauvaise ne pourrait être, car le mal ne lui serait pas extérieur. . . .

[In Mlle Vinteuil's soul, at least in the earlier stages, the evil element was probably not unmixed. A sadist of her kind is an artist in evil, which a wholly wicked person could not be, for in that case the evil would not have been external.]

Mlle Vinteuil's performance corroborates the suspicion that the shock in "La Confession" stems from the realization that regret has always been a part of her pleasure—and perhaps even its source. Already in her first adventure, her cousin's advances made her tremble "aussitôt de remords et de volupté," reflecting her own mixed feelings. Significantly, her first seducer succeeded by proceeding in a manner at once gentle and bold: "Il avait des manières à la fois douces et hardies. . . . Il m'induisait à mal faire presque par surprise." Only the image of her mother's purity saves the narrator from the troubling mixture of pleasure and remorse, for her mother represents the principle which distinguishes the categories of virtue and sin, purity and corruption, pleasure and pain, truth and deception. The narrator fears that with her mother's death, the "necessary support" keeping these categories distinct would fail her, and she would be over-whelmed by irresistible transgression. But this leaves her in an impossible situation: successful conduct seems to depend on resisting one crucial separation (from her mother), in order to maintain another, that between moral categories.

Her solution is a marriage in which the bounds of propriety will be redrawn, yet retained, and the inevitable separation enacted on a ceremonial level, so that the actual, physical departure may be indefinitely deferred. The misplaced object of desire, the mother, will be replaced, by a virtually absent husband, finessing the inescapable loss by a negligible addition. In the ideal solution, her husband will become an appendage of her mother: "Il était, de plus, décidé à habiter avec nous. Je ne serais pas séparée de ma mère, ce qui eût été pour moi la peine la plus cruelle." The narrator will at once be satisfying her mother's desire to see her settled, yet retain the essential contact. In the context of this perfect resolution, the narrator experiences a glorious reconciliation and fullness, recapturing, it would seem, the kiss of absolution of her childhood. The experience strikingly anticipates Marcel's taste of the madeleine:

> Le baiser de ce soir-là fut aussi doux qu'aucun autre. Ou plutôt ce fut le baiser même des Oublis qui, évoqué par l'attrait d'une minute pareille, glissa doucement du fond du passé et vint se poser entre les joues de ma mère encore un peu pâles et mes lèvres.

> [The kiss of that evening was as sweet as any other. Or rather it was the same kiss which, evoked by the attraction of a similar moment, had glided softly out of the depth of the past to alight between my mother's cheeks, still a little pale, and my lips.]

In this moment, innocence seems once again possible. However, just after, at the party celebrating this union, the girl is approached by a young man "qui avait la plus grande responsabilité dans mes fautes passées [who had the greatest responsibility in my past faults]." The wine has dissolved the bounds between the permissible and impermissible, and the narrator feels a sudden "mixed" urge, "à la fois besoin de me reposer et de dépenser mes nerfs [a need to rest and, at the same time, to expend my nervous energy]." Unable to tolerate these conflicting drives, nor able to keep them separate, she falls into the scandal of sensuality and remorse once again. But with the ensuing death of her mother, the recovery of innocence is no longer possible. The only means for reinstituting the separation essential to meaning are death and writing, but the confrontation in the mirror questions whether "purity" was not always tainted, whether the "proper" was not always a part of the "improper," and whether the return to innocence was not always impossible.

For the object of the girl's passion, her mother, has always been impermissible, and her purity notwithstanding, the pleasures she offered were inevitably a mixture of sweetness and cruelty, like the bedtime kisses which occasioned "too much pleasure and too much pain." The aura of "Les Oublis," in which the mother became perfectly herself, has been created by the child's imagination, or the narrator's memory. Even at their apparent origin, these kisses were cherished because they recalled a yet more distant joy, "l'ancienne habitude qu'elle avait perdue [the old habit which she had lost]." The only innocent world is one remembered, one seen through the anticipation of return. Those days of remembered fullness were also days of "angoisse joyeuse [joyful anguish]," and the visits were at once "la chose la plus douce et la plus cruelle [the sweetest and the most cruel]." The figure of the mother, seen as free of deception, is itself born of the girl's paradoxical conviction that her coldness is proof of her love. Even at the moment of greatest plentitude, her mother's love must be intuited, and her sincerity "démêlée au milieu du feint." As in Marcel's first view of the Duchesse de Guermantes in the church at Combray, a creative act of reading must be interposed to preserve the vision. Up to now, transgression has been seen as a separation from the mother, and innocence a return. But if the fullness of the mother's presence is created by the narrator's anticipation of her return, we must conclude that the guarantor presence against separation is itself a product of separation.

The source of the mother's perfection lies in the proximity of disappearance. When the Duchesse de Guermantes disappoints Marcel's expectations by failing to embody everything he imagined, he reinscribes in her material appearance all the magic previously invested in her image. Similarly here, the young girl's imagination is so vivid that her mother's arrival can only verify the vision carefully nurtured in her absence. Disappointment is precluded, since her presence is already foreseen as a vindication of the anticipation. Nor is she remembered as she was experienced, but rather recalled as she was anticipated. Truly, *no* figure could fill "Les Oublis" so richly and faithfully as her absent mother, and only this virtual figure, discerned behind a mask of *froideur* [coldness], could describe the principles of fullness, purity and propriety, replacing, as it were, the mother who does appear. The mother's image is actually doubly inscribed by absence:

in expectation of her arrival, and in the fear of her departure, locating presence always in the project of recovery, at the imagined moment of recapture.

The complementary nature of presence and absence recalls the pleasure disturbingly close to remorse. Looking in the mirror, the narrator was stunned to discover that her pleasures were corrupt, not because they were "evil," but because they found their source in the ostensibly redemptive quality of remorse. Later, in his reading of Ruskin, Proust explored this mixed pleasure, for he was troubled to find examples of his mentor's most profound idolatry among his most beautiful pages: "Je vais citer une de celles que je trouve les plus belles et où ce défaut est pourtant le plus flagrant [I will cite one of those which I find the most beautiful and in which, however, this defect is most apparent]." His difficulty was in locating the reasons for such beauty in the idolatrous context, and finding "à quel ordre de vérité peut correspondre le plaisir esthétique [to what order of truth aesthetic pleasure may correspond]." Proust comes to sense sympathy between Ruskin's idolatry and his own, as he reads the Ruskin text inside St. Mark's, as though one could better seize his insights in that mysterious semi-darkness:

> L'émotion que j'éprouvais à lire là cette page . . . était très grande et n'était pourtant peut-être pas très pure. . . . Et peut-être cette page des *Stones of Venice* était-elle belle surtout de me donner précisément ces joies mêlées que j'éprouvais dans Saint-Marc.

> [The emotion I felt in reading this page . . . was very great and yet perhaps not very pure. . . . And maybe that page of *Stones of Venice* was beautiful above all for giving me those mixed joys I experienced at Saint-Marc.]

As it is for Proust, "untroubled pleasure" is a difficult concept for the narrator of "La Confession," since pleasure seems to arise from a context of *trouble,* in which the regret, the sense of transgression, shows itself an essential part of the pleasure. Evil can hardly have corrupted an original purity, if the purifying remorse was at the heart of the "corrupt" pleasures.

The scandalous realization that remorse is a necessary part of her pleasure is one that the narrator must postpone, just as she postponed her mother's departures. Her strategy will use writing to recall the lost moments of innocence, much as she once used disease to call back her mother's presence. The sweetest moments of "Les Oublis" sustained the mother's ideality by extending the recovery (which is to say, extending the disease) that had recalled her:

> Mes plus douces impressions sont celles des années où elle revint aux Oublis, rappelée parce que j'étais malade. . . . Elle n'était plus alors que douceur et tendresse épanchées sans dissimulation ni contrainte.

> [My happiest recollections are of those times when she would be called back to *Les Oublis* when I was ill. . . . During that time she was all overflowing gentleness and tenderness, undisguised and unrestrained.]

Yet actual recovery may be undesirable, since it would cause a new separation. Recovery therefore ironically implies loss, for the narrator would become "well enough for my mother to be able to leave." The only alternative is to extend interminably the special moment of convalescence, maintaining a delicate balance between irrevocable loss and complete recovery. This would put her always between illness and health, like the "moral convalescence" during which she would recover her innocence; when the fullness of virtue could be appreciated through its absence, but when absolution was not beyond her reach.

Like a perpetual convalescence, writing will extend these moments indefinitely, recalling lost fullness from the perspective of loss. And presumably, like Marcel's Tante Léonie, the narrator would remain in a state always bordering between serious illness and perfect health, constantly receiving the undisguised kind consolation of her mother. Illness would remove her from the demands and temptations of life, replacing the deceptions of living with strategies of writing. Those strategies would have become translated to a different level, and like a writer of fiction, she would become a privileged spectator on the world, neither an active participant, nor an isolated outsider. The language of fiction, locating itself between presence and absence, truth and deception, provides the room for re-inscribing the possibility of recovery in the story of loss, the special ground, which is the space of Proust's *Recherche*. Baudelaire was surely looking ahead to Proust when he placed the artist "à l'état du convalescent [in the state of the convalescent]," and Proust may well have had this remark in mind when he created the grounds for a "sincere" confession in the suspended time between a nearly unsuccessful suicide attempt and presumed death from its complications.

RANDOLPH SPLITTER

Proust, Joyce,
and the Theory of Metaphor

One of the most significant propositions of the French psychoanalyst Jacques Lacan is that "the unconscious" is structured like a language, that (for example) the workings of a dream may be defined in terms of linguistic concepts like metaphor and metonymy. Roman Jakobson, analyzing two different types of aphasia, had specifically divided rhetorical functions into the two poles of metaphor and metonymy, and this divison has proved influential in structural/semiological theory, despite the fact that no one agrees on what actually fits into either category. Lacan's psychoanalytic corollary to Jakobson's hypothesis, which equates metaphor with the Freudian mechanism of condensation and metonymy with displacement, breaks down the distinction between literary and psychoanalytic catego-ries, suggesting that Freudian interpretation and literary analysis are analo-gous processes. In this paper I would like to pursue that suggestion by examining certain metaphorical structures in the work of Proust and Joyce, beginning with one particular metaphor—namely, flowers—that appears, with surprisingly similar connotations, in the work of both writers. I am concentrating on the idea of metaphor, defined broadly, because it seems to me more basic, more essential (than metonymy) to the construction of meaning in literature. Indeed, the idea of metaphor is essential to Proust's (or at least his protagonist Marcel's) theories about art and literature. I don't intend to blur the differences between Proust and Joyce, but I think the remarkable structural parallels between their work can help us to draw

From *Literature and Psychology* 29, nos. 1 and 2 (1979), © 1979 by Morton Kaplan.

certain conclusions about the possibilities of literary meaning and literary interpretation. In fact, this examination of metaphor—which does not limit itself to Lacan's definitions—may enable us to see both Freudian interpretation and literary analysis in a new light.

Both Proust and Joyce explore the ambiguities of sexual relations, make jealousy a condition of friendship and love, imply (in Joyce's words) that *armor matris* may be the only true thing in life, investigate "mourning and melancholia," associate death with the transcendence of art, try to stop time or reverse it or escape it, try to solve the riddle of male/female differences, blur the distinction between inner and outer worlds, pretend to believe magical substances or essences, and invent their own myths of artistic creation or "procreation." The differences between Joyce and Proust—in the treatment of homosexuality, in Joyce's emphasis on fathers as well as mothers—are revealing and significant, but their complex, dialectical "theories" of the relation between art and life, between inner and outer worlds, set them apart from most other writers, who tend either to idealize art or to define art as a direct representation of "life."

A l'ombre des jeunes filles en fleurs, the title of the second volume of Proust's *Recherche,* turns flowers into a metaphor for the incipient, emerging, budding sexuality of adolescent girls, but this association is already implied by the "real" flowers, the pink and white hawthorns, of Combray, which move the young Marcel by their visual beauty. Marcel associates the festal flowers with celebrations of the Virgin Mary—"in its cool, rosy garments, a Catholic bush"—and just as he earlier imagined the blossoming of the flowers in church as the careless, spontaneous movement of "a young girl in white," so now he identifies the pink hawthorn with the little girl (Gilberte), with reddish hair and pink freckles, that he sees behind the hedge. Gilberte's mother, who appears now as "a lady in white," is actually the same mysterious "lady in pink," an actress or courtesan and not quite a lady, whom Marcel has met at his uncle Adolphe's. The color of the hawthorns is, like the color associated with the women, ambiguous, variable, and deceptive. In fact, the pale buds of the hawthorn, when they open, disclose a "blood-red stain," which suggests "even more strongly than the full-blown flowers the special, irresistible quality of the hawthorn-tree."

The opposition between pink and innocent white, the association with the Virgin Mary, with young girls, and with a lady who isn't an innocent young girl, the particular emphasis on blossoming, the opening of buds into mature and beautiful flowers, the glimpse of the girl behind the hedge, through an arch of pink flowers, and the crucial exposure of a blood-red stain on the inside of pale buds all imply an underlying preoccupation with the mysteries of virginity and sex: with the loss of virginity in intercourse (the blood-red stain caused by "deflowering"), with the disillusioning metamorphosis of an innocent virgin into a not-so-innocent lady (her mother!), with the equally mysterious metamorphosis of a girl "blossoming" into a sexually mature woman (marked, on the most literal level, by the blood-red stain of menstruation), or simply with the mysterious, frightening, barely glimpsed sight of a girl's genitals, which seems to disclose (in the fantasy of a boy familiar with his own anatomy) a blood-red wound. In short, the pink hawthorns, white flowers tinged red, are reassuringly innocent and yet ambiguously seductive at the same time, like the young, pubescent girls "in bloom" who will be Marcel's special province in love.

The *Jeunes filles en fleurs* of Balbec, spontaneous, youthful, alive, unselfconsciously natural, like seagulls or flowers, are adolescent girls on the verge of sexual maturity, their frank, uninhibited manners less sexual than tomboyish. In fact, these athletic, tomboyish girls—the cyclist Albertine who plays golf and "ferret" and wears a polo cap, the girl who plays leapfrog with the old gentleman, as well as the Gilberte who plays prisoner's base—may remind Marcel of his own boyish, adolescent self. This narcissistic desire for someone like himself reduces (but does not eliminate) the mysterious and alien "otherness" of the other person, helping him to close the gap between himself and the unpossessible person that he loves. In many ways, however, these healthy, tomboyish girls are the exact opposites of sickly, nervous, overly mannered, possibly even effeminate(?) Marcel, presenting him with the self-sustaining "life" that he both lacks and desires. In fact, "life" seems to be a magical quality that the *other* person always possesses, the mysterious essence of the life that person leads when one is not around, the evanescent, insubstantial quality that one tries to possess for oneself. Ironically, Marcel takes Andrée for a "healthy, primitive creature" like the rest of the band, but she turns out to be "too intellectual, too neurotic, too sickly, too much like myself." The narcissistic element in love has to contend with the desire to possess what one doesn't have, the attraction for one's opposite.

The confusion about the appearance, the identity, even the sex of the person one loves—the ambiguous, transitional condition of *Jeunes filles en fleurs*—is illustrated by Elstir's remarkable portrait of "Miss Sacripant," who turns out to be Odette in her pre-Swann days. With short hair, a "mob-cap," and a cigarette in her hand, the model seems to be an actress "half dressed for a part [*en demi-travesti*]," and her appearance is so ambiguous that she seems to be first "a somewhat boyish girl" and then "an effeminate youth, vicious and pensive." Marcel likens the meeting of two homosexuals to the pollination of a flower by a bee, as if the flower represented the "female" side of the relation, but the literal/imaginary token of virginity represented by the flower (of the *Jeunes filles en fleurs*) is itself sexually ambiguous, an imaginary, "poeticized," feminized phallus—in Freudian terms, a fetish—which might suggest that young girls are not so different from boys after all. Marcel may like to think of mothers as pure and virginal, but the metamorphosis of an innocent girl into a sexually mature woman frightens him. The fantasy that sexual "flowering" is not incompatible with possessing a "flower" reassures him on two counts: because it reduces the difference between himself and the "other" and because (like any fetishistic fantasy) it reduces his fear of losing his own "flower." Conversely, the fact that women don't have penises is disturbing, and so Marcel makes a fetish of virginity, of sexual innocence, as if women lost their quasi-phallic "flowers" in sexual intercourse and only then became an alien species, the opposite sex.

For Joyce's Stephen Dedalus, as for Proust's hero Marcel, the ideal object of love is a kind of virgin temptress who appears ambiguously innocent and seductive at the same time. Marcel can't tell whether Gilberte and Albertine, with their equivocal looks, gestures, and responses, are "virtuous" or not, but the uncertainty appeals to him. Stephen thinks that the girl on the tram, Emma, is trying to seduce him, and ten years later she becomes the "temptress" of his villanelle. Even as temptress, however, she is the object of praise and homage, as if he were simply adapting a hymn to the Virgin Mary. The birdlike girl on the beach—the identical image in which Albertine first appears to Marcel—makes a mute appeal to him, without shame, as Gilberte may have been doing from behind the hawthorn hedge, but she is innocent and childlike, beautiful rather than sexual, something to see rather than touch. The flirtatious, nymphomaniacal, vain, narcissistic, and essentially infantile character Issy in *Finnegans Wake* is an exaggerated, caricatured version of these virginal temptresses, of Gerty MacDowell in *Ulysses,* a Lolita-like nymphet who seems to be two and twelve and twenty-two years old at the same time. In fact, Issy and her seven or twenty-eight alter egos, the flower-girls, bear a remarkable resemblance to Marcel's *Jeunes filles en fleurs.* In both cases, the girls' childlike innocence is reassuring, promising harmless childhood games like "ferret" or dancing around the maypole in place of the dangerous sexual complications of an experienced *femme fatale.*

In Joyce's work as in Proust's the image of flowers is closely associated with the sexuality of women. The last two pages of Molly's monologue in *Ulysses* are strewn with references to flowers: she says she loves flowers, would like to see the place swimming in roses, remembers Bloom (in their famous rendezvous on the hill of Howth) calling her a flower of the mountain, tries to decide (playing upon the first line of a song) "shall I wear a white rose . . . or shall I wear a red," and agrees with Bloom that a woman's body is like a flower. Moreover, the swimming roses seem to be associated with the Bay of Gibraltar at sunset, "the sea crimson sometimes like fire," and the crimson sea with "that awful deepdown torrent," the bloody menstrual flow "pouring out" of Molly "like the sea." Bloom speculates that Martha has a headache because she has "her roses," and in his notes for *Ulysses* Joyce confirms the identification "rose—menses." But Bloom, playing upon the floral connotations of his name, signs his love letters to Martha "Henry Flower," which makes us question whether flowers are exclusively feminine. At the end of the "Lotus-Eaters" chapter, Bloom imagines his penis as a "languid floating flower" on the surface of the bath water. The implication seems to be that, as in Proust, these swimming menstrual flowers are fetishistic substitutes for a missing phallus, like the drawers Bloom carries around in his pocket or "the pin of her drawers. / She didn't know what to do / To keep it up / To keep it up." *It*, not them, as if she were keeping her phallic pin up: there are many jokes in *Ulysses* about keeping it up, from "U. p.: Up" to "who's getting it up." Bloom's thoughts about the pins in women's clothing lead him to reflect that there are "No roses without thorns," as if a woman's body were protected by sharp, prickly spikes, as if the menstrual "roses" themselves were thorny and phallic.

In the first variant of the prankquean tale, in *Finnegans Wake*, just before the prankquean urinates on the door of Jarl van Hoother's castle, she "pulled a rosy one," as if pulling a rabbit out of a hat or picking a card out of a deck (in the third variant, she "picked a blank"). The context of sexual references in the story, the fact that she is just about to urinate ("made her wit"), lead us to imagine that there is a rose growing out of her vagina, and in the second variant she "nipped a paly one," as if nipping a flower in the bud. Like Molly who wonders whether she should wear a white rose or a red one, the prankquean has a pale or rosy flower in her bag of tricks (pranks), a magical token of potency as well as virginity, and she pulls it out in order to show it to the Jarl. If she can pull it out, she can also cut it off, nipping it like a flower: this is just one more magic trick for her—it grows back again—but for the Jarl it represents the dangerous, frightening possibility that the fantasy of a female "flower" can help to ward off. The rosy/pale dichotomy suggests a contrast between menstruation and micturition, but any fluid that comes out of a woman's body seems to become a fertile, magically powerful substance, a kind of inflammatory "firewater" which enables the prankquean not only to set the hills on fire but also to inflame the Jarl's passions.

The pink and white hawthorns of Combray are Proust's version of Joyce's red and white roses, and it is the pink flowers, the pink freckles on Gilberte's face, the lady in pink herself, that are especially seductive. The "blood-red stain" on the inside of the hawthorn buds suggests what one will find when one cuts off the flower: the imaginary flower of *Jeunes filles en fleurs* only hides the possibility of a bloody wound, as if the fact that girls don't have penises meant only that they had lost what they had once had. The blood associated with the loss of virginity (of one's "flower") or with the onset of menstruation at puberty seems to mark the metamorphosis of girls into sexually mature women. As such, it also divides women from men: like anything alien, different, "other," it provokes both desire and fear. In "Combray" there are "real" flowers, "real" hawthorns, while the prankquean's "rosy" and "paly" ones are only props for a tricky sleight-of-hand, magical, metaphorical signs of purely imaginary possibilities. Even the metaphorical flowers of *Jeunes filles en fleurs* are, among other things, signs of youthful beauty and innocence, while Joyce's menstrual roses are a metaphor that must be taken literally or not at all, signs of a fictional, imaginary anatomy. But Joyce's emphasis on fantasy helps to explain how metaphors work, leading us to take even Proust's elegant, idealizing metaphors "literally."

If the prankquean takes the jiminies to the land of the dead, symbolically crucifies them "with the nail of a top," baptizes them, and carries them back again under her apron or pinafore (as if she were pregnant), they seem to be reborn through her, as if she were their mother. Who, after all, is their mother? Is the Jarl really their father? The prankquean tale might be trying to explain how children's parents come to be their parents, as if the children were there first. One of its major themes is, in fact, the question of why we need two parents. As Stephen says in *Ulysses,* feigning a child's ignorance of a father's role in producing children: "Boccaccio's Calandrino was the first and last man who felt himself with child. Fatherhood, in the sense of conscious begetting, is unknown to man. . . . Paternity may be a legal fiction." A mother gives birth to, nurses, and takes care of a child, but (Stephen seems to be saying) a father just gets in the way. When the son grows up to be a father, however, he may feel differently, and, fearing the life-and-death powers that mothers seem to possess, he may even try to assert that the "only begetter" of children is a father, not a mother, the Jarl, not the prankquean. The myths of Zeus giving birth to Athena out of his head and to Dionysus out of the "secret womb" in his thigh try to prove the same thing; Zeus's own father Kronos had a habit of eating up his children, but when Zeus gave him a rock to eat, he threw up all the children he had swallowed, as if giving birth to them once more.

Indeed, the prankquean tale is a battle of the sexes which tries to decide who is more powerful, men or women. And at the same time it tries to figure out what the difference between them really is. The prankquean, asking the Jarl for the pot of porter (please) that he as a good host should give her, also asks him a riddle about the difficulty of telling things apart: "why do I am alook alike a poss of porterpease?" She is a lookalike, like the twin jiminies (if they are identical) or like Issy's mirror-self, but is she divided by sexual differences from the Jarl? The pot of porter or peas (pease porridge hot . . .) is also the piss (wit/witter/wittest) that she spills on the Jarl's doorstep before she goes raining in the wilderness. Confusing semen with urine, she wants to know why her piss isn't the same as—and just as good as—his. A man's and a woman's urine look alike, although their urinary organs don't. Throughout *Finnegans Wake,* where the prankquean rains, Anna Livia becomes a river, and Issy tells us to listen to the sound she makes when urinating, a woman's urine becomes a fertile, lifegiving, sexually arousing, magically potent substance. The Jarl, who has been busy masturbating (laying warm or cold hands on himself), may simply be drowning in his wet bed: the children in the nursery have an oilcloth sheet to protect their bed, like the oilsheet Stephen's mother puts on his bed on the first page of *A Portrait.* According to the prevailing infantile theory, all sexual activity can be reduced to urinating. When the prankquean pisses on the "dour" Jarl's doorstep, trying through her wit to make him laugh—a traditional fairy tale motif (as in the Grimm brothers' "The Golden Goose") equates laughter with release from sexual inhibition— he shuts the door in her face, rejecting her advances. But the third time around he opens the door, extends his phallic guns ("to the whole longth of the strongth of his bowman's bill"), and violently, thunderously shuts the door again. In short, he shits ("ordurd," "shut up shop," "shot the shutter"), unless he simply spills more water: "And they all drank free. . . . And that was the first peace of illiterative porthery in all the flamend floody flatuous world." Despite the Jarl's noisy, phallic pretensions, the climax of the tale suggests a reversal of sexual roles: the prankquean splashes her fertile urine on the Jarl and he, as if impregnated by her, as if he were Proust's Marcel becoming a mother to his novel, gives birth to a piece of pottery, poetry, or shit. Just as the confusion of semen and urine eliminates the difference between women and men, this infantile "anal birth" fantasy enables men to give birth as well as women.

Still, the tenuous sexual relations between the Jarl and the prankquean amount to nothing more than a series of ambiguous exchanges. The Jarl ought to offer the prankquean the pot of porter but it is more likely she who offers him the ambiguous drink, the love potion intended for King Mark. He rejects her offer, she steals a jiminy. But in shutting the door, he is also literally handing her an answer—a piece of shit or simply the word *shut*. From one point of view, the Jarl and the prankquean exchange nothing but words. She asks him a riddle or tells a joke in her "perusienne" dialect and he, answering her in thick Germanic "dootch," roaring like thunder, issues a thunder-word, a piece of poetry. When Beckett said that *Finnegans Wake* "is not about something, it is that something itself," did he mean that it is only about language (how to have fun with words)? Or that words, which seem to signify "things," even more than one "thing" at a time, can take the place of the things they signify? When Joyce has the Jarl "handword" an answer, he asks us to take that answer literally, as if it were not just a word but a thing. Saying "shit!" to someone is tantamount to throwing it (hurling abuse, slinging mud), and the idea of "shitting on" someone is, conversely, a metaphor for expressing contempt. One of the projector's schemes in *Gulliver's Travels* is to replace words by *things*, having everybody carry a supply of conversational items on his back, but another scheme is to learn propositions by writing them down and eating them, which might have the result of turning words into shit, the "heaviest," earthiest, most material thing of all. The prankquean's witty double entendres may inspire the Jarl to create poetry, but the context suggests that his final, illiterate, "flatuous" word is just a fart ("git the wind up"), reminding us of Swift's Aeolists (*A Tale of a Tub*), who are literally inspired by hot air.

As in Swift's case, Joyce's identification of words and things, his anal humor, betrays a serious fear that there is no such thing as "spirit" after all, that the world is nothing but matter, earth, garbage, rotting corpses, shit. The garbage "tip" or middenheap or prehistoric barrow where Finn MacCool lies buried, the earth to which dead matter returns, destroys any distinction between the "waste matter" a man (Earwicker) leaves behind him and the corpse that he finally becomes. As Mulligan says, "I see them pop off every day in the Mater and Richmond and cut up into tripes in the dissecting room." Instead of the pure ether where Icarus would like to soar, there is only "bad gas": "they have to bore a hole in the coffins sometimes to let out the bad gas and burn it." But this gas is the only spirit or soul a dead man has left: "Much better to close up all the orifices," thinks Bloom in the cemetery. "Yes, also. With wax. The sphincter loose. Seal up all." The fear of losing breath or spirit or conscious life stands behind Joyce's lifelong attempt to turn base matter into gold, into air: to give life to the wildest fantasies and turn gross reality into self-sustaining art. Bloom's quasi-scientific interest in physical "facts," the impulse behind the "Ithaca" chapter, is well illustrated by his favorite natural law, the law of falling bodies: everything returns to earth, "brightness falls from the air," and as Stephen/Icarus decides, "Not to fall was too hard, too hard." ("This was the Fall," writes Mann in *The Magic Mountain:* "that first increase in the density of the spiritual, . . . the transition from the insubstantial to the substance.") But everything Joyce wrote is designed to disprove this, to prove that "Phall if you but will, rise you must." Stephen, who imagines that his "soul had arisen from the grave of boyhood," believes that he can create "out of the sluggish matter of the earth a new soaring impalpable imperishable being," which is, in one sense, himself. Recreating life out of life, Stephen's androgynous artist (in *Ulysses*) not only gives birth to art but, identifying himself with his creation, becomes his own "consubstantial" son. Godlike, ghostlike, seemingly dead, he may have escaped life's dangers and become invisible, impalpable, immortal, pure spirit.

As Joyce's aloof irony turns to self-mocking humor, he describes Shem's writing as his "wit's waste" and reduces the Jarl's poetry to a piece of shit, as if Keat's ode were identical with the Grecian urn and the urn itself just a piece of "illiterate pottery." But his puns do not merely reduce words to material things; they make words seem "real," alive, as if in the "virgin womb" of the imagination the word really could become flesh. Indeed Joyce (in *Finnegans Wake*) specifically identifies words—the spontaneous flow of spoken language—with the babbling sound of the "river" Anna Livia, with the hissing sound of Issy's micturition, so that the magical, lifegiving power of a woman's urine is also the power of language. Just as the prankquean inspires or impregnates the Jarl, Anna Livia pours her babbling flow of words into the ear of sleeping Earwicker—the words of his dream, his "stream" of consciousness—with the implication that this living, fertile stream (like the whiskey splashed on Finnegan) will wake him up some day. Shem, borrowing his mother's verbal potency, "lifts the lifewand and the dumb speak," but Joyce's male artists, despite their pretensions of being autonomous, self-sufficient, androgynous creators, seem to need the literal inspiration of a maternal muse. They can create their written (silent) artifacts only by listening to the sound of living voices, particularly women's voices, as if they subscribed to the myth of the written word's dependence on the spoken that Jacques Derrida has been at such pains to dispel. In fact, the Joycean artist fears that he himself is dead, alienated from life, that "life" is something which belongs to others, to the other sex, to mothers, and his whole project is, while insulating himself from life, from other people, to steal that "life" (Derrida's "presence") and instill it into his art. So Joyce tries to make *Finnegans Wake* seem as spontaneous, accidental, and alive as possible, as if it were an uncensored stream of consciousness, a babble of voices that has to be heard rather than read, even though it is, in reality, a dense, clotted, carefully constructed verbal artifice that has to be *read* rather than heard. Pretending to imitate the immediacy of life, Joyce either freezes the present moment or lets time flow by in a continuous present, turning the last chapter of *Ulysses* into an unpunctuated stream of consciousness (a woman's). It is Joyce who constructs Molly's monologue, but he pretends that he is only recording her words.

If artistic inspiration is sometimes conceived of as a divine afflatus, it may not be too surprising that Joyce's myth of the dreaming father, in *Finnegans Wake*, resembles the medieval legend of "The Madonna's Conception Through the Ear." According to the legend, the Virgin Mary was impregnated through the *ear* by the breath or Word of God. In the *Wake* the roles are largely reversed: a woman's words penetrate a man's ear, and it is in the virgin womb of the artist's imagination that the word is made flesh. Some medieval paintings show the Virgin Mary being "impregnated" through the eye, not the ear, by a divine beam of light, and Proust's Marcel, whose eyes are pierced by the light cast from Mme. de Guermantes's eyes, who fears the darkness because whatever he can't see may no longer be there, seems to share the belief that light (like the light projected by the magic lantern) is a magical, fertile, almost supernatural substance. Like the Impressionist painters, Proust realizes that we see not the object itself but the (changing) light reflected from it, and yet this does not mean that we are condemned to a world of unstable, unreal appearances: light appears, instead, to be the highly distilled essence of the object, the Joycean *claritas* that the image projects. More mystically, the Berkeleian archdruid in *Finnegans Wake* claims to see the inner light that is *not* reflected from the object, the inner reality or "inscape," and in *A Portrait* Stephen decides that he is not interested in the *colors* of words after all. Marcel too implies that the essence of the object is hidden inside it, but ultimately his quasi-platonic essences are the rarefied, refined distillations of a physical, "sensible" world, tokens of exchange between the world and himself. Like Joyce, like his favorite con-artist Lemoine pretending to turn earthy carbon into dazzling, light-reflecting, valuable diamonds, Proust would like to turn base matter into light, into air, to make the dense substance of the world almost insubstantial—but not quite, because then it would no longer be real.

As a child Marcel thinks that his mother's presence is a kind of magical substance (her kiss) which he can literally assimilate into himself and without which his life has no real meaning. This magical substance belongs to his mother but can become independent of her, something to comfort him in her absence, and if he manages to possess it, it comes to signify not his mother's presence but his own, a kind of self-presence which convinces him of his own existence. We might say, at the risk of sounding like a parody of Derrida, that this presence is the presence of an absence, of an "other" who is not there or, at the least, will not always be there. Marcel's attempt to possess this other, to possess its mysterious "otherness," is of course unsuccessful, but this is the only way that he can free himself from dependence on his mother—or others generally—and create an independent self. In later life the magical substance that penetrates Marcel's senses appears under the guise of the taste of the madeleine dipped in tea, the sound of the musical phrase in Vinteuil's sonata and septet, the cold, damp, musty smell of the little pavilion in the Champs Elysées, the color of the pink hawthorns, or light itself, emanating from the eyes of the Duchesse de Guermantes or from the aptly-named magic lantern or reflected off the tops of church steeples at sunset. But always the magical substance is the highly distilled essence of an "other" one would like to possess—the world outside oneself, or deep inside oneself, out of reach, forgotten. And, once possessed, this foreign substance always turns out to be, simply, oneself, the mysterious essence that one likes to think of as one's "self": as Marcel remarks after tasting the madeleine, "this essence was not in me, it was myself." So it is not simply his mother that Marcel wishes to possess but the "otherness" in which he hopes to find the secret of his own identity.

Like Stephen Dedalus, who is fond of the odor of "horse piss and rotted straw," Marcel likes the musty, sooty, down-to-earth smell of the little pavilion (that is, the public toilet) as much as the fragrance of flowers or the "perfume" of the tea-soaked madeleine. In fact, the odor of the little pavilion is associated with the adjacent gardens of the Champs Elysées, and after "wrestling" with Gilberte in the bushes, Marcel comes down with an illness that may be related to his asthmatic choking fits. Moreover, the "perfume" of his Aunt Léonie's lime*flower* tea conjures up the image of another "little pavilion" behind his aunt's house, which also opens onto a garden, as well as "all the flowers in our garden and in M. Swann's park, and the water lilies on the Vivonne." Breath means life to Proust, but all these volatile, ephemeral essences represent tiny, homeopathic doses of the "life" outside him that the Proustian artist (like the Joycean) both fears and needs in order to survive, the magical, supernatural *mana* that animates an animistic universe. He too seems to feel that "life" belongs to others, to mothers, and the dangerous, uncontrollable *mana* that animates the universe originates for him in a mother's unpredictable love. Proust's metaphor of the artist becoming a mother to his work is less graphic, less literal-minded than Joyce's, but he too seems to imagine the artist impregnated or inoculated—through the eye or mouth or nose or ear (or somewhere else?)—by the fertile, lifegiving essence that enables him to give birth to art. This artist is not impregnated by words, like Joyce's dreamer, but Marcel specifically identifies the "essence" of life with the idea of metaphor.

Elstir's paintings, for example, "recreate" the world by extracting, "from the chaos that is all the things we see," isolated images detached and set apart from everything else, like the discrete, self-contained images that become Stephen Dedalus's epiphanies. But these images undergo a kind of metamorphosis—"analogous to what in poetry we call metaphor," says Marcell—whereby they are transformed from our conventional representation of them into our original, immediate, sensory impression of them: "according to the optical illusions of which our first sight of them is composed." It is this kind of metamorphosis, not merely a blurring of vision, that makes Elstir, in his picture of Carquethuit harbor, paint the town in "marine terms" and the sea in "urban terms," just as a poet might describe church steeples in terms of the masts of ships or young girls in terms of blossoming flowers. The replacement of the land by the contiguous sea, or vice versa, seems more like metonymy than metaphor, but the exchange of signs between two completely different things, the transformation of one into the other, is more clearly metaphorical. Even the isolated images that Elstir seems to extract from the world around him are not just random snapshots but, in effect, metaphors for the real world. In a more complex and subtle way, Elstir's portrait of "Miss Sacripant," rather than merely (metonymically?) blurring the distinction between male and female, endows one with the "signs" and attributes of the other, transforms one into the other, and turns that boyish, girlish face topped with short hair into a metaphor for the opposite sex, for the ambiguity of sexual identity. In short, Elstir's paintings are not strictly realistic but neither do they abandon reality for a strictly imaginary world; instead, they transform ambiguous images into signs or metaphors of a hidden, underlying reality.

As Proust finally formulates it, the task of the artist is not simply to escape into a private world, no matter how beautiful, but to discover the complex structures that seem to govern our lives. In Marcel's words:

> What we call reality is a certain connection between these immediate sensations and the memories which envelop us simultaneously with them—a connection that is suppressed in a simple cinematographic vision, which just because it professes to confine itself to the truth in fact departs widely from it—a unique connection which the writer has to rediscover in order to link forever in his phrase the two sets of phenomena which reality joins together.

The writer's prototypical *phrase,* microcosm of the writer's art, is not just an ineffable, airy nothing, the sign of a fine style, but a locus or condensation of meanings, like the puns and wordplays of *Finnegans Wake.* Again Marcel uses the word *metaphor,* this time to mean not the identification of two things separated in space but of two sensations separated in time: "by comparing a quality common to two sensations, we succeed in extracting their common essence and in reuniting them to each other, liberated from the contingencies of time, within a metaphor." The "common essence" revealed in a metaphor is finally the magical "otherness" which impregnates the self, the essence common to self and other, just as in *Finnegans Wake* language itself is equated with a woman's urine, which, endowed with magical properties, fertilizes a man's imagination.

Proust's "metaphor" is like a multiple-exposure image which does not simply blur the outlines between contiguous things but, by superimposing discrete images, establishes a structural, paradigmatic connection between them. In these terms art reveals the kind of underlying relations which give reality a human meaning, specifically a structure of recurrence whereby, as in Freudian psychology, lost or forgotten "impressions" underlie current ones. Freud interprets this structure of recurrence in terms of the return of the repressed, repetition compulsion, the uncanny, and even the death instinct, but Marcel finds this "uncanny" repetition joyful. Instead of feeling bound to the past, Marcel feels liberated from time, and it is the structure of metaphor that makes this liberation seem possible.

Proust's name of metaphor for the bit of reality that we discover, already existing, in ourselves may seem arbitrary and imprecise, but he is underscoring a fundamental truth about the nature of imagination: there is no such thing as pure fantasy, nor can we perceive a pure reality unstructured by our past experience. As Lacan implies, metaphor is not just a figure of speech but the essential structure of imagination, which means that we assimilate new experiences into old ones, take one thing for another, and treat "real things" as signs of our own fantasies. In the most "fantastic" works of fiction, such as myths, fantasies that cannot really happen purport to be real, but there is always some semblance of reality: giants are like men, only bigger; a man whose head has been cut off picks it up and walks away, which is conceivable but not likely. The most "realistic" works take verisimilitude, semblance to reality, as their basic principle, but this reality is composed of the "signs" the writer expects to find in the real world, metaphors for "real" things, like Joycean epiphanies that claim to capture the "whatness" of reality. We have seen how the multiple-meaning puns and double entendres of *Finnegans Wake*, which imitate the logic of dreams, seem to make words and things (shut/shit, wit/wet) interchangeable, as if words were metaphors for things and "things" were metaphors for the imaginary elements of fantasy. Joyce specifically identifies words with urine as magically fertile substances, but which is a metaphor for which?

In the first chapter of *A Portrait*, "real life" seems to be represented for Stephen by the cold slimy water in the ditch behind the outhouse, the dirty water sucked down a drain, the "earthy" rainwater of the country-side, and the warm turfcolored bogwater of the bath; these are the signs of the reality that attracts and repels him at the same time. This recurrent, almost obsessive image of "dirty water," alternately warm and cold like the bed after he has wet it, becomes the "sordid tide of life" that threatens to overflow the "breakwater of order and elegance" that he has erected, that threatens to drown him. Here the "tide" is merely a metaphor for the squalid disorder of "real" life, but later he walks near a real breakwater and dreads "the cold infrahuman odour of the sea" as if it might literally drown him: "O, cripes, I'm drownded!" cries one of his friends splashing in the water. In *Ulysses*, where a drowned man is fished from the sea, Stephen's fear of drowning is so great, so irrational, so phobic, that he doesn't even like to wash. It is not simply the sea that he fears but the metaphorical "tides within him," the dangerous, uncontrollable impulses that threaten to overwhelm him: "From without as from within the water had flowed over his barriers," just as he couldn't prevent the water from literally wetting his bed. In *Finnegans Wake* the water tends to come from without, from someone else, but it is still identified with bodily fluids.

In short, language seems to take the place of life in *Finnegans Wake*, but words themselves are identified with the sordid, seductive tide of life, as if one could take possession of life (could live) by assimilating words and using them to replace the life they seem to represent. So, in the first chapter of *A Portrait*, Stephen is obsessed not only by squalid images of life but by the mysterious meanings of words, especially words with more than one meaning, and if words do not always enable him to make sense of reality, they can always be used to construct a new reality (out of the pieces of the old), like the "green rose" he unwittingly creates out of the wild rose and the green place in the song. Like an alchemist or a primitive shaman, Joyce turns wet, "dirty," bodily life into art, but his literal use of metaphor appears to imply that words are literally urine, art is literally shit. Joycean puns (shut/shit, wit/wet) condense more than one meaning, but the point is not that one meaning is "manifest" and the other "latent," one conscious and the other unconscious, one real and other imaginary. The very idea of metaphor, which makes hypothetical or imaginary possibilities seem real—a sea of dirty water threatening to drown us, a man giving birth to poetry—also translates "reality" into the signs of fantasy. Joyce's magically fertile substance (urine) signifies, like Proust's precious essences, the animistic "life" that belongs to the world outside oneself, which one has to try to make one's own, and it is the metaphorical possibilities of language—of literature generally—that make this appropriation seem possible.

As I have suggested, Lacan's argument that "the unconscious" has the structure of language breaks down the distinction between literary and psychoanalytic categories. The jokes and slips of the tongue that Freud analyzed are miniature verbal structures like the puns and wordplays of *Finnegans Wake*, and dreams, while not expressly verbal, reveal the same quasi-linguistic structures of substitution, condensation, and displacement. Even neurotic symptoms reflect the substitution and displacement of unacknowledged desires: phobias like little Hans's turn animals into symbolic, metaphorical substitutes for something else; a fetish, if it is not simply a metonymic displacement of desire (from body to clothes), is a symbolic, metaphorical substitute for a phallus. Indeed, the infantile sexual theories that Joyce appropriates in *Finnegans Wake* depend upon complex transformations of something into something else, like the literal/metaphorical identifications of feces, gift, money, baby, and phallus that Freud analyzes in a famous essay on anality. Beginning with the "Project for a Scientific Psychology," Freud kept trying to construct a mechanistic, physical-science model for psychological processes, but the heart of the Freudian enterprise is not the shaky, pseudoscientific instinct (libido) theory, nor even the facile, allegorical model of ego, superego, and id. The most significant discovery that Freud made, anticipating the quasi-linguistic models of structuralism, is his theory of symbolic identification, of the transformation of meanings, of the metaphorical substitution of fantasy for "reality." From this point of view the central Freudian texts are the "semiological" studies of dreams, jokes, and verbal slips, the case histories that "deconstruct" and interpret private, individual "myths," as well as many shorter studies of how fantasies work, how meanings are transformed.

Moreover, reading literature ought to make us realize that the metaphorical structure of fantasies is not necessarily a property of unconscious thought. The metaphorical, "linguistic" structure that Lacan is talking about is the structure of what poets used to call the imagination, which, in seeming to bridge the gap between reality and fantasy, puts unconscious fantasies into conscious terms: the intense self-absorption of both Joyce and Proust is, in effect, an attempt to make the unconscious conscious. But there is no such thing as *the* imagination just as there is no such thing as *the* unconscious: imagination is simply the structure (the logical process) of identification and transformation, whose basic paradigm is the metaphor. This is not the place for a wholesale reinterpretation of Freud, which in its own way the French "return to Freud"—admirably exemplified by Jean Laplanche and J.-B. Pontalis's thorough, lucid, and indispensable "dictionary" of psychoanalytic concepts, *The Language of Psychoanalysis*— has already begun. But we may use the examples of Proust and Joyce to illustrate a Freudian theory of metaphor and, at the same time, a metaphorical, "semiological" theory of Freud.

We should recognize, however, that the definitions of metaphor proposed by Proust, Lacan, and modern linguistic theorists are not identical. The disparity between the "signifier" and what it seems to signify opens up a field of metaphorical possibilities, as if any signifier were already a metaphor for the "signified." Lacan equates metaphor, the substitution of one signifier for another, with the Freudian process of condensation in dreams, in which one signifier is superimposed on another, as in verbal puns. But as Jean Laplanche warns us, in a postscript to an article focusing on the metaphorical structure of dreams: "To proclaim hastily that Freudian displacement *is* metonymy and condensation metaphor is to choose to ignore much information and many developments for which we are indebted to Freud as well as to the linguists, to skip (to say the least) numerous meditations." Rather than insist on a strict interpretation of metaphor and condensation, it might be more fruitful to consider metaphor (like the images in dreams) as a condensation of literal and figurative meanings which undermines the distinction between literal and figurative meaning, a condensation of signifiers in which each one signifies the other. The deliberate confusion of words and "things" in Joyce's prankquean tale, where verbal "wit" signifies something wet and the answer "shut" signifies a piece of shit, is a case in point. For both meanings appear to be "present," and it is in fact the interplay between literal and figurative meanings, between *wit* and *wet,* which is the source of the wit, which makes the joke (for the reader) both funny and meaningful.

We have seen how the traditional literary identification of flowers and women (as in the medieval *Roman de la Rose*) becomes in Proust a complex metaphor for sexuality. There are "real" flowers in the *Recherche,* but the flowers in the phrase *jeunes filles en fleur,* (the signifier) signify as well the emerging sexuality of adolescent girls. The metaphor *en fleurs* includes a literal meaning (flowers) and a figurative one (sexuality), but this is not merely an abstract analogy between plants and people. As the corresponding metaphor of "deflowering" suggests, flowering may signify the presence of a specific, literal "flower," the literal sign of an imaginary anatomy. Moreover, the imaginary token of virginity that is lost in the sexual act of "deflowering" signifies an ephemeral presence that can, by definition, turn into an absence. Reversing the usual rule that males possess visible, prominent sexual organs and females don't, Proust endows women—at least adolescent girls—with an ambiguous sexual possession which men desire to "steal." If Marcel finds himself *à l'ombre des jeunes filles en fleurs,* in the *shadow* of these flowers, it may be because—as in the opening pages of the *Recherche*—he is not able to see just what is there and what isn't.

The ephemeral possession signified by the flower becomes finally—like the flower that Joyce's prankquean pulls out of her bag of tricks—the ambiguous sign of the opposite sex, the magical, even illusory "presence" of the "other" which one would like to have for oneself. In these terms the male/female dichotomy is reduced to a distinction between self and other, and the self/other dichotomy becomes simply a distinction between presence and absence, the *mana*-filled presence that (because it always belongs to the "other") is always absent, signified by its own absence. The red/ white, rosy/pale contrast in the prankquean tale becomes finally an opposition between colored and "blank" (Fr. *blanc,* white). These binary oppositions remind us that the two terms joined in a metaphor are not only similar but different, just as Proust's pink hawthorns are different enough from the white ones to make them seem new and special. By the same token, the present impression (in Proust's metaphorical structure of reminiscence) repeats the past impression, but in a new context, in a new way. The task of the metaphor is to find the "common essence" uniting the two impressions, to overcome the difference between them, but the difference—like the difference between pink and white hawthorns—helps to reveal the essential meaning of the impression, of the hawthorns. Derrida's radical notion of "*differance*" emphasizes, at the very least, the role of differences in the production of meaning, and "structuralist" theories are commonly based on binary oppositions like the one between metaphor and metonymy. The purpose of myth, according to Claude Levi-Strauss, "is to provide a logical model capable of overcoming a contradiction," but we may add that every metaphor is itself a logical model that attempts to overcome a contradiction, the contradiction between two terms that are different yet essentially the same. The opposition between pink and white, rosy and pale, is only a sign of the deeper, more fundamental opposition between "literal" and "figurative" meanings, between "real" and "imaginary" possibilities.

In one sense the metaphor of the flower signifies (condenses) two opposite, reciprocal meanings (presence and absence), but in a deeper sense it signifies nothing at all (an absent presence). This conclusion should underscore the primacy of the signifier over the signified, but we should realize that the "nothing" that is signified is the elusive, ephemeral "presence" that metaphor itself tries to bring into being. Derrida justifiably warns us against applying a metaphysics of presence to the universe of the written text, but every writer (every text) *tries* to create—out of the difference between signifier and signified, between literal and figurative meanings, between presence and absence—a new presence. A quixotic task? The "fetishistic" flowers of *Jeunes filles en fleurs*—or of the prankquean—do not really exist, but they are not mere delusions by which Proust or Joyce hides from himself (represses) the painful truth about women. They represent an attempt to understand what women mean to men, to overcome the mysterious "difference" and disturbing "otherness" of women. The "logic" of metaphor makes this possible, not simply by turning "presence" into a fictional problem rather than a physical one but by revealing that it—the seductive, elusive, and disturbing presence of the "other," of the other sex—always was a fictional problem, a problem of imagination, a problem in the construction and interpretation of signs.

Proust: A Retrospective Reading

There is no such thing as a direct reading. There is no such thing as an innocent reading. There is no such thing as a spontaneous reading. Our reading of any text always takes another for a starting point, for its background; we always read a text by comparison with another. In short, to use today's language, reading is an intertextual activity. A Balzac fan bases his reading of Proust on Balzac. A Proust fan bases his reading of Balzac on Proust. The naive reader will unwittingly base his reading of any book he opens on the amalgamation of everything else he has already read. Conversely, the enlightened reader may choose to read a text methodically with glasses whose focus has been adjusted for Balzac or Proust or Mallarmé.

Is that to say all intertextual readings are equivalent? Such is hardly our view. Over the naive reading, based on a random cluster of texts, the undifferentiated library insidiously at work in the mind of the reader, preference must no doubt be given to the enlightened reading, which considers a text in the light of another, clearly defined one. However, a further distinction here between two types of enlightened reading may perhaps be useful.

Deliberately employing rather vague terms, let us postulate a literature of the past and a literature of today.

Two very simple ways of bringing them into relation are conceivable. One might adopt a *prospective* attitude, which would consider today's literature in the light of the past's. Or one might adopt a *retrospective* attitude, which would consider the literature of the past in the light of

From *Critical Inquiry* 8, no. 3 (Spring 1982). © 1982 by Jean Ricardou. Translated by Erica Freiberg.

today's. The two positions are not equivalent. The prospective attitude is threatened with sterility: it may well find itself mainly seeking in today's literature the trace of that which was active in the literature of the past, that is, the persistence of something which is now perhaps fading away. The retrospective attitude, on the other hand, has a good chance of proving fruitful: what it tends to seek in the literature of the past is a foreshadowing of that which is alive in the modern text, that is, the beginnings of what is now in effect. In short, the former tends to minimize the innovations of today's text; the latter tends to stress the innovations in the text of the past.

Clearly, this does not mean that today's text has a metaphysical role—that of containing a truth which would illuminate its inarticulate beginnings in the text of the past. Rather, today's text has an operative role—that of an instrument with which to analyze the text of the past. And this retrospective analysis is threefold: it *detects* the way the text works; it *explains* the way the text works; it *specifies* the way the text works. In the first two operations, detection and explanation, the *resemblances* between a highly active process in a recent text and a less intense one in an old text are turned to account. In the third operation, specification, the *differences* between the two are stressed.

If we subject Proust's *Remembrance of Things Past* to a retrospective analysis in the light of the recent literary movement that has been named the New Novel, we immediately perceive, in Proust's work, a highly significant process. We are, in fact, witness to the beginnings of a monumental metamorphosis: a famous linguistic operation, metaphor, undergoes a radical change in function. It used to be mainly *expressive* or *representative*; with Proust, it becomes *productive*. Let's see how.

We know that the principle of metaphor is a kind of *exoticism*. Whenever the figure appears—in the *here and now* of what we are reading—it brings with it something *foreign* which, perhaps, had never before been mentioned.

Let's take an example. Imagine a scene in a courtyard, in the Guermantes's mansion, for instance, with some uneven paving stones that cause the narrator to stumble. It is of course quite possible simply to describe the stones' unevenness. That is what Proust first does toward the end of *Time Regained*: "But as I moved sharply backwards I tripped against the uneven paving stones in front of the coach-house." However, it is also quite possible to formulate that unevenness in a different way, either by a short comparison (i.e., a metaphor) or by a long metaphor (i.e., a comparison). If there are uneven paving stones in some other place, the baptistery of

Saint Mark's in Venice, for instance, I might write, insisting on the common point of the uneven paving stones: But as I moved sharply backwards
I tripped against the paving stones as uneven as those in the baptistery of
Saint Mark's in Venice. What then tends to occur, as we can see, is a
veritable *aggression*. One cell of the fiction, the place under discussion, the
courtyard of the Guermantes's mansion, is attacked by an entirely different
place, the baptistery of Saint Mark's in Venice, which had not previously
been mentioned. The reader is taken from Paris to Venice in no time. Yet
the attack is limited; it is what one might term a *minuscule aggression*.

There are two reasons for this. For one, the assailant, Venice, has seen
its importance diminished: the few words accorded it ensure the reader of
the intervening city's temporary character. Second, this assailant, Venice,
has seen its nature belittled: the formula "*as* uneven *as* those in the
baptistery of Saint Mark's" ensures the reader of the intervening city's
phantom character. Venice is presented less as a new place in the fiction
than as a simple figure of speech. In fact, the narrative has not left Paris,
and the protagonist has merely entered the Guermantes's mansion. In
short, the Venetian baptistery was not brought up for itself; it was only
mentioned in order to permit the *representation* of the uneven paving stones
in the Guermantes's courtyard. Such, very schematically, is the way the
expressive or representative metaphor works. On the one hand, it en-
hances the point, or the quality, that the comparer and the compared have
in common. On the other hand, it establishes an *inequality*: the fiction's
here and now, the compared, remains in a fundamentally dominant
position, whereas the foreign place, the comparer, remains in a fundamentally dominated position.

Now, we all know that *Remembrance of Things Past* does not contain
the sentence we just examined; it is apocryphal, invented purely for the
purposes of demonstration. What Proust really accomplishes is not a
metaphorical representation (of the uneven paving stones). What Proust
really accomplishes is a *metaphorical telescoping* (of the two cells of the
fiction). We have seen that metaphorical representation emphasizes a
common point by means of a duel with a foregone conclusion between
two unevenly matched cells. Metaphorical telescoping does just the opposite: a combat beween two evenly matched cells is carried to its unpredictable
climax by means of the point they have in common. This time the narrator
is led to *forget* the fiction's here and now, the Guermantes's courtyard, to
the extent of finding himself *besieged* by a foreign place, Saint Mark's
baptistery. Or, if you prefer, the narrative order undergoes a metamorphosis: on the way to a party at the Guermantes's, we suddenly find ourselves

in Venice. The metaphor is no longer used for an expression or a *representation*; what is important is no longer the unevenness of the courtyard paving stones. The metaphoric principle is used to *organize the narrative order*; what is important is the passage from one place to another:

> the chauffeur gave a shout and I just had time to step out of the way, but as I moved sharply backwards I tripped against the uneven paving stones in front of the coach-house.

> Every time that I merely repeated this physical movement, I achieved nothing, but if I succeeded, *forgetting the Guermantes's party,* in recapturing what I had felt when I first placed my feet on the ground in this way, again the dazzling and indistinct vision fluttered near me. . . . And almost immediately I recognized the vision: *it was Venice,* of which my efforts to describe it and the supposed snapshots taken by my memory had never told me anything, but which the sensation which I had once experienced as I stood upon two uneven stones in the baptistery of Saint Mark's had, recurring a moment ago, restored to me complete *with all* the other sensations linked on that day to that particular sensation, all of which had been waiting in their place—from which *with imperious suddenness a chance happening had caused them to emerge,* in the series of forgotten days.

Clearly, we are no longer dealing with a *representative* metaphor whose purpose would be to evoke the uneven paving stones. We are dealing with what I propose to call an *ordinal* metaphor which elaborates a narrative order and leads one fictional cell (the Guermantes's mansion) to be interrupted by another fictional cell (Venice). In other words, the ordinal metaphor does not express, or represent, an aspect of the fiction; rather, it is *productive of a narrative order*.

Here, however, we need to be very clear. Between the representative metaphor and the ordinal metaphor, there is not merely a *difference* in function—the one representing an aspect of the fiction (the paving stones' unevenness), the other ordering the fictional cells (the Guermantes's mansion interrupted by Venice). Between the representative metaphor and the ordinal metaphor there is mainly a *contradiction* in function: whereas the *representative* metaphor obviously obeys the mechanism of representation, the *ordinal* metaphor has a curious way of challenging this very mechanism. Or, to put it more plainly, *the ordinal metaphor has an antirepresentative function.*

While each of the fictional cells is indeed obtained by an effect of representation, the substitution of one cell for another by means of an ordinal metaphor is not an effect of representation. The first cell, qua representation, is attacked by another cell, qua representation, and the attack shakes the solidity of the representation itself. The reason is obvious: by resting on a resemblance, the ordinal metaphor causes two fictional cells, which were remote in space and time, *to be telescoped into a single instant.* In short, the ordinal metaphor volatilizes time and space, the two categories on which the effect of representation depends.

This antirepresentative effect of the ordinal metaphor is marked in various ways. One of the most spectacular, no doubt, concerns the function of the narrator. As we know, in this and many other novels the narrator resolutely belongs to the activity of representation: as a character, he participates in the events represented; as the narrator, he represents the events in which he has taken part. His identity, his consistency, his integrity, his presence are, then, indispensable to the smooth working of the representation. Now, it is just this presence, this integrity, this consistency, this identity which are incontrovertibly challenged as soon as an ordinal metaphor goes to work on the narrator's body. The reason is simple: insofar as he constitutes the place where two different fictional cells are telescoped, the narrator finds himself forced to belong, *simultaneously*, to two points in space and two moments in time. In short, he undergoes an intolerable division of his own self, which he experiences, on the fictional level, as that perfect challenge to his own being: the loss of consciousness.

This is exactly what happens a little further on, in the Guermantes's library, in a delightful passage where, on the one hand, one cell's attack on another is emphasized by a vocabulary full of conflict terms and, on the other, the battlefield is the narrator's own being:

> In this case as in all the others, the sensation common to past and present had sought to *re-create* the former scene around itself, while the actual scene which had taken the former one's place opposed with all the resistance of material inertia this *incursion* into a house in Paris of a Normandy beach or a railway embankment. The marine dining-room of Balbec, with its damask linen prepared like so many altar-cloths to receive the setting sun, had *sought to shatter the solidity of the Guermantes's mansion*, to *force* open its doors, and for an

instant had made the sofas around me *sway and tremble*. . . .
And if the actual scene had not very quickly been *victorious,* I
believe that I should have lost consciousness; for so complete
are these resurrections of the past during the second that they
last, that they not only *oblige our eyes* to cease to see the room
which is near them in order to look instead at the railway
bordered with trees or the rising tide, they even *force our
nostrils* to breathe the air of places which are in fact a great
distance away, *and our will* to choose between the various
projects which those distant places suggest to us, they force our
whole *self* to believe that it is surrounded by these places.

Let us now recall the principle which underlies our reading: rather
than going naively to Proust with a clutter of baggage from our personal
library, we propose to read Proust in the light of a specific recent literary
activity, that of the New Novel. Now, we know that the ordinal metaphor
is particularly active in the texts of the New Novel. We find it at work in
Alain Robbe-Grillet's *Jalousie,* in Claude Simon's *Triptyque,* as well as in a
novel I committed myself, *La Prise de Constantinople.*

In *Triptyque,* for instance, an initial fictional cell, centered around a
place in the country, is brutally assailed by a completely different fictional
cell, centered around a place on the Mediterranean. The attack is instanta-
neous: no warning precedes it, not a comment, nor even the indentation of
a new paragraph. (We indicate it with a slash in the quote from *Triptyque*
here.) At least this attack is based on a common feature: a *leg*—of a rabbit
on a plate, of a woman on a bed:

> Half the rabbit's body is now bared. The pink muscles of the
> *legs,* [/] the buttocks and the stomach look like an anatomy
> plate. Her foot resting flat on the bed, with a sudden stretch of
> her *leg* the woman pushed the closet door.

At this point, we can provide examples of the three operations which
characterize retrospective reading. The *first operation,* as we have already
stated, consists in *detection:* based on the frequency with which this
phenomenon appears in the New Novel, it is easy to point out, insofar as
they are similar, the various ordinal metaphors at work in the Proustian
text. The *second operation,* we repeat, is on the order of an *explanation:*
based on the radical nature of this phenomenon in the New Novel, it is
easy to point out, insofar as they are embryonic in the Proustian metaphor, both a *productive aspect* (there is elaboration of a narrative order)

and an *antirepresentative aspect* (there is elimination of time and space). The *third operation* is a kind of *specification:* based on the radical nature of this phenomenon in the New Novel, it is easy to point out, insofar as they are different in the Proustian metaphor, three mechanisms which each result in an undeniable *restriction.*

The *first restriction* establishes an *attenuation* of the phenomenon: where the New Novel operates incisively and without warning, Proust's novel attenuates the mechanism by all sorts of comments which soften the blow. The *second restriction* leaves the phenomenon incomplete: where in the New Novel the attacking cell prevails, in Proust's novel the cell which is attacked, the present, is "very quickly victorious." The *third restriction* leads to a *reduction* of the phenomenon: where the New Novel uses it as the decisive operation producing a particular narrative order, Proust's novel implies, in more ways than one, that the origins of the phenomenon could very well be psychological. We are, of course, referring to his frequent allusions to the famous "involuntary memory."

Thus the time has come to make the following observation. Retrospective reading is not limited to detecting a process in the text of the past (the ordinal metaphor). It is not content with emphasizing certain functions which had previously gone relatively unnoticed (the production of the narrative order and the role of antirepresentation). Rather, retrospective reading tends mainly to point out, in Proust's text, the particular mechanisms which serve to weaken this process. We have already described them: attenuation, incompletion, reduction. In so doing, retrospective reading authorizes a noteworthy event: a complete reversal of perspective as regards the role of "involuntary memory." Far from founding the mechanism which it is supposed to induce, involuntary memory on the contrary is one of the various tactics of an obvious strategy, the goal of which is to restrict the explosive effects of the ordinal metaphor. In other words, Proust, in *Remembrance of Things Past,* is not a psychologist who, with the ordinal metaphor, found a powerful formulation for the phenomenon of involuntary memory. On the contrary, in *Remembrance of Things Past* Proust systematizes a new narrative process, the ordinal metaphor, and proposes, with involuntary memory, a *fictional justification* enabling this explosive phenomenon to be assimilated in the course of the novel.

If our hypothesis is correct, its fertility should be demonstrable along several *axes of fructification.* We shall indicate four of them.

The *first axis* is *the fictional extension of the ordinal metaphor.* Our previous hypothesis was that the fiction calls upon involuntary memory because the latter is patterned, in its particularity, on the functioning of the ordinal metaphor. If this hypothesis is correct, it should be possible to find other fictional subjects in Proust's novel which are invoked because they, too, conform, in their particularities, to this same ordinal process. These, as we know, are legion. We shall enumerate three of them. The *first* one is *love.* When Swann realizes Odette's resemblance to a Botticelli painting, the shock of the encounter between the two remote realities awakens the ardor of his love. The *second* one is *diplomacy.* When King Theodosis defines the principle of the rapprochement between two powers, he employs the term "affinity," that is, "possession of common features." The *third* example is *geography.* When the narrator, at the end of *Remembrance of Things Past,* discovers the particularities of the Combray countryside, he does so in the following manner: two cells which had up to that point been inaccessibly remote, Swann's way and Guermantes's way, are suddenly brought into relation through what is common to both—Gilberte, Swann's daughter, becomes a Guermantes through her marriage to Saint-Loup.

The *second axis* is *the extension of the ordinal metaphor to the configural metaphor.* We have had to recognize that a metaphor can become an *ordinal* metaphor insofar as it brings about the attack of one cell by another. We shall now have to admit that a metaphor may become a *configural* metaphor insofar as it brings about the organization of a cell, in relation either to another cell or to itself. These phenomena, which at times grow highly complex, are legion in *Remembrance of Things Past.* We shall provide two examples. The *first* is well known: it is a case of *reciprocal assimilation.* When Elstir paints the harbor at Carquethuit, he does it in such a way that the land mimics the sea, and the sea, the land:

> It was, for instance, for a metaphor of this sort—in a picture of the harbour of Carquethuit, a picture which he had finished a few days earlier and at which I now stood gazing my fill—that Elstir had prepared the mind of the spectator by employing, for the little town, only marine terms, and urban terms for the sea. Whether its houses concealed a part of the harbour, a dry dock, or perhaps the sea itself came cranking in among the land, as constantly happened on the Balbec coast, on the other side of the promontory on which the town was built the roofs were overtopped (as it had been by mill-chimneys or church-steeples) by masts which had the effect of making the vessels to which they belonged appear town-bred, built on land, an impression which was strengthened by the sight of other boats, moored

along the jetty but in such serried ranks that you could see men talking across from one deck to another without being able to distinguish the dividing line, the chink of water between them, so that this fishing fleet seemed less to belong to the water than, for instance, the churches of Criquebec which, in the far distance, surrounded by water on every side because you saw them without seeing the town, in a powdery haze of sunlight and crumbling waves, seemed to be emerging from the waters, blown in alabaster or in sea-foam, and, enclosed in the band of a particoloured rainbow, to form an unreal, a mystical picture.

The *second example* is one we have implicitly suggested: it is a case of *serialization*. When the narrator goes to the Guermantes's party, the entire sequence tends to take shape as a series of similar events: first, the uneven paving stones bring back Venice; then, the metallic sound of the spoon recalls a railway trip; finally, the starched napkin resurrects Balbec.

The *third axis* is *the extension of the ordinal metaphor to ordinal consonance*. We have seen that, with the ordinal metaphor, one cell is attacked by another on the basis of a common point *located at the fictional level*. We can see that, with ordinal consonance, one cell is attacked by another on the basis of a common point *located at the narrational level*. It is no longer a question, this time, of a resemblance between two of the events narrated; it is a question, this time, of a resemblance between the words employed to narrate them. At least some traces of ordinal consonance can be found in *Remembrance of Things Past*. We shall provide two examples. In two of the above quotations, the text states that the solidity of the Guermantes's mansion is attacked by a common *sensation,* by the baptistery of Saint Mark's and by the Balbec dining room. We can now observe that it is also attacked by certain common *words*. The baptistery of Saint Mark's is in *Venise* ("Venice"), and the uneven paving stones at the Guermantes's mansion are in front of a *remise* ("coach-house"). Balbec's dining room is termed *marine* and, in the Guermantes's mansion, it is the narrator's *narines* ("nostrils") which are forced to breathe the air of far-off places. Balbec's linen is prepared like so many *nappes d'autel* ("altar cloths"), and the place that is attacked is the Guermantes's *hôtel* ("mansion").

The *fourth axis* is *the extension of the configural metaphor to configural consonance*. We have stressed the fact that, with the configural metaphor, one cell organizes certain of its fictional aspects according either to certain *fictional* aspects of itself or to certain fictional aspects of another cell. We can now see that, with configural consonance, one cell organizes certain of its fictional aspects according either to certain of its own *words* or to certain words of another cell. Although they remain somewhat clandestine, these phenomena can be found in *Remembrance of Things Past*. On some pages, for instance, the fictional cell tends to construct itself around the insistent conjunction of churches and pastries. Judge for yourself with the following quotations from *Swann's Way* (my italics):

> She sent out for one of those short, plump little cakes called "petites madeleines," which look as though they had been moulded in the fluted scallop of a pilgrim's [*Saint Jacques*] shell.

> The taste was that of the little crumb of madeleine which on Sunday mornings at Combray (because on those mornings I did not go out before *church-time*).

> Including that of the little scallop-shell of *pastry*, so richly sensual under its severe, *religious* folds.

> I would turn to and fro between the *prayer-desk* and the stamped velvet armchairs, . . . while the fire, baking like a *pie* the appetising smells with which the air of the room was thickly clotted, which the dewy and sunny freshness of the morning had already *"raised"* and started to *"set," puffed* them and *glazed* them and *fluted* them and *swelled* them into an invisible though not impalpable country *cake*.

> A maid, one who looked as smart at five o'clock in the morning in her kitchen, under a cap whose stiff and dazzling frills seemed to be made of *biscuit*-ware, as when dressed for *churchgoing*.

> You might see Mme. Sazerat kneel for an instant, laying down on the *prayer stool beside her own a neatly corded parcel of little cakes which she had just bought at the baker's*.

> And again, *after mass*, when we looked in to tell *Théodore* to bring a *larger loaf* than usual because our cousins had taken advantage of the fine weather to come over from Thiberzy for luncheon, we had in front of us *the steeple, which, baked and brown itself like a larger loaf still of "holy bread,"* with flakes and sticky drops on it of sunlight, pricked its sharp point into the blue sky.

Now, this configuration of the cell becomes clearer once we see that the pattern for the rapprochement is a play on words between the little cakes (the "petites madeleines") mentioned here and the church (the Madeleine) often mentioned elsewhere in the text.

One last remark will close this paper: it concerns our demonstration of the axes of fructification. Two methods enabled us to perform it. One uses logic: with the ordinal metaphor, it is possible to conceptualize, at least in the abstract, the mechanisms of configural metaphor, ordinal consonance, and configural consonance. The second method uses retrospective reading: the latter two mechanisms are clearly active in the New Novel—ordinal consonance, for instance, in *Triptyque,* by Simon, and in *La Prise de Constantinople,* signed by myself; configural metaphors appear as variants in *Martereau,* by Nathalie Sarraute, and in *La Maison de rendez-vous,* by Robbe-Grillet.

Thus our purpose here has been twofold. One aim, obviously, was to reveal certain aspects of Proust's text and their place in the modern challenge of expression and representation. The other aim, more generally, was to convey the following. There is a way of enjoying the literature of the past that prevents one from understanding the literature of today. There is a way of enjoying today's literature that gives one a better understanding of the literature of the past.

DIANA FESTA-McCORMICK

Clothes as Masks

I. THE LANGUAGE OF DECEPTION

Masks are by definition a means to hide, at the surface, something that lies within. When a mask is recognizable (like a perforated band worn over the eyes) it may be an incentive to discover what lies beneath. The most commonly used masks, however, are those that are not clearly detectable and which under the guise of truth are indeed lies. Since almost anything can be used for this purpose, it follows that the role of masks is as wide and as complex as that of truth and reality. Masks may be used for purposes as devious as those adopted by sincerity. Literary masks are particularly problematic. They are deceptive façades for character traits or feelings, and instruments that reveal what they purport to conceal. A kind of complicity may be established through them between author and reader. When clothes are used as masks, their role is to disguise the personality of the wearer. Simultaneously, the prominence accorded a supposedly inconspicuous detail serves the opposite purpose. Clothes used as masks are thus a language of communication that reinforces a premise and emphasizes traits, instead of hiding them.

In a work where memory is the central device for bringing to life a whole world, the importance accorded some minutiae of sartorial fashion is particularly revealing. Impressions surge from the unconscious where they have been stored, but they are also shaped by knowledge accumulated during intervening years. Proust does not allow the reader to attempt a

From *Proustian Optics of Clothes: Mirrors, Masks, Mores.* © 1984 by ANMA Libri and Co.

separation of a verifiable outer reality from the psychological perspective that helps shape that reality. If Albertine's polo hat were to be considered a mask, for instance, it would not be so important to see the dark area on the girl's face as an indication of the boy's awareness of a mystery surrounding her from the start. One would be more likely to concentrate on the presumed reality of the hat itself. What is it supposed to hide? And if it is meant to hide something, what does that intention reveal about the wearer of the hat? The answers one would attempt to find would aim at throwing some light upon the personality of Albertine and not of Marcel. [Elsewhere I have] centered on the role of memory and not on that of masks. I shall now consider the question of clothes viewed as masks, and what they reveal about the intention of the wearer.

At the core of *Remembrance of Things Past* there is the subject of homosexuality. However, the opening of the novel not only avoids the subject but emphasizes aspects that become misleading when considered in retrospect. The author builds a system of masks in the very structure of his work, so that the deviousness of homosexual behavior may be more fully appraised once it is uncovered. The need to hide a homosexual proclivity in a society unprepared to accord it a modicum of sympathetic recognition, dictates sham on the part of the characters involved. A striking number of people in the world of *Remembrance* (with the exception of the narrator's family) emerge colored by sexual ambiguity: Odette de Crécy, Albertine, Andrée, Madame Verdurin, Gilberte, Saint-Loup, the demoiselles Bloch, Mademoiselle Vinteuil, Morel, etc. But it is through Charlus, primarily, that Proust reveals the ambivalent nature and all the contradictory elements he saw at the heart of homosexuality.

There may seem to be a discrepancy between Marcel's personal realities and the events that he presents. Germaine Brée writes that these latter "appear to an observer simply as patterns or designs which do not in the least convey their real inner motivation." The disconnected gestures to which she alludes are integrated with an "inner discourse," however, and are assimilated into the characters' personality. This is done thanks to the omniscient narrator who decodes the patterns and bridges the gap between the inner and the outer reality. But the narrator's intent to mislead the reader, and his temporary success, are also important. Hence the mask can occasionally be separated from the reality underneath. That separation accords the mask its intended function to deceive by establishing a double identity: one perceived initially, and the other disclosed later. The deception may be twofold. Its first effect is registered by the narrator, who is duped into accepting things at face value. But the Marcel who saw at first the world somewhat differently from the one he subsequently discovers, the reader remembers, is the same narrator who evokes the past from the perspective of the present.

Marcel recounts things of the past not in the light of his later discoveries but of his initial misconceptions. Yet at certain times he also allows his knowledge to intrude upon the retelling of past events. "The novelist narrator," remarks René Girard, "is the only one capable of going beyond the abyss between divergent perceptions of a same object." But if Marcel often chooses to enlighten his readers about details he himself was unable to decipher when they occurred, he rarely does so in the context of homosexuality. The narrator allows sexual ambiguity to go undetected until the story leads to the discovery of it. He has meanwhile permitted the mask to conform with the intention of the wearer. Narrator and reader thus experience the same misconception, sustained until the time comes for both to discover the truth. This establishes a complicity between them different from that provided in other instances. That complicity has its source in their simultaneous experience and not in the sharing of information available to the narrator when he begins to tell his story.

The introduction of Baron de Charlus is preceded by his reputation as a womanizer. The notoriety of that distinguished and haughty man comes primarily from some outrageous escapades during his youth. Charlus is considered favorably for his escapades with women. Everybody "knows" that he is Odette Swann's lover, and his nephew Saint-Loup recounts with undisguised pride how, when his famous uncle was young, he "used to bring women to his bachelor quarters every day." Charlus is thus introduced with his social mask, through rumors calculated to mislead the reader. Marcel will leave readers with that misconception for a while, before he allows them to see through it.

The first time Charlus actually appears is at Tansonville, when young Marcel also catches an initial glimpse of Gilberte and is startled by a strident call from "the lady in white." Standing a little apart from that lady, "a gentleman dressed in twill and whom I did not know, fixed upon me eyes that seemed to come out of his head." The scene blends reality with the workings of the imagination. The impressions that the narrator retains of it are so strong that even after he learns, for instance, that Gilberte's eyes are black he still thinks of them as deep blue. What he catches of the three persons is a sensed, more than perceived, reality. Vague forms take shape in his memory, delineated in a splash of white or an imagined blue, and give substance to his impressions of Charlus. He remembers the intensity of his glance and the type of material of his suit. That he should

remember that detail would seem preposterous, were it not that he had
already suggested that his ability to register any verifiable reality was
inextricable from the expectations nourished in his imagination. The reader
may now add to this what Marcel is not yet prepared to say, but is well
aware of at the time he records these events: that Odette's companion is
not susceptible to feminine charms.

Standing as if frozen along the garden path, the man who rivets his
eyes upon the boy wears a duck suit. In retrospect, his intense look is easy
to decipher. What Marcel does not say yet is that Charlus takes a marked
interest in young ephebes. Although the suit is hardly described, it may be
equally revealing of the wearer's personality if it is analyzed in the light of
the homosexuality that eventually becomes apparent. The reader does not
know if it is light or dark. Still, one may assume that it is neutral in color,
for the narrator later discusses Charlus's reluctance to wear clothes that
might reveal his predilection for bright tints. He fears that such a predilection might be construed as being effeminate. But the twill of the material is
striking. It is a type of ticking, often accompanied by very thin stripes, very
tightly woven and ideally used for covering mattresses and pillows. Marcel
must have noticed the neutral greyish cloth primarily for the ridges, for it
would be inconceivable otherwise that he could guess at the actual kind of
the material. There must have been lines that both blended with and stood
apart from the background. Twill is also quite stiff and hence in keeping
with Charlus's public image. Later, stripes will recur in allusions to his
clothing. One might remember by then that Swann had once observed that
he felt quite at ease when Charlus was with Odette, for "between M. de
Charlus and her, Swann knew that nothing could happen." By then,
stripes have become associated with Charlus's natural preference for patterns and colors in his clothing, disguised in the barely perceptible lines of
generally dark suits. His homosexuality, which is hardly dependent upon
his taste for colors, has made Charlus vulnerable and fearful of anything
that might betray him.

In that initial picture of Charlus, stripes are not mentioned. All the
reader knows is that he wears a stiff-looking suit. That stiffness, whether
of material or of stance, conforms with the unbending pride and underlying arrogance of Charlus's public image. It is the means he consciously
seeks in his effort to hide his vulnerability, a wall erected to protect his
secret. The lines (assuming that the material is indeed striped) indicate the
rigidity of his social posture and, at the same time, a contradictory element
in the strict severity he intends. But they are not clearly detected at this

time, and so they may stand for the still undiscovered nature of the wearer, of the mask that dupes both the young Marcel and the reader.

The next time Marcel runs into Charlus, it is also by accident. This second meeting expands on the motifs introduced with the first. The shock of the encounter in the Tansonville garden was vaguely at odds with the reputation of the gentleman. He appeared symbolically "at some distance" from his presumed mistress, and his eyes seemed to lunge out of their sockets in the effort, one is already tempted to conclude, of coming nearer to the boy. The twill suit mentioned seemed in keeping with the dandyfied elegance. Yet the very fact that it was noticed appears extraordinary. It both blends with the image one might have had of him, and stands apart.

The second meeting is also orchestrated against a carefully built background. Here, too, Charlus's arrival is preceded by a reputation that can only create confusion when it is measured against the impact of direct encounter. He is described by Saint-Loup in a highly flattering manner—as an athlete who relishes physical exercise, risks discomfort, walks long hours, sleeps in some country hut along the way. He is also described as kind and unassuming with simple people, and responsible for the advancement to advantageous positions in Paris of many a young man from the country. Allusions are made to his escapades with women, and to his unforgiving pride. A story is also recounted of his having once beaten, and within an inch of his life, a friend who had dared make "bizarre" advances to him. Palamède de Charlus is also called a trend setter in fashion. Merely because he wanted something warm one summer, he had his tailor make him a coat out of a vicuna cloth, which until then had only been used for blankets. It became a rage, and soon enough all Paris was wearing those "blue and fringed, long haired coats." Since after he meets the Baron, Marcel notices that he wears only the darkest of tints, one wonders if the colorful vicuna mentioned by Saint-Loup proved puzzling to him in retrospect. There is little doubt that Marcel remembers the details of that conversation, for he includes them in his memoirs. Yet he never questions the discrepancy between that blue color and fringe of the long haired wool and the unrelievedly somber suits that he is soon to accept as Charlus's distinctive marks. One may conclude that his silence in this case is hardly accidental, and that it is meant not to alert the reader to the problematic identity of the wearer.

Charlus is to come to Balbec to join his nephew and Aunt Madame de Villeparisis at the Grand Hotel. Since Marcel is Madame de Villeparisis's friend, he will no doubt have occasion to meet the Baron. Marcel makes no reference, however, to having already seen Charlus (whose identity he clearly knew) long ago at Tansonville. It is as if that memorable day—of which he has kept every particle intact in his memory—were completely forgotten. But the narrator's lapse here is a necessary device for the setting of the scene that is to follow. A little pantomime not devoid of humor is to take place, in which Marcel and Charlus study each other surreptitiously. They have not met yet, and they do not know each other's identity. But the scene comes too closely on the heels of a discussion with Saint-Loup for the reader not to realize that the gentleman Marcel catches staring at him is the famous Baron. The evidence that has been accumulated against Charlus's public posture, meanwhile, is indirect and surrounded in mystery. Only in retrospect do details emerge that point to his sexual preferences, and to his effort to hide them. Swann's reference in the past to "that type of man" being "the worst of all" may have alerted the reader for a moment. The narrator's discomfort at the insistence with which a man dressed in black scrutinizes him in a public place conveys a feeling of oddity. Yet the impact of these details is assimilated only by osmosis, as they gradually seep into the readers' consciousness instead of appearing in any logical sequence open to analysis. The narrative has so blended form and content that one follows the same perceptive path as the narrator in the evocation of past events.

II. FIRST TELLTALE SIGNS

The second meeting with Charlus is introduced with the words "the morning after the day Robert had thus spoken of his uncle . . . I had the sensation of being looked at by somebody not far from me." The association is indirectly but clearly made between Saint-Loup's discourse about his uncle and the person whose baffling behavior Marcel suddenly notices. In a work that emphasizes the subjective and intuitive nature of reality, the role of the eyes helps fulfill the narrator's (and reader's) trajectory from an unconscious perception of truth to his conscious weighing of it. Eyes register details before they are put into intellectually understandable contexts. Marcel had noticed that Charlus's eyes at Tansonville seemed about to pop out of their sockets, so intense was their gaze. But the look itself can be understood only later, when the narrator reflects upon the man's interest in young men. Charlus's eyes are an effective means of revealing both his social lie and his inner truth. In Marcel's second encounter, the boy senses he is being looked at before he actually notices the man staring at him. He then watches in amazement the strange man who, seeing himself looked at in turn, improvises a sequence of motions designed to erase whatever impression he fears he may have produced. At the same time, he scrutinizes the effect he makes upon Marcel who is watching him. The pantomime is complex, pointing to the boy's innocence, and hence to his inability to make any sense of the unusual behavior he witnesses. Marcel does not understand the maneuvers of a homosexual who hesitantly approaches someone who has caught his fancy, but who also prepares for a retreat, in the event of a rebuke. The narrator uses the dumb show in order to allow readers to recognize elements that he could not yet understand at the time. Clothes play a role here which is worth analyzing.

Marcel is tempted to interpret Charlus's successive gyrations, audible sighs, display of indifference or attentive scrutinizing, as manifestations of either a thief or a madman. But he hesitates to arrive at a conclusive judgment that might be at odds with the man's simple yet striking elegance.

> However, this extremely neat attire was more serious and much simpler than that of all the bathers I saw at Balbec, and reassuring for my jacket so often mortified by the glaring and banal whiteness of the beach.

The "serious" suit produces the intended reassuring effect. Its simple elegance is not meant to hide the presence of either a thief or a lunatic, but the more shocking one of a homosexual. Still, while it quiets the onlooker's misgivings, it also serves to alert him to the disharmony between the man's outer appearance and his behavior. If it comforts the boy—who admits having felt mortified by the darkness of his own costume—it points to the striking difference between the gentleman in question and the rest of the summer residents at Balbec. Furthermore, the French adjective "soigné" ("une mise extrêmement soignée" or a very scrupulously chosen attire) suggests deliberate intention in the care taken over the choice of clothes that is perhaps not fully implied by the word "neat." Charlus's dark suit, in fact, has the connotations of an adopted mask, serving the double purpose of deceiving and of revealing the deception. In this it underscores both the point of view of the man who wears the mask, and the perspective of the author-narrator ready to decode its meaning. What follows reinforces all previous doubts. It also emphasizes the crucial role of clothing in revealing sham.

Marcel's considerations as to the identity of the strange gentleman are interrupted by the arrival of his grandmother. Yet they are taken up again in seemingly continuous flow an hour later, when he sees the man again.

> I saw that he had changed his suit. The one he was wearing was even darker, and no doubt this is because true distinction is less removed from simplicity than false distinction. But there was something else: when drawing nearer one felt that if color was almost entirely absent from these garments, this was not because the person who had banished color from them was indifferent to it, but rather because, for whatever reason, he abstained from it. And the sobriety which they displayed seemed of the kind that comes from compliance with a diet, rather than from want of appetite. A dark green thread harmonized in the cloth of the trousers with the stripes on his socks, with a refinement that betrayed a vivacity of taste subdued everywhere else and to which this single concession had been made out of tolerance, whereas a red spot on the necktie was imperceptible, like a liberty one dares not take.

The light of involuntary recognition in Charlus's eyes when meeting the boy he had so attentively examined a while ago, is quickly subdued. He stands, in the passage just quoted, as if caught within a frame, with gestures and expressions immobilized and inseparable from the rest of his appearance. The first impression he makes is one of severe elegance. A few details are then noticed, with the emergence not so much of color but of the suggestion of color. At first, the most evident feature is the intense darkness of the suit. Next, inconspicuous traces of color come to the fore.

The reader's attention is directed to the suit. What has been called "serious" a while back, now becomes "even darker." An interpretation is, however, quickly supplied. "Real elegance," it is suggested, is particularly evident when not encumbered by the usual embellishments. Implicitly, light colors are commonplace, as stated earlier ("the banal whiteness"). The gentleman's refinement thus rests on what one might call a harmony in black. Without this subtly suggested explanation, the presence of the green threads and the minute splash of red would have had little significance. They are fittingly introduced with the qualifying "but" ("but there was something else").

Charlus's first brief appearance in his twill outfit suggested the presence of stripes. What must have impressed Marcel at that time probably was a stiffness in the man, which in turn must have suggested that the suit was made of ticking material. A reverse emphasis now occurs. The suit stands out against the radiance of the sun, delineating a stark silhouette. But if its somber quality is immediately registered, this time Marcel's eye lingers on the thin stripes in the trousers that match the piping in the socks. The movement of the legs in walking must have directed his glance, yet the image appears as if still. The suggestion of motion comes not from the implicit walking, but from the stripes. These create a double contrast, in their hue and in the series of lines they trace against the dark uniformity of the background. The background is what is first perceived, and hence may be considered a surface. The stripes are the hidden reality that slowly emerges.

The identity that Charlus wants to hide comes through in his very effort to hide it. But he exaggerates. The unvarying darkness of his clothes draws attention and conveys the impression of punctiliousness, particularly at a seaside resort where light colors are dominant. Still, the stark outfit could be accounted for by his reputation of elegance and a certain originality. In this context, the tenuous presence of color is a divergence, betraying a self-imposed restriction rather than distaste for it. Hence Marcel's impression of abstention rather than "want of appetite" in his reaction. Charlus's natural bent becomes associated with "a vivacity of taste" that would not have shown through, had he used colors in a less disguised manner. The green stripes and the daring spot of red are removed from the image of masculinity they would presumably destroy if put in evidence, and from that of the homosexual they only indirectly suggest. They emerge as mask and as Charlus's secret truth.

Proustian masks are, in Germaine Brée's words, both imperfect and forever changing. The fact is that a whole system of masks is used to show layers that are to be lifted at every turn. In the case at hand, a clash is suggested between the narrator's expectations and his discovery. Marcel and Charlus are deliberately isolated. A stage is visualized, with a corresponding atmosphere of theater. There, the central actor plays his role, which is indeed clearly a role. The spectator is, however, also on the stage, and he both acts and serves as interpreter for the movements of the other. He also creates the buffer zone needed to show the fluidity and the interchangeability between theater and life. On the outer side stand the public, or the readers of the novel. With the intermediary help of the narrator-actor, readers react predictably on a double level, both accepting the suggested reality and never quite losing sight of its fictional quality. Hence the "imperfection" of the mask, its evolving and revealing function. Charlus's "perfectly composed features to which a light coat of powder conferred the aspect of a theatrical face," could have presented an inscrutable, or perfect mask. The restlessness and fixity of the eyes at the same time betray a hidden frailty. Likewise, the dark costume could be convincing in merely denoting adherence to a personal taste, were it not that the thin ridges of green and the surprising spot of red repudiate that premise.

A frown or a shrill voice caught in passing, a moss rose whose delicate petals are conspicuous against the unvarying darkness of Charlus's outfits, a remark one remembers about his innocuous presence next to a pretty woman, or the obstinacy with which "he did not even allow that a man wear a single ring," gradually form a frame of reference with different connotations from the ones readers were led to expect. It is not changes that occur but patterns that gradually evolve and contribute to the defini- tion of the character. If the definition remains fluid and complex to the end—for Charlus as well as for all others—that is only because it reflects the essential impenetrability of every individual in real life. The narrator's perceptive eye appears to remove layer after layer of coverings. But each layer is not merely a cover but also a component of what it hides beneath, and therefore part of its essence. The black suit with the bright rose is a mask without which one could never guess at the nature of what it hides. It is the needed stage without which the presence of an actor would be incongruous. It thus proffers truth by making the mask itself eloquent.

If Marcel is merely baffled by what eludes his understanding at this point, the indelicate Bloch has no compunction in articulating all that has been suggested. When he asks who "that excellent puppet in the somber outfit" is, his function is that of the interpreter for what the narrator is still loath to avow. The dark suit is the factor that identifies the actor in Charlus. But the stage upon which the "puppet" moves in grotesque imitation of truth is life itself. Hence the suggestion of pathos that begins to appear, and the duality where the comic and the tragic blend in a single entity.

The movement that shapes initially unsuspected identities is progres- sive. The reader is alerted from the beginning to the possible meanings that inconspicuous details may be hiding. These acquire the value of symbols, as they are increasingly focussed upon. The motif of the stripes, for in- stance, is signalled with some insistence by the green lines across the dark pants seen at Balbec, and it is finally given prominence in a fleeting sight of Charlus later on. Meantime, Charlus's behavior has swung from the insultingly haughty to the graciously helpful, his voice has varied from the shrill to the mellifluous. When readers next catch a glimpse of him, their attention is drawn to the "white gloves striped in black." Far from neglect- ing the suggestive value of those stripes, they may now grant them the importance they deserve and see in the black and white lines across the gloves hidden significance.

The image that finally emerges on the occasion following those already mentioned reverts to the nondescriptive impression of the first encounter. Instead of a silhouette that briefly appears at a bend of the road, the man now sits inside a carriage. His very identity this time appears linked to the striped gloves he wears. He is in fact invisible "at the back of his coupé," and all that can be noticed are "his hands held within white gloves striped in black, a flower at his buttonhole." Yet those gloves and the flower are enough for Saint-Loup to recognize his uncle. They are the element that gives him away. They are no longer mere contrasts of color, but the illustration of the duality for which they stand. Their outline is particularly stark when seen next to the flower's soft petals. One may see in them a silent voucher for the androgynous nature Charlus seeks to conceal.

Marcel is not only young but quite naive during this period. He is quick to catch a look of worry or disappointment on the face of friends when he mentions that he is to see the Baron, but he fails to detect any warning in it. He simply stores those looks in his memory without so much as wondering why they exist. He also notices that one time Charlus seems so anxious to be with him that in his haste he grabs the wrong hat. He explains the obstinacy with which that hat is clutched even after the mistake is pointed out, but he does not see in it a confirmation of his initial suspicion—that Charlus chooses to follow him at the cost of taking someone else's hat. The incident points symbolically to the false identity to which the Baron clings, and shows the mask he assumes not only to protect his intentions from scrutiny, but to allow them realization.

III. THEATER

The action, passions, dénouement of a play cannot be fully appreciated until they evolve before a spectator upon a stage, where they unite visual and auditive perception to all preconceived notions. There, the anticipation that preceded the experience of theater and the actual experience come together. Memory retains both of them, and compounds them within the imagination. That is what happens in Proust's *Remembrance of Things Past*. Marcel's recollections follow the pattern of a theater experience, alternately presenting periods of wait, actual events, and new perspectives gained through distance. But the narrator is simultaneously director and actor, and the scenes he both witnesses and recounts are at one remove from the spectator's (or reader's) direct appreciation. The distance thus created diminishes the dramatic impact, while it emphasizes the theatrical setting. A theater within a theater emerges at each turn. At the same time, readers add their own understanding to a partially explained context. Actors fulfill their roles with fidelity and conviction; they convey mimetic reality to words, and intellectual implications to gestures. They display sincere imitations of characters and a forged earnestness of emotions. "It is at the theater that one gets to say everything without making anything known, without making oneself known," remarks Rosette Lamont. The narrator-author implies a wealth of things, without specifying any of them.

The next time the motif of clothing is used to help define Charlus's personality, it appears quite strikingly within a theatrical setting. The importance of the scene is increased by the fact that the actor himself (Charlus) has designed the stage setting and the action, and has contributed direction and interpretation. Unfortunately, he does not know the complete script, and the other actor's (Marcel's) role does not fulfill his expectations. The other actor is once again spectator and performer, a narrator consciously retelling events and the participant in an unwritten script. At one remove from both action and direction, stand the real spectators or the readers of the novel. They command a view of the whole proscenium, and have at least an intuition of backstage directions. All the while knowing that a fiction faithful to life is being enacted, they remain mesmerized by the action. The passage that follows is well known. Marcel has been invited to come and see the Baron at eleven in the evening, following a reception at the Guermantes. He arrives punctually, but after waiting for about an hour, he is ready to leave. A valet appears at that point and assures him that he is doing his best to work him in among other visitors.

> I waited ten more minutes and, after having asked me not to stay too long, because since M. le Baron was tired, he had to have several most important people who had made appointments many days earlier sent away, they let me in where he was. That "mise en scène" around M. de Charlus seemed to me much less impressive than the simplicity of his brother Guermantes, but already the door stood open, I just noticed the Baron in a Chinese dressing gown, his throat bare, stretched on a sofa. I was struck at the same time by the sight of a shiny top hat on a chair with a pelisse, as if the Baron had just come in. I thought M. de Charlus was going to come toward me. Without making a single motion he fixed upon me a pair of implacable eyes.

Before even being admitted into the sanctum—where the Baron is revealed more like a terrible sphinx chastising visitors for unknown offenses than like a gracious host—Marcel is aware of a prevailing theatrical atmosphere. His considerations on the *mise en scène* reveal his reluctance to be drawn into some kind of unknown ritual—in which he eventually participates all the same, as he is drawn within the radius of Charlus's dominion, in his stage-like chamber.

The opening of the door in the passage quoted is the equivalent of the lifting of a curtain at a theater. It shows the stage beyond the proscenium where Marcel is standing and reveals to the public the resulting double perspective. All has been prepared in advance for this moment and a concerted effort must have gone into the final dramatic effect. The young man still stands in the foreground, while beyond him another view opens framed around an immobile man. Particular care has been given to arranging a few details. Marcel's startled attention is drawn to them, to the robe Charlus is wearing, and to the furlined coat and top hat displayed on the chair.

What Marcel does not understand (and one might wonder at his protracted wonderment, but that would be another subject) is that the stage has been set for a seduction scene. The intended seduction rests here not on appeal through endearment and charm, but on manipulation through intimidation. The long wait imposed is the first step in the effort to weaken the boy's defenses. He is tired, frustrated, somewhat resentful by the time he is received by the man who had invited him. That he is abused and chastised is not surprising, once one learns to interpret available clues. The main clues are contained in the clothes so ostentatiously exhibited, and in their contrasting implications. On the chair, discarded but prominent, are the vestiges of a social mask; on the sofa, lies the allurement of promised intimacy. With the robe and its exotic character on the one hand, and the coat and hat in keeping with the canons of severe elegance, on the other, the inference is that Charlus uses these devices consciously, and counts on their mysterious power in order to obtain the desired effect.

His contrived behavior and manner of dressing have until now been used by Charlus to hide his androgynous nature. That he has not always been convincing cannot be attributed to a lack of trying. In fact, failure to convince can be imputed to too much trying. In this scene, however, Charlus's intention is not to hide his homosexual inclinations, but to reveal them. The very nature of his sexual preferences dictates nonetheless that the language of communication be tortuous and that it be seized through innuendoes. His grotesque appearance (the reclining position of the body, the terrible eyes, the bare neck emerging from the Oriental robe, all within a frame of reference that does not justify them in the house of a nobleman receiving an expected visitor) conveys a sense of distortion parallel to that of a ritualistic and grimacing mask. But the mask is meant to be recognized and appreciated in its just connotations here. It is to be seen as a helping device in a rite of passage for the young man, as the key that should usher him into the world of adulthood. That world, however, differs from the traditional heterosexual one. Hence the innuendoes and devious presentation.

Ritualistic masks contain arcane meanings that are intelligible only to those already instructed in their language. "A masked character," writes Jean-Louis Bédouin, "whoever he is, is not simply a character whose real identity remains unknown. He is more than that; he is above all something else, since he posits himself as an enigma, and he defies all others to decipher his language. He thus places himself outside common law, claiming for himself the use of a freedom all the larger for not being limited any more, momentarily, by social conventions." Charlus's mask is clearly visible, and Marcel is not blind. Its challenge to the onlooker to interpret what lies beneath the disturbing surface, however, falls short of the desired effect. If the boy understands that the claims being made are not "limited any more, momentarily, by social conventions," he is still at a loss to interpret their message. He does not know what to make of the pelisse and hat on the chair, "as if the Baron had just come in." He should recognize that they are there solely for his benefit, since Prince Von Faffenheim had mentioned a dinner invitation at Charlus accompanied, however, by the instruction "not to come after a quarter to eleven." The Baron could not have made himself available to dinner guests and have been out at the same time, Marcel probably senses. He had expected to be greeted upon his arrival, and all social conventions have been violated. The Chinese robe seems out of place, and the bare neck must have looked outright indecent in a man usually buttoned up in severe outfits. Still, the boy's bafflement here could have been absorbed in the invisible script, had it been part of an act. But Marcel's reaction is genuine. He partakes of a rite, in fact, without guessing at the intricacy of its language. His own truth is thus caught in a lie, and Charlus's increasing dissatisfaction with his incomprehension is no longer feigned.

The scene revealed with the opening of the door focuses upon the Baron and the few items of clothing mentioned. These may be divided into three categories, with the robe and top hat at the opposite extreme, suggesting the world of salon and boudoir. On the other hand, the fur-lined coat (referred to simply as "a pelisse") is elegant but not particularly distinguished. It may therefore represent yet another aspect of Charlus's life: his blending with an anonymous crowd. The dressing gown, however, presumably of silk, suggests a kind of opulence with exotic undertones. The fact that it leaves the throat bare (a detail that Marcel is quick to notice) subtly shifts attention from the loose wrap itself to the body it half reveals. The Chinese robe thus stands for a hardly disguised invitation to the flesh beneath. Since the Baron's manifest intention is to seduce Marcel, and to humiliate him into prostration before presumably receiving him in his open arms, the dressing gown stands as a recognizable mask with ritualistic value.

The hat is referred to in the original as a tall shaped "eight reflec-tions" hat (*un chapeau haute forme "huit reflets"*) and thus of rarefied elegance, with silk nap of such luster that it reflects many lights. It is a symbol of Charlus's nobility and public demeanor, haughty (the tall shape underscores that quality), impenetrably dark and prismatic at the same time. It represents a type of mask quite distinct from that of the robe, one that is designed to create illusions that diverge from hidden truths. When, contrary to the Baron's expectations, Marcel becomes incensed instead of vanquished by the indignity of Charlus's language, it is instinctively against the hat that he vents his rage.

> With an impulsive movement I wanted to strike something, and since a remnant of discernment made me respect a man so much older than myself, and even, because of their artistic dignity, the German porcelains placed around him, I rushed to the Baron's new tall hat, I threw it on the floor, I trampled on it, set upon tearing it to shreds, wrenched off the lining, tore the crown in two, without listening to M. de Charlus's vocifer-ations that continued and, crossing the room in order to leave, I opened the door.

The valet's earlier insinuation that the Baron was tired from having re-ceived many guests, is especially unconvincing once Marcel has been admit-ted to the room. But what he suspects to be a lie could be ascribed to Charlus's reluctance to admit that he had been out when expecting a guest—as the hat and coat would indicate. Still, had the Baron wanted to hide that fact, he would not have left such revealing clues in full view. The stage has undisguisedly been set to create a mystifying atmosphere. All disguises appear intentionally displayed here, and that includes the spying of the two valets and the poor delivery of their appointed lines. They are *not meant* to convince but, on the contrary, to denounce their own presence as masks, to make themselves visible to the newcomer in the realm of Sodom. Marcel's obtuseness in failing to decipher the multiple signs does not prevent him from seizing impulsively the one item that most reflects the lie given to the outside. He tramples the hat as he would the man who has misled him, he wants to obliterate its sheen and the imperturbable arrogance for which it stands. His rage and frustration are wonderful, and could not have been more effective. Charlus and the two spying valets must have been silently applauding. But the naive boy then ruins the whole thing for them by crossing the room to go away, instead of falling weeping into the Baron's arms. The script was not understood. The masks were taken at face value, in adherence with standard language. Their voice has gone unheeded, and their symbolic value is thus reduced to a commonplace object of disdain.

Charlus cannot be insulted by Marcel's reaction, but he is nonetheless annoyed. He is so accustomed to the deviousness of his own behavior and of the signs he employs, that he has lost a just perspective of what these may convey to an uninitiated person. He is equally surprised, in fact, when his mask shows through and when its eloquence goes undiscerned. A bit piqued, he confides to Jupien that he is somewhat taken with a young bourgeois who hardly deserves the honor. "After all what does it matter," he protests. "That little jackass may bray all he wants before my august Bishop gown." Charlus's language is in keeping with the idea he would like to suggest and not with its literal meaning. The Bishop gown he evokes here is meant to project an aura of respectability. Had he wanted either to hide or to reveal his homosexuality, the problem would be simple enough. But he wanted to be many things at once, a master, a nobleman, a slave, a vulgarian, an example of probity, a hedonist, a rebel above the law, and a "Bishop" promulgating his faith.

Charlus's masks are all intensely lived and forcefully projected. Each mask upon his face does not merely mirror the character impersonated but also his own intimate wishes and dreads. Each is not only a segment but a microcosm of his whole person. Each is also revealed through his clothing— whether it be a dark suit, a top hat, or the imagined vermilion garment of a Bishop he mentally dons for a moment. "Hypocrisy, in the masked ball, becomes the rule of the game," writes Starobinski, "The struggle for power or for money is then found transposed on the level of festivity, and through a supreme return to gratuity, the hypocrite has no other ambition outside the perfection of his own game. All he has to do is to enjoy his being in itself so perfectly outside of himself." This would explain how Charlus can alternately impersonate a vigorous gentleman living up to social demands of masculinity, or display a body wrapped in soft silk and reclining like an odalisque. Both the black outfit and the Chinese gown are faithful to a reality whose scope is the "perfection of the game" itself. In either case, all doubts and inner instability are silenced, so that Charlus can live his carefully composed mask.

IV. EMERGENCE OF THE TRANSVESTITE

The old adage that truth will out is nowhere more applicable than to literary masks. Since by its nature literature aims at communicating, the reader cannot forever be left out of plots, no matter how intricate these may be. The narrator in *Remembrance* holds out his revelations as long as possible. He builds his story around a gradual awakening that ushers his own conscience and that of the reader into an increasing awareness and perception of truth. From the initial "for a long time I went to bed early" to the closing line "within the dimension of time," that awareness takes shape and removes one by one all masks, until the essential truth is left. Charlus's mask too is slowly pushed aside and the vulnerable man beneath begins to show.

Straddling precarious and contradictory alliances, Charlus is a poignant illustration of the social outcast. Intimately drawn to express his desires but wanting to compensate against his natural bent through scrupulous adherence to accepted codes, he vacillates between earnestness and bravado, humility and arrogance. He is ostensibly set upon squelching all visible marks of those female qualities in him that have wrought havoc in his life, but allows them to show through nevertheless. An exaggerated movement, an unexpected coquettishness in dressing or demeanor, become the denouncing signs of both his inadequate femaleness and his perverted maleness. He can neither proclaim his homosexuality openly, nor sublimate it, and belongs therefore among the "solitary," as the author defines them, for whom solitude is both a comfort and a cover up. When he feels pushed into the realm of Sodom, he is no more in harmony with it than with accepted norms.

And one must admit that in some of these newcomers [to Sodom] woman is not only inwardly linked to man, but hideously visible, agitated as they are by a hysterical spasm, by a shrill laugh that convulses their knees and hands, looking no

> more like average men than those monkeys with melancholy
> and shadowed eyes, with prehensile feet, who don a tuxedo and
> wear a black tie.

Charlus's mask now reveals him as a caricature of himself, no more like a man than a dressed-up monkey, displaying all the vulnerability of a woman but none of her prerogatives.

Suddenly, all that has been presented in veiled terms holds no more mystery. The incident of Charlus's meeting with Jupien discloses a language until then indistinct. From now on the Baron's mannerism, his clothes and voice, no longer act as screens but as mirrors to his nature. Against all that contrived evidence, Marcel suddenly understands, the truth is now visible, and the homosexual cannot hide forever beneath a virile façade.

> Even if—for so many possible reasons—he lives with a woman,
> he may deny that he is himself one, he may swear that he has
> never had any relation with men. But let her look at him as we
> have just shown him, lying in bed, in a pyjama, his arms bare,
> his neck bare beneath black hair: the pyjama becomes a wom-
> an's camisole, the head that of a pretty Spanish girl.

Symbolically, it is the nakedness of flesh, the arms and throat left uncovered by a pajama, that show the lie of the masculine garment. One brief moment of abandon measured against stratagems worked out over a lifetime, and the mask acquires a transparency that can never again be covered.

Reason indicates that there is no point in keeping up a pretense if it can no longer convince—unless the pretense is duplicated on the receiving end which feigns to believe. A chain of lies hence develops that resembles a social minuet, in which each side follows invisible directives of hypocrisy and gentility. Young Marcel has taken a long time to understand Charlus, but the other characters in the story have known all along. Yet it is for their benefit that the Baron has cultivated his athletic demeanor and wears dark suits. Both he and those around him thus continue to accept the illusion of his virility, as long as the unwritten script is respected and social codes are not betrayed. Marcel watches in fascination this world of make-believe, in which masks need not be either lies or symbols, but may suggest a balance between the two. Charlus wears his recognizable mask with a certain dignity and a semblance of truth. Gingerly poised upon a stage that demands fidelity to roles, he continues to command respect until he blatantly oversteps assigned boundaries.

Concessions are made on both sides. Charlus does not wear flamboy-
ant silks in public, and his influential relatives bow to his capricious predilection for, or sudden ostracism of, various people. He still reigns as a
monarch in a world that appreciates discretion. Only on the sly does he
survey the field in search of affinities among the bystanders, or of tacit
consent to unworded overtures.

> I had all the time (as he pretended to be absorbed in a simu-
> lated game of whist that allowed him not to appear to see
> people) to admire the contrived and artistic simplicity of his
> evening coat which, through mere nothings that only a dress-
> maker could notice, seemed like a Whistler's "Harmony" in
> black and white, black, white and red rather, for M. de Charlus
> was wearing, hanging from a large cordon upon the frills of his
> dress coat, the cross in white, black and red enamel of the
> Knight of the religious Order of Malta.

Marcel now unhesitantly calls Charlus's demeanor "pretended" and "sim-
ulated." The simplicity of his dressing is not a mere mark of good taste but
a "contrived" effort to appear so. The touch of red that breaks the overall
Whistlerian impression of grey is a disguised replica here of the minute
spot on his tie, earlier deemed daring. Ironically, it is through a symbol of
honor and incontestable claim to integrity (the cross of Malta) that the
Baron both hides and displays his preference for brilliant colors, that he
affirms his own beliefs while respecting the "religious order" of old.

Rigid masks were worn on stage in ancient Greece, holding each actor
to specifically assigned and stylized roles. Wood and metal gradually gave
way to more flexible material through the ages, so that coverings upon
faces could follow more natural contours and reflect rather than dictate
interpretations. The modern actor has come to rely upon his own controlled expressions to convey a sense of truth for various impersonated
characters. Charlus's function in the novel is that of an actor who is finally
recognized as such by the narrator. His costumes may vary, but only
because the setting demands it, and not in order to project actual changes.
His mask thus resembles those worn in ancient times, rather than the more
modern and flexible ones. The stare of the eyes or the lowering of his lids
are as exaggerated and conspicuous as if they were carved in brass. The
only variation in his single role is to alternate twill with silk, or an evening
coat with a loose robe. His clothing thus reflects moods and tempo within
his tragicomic role, fluctuations of desires and the pathos of unresolved
tensions.

At the Princess of Guermantes's soirée, Charlus is obviously at home. He makes guarded gestures or bestows impassive glances, he uses chastising or mellifluous words to condone the presence of one guest or disapprove that of another. M. de Vaugoubert, Marcel can now guess by the mere timbre of his voice, shares the Baron's sexual preferences, and smiles to him with unmistakable innuendoes of recognition. Charlus, "enveloped by the Countess of Molé's immense skirt," is annoyed at Vaugoubert's indiscretion. The observation about the skirt is placed in parenthesis, as an aside provided by the narrator. The resulting tableau illustrates visually what is being discussed. Marcel points to a frame within the larger context of the crowd around, which encompasses a single element—that of a man who reigns not so much as a monarch, but as a queen wrapped in cascades of cloth. Everybody can see him and recognize him for what he is, without there being, however, any infringement of decorum. The Countess of Molé next to him provides with her gown the feminine adornment that reveals Charlus as a transvestite. But she also acts as a decoy that permits his male identity to endure. Such is the tenuous balance required by the role, one that allows a recognizable mask to be publicly displayed so that identities be manifest. But no open proclamation of those identities is possible, without there being an implicit deterioration of the mask's value. When the Countess leaves, Charlus looks "totally helpless," in Saint-Loup's words, ostensibly because of his romantic attachment to the lady, but in reality because her gown had provided a needed frame, the mask that half concealed his complex truth and yet made it come to life.

In a work where events are told through the mediation of a narrator, masks can only be discerned from the perspective of that narrator. If readers have been allowed to understand the true nature of Charlus before Marcel avows his own understanding, that is only because of the multiple layers of time woven into the narrative. The faraway past that is evoked can sustain a pattern of mystery, expectation, even surprises, by being inserted into an amorphous present. There, personalities are shown not as Marcel eventually sees them, but as they appeared to him at the time. There is no drastic change anywhere, only the maturing of views with corresponding insights into the characters around. Aside from his opinions about the members of his household, who because they are familiar do not lend themselves to misconception, young Marcel's views of the rest of the world are understandably inadequate as the narrator describes them when beginning his reminiscences. That world thus appears as if it wore a mask that can be deciphered only slowly. Marcel's growth may be envisaged as the act of lifting those masks one by one, each time coming closer to the truth within. In order to recreate the mystery of old he isolates time within the confines of the past, separate from the present. There he reigns for a while suspended in his tenuous youth, before he ushers events to their appointed truth.

Once he understands that the dapper figure of Charlus is a semi-female in disguise, all new encounters with the Baron are colored by that discovery. As he waits on the platform beside the train at Doncières one day, Marcel suddenly sees the Baron advance in a grotesque imitation of his earlier images. Summer light shines mercilessly upon his undulating, quasi-deformed body that appears to be in process of disintegration. His figure seems to display the many layers that went into its composition. Truth and lie are shown meshed into one.

> In Paris, where I only met him at evening functions, immobile, tightly fitted in a black coat, kept in a vertical posture by his proud straightening up, his urge to be admired, the pyrotechnics of his conversation, I had not realized to what extent he had aged. Now, in a light-colored traveling suit that made him appear larger, as he walked swaggering, balancing a stout stomach and an almost symbolic behind, the cruelty of daylight decomposed, on his lips, into makeup, rice powder affixed with cold cream on the tip of his nose, in black on the dyed mustaches whose ebony color contrasted with his grizzled hair, all that in artificial light would have seemed the animation of coloring in someone still young.

The swagger in Charlus's walk is emphasized by his loose garment. Marcel contrasts the present suit with the "tightly fitted" ones worn at Parisian gatherings. The swaying movement of the hips puts in evidence the large stomach and pronounced buttocks. This explains the adjective "symbolic" next to "behind," pointing to the round feminine shapes thus displayed. It is the light color of the suit, Marcel remarks, that makes the Baron "appear larger," and hence accentuates the curves of his body. Charlus has taken care to put makeup on his lips and face, and to dye his moustache. The glaring light exposes his sham, much as it had done earlier. The role has not changed, but the reverse of the medal is now shown.

Marcel's first actual meeting with Charlus was in Balbec, only a little way from the Doncières station where he has now run into him. It was summertime then too, and the Baron's outfit stood out like a dark blotch against the broad daylight. Yet now the narrator explains the presence of "the light-colored traveling suit" as due to the place and time of day. The light outfit is possibly meant to suggest something quite different and to reveal the woman within Charlus. Whereas female qualities showed through the severity of his suit years before, Marcel now sees in the Baron a counterfeit man—someone who displays customary feminine attributes, as if wanting to camouflage his male identity. What he has learned during the years since he first met Charlus helps him see the transvestite in him.

Transvestitism shows "the abnormal desire to dress in the clothing of the opposite sex." Ostensibly Charlus does not dress like a woman, and he cannot be called an outright transvestite. But his clothing suggest a not altogether unconscious manner of both hiding and revealing his homosexual identity—so that male characteristics show through when he is enfolded in the Countess of Molé's gown, and an undulating female impression issues from his loose fitting summer coat. Clothes fulfill for him functions dictated by inner needs, and since they often project his feminine characteristics they define him to a degree as a transvestite. If the Baron's obstinate wearing of dark suits in the first part of the narrative denotes his concerted effort to appear virile, one may by inference conclude that his donning a light-colored outfit now intentionally manifests an opposite desire. He wants to look like a woman, to use dye, powder, and cold cream, to put on loose fitting clothes that highlight the oscillating motion of his walk. If Charlus's role forbids him to put on an unmistakable feminine attire, he can imitate it, and achieve thereby all the approximate values and shortcomings inherent in the miming of truth. His costume cannot be completely faithful to his intent, except on a symbolic basis. Its power thus emerges from its ability to suggest, if not to portray, the woman within him.

The narrator claims that feminine qualities are not merely acquired but inherent characteristics in the homosexual's nature. Hence it is that these are manifest above all when homosexuals are completely relaxed, away from social scrutiny, or when emotions become a directing force. The first time Marcel clearly remembers thinking of Charlus as being feminine is when he catches him unawares near the home of Madame de Villeparisis. Soon after, when Jupien arrives on the scene, a kind of ritualistic dance between the two, enacted before Marcel's eyes, explains the Baron's nature. It also becomes gradually evident that the narrator's intent is to establish that Charlus's disguise has maintained an uninterrupted correspondence with the female nature that had transpired. Once this is recognized, the eye naturally selects those details and mannerisms that corroborate the hypothesis. With Marcel's discovery of Charlus's disguised truth, something that was poorly understood until then suddenly emerges with unambiguous clarity.

> It is all fidgeting, with affectation and the same amplitude with which the wrapping into petticoats would have widened and checked his swinging gate, that he advanced toward Madame Verdurin.

The sweeping of a nonexistent petticoat here is in keeping with Charlus's image of himself and with his projection of that image upon the bystanders. It is the *grande dame* who advances, whose gracious steps bring her to the attention of the guests around. For there is, among the guests, someone whom he wants to impress. The Baron is only guided by his emotions here and by his desire to be seductive in front of Morel. The narrator's eye has been unsealed. He now sees what his imagination alone can supply, and knows that the "fidgeting" and the "amplitude" in Charlus's movements are dictated by an evoked presence of the wide petticoats he might elect to wear if left to his taste. Severe suits and light petticoats reflect simultaneously Charlus's social and personal realities. He lives in the constant contradiction of intent and result, in which his efforts to be casual about a subject of obsessive importance for him often become an instrument that reinforces the doubts of his listeners. He knows that he is a homosexual, and he also knows that his entire awareness of himself and of the world around him is modified by that knowledge. Hence the mask he seems to wear is actually a reflection of that truth. He appears with the swinging motion of his hips, as if he were imitating a lady, but that imitation projects his true identity. The petticoats can thus be considered as no more imagined than that identity, since they are as deeply felt and experienced.

V. TECHNIQUES OF PRESENTATION

Marcel's recollections show, more than transformations, differing perspectives. Life does not stand still, emphases do switch with the passing of years; modes, manners, and traditions are altered. But the slow movement that ushers in one epoch after another can hardly account for the complete metamorphosis of most of the characters in the novel. Those dramatic changes reflect the narrator's own evolution from the dormant and idealized reveries of early youth to a gradual awakening. The world that is initially captured is that of a boy who, from a secure position within the confines of his family, looks out and recognizes the shapes of his expectations, dreams, and fears. Slowly, he emerges from the protective shade of his home and advances as if in growing daylight, toward the world on the outside. The magic lantern of his reveries had revealed the surface of things, the masks that gave reason to his dreads and his hopes alike. Out in the open, the opacity of his room vanishes. He approaches all familiar shapes from one side and then another, and records what he sees. He senses the mystery that each being contains, and comes closer in order to see more clearly. Silhouettes begin to reveal traits that were indiscernible from afar. His eye lingers on one and then the other, before he starts to reassemble them in a new and complex whole. The mystery disappears, replaced by another enticement, which is that of a personal truth. Each facet there contains its own mirror and the reflection of what lies behind.

Marcel's presentation of Charlus's clothes follows his understanding of the man. The vague outline he first caught sight of in his twill suit, in the Tansonville garden, acquires, in the space of a few years, features that he could not have seen initially. As he draws closer, Marcel observes the Baron from all angles. When he comes full face again, all sides and surface variations have been revealed to him. But as the perspective of his diagnosing eye changes each time he switches position, so does the technique of presentation. Mary Ann Caws's discussion of what she calls "the outlook and the inscape" may be applied here. "It is as if the outlook were first a specific location for the vision, like a lookout point on a scenic highway, and then a perspective adopted" she says. And she adds that the person seeing or the poet recounting "is where he sees from, and he is his judgment." In the early sections of *Remembrance*, the reader understands far more than the narrator is ready to admit about Charlus's nature, but still less than the other characters. Readers stand at a vantage point from which it is possible to observe the boy and what he is looking at, but without yet as much access to the world of *Remembrance* as the characters who compose it. As Marcel advances into that world, he catches up with his readers, and gradually reverses the procedure used in the interpreting of signs. He learns more and more, and in sharing his learning he establishes a certain complicity with his readers. Together, they alone fully understand the recondite maneuvers of the characters, each of whom remains a prisoner of his own myopic vision.

When Charlus comes to the Verdurins wearing a light suit and swinging his hips, the reader is not surprised, for the various sections that comprise the evocation have all been shown previously. But each had revealed only a segment of the whole, while now they are brought together in full view. A man, somewhat different from and still very much like all the portraits that have been sketched, is revealed. He is at the same time the Baron of the Parisian salons conscious of his prestigious position, and the effeminate dandy who eyes a conquest and enacts a pantomime of seduction. Marcel and the readers are aware of both his masking of the truth and of the truth that shows through the mask, while the rest of the bystanders are either baffled by what they cannot understand, or see in Charlus a reflection of their own preconceived notions. "The testifying of the senses is also an operation of the mind where conviction creates evidence." Everyone "sees," but optics are dictated by focusing angles. The same man thus projects different images for each viewer, but each image is a partial lie or an incomplete truth for all except the narrator and the reader.

The relatively short span of time that has gone by from *The Budding Grove* to *The Captive* has not truly brought about a metamorphosis in Charlus's behavior. A combination of chance encounters and a more mature understanding on the part of Marcel are responsible for an increasingly clear manifestation of the Baron's tastes. The outfits he wears appear to the narrator as explicit denunciations of those tastes. He remarks that "M. de Charlus used to wear at this time—for he was changing very much—very light trousers recognizable a mile off." The reason the Baron is now wearing clothes he would until recently have shunned is that "he was changing very much." Yet he is still quick to take offence at the slightest innuendo about his mores. It is thus hard to believe that, though in the recent past he wore dark suits in order to camouflage his tastes, he now dons colorful apparel as if in open declaration of his homosexuality. The reader can only conclude that it is Marcel who now notices what was previously invisible to him. It must have been his blind acceptance of the nobleman's reputation for severe probity that had impressed upon his memory images of a Charlus always in black. When knowledge of his true nature supersedes that reputation in his mind, the "testifying of the senses," in his own words, then seeks the needed evidence.

When Marcel was still looking for explanations of all the apparent contradictions, emphasis rested on the psychology of Charlus. Since his clothes were part of a mask, the search was directed toward the unrevealed facets of the wearer's personality. When that becomes clear, the focus is shifted. The view is now broader and it embraces, together with the figure of the Baron, other people around him. The analysis of the central figure's psychology is not abandoned, but it appears reduced in scope and is only indirectly considered. To illustrate this, one might look at a vividly painted scene, that is recorded only at second-hand by Marcel. He allows someone else to speak, so that images may contain another's point of view. The direct witness in this case is the butler, whose interest in Charlus's psychology is minimal, and whose understanding of what he sees rests on notions that both narrator and reader know to be false. He tells of having seen the Baron and makes casual comments that are reflective of general views rather than personal observation.

> Surely Baron de Charlus must have caught some disease to stay such a long time in a public urinal. That's what comes from being an old pursuer of women. He wears the pants of one [of a womanizer]. This morning Madame sent me out for an errand at Neuilly. I saw Baron de Charlus go in at the urinal of Rue de Bourgogne. Coming back from Neuilly, a full hour later, I saw his yellow trousers at the same urinal, in the same place, in the middle, where he always goes so as not to be seen.

Optics are colored by assumptions—or, in popular diction, by the lens one wears. Marcel's narrative at this point is doubly subtle, for, rather than tackling directly the butler's mistaken analysis of the situation, he introduces the incident here recounted with a linguistic disquisition on the misconception of sounds. He indicates that, no matter how many times the butler may have heard the word "urinal" pronounced correctly, having once seized a wrong version of it, he continues to hear it and to repeat it incorrectly. (The butler hears the word *pistière* instead of *pissotière*.) The veracity of sensory perception is hence challenged, for it too is manipulated by the mind. Just as sounds continue to be fitted within familiar and preferred structures in spite of all evidence to the contrary, as is clearly implied by the narrator, so do images of people, once their reputation has been blindly accepted, retain for many their initial cast.

A full understanding of the Baron's disguise encompasses three levels: First, there is what strikes the eye, a surface deprived of depth and interpretation—such as was suggested by the original twill suit. Second, there is what lies beneath, and hence involves the psychology of the wearer—as was illustrated by the deep black pants with the thin green lines. Third, there is an overlay imposed from the outside mirroring the notions and attitudes of onlookers—as they now appear through the butler's reference to the yellow trousers. All three levels now appear simultaneously. The resulting complexity of view allows Charlus to emerge as no longer fragmented—the athletic dandy, the haughty nobleman, or the glaring homosexual—but as a whole.

The yellow pants in the passage just quoted become the vehicle for expressing a prismatic point of view. Charlus approaches the *vespasienne* somewhat furtively, but the striking color of his trousers catches the butler's eye. One hour later those same pants are noticed again, in the same spot, showing beneath the elevated surface of the urinal's wall. The clear implication is, of course, that a more conservative shade would not have been noticed, let alone recognized, after an hour's lapse. Since the general assumption is that the Baron is a womanizer, the butler concludes that he must have caught some disease in the pursuit of his vice. The bright pants serve the dual purpose of denouncing Charlus's presence where secrecy is sought, and of bolstering with their fulgent tint his presumed addiction to women and resulting complications. The trousers are perceived from a position where social view and personal intent are on the same plane. More specifically, the social Charlus with his surface mask, and the butler with his superficial assumptions, stand on the same level. Within that limited perspective, the yellow pants are the symbol of an assumed role, which is that of a ladies' man. But where notions of sportive virility had dominated Charlus's earlier social images, an element of depravity is now insinuated, with the allusion to some venereal disease that he must have caught. With the readjusting of emphasis, the mask has acquired some of the characteristics of truth, and a vitality not controllable by the intention to misguide.

Such is the scene that emerges from the butler's point of view. The color of the pants is interpreted in keeping with preconceived notions, and the Baron's resulting deviousness is exposed accordingly. If Charlus could have defended himself against the butler's accusation of being contaminated by some sexual illness, he would have probably done so only half-heartedly. He would have feared far more a suggestion of irregularity in his sexual preferences. Marcel, however, enjoys a deeper understanding of events. He can see the multiple layers where masks have the role of hiding and of revealing the elements they shelter. The narrator reconstructs the scene allowing the butler's perspective to emerge, but implicitly adding to it his own. The yellow pants do not represent the tastes of a man who runs after women, it is intimated, but those of an effeminate man in search of male conquest.

The butler's remarks evoke a scene that was visually perceived. The details are placed within an objective frame of reference, with verifiable dimensions of time, place, shape, color. The resulting image is in harmony with what Marcel has retained of Charlus during the earlier Balbec days, resting on a hypothesis of aggressive manhood. But objectivity is not easily verifiable, and the two images (the butler's and Marcel's earlier one) coincide in intrinsic aspects. Bright yellow has replaced severe black, yet the two contrasting tints are given equal weight. A similar conclusion as to Charlus's presumed virility is reached from diametrically opposite sides. The reader's understanding, however, is that since all these apparels are masks, their language is symbolic. When perspectives change, so do analyses and interpretations. The narrator can now convey a picture in which decadence and corruption have invaded the realm of a previously robust vitality, without betraying individual premises and contrasting optics. Both he and the butler are thus able to see Charlus as a pathetic man in hiding, given away by the color of his pants.

VI. THE SEARCH FOR TIME AND TRUTH

Since all truth is of a subjective nature in the Proustian world, it follows that the demarcation line between appearances and reality is nonexistent. What appears to be, is. But truth must be indivisible, and appearances cannot therefore be splintered and still convey a sense of accuracy. Yet the preceding discussion has pointed to the various levels of understanding and contrasting optics. The problem for the reader is how to reconcile the evident multiplicity of views with the single and all-inclusive vision of the narrator, and how to allow the latter to be personal (and hence limited) without depriving him of the extended optics that other people may provide. The solution is found in part through a shift in the narrator's focus allowing him, through the dimension of time, to look at objects from different angles. Those angles include other characters' perspectives assimilated within Marcel's field of perception. But that is not all. Time does not operate on a single level, and the narrator's eye is not alone in being affected. The object of perception itself must be transmuted, through a slow wearing off of certain elements and the buttressing of others. The movement is fluid, with the narrator's understanding swayed by outside events, and events molded by his apprehending eye.

The narrator's assumption that truth excludes lies and vice-versa (that masks are hence a cover up for some integral truth beneath) must also be placed within the scope of a personal vision. Broad as that vision may be, it must arrive at some cohesive understanding. Marcel notices an increased display of revelatory signs in Charlus, where the latter's attention to all details had earlier protected the secrecy of his sexual habits. His growing awareness within the passing of time is always implied and lies at the heart of the narrative. But the presentation underscores the importance of sensory rather than psychological perception. Hence the change appears to be almost exclusively on Charlus's side.

> Had M. de Charlus contracted during the burning trips from Doncières to Deauville the dangerous habit to relax and, just as he pushed back his straw hat to cool off his enormous forehead, to unfasten, at the beginning only for a few moments, the mask that for too long had rigorously been attached to his real face?

Marcel's consideration here implies a definite distinction between a natural and a superimposed expression. The hat in the passage quoted, symbol of the screen Charlus has for so many years interposed between himself and any outside scrutiny, is lifted a little. Fatigue, after the sustained effort of a lifetime, relaxes the Baron's grip upon the effeminate features he has sought to hide. At the Verdurins where he displays his predilection for Morel and teases people with a daring manner of speech unnoticed before, his behavior becomes shocking. Still, what is attributed mainly to Charlus's diminishing care for appearances, must be measured through the narrator's deepened awareness and the changed condition of the Baron's social circle. The great salons with the rarefied atmosphere of nobility have until now helped him shelter his secret, in tacit acquiescence with his transparent lies. But the new surroundings, composed essentially of vulgar *nouveaux riches,* will not allow any overt challenge to go unpunished. There, the overwhelming obsession is to arrive at the worldly peak the Baron has ostensibly relinquished. A new set of rules must be respected. Charlus is not flexible enough to accommodate to the needs of the moment. Amidst the unaccustomed ways of the Verdurin crowd, he appears naked to the unforgiving eye. The distinction is thus not simply between his real and unreal features, for the same truth that now becomes evident had been suggested earlier. But then the world around him had helped by accepting his feigned reality.

Masks are powerless to convey meanings without receptivity from the outside. It is a matter of accepting a sign while rejecting another, of bowing to a certain extent to the prescribed rules of a social condition.

> In reality—and this is what all that fuss from within revealed— there was between the severe Charlus dressed all in black, with his hair in a crew cut, whom I had known, and the young men with makeup, laden with jewelry, only that purely imaginary difference that exists between an agitated person who talks too

fast, moves all the time, and the neuropath who talks slowly, keeps his eternal phlegm, but is affected by the same neurasthenia in the eye of the clinician who knows that this one, like the other, is devoured by the same anguish and hit by the same flaw.

The narrator points to the fallacious surface of things. By conforming to accepted notions, these often do little more than deny the very premise upon which they stand. Charlus's dark outfits conveyed images of respectability that were in keeping with the associations society itself had conferred upon such garbs. His too rigorous adherence to these conventions, however, revealed the Baron's fear that if the slightest exception were to be made the whole structure might disintegrate. But the sensitive eye could easily have read in the severe suits the same revelatory signs as those conveyed by garish outfits. The only difference is that the latter follow to the letter what popular belief has assigned to homosexual taste, while the others echo a more subtle language. They are both masks to the degree that they are in harmony with recognizable patterns of interpretation. Through either mask, psychological truths become evident in contrast with (rather than adherence to) purported meanings.

The truth of all this sign-play rests on the tenuous balance between reality and appearance, and on the oscillatory movement of the eye focussing on one aspect or the other. The Guermantes were eager to accept certain signs as most revealing of Charlus's personality, the Verdurin clan does not share their concern to protect his name. Essentially, the two worlds operate on a similar basis of self-interest with slight variations in emphasis. Only a glaring disavowal of their respective idea of decorum—or an affront to their vanity—will tip the balance against the culprit. Charlus's continued identification with the Guermantes's ways thus elicits a certain loyalty from the Guermantes, while it makes him suspect in the eyes of the Verdurins. Added to this, there is the normal wear and tear of time, which alters both the perspective and the object focussed upon. The result thus appears as a new image, emerging from the change of surroundings (the passage from the Guermantes to the Verdurins), the more alert eye of the narrator, and Charlus's own relaxation of his unbending social mien. These compounded elements force the attention upon the significance of yellow rather than black pants, and of the Baron's sweeping gestures where rigid attitudes had dominated.

Critics have long been dissatisfied with the poetic but unfaithful translation of the Proustian title as "remembrance" of things past. Proust's choice of the word "search" (*à la recherche*) emphasizes the struggle of the protagonist to pierce the mystery of time and the anguish that accompanies it. That mystery is akin to every individual's hidden vitality, the coalescence of thoughts, feelings, palpitations at the core of existence. All that breathes operates within the dimension of time. Hence the search for the definition of each entity in the limited span of a lifetime. Correspondingly, if an individual's secret being cannot be reached, neither can the essence of time, which is the repository of that secret. Thus the word "search" rather than "remembrance." That search is imbued with tension, for every step forward in the unravelling of life's mystery uncovers what lies ahead. Still, each step comes a bit closer to some sought for verity.

As the narrator's eye seeks out details in Charlus's hidden mechanism, the Baron's armor is correspondingly penetrated. In the optics of clothes, the first step that brings one closer to the Baron's nature has transmuted dark cloth into colorful substance. Symbolically, the light tints become the instrument for divulging secrets previously wrapped in shadow. A second step, removing yet another layer of Charlus's protective mantle, brings into focus not so much the clothes he wears, as the act of taking them off.

> M. de Charlus unbuttoned his overcoat, took off his hat; I saw that the top of his head was greying in spots.... M. de Charlus was about to give his coat with the instructions of a familiar guest. But the footman to whom he was handing it was a new one, quite young.

The above quotation points to what may be seen as an act of disrobing, which coincides with the soirée in which Charlus falls from grace. Marcel may well assert the fact that "the face of M. de Charlus continued to keep quiet for practically everybody what to me appeared to cry out." The fact is that "practically everybody" is aware of the Baron's sexual mores and is prepared to go along with his comedy of pretenses, just so long as it proves worth one's while. When Madame Verdurin no longer sees any advantage, and suspects there may be a distinct disadvantage, in welcoming him amidst the faithful in her clan, she begins to find intolerable his predilection for young men. It is then that she dismisses him, brutally plunging him into the indignity of the moral disobedience that has been haunting him all along. The relevance of a black or yellow garb is of no consequence now. The value of both masks is invalidated by Madame Verdurin's refusal to acquiesce to either of them. Coat and hat, which had symbolically protected Charlus's vulnerable nature, are now removed. One assumes they are dark here since this is a formal reception, but the color remains undisclosed for it no longer plays any role.

Students of Proust have been fascinated by the integration of spatial/temporal elements throughout the saga novel. Marcel's time resides outside the grasp of calendars, it remains blended with space. How many years have gone by since he saw Charlus at Balbec? Not many, presumably. Yet the youthful Baron of those years now looks old. As he takes off coat and hat, the distance that separates him from the early figure in the thinly striped pants is marked by the grey in his hair. Marcel notices that as he hands over his overcoat he becomes visibly intrigued by the young footman. But Charlus's suddenly arrested attention here is not different from the pantomime enacted at the sight of young Marcel. The narrator's increased consciousness makes him perceive what was earlier shielded by his innocence. He can now detect pathetic contrasts in the Baron where only irritating inconsistencies had appeared. Charlus's act of abandoning his coat is associated in Marcel's mind with fatigue and age. The handing over of hat and overcoat subtly infers the forsaking of a mask—for, as the Baron lets go of the outer wrap, the old man coveting the young blatantly shows through. The relation of one act to the other resides in the composition of the text, and is verified by Marcel in a visual manner. The first set of assertions ("... took off his hat; I saw that the top of his head was greying ...") brings together, with the insertion of the semicolon, two actions of which the second appears as the result of the first. The lifting of the hat becomes the visual means for showing the aging of the Baron. The other set of actions is ostensibly separated by a period ("... a familiar guest. But the footman ...."). Yet the initial "But" of the second sentence bridges all supposed gaps, and assimilates the familiar act of surrendering a coat to one equally familiar of greedily eyeing a young ephebe.

VII. TIME RECAPTURED

Such are the ways of perception, and such are Charlus's masks. What Roland Barthes calls the element of surprise, dictated by an initial false steering in the understanding of all the characters of *Remembrance*, is in reality a gradual and consistent unraveling of truths only vaguely sensed at the start. The "inversion" of which Barthes speaks (evident in the presentation of people both in their psychological nature and, ultimately, in their sexual behavior) is not necessarily calculated to misdirecting readers as to surprising them. It is meant to instruct them on the danger of preconceived notions where personal entities are concerned. First impressions hold the

key to further discoveries and act as a challenge to solve enigmas that are
barely sensed. In looking back, one sees that the lady in pink is quite
reconcilable with the subsequent and seemingly contradictory images of
Odette; that the dark-suited man staring at a boy on a street in Balbec is
the very same as, and explained by, the mimic of the gentleman in yellow
pants; and that the girl in the polo hat announces all the mystery of the
enticing young lady later seen in her Fortuny gowns. From the first, each
of these figures suggests its true essence, even if their entity is too complex
to be immediately comprehended. Each of them has, at first sight, suggested the presence of masks symbolically worn over their countenance.
Only time helps transmit the significance of those masks, and offsets what
has intruded upon the immediate first impression through a process of
reasoning. Understanding is linked with the element of time, and can only
be grasped through time. Reputations, or what people say about someone
should not mislead the reader. On the contrary, words are measured
against the verity of sensory understandings. Hence the importance of
clothes in Marcel's world, on a scale with that of voices and the prominence accorded to eyes, in revealing the characters' complex truths.

Charlus's words had always been in disagreement with his actions, at
least to all appearances. Suffice it here to remember the baffling scene in
which every detail in the room was arranged in the hope of winning
Marcel's favor, while invectives were unceremoniously hurled at him. The
reader knew then that what was said had no real importance when
measured against the Baron's reclining position and the sheen of his silk
robe. Later, the narrator understands that protested innocence does not
necessarily imply guilt, but it expresses resistance and, at the same time,
surrender to temptations. When Charlus assures Marcel of his loyalty to
Morel, for instance, and still cannot restrain his hand from fondling the
young man, Marcel knows that actions and words merely appear to be
contradictory. A case in point may be cited when Brichot is to fetch the
narrator's coat and brings instead that of Charlus—who has been expressing his gratitude to the young man for having spurned his advances in the
past.

> "What is going on? it's my overcoat that he brings," he said in
> seeing that Brichot had been searching so long to attain such a
> result. "I would have done better to go myself. Anyway you are
> going to put it on your shoulders. Do you know that it is
> highly compromising, my dear? it is like drinking from the
> same glass, I shall know your thoughts. But no, not like that,

come, let me do it"; and while putting the coat on me he
pressed it against my shoulders, drew it up along my neck,
pulled up the collar, and with his hand he brushed my chin,
apologizing. "At his age, this thing does not know how to
cover himself, one must coddle him; I missed my vocation,
Brichot, I was born to be a nursemaid."

The coat that was surrendered at the beginning of the Verdurins's party is
now adjusted on Marcel's shoulders with a mixture of contained lust and
tenderness. The same item of clothing that contributed to exposing Charlus's
weakness when removed (and one recalls that this is the time when he is
publicly chastised) reinforces the impression of nakedness he has conveyed.
But another element is added to it.

The kindness that has often been mentioned in connection with Charlus,
but which was just as often belied by the sharpness of his verbiage, finally
shows through. His act of patting the young man here does not merely
denounce the incorrigible reprobate in him, but allows a degree of tenderness to show through—a quality, one realizes, that has been camouflaged
more systematically than his sexual preferences. Words and acts have
followed a circuitous path in opposite directions, but are brought together
at the end. The vaunted gentleness of the Baron is finally communicated to
readers in the only possible manner consistent with the work as a whole,
visually. What one now sees is the young Marcel wrapped in the large coat
of old Charlus, who coddles and comforts him. In relinquishing his mask,
he exposes his weakness beyond the fact of being a homosexual. He shows
his vulnerability through sentiment. As he pats the cloak that protects the
young man, he is more like an old mother caressing a frail and hurt child
(and Marcel is suffering deeply at this point) than like an old lecher
incapable of holding vice in check. It is true that his protestations as to his
avocation as nursemaid make one smile, in view of the lingering pressure
of his hand upon the boy's collar and neck. But that is due more to the
reader's rational diffidence than to natural reaction. Simultaneously, readers can hardly be blamed for being a little skeptical in hearing his salacious
innuendoes on the "compromising" situation through the shared intimacy
of an overcoat. Words and actions cannot be separated, for they find in
each other a resonance of truth. Visually, the overcoat protectively laid on
Marcel's shoulders illustrates the tension at the basis of that truth.

One may wonder at this point if the definition of masks as elements
meant to mislead is at all justifiable. Their existence is time and place
bound, and dependent on conventions. Any imbalance brought to the

interdependent forces upon which they rest, dismantles their architecture and bares pretenses. Charlus's mask can only be seen as an expression of his inner weakness; its efficacy depends upon the acquiescence of those around him for survival. The problem is compounded by the fact that he himself is time and place bound, an heir both to his generation and to the values of his caste. His mask falls when sympathy is denied, vanquished by the world in transition to which he cannot adapt. "They had caught and hit him suddenly at the moment when he was without arms." His affection for Morel has made him vulnerable to attack; the fact that he is not receptive to the needs of a climbing bourgeoisie has turned him into a victim of its resentment. The Verdurins pounce on him—not because he has changed, as Marcel implied, but because he has not changed, caught in the double vise of his aged body and yet immutable longings. Sadly, sensing perhaps that he would soon be deprived of his protective social mantle, he laments:

> But there is no more society, there are no more rules, no more decency, not any more for conversation than there are for dressing. Ah! it's the end of the world.

The world in which a delicate balance of gentility and equivocation has held sway for years is crumbling. The ephemeral stance of a moribund aristocracy is subverted by the interests of *nouveaux riches*. Charlus lacks the strength either to restrain himself from crossing the new boundaries, or to adapt his manners to them. Dress codes too have changed in this society of Philistines, and he has not learned the rules.

The author's repeated allusions to Charlus's masks are a technique of presentation. The element of "surprise" alluded to by Barthes is a device to expose the multiple layers of a character's personality. There are, indeed, no surprises. What may appear as change is only an oscillation caught within the pendulum of time. The subtle synchronization of traits to the process of aging through time, points to yet another aspect of truth. Physical deterioration and the ensuing grotesqueness in Charlus's appearance are fruits of his spiritual decline and impoverishment of will. Age is a mirror of his unvanquished passions, and not the element responsible for the visible ruin of his personality. Time itself is not to be taken literally. The Bergsonian sense of "duration" is the element that contributes to the decaying of a construction, and allows the skeleton underneath to show through. What is at stake is no more the Baron's aging than that of the narrator—no more the dropping of masks than the shrinking of illusions. The "given" upon which youth rests—the orderly world of Combray and the promises perceived in the expanse of sun and sea at Balbec—crumble, as Marcel comes ever closer to the mysterious existence beyond the periphery of friends and family. There, Charlus's upright posture and nobility emerge as the fabric laid over his all too human flesh, while clothing itself begins to adhere to his skin.

Marcel can now summarily dismiss Charlus's endeavor to avoid wearing light ties as representing a concession to some presumed criteria of seriousness. The Baron's effort to show manliness is more pathetic than Saint-Loup's rush to patriotic militarism. But desultory attitudes are visually transmitted in the choice of clothing. The message is quite clear, whether the ties be light or dark. "The dialectic of cloth and body is the secret of Greek art," writes Anne Hollander, "as it may have been the key to Greek gesture and manners; and in those works of art in which no drapery appears, its absence is expressive." From time immemorial, ornaments have been used as a system of communication both ethical and aesthetic, based on conventions, but projecting personalities and individual expressions. Hence, an intuitive perception of truth may arise from the tensions or the harmony established between the wearer and his clothing—or even between the person and the absence of clothing.

The narrator has steered the reader to *Time Recaptured,* where his search becomes momentarily suspended, reconciled with the full acceptance of human frailty—before it can be renewed in the flux of time and joined to a new beginning in the mystical presence of Combray. In the limbo of declining illusions, life emerges as a series of grotesque parodies, with loves, joys, and desires appearing as macabre dances where dreams of old are unrecognizable.

> Walking behind two Zouaves who paid no attention to him, I saw a tall stout man, with a soft felt hat, a long greatcoat, and on whose purple face I hesitated if I should place the name of an actor or of a painter equally known for innumerable sodomist scandals.

A soft felt hat has replaced the rigid sheen of a top hat, a long overcoat the dapper pelisse of old. A general feeling of sluggishness prevails, as the now shapeless body of the Baron ambles unrestrainedly after young soldiers. The long coat seems inadequate to cover the large frame, the flabbiness of the felt hat can no longer simulate an upright posture. It is as if the abundance of flesh had finally put all spirit to rest, and were now ready to burst in scandalous display beyond the dignity imposed by cloth. One guesses a lamentable nudity that coat and hat can no longer protect. The next step will thrust all clothing aside and reveal a wounded flesh whose only coverings are blood and welts.

As the reader approaches what may well be one of the most audacious scenes in the whole of *Remembrance,* masks seem suddenly dropped and all pretences abandoned. It is only an illusion. Masks have by now adhered to the very traits that were to be covered, and have been permeated by the vulnerability they were supposed to shelter. In the homosexual house of prostitution, even Marcel's meager justification for voyeurism appears irrelevant as, unseen, he witnesses a show of masochistic brutality.

> Tiptoeing in the darkness, I crept to the round window and there, chained upon a bed like Prometheus to his rock, receiving from a cat-o'-nine-tails studded, in fact, with nails, lashes administered by Maurice, I saw, already all bloody, and covered with ecchymoses that showed that the torture was not taking place for the first time, I saw before me M. de Charlus.

The sense of revulsion that the prostrate figure elicits is mitigated by the pity it inspires. Truth seems finally revealed, with its core of suffering that no dress can hide. And yet that truth is insidiously associated with the initial dark suit, like the reverse side of a same medal. The Maurice who wields a murderous whip is only a poor devil earning his keep, and Charlus's moans are part of a chosen script where pain and pleasure are inseparable. The only difference is that bloody weals have now replaced all other clothing, while chains simulate the rigid exterior of old. But the same masks are present, coverings in which lies and truth are blended, for they follow the devious dictates of a man's endless search for identity.

Fittingly, the last sight of M. de Charlus at the large reception at the end, points simultaneously to his flimsy covering and pathetic nudity. Age is revealed as another facet of the masks worn in a lifetime. Knowing observers—the narrator and the readers—perceive all the elements that have gone into this final image, and may dissect virtues and vices. The large flabby man they see appears as someone who ought to be immune to the dictates of the flesh. On the road where Marcel meets him led by Jupien, he wears a straw hat, as if to cover the ravages of passions with a residue of youthful decorum. "But beneath his straw hat a forest of untamed hair entirely white showed through." The hat shields no secret. As a mask, it is still a mere symbol easily decoded by those who have learned its meaning. Charlus's untamed urges show through, undiminished by the white in his hair. At the party itself—where Guermantes with ancestral lineage mingle with newly arrived climbers so disdained in the past—Charlus meekly bows to the Pharisees of old and uncovers his head.

> And immediately, with infinite care and all the endeavor of a
> sick man who wants to show himself capable of all movements
> still difficult for him, M. de Charlus uncovered his head, bowed,
> and greeted Madame de Sainte-Euverte with the same respect as
> if she had been the Queen of France.

The lifting of the hat expresses here a primordial sense of humility, not unlike the fustigations Charlus received when chained upon a bed. In both instances, surrender not devoid of pleasure is evident. Where blood and bruises had reflected the Baron's misery, "torrents of silver hair" now show his vulnerability. A cavalcade of masks emerges in retrospect in these final pages of *Remembrance*. But masks are exposed for what they truly are, mutable and elusive entities perceived in all their complexity. Captured for a brief moment in the readers' collective memory, they can soon resume their cyclical variations—back in Combray, in Swann's world, and in the world of Sodom and Gomorrah.

Chronology

1871   Marcel Proust is born on July 10 in Auteuil to Doctor Adrien Proust, the son of a grocer from Illiers, and Jeanne Weil Proust, the daughter of a wealthy Jewish stockbroker. The family lives in Paris and spends summers in Illiers.

1873   On May 24 Robert Proust, Marcel Proust's younger brother, is born.

1879   Proust plays with Marie and Nelly Benardaky in the Champs Elysées. Marie is presumably an early model for Gilberte.

1880   Proust has his first asthma attack.

1882–89   At the Lycée Condorcet, Proust studies with the philosopher Alphonse Darlu, who has a profound and permanent influence on him. He begins visiting the fashionable salon of Mme. Straus, the mother of one of his schoolfellows. He also makes the acquaintance of Laure Hayman, a celebrated courtesan, who probably contributed much to Proust's portrait of Odette.

1889–90   Proust joins the army and is sent for his year of military service to Orléans, where he meets Robert de Billy, who is probably the model for aspects of Robert de Saint-Loup. He also meets Anatole France in a fashionable salon.

1893   Proust meets Robert de Montesquiou, who sees that Proust is invited to the most exclusive salons. Montesquiou also suggests to him many aspects of the Baron de Charlus. In the fall, Proust receives a law degree from the Ecole libre des sciences politiques.

1895   Proust receives a degree in literature and is hired by the Bibliothèque Mazarine, but leaves immediately in order to travel with the composer Reynaldo Hahn.

1895–99   Proust works on *Jean Santeuil*, which is not published until 1952, well after the author's death. Usually considered an initial draft of *A la recherche du temps perdu*, *Jean Santeuil* is, however, more directly autobiographical.

1896   Proust publishes *Les Plaisirs et les jours*, a collection of prose pieces mostly written between 1892 and 1893. The book is illustrated by Madeleine Lemaire and introduced by Anatole France.

1898   During the Dreyfus Affair, Proust's passionate support of Dreyfus puts a strain on many of his relationships in society.

1899   Proust begins translating Ruskin. His English is very poor but his mother, anxious that he commit himself to his literary work, helps him. Proust's asthmatic condition has worsened considerably.

1900   Proust travels to Venice with his mother in May; he takes another trip there in October.

1902   After traveling around France for most of the year, Proust visits Holland.

1903   Proust's father dies on November 26.

1904   Proust publishes his translation of Ruskin's *Bible of Amiens*.

1905   Proust's mother dies on September 26.

1905–6   Proust spends six months in a sanatorium. He continues to translate Ruskin. He moves to 102 boulevard Haussmann in Paris.

1907   Proust travels by car through Normandy. Alfred Agostinelli, who was in many respects Proust's model for Albertine, is his chauffeur.

1908   Proust begins some sketches for *A la recherche du temps perdu*, and starts working on *Contre Sainte-Beuve*.

1909–10   Proust finishes *Contre Sainte-Beuve* but has trouble finding a publisher. In 1910, he has the walls of his bedroom lined with cork for soundproofing.

1913   Bernard Grasset agrees to publish Proust's novel, which he has been writing almost continuously since 1908, at the author's expense. *Du côté de chez Swann* appears on November 13. In November, Alfred Agostinelli leaves Proust to go to the Côte d'Azur. The "fugitive" takes up aviation and dies in a plane crash on May 30, 1914.

1914–19 Proust leads a secluded existence and works on his novel. The Nouvelle Revue Française has taken over the publishing of Proust's work, and produces *A l'ombre des jeunes filles en fleurs* in November 1918. This volume receives the Prix Goncourt in December 1919, when the N.R.F. also publishes *Pastiches et mélanges*. Proust is forced to move out of his apartment; he moves to 44 rue Hamelin.

1920 *Du Côté de Guermantes I, Du Côté de Guermantes II*, and *Sodome et Gomorrhe I* are published by the N.R.F.

1922 *Sodome et Gomorrhe II* is published. On November 18 Proust dies of pneumonia.

1923 *La Prisonnière* is published.

1925 *Albertine disparue* is published.

1927 *Le Temps retrouvé* is published.

Contributors

HAROLD BLOOM, Sterling Professor of the Humanities at Yale University, is the author of *The Anxiety of Influence, Poetry and Repression,* and many other volumes of literary criticism. His forthcoming study, *Freud: Transference and Authority,* attempts a full-scale reading of all of Freud's major writings. A MacArthur Prize Fellow, he is general editor of five series of literary criticism published by Chelsea House.

SAMUEL BECKETT was an Irish poet, playwright, and literary critic. He is best known as the author of *Waiting for Godot, Endgame,* and the Malone trilogy.

WALTER BENJAMIN was a journalist and literary critic, and the author of *The Origins of German Tragic Drama, Charles Baudelaire,* and two collections of essays, *Illuminations* and *Reflections.*

GERMAINE BRÉE written extensively on Proust, Albert Camus, and André Gide. She teaches at Wake Forest University.

RENÉ GIRARD is University Professor of the Humanities at Stanford University. His books include *Mensonge romantique et vérité romanesque,* *(Deceit, Desire and the Novel)* and *La violence and le sacré,* *(Violence and the Sacred).*

HOWARD MOSS is Poetry Editor of *The New Yorker.* His books include *Selected Poems* and *The Magic Lantern of Marcel Proust.*

ROGER SHATTUCK has written extensively on Proust and other modern French authors.

GILLES DELEUZE teaches philosophy at the University of Paris and has written two books on Nietzsche, as well as texts on Bergson, Hume, Sacher-Masoch, Spinoza, and Kafka. His *Nietzsche and Philosophy* has been translated, as have *Proust and Signs, Kant's Critical Philosophy,* and two books written with Felix Guattari *Anti-Oedipus* and *A Thousand Plateaus.*

GERARD GENETTE is the author of *Figures of Discourse* and *Narrative Discourse: An Essay in Method,* both seminal works of structuralist methodology.

LEO BERSANI is Chairman of the Department of French at the University of California, Berkeley. He is the author of several books including *Marcel Proust: The Fictions of Life and Art, Balzac to Beckett: Center and Circumference in French Fiction, A Future for Astyanax: Character and Desire in Literature,* and *The Death of Stephane Mallarmé.*

PAUL DE MAN was, until his death in 1983, Sterling Professor of Comparative Literature at Yale University. He is the author of *Blindness and Insight: Essays in Contemporary Criticism, Allegories of Reading: Figural Language in Rousseau, Nietzsche, Rilke, and Proust, The Rhetoric of Romanticism,* and the forthcoming collections *The Resistance to Theory, Aesthetic Ideology,* and *Fugitive Essays.*

WALTER KASELL is Assistant Professor of French and Comparative Literature at Brandeis University. He has published on Proust and Gérard de Nerval.

RANDOLPH SPLITTER is the author of *Proust's Recherche: A Psychoanalytic Interpretation.*

JEAN RICARDOU is the author of *Claude Simon: Analyse, théorie, Revolutions minuscules,* and other works.

DIANA FESTA-McCORMICK teaches in the Department of Modern Languages at Brooklyn College. Her books include *The City as Catalyst: A Study of Ten Novels, Honoré de Balzac,* and *Proustian Optics of Clothes, Mirrors, Masks, Mores.*

Bibliography

Adam International Review 25, no. 260 (1957). Special Marcel Proust issue.

Albaret, Celeste. *Monsieur Proust*. Edited by Georges Belmont, translated by Barbara Bray. New York: McGraw-Hill, 1976.

Atget, Eugene. *A Vision of Paris: The Words of Marcel Proust*. Edited and introduced by Arthur A. Trottenberg. New York: Macmillan, 1980.

Barker, Richard Hindry. *Marcel Proust: A Biography*. New York: Criterion Books, 1958.

Barthes, Roland, et al. *Recherche de Proust*. Paris: Editions du Seuil, 1980.

Bataille, Georges. "Proust." In *Literature and Evil*, 109–123, translated by Alastair Hamilton. London: Calder and Boyars, 1973.

Bell, Clive. *Proust*. London: Hogarth Press, 1928.

Bell, William Stewart. *Proust's Nocturnal Muse*. New York: Columbia University Press, 1962.

Benoist-Méchin, Jacques Gabriel Paul Michel. *Avec Marcel Proust*. Paris: A. Michel, 1977.

Bersani, Jacques, ed. *Les Critiques de notre temps et Proust*. Paris: Garnier, 1971.

Bersani, Leo. *Marcel Proust: The Fictions of Life and of Art*. New York: Oxford University Press, 1965.

Brée, Germaine. *Marcel Proust and Deliverance from Time*. Translated by C. J. Richards and A. D. Truitt. New Brunswick, N.J.: Rutgers University Press, 1955.

————. *The World of Marcel Proust*. Boston: Houghton Mifflin, 1966.

Bucknall, Barbara J. *The Religion of Art in Proust*. Urbana: University of Illinois Press, 1969.

Casey, Edward S. "Literary Description and Phenomenological Method." *Yale French Studies* 61 (1981): 176–201.

Cattaui, Georges. *Marcel Proust*. Translated by Ruth Hall. New York: Funk and Wagnalls, 1968.

Cocking, John Martin. *Proust*. New Haven: Yale University Press, 1956.

Coleman, Elliott. *The Golden Angel: Papers on Proust*. New York: C. Taylor, 1954.

Culler, Jonathan. "The Problem of Metaphor." In *Language, Meaning, and Style: Essays in Memory of Stephen Ullmann*, edited by T. E. Hope, T. B. W. Reid, Roy Harris, and Glanville Price, 5–20. Leeds: Leeds University Press, 1981.

Curtius, Ernst Robert. *Marcel Proust.* Translated into French by Armand Pierhal. Paris: La Revue Nouvelle, 1928.

De Billy, Robert. *Marcel Proust: Lettres et conversations.* Paris: Editions des portiques, 1930.

Deleuze, Gilles. *Proust and Signs.* Translated by Richard Howard. New York: Braziller, 1972.

Descombes, Vincent. "La Révélation de l'abîme." *Degrés* 26–27 (Spring–Summer 1981): c1–c15.

Doubrovsky, Serge. "The Place of the Madeleine: Writing and Phantasy in Proust." *boundary 2,* no. 4 (Fall 1975): 107–34.

Ellis, Havelock. "Marcel Proust." *Atlantic Monthly* 156, no. 4 (October 1935): 421–32.

L'Esprit Créateur 11, no. 1 (Spring 1971). Special Marcel Proust issue.

Fernandez, Ramon. *Messages.* Translated by Montgomery Belgion. New York: Harcourt, Brace & World, 1927.

Festa-McCormick, Diana. *Proustian Optics of Clothes: Mirrors, Masks, Mores.* Saratoga, Calif. Anma Libri, 1984.

Feuillerat, Albert. *Comment Marcel Proust a composé son roman.* New Haven: Yale University Press, 1934.

Forster, E. M. "Proust." In *Abinger Harvest,* 96–102. New York: Harcourt, Brace & World, 1964.

Fowlie, Wallace. *A Reading of Proust.* Garden City, N.Y.: Anchor Books, 1964.

Frank, Joseph. "Spatial Form in Modern Literature." In *The Widening Gyre,* 3–62. New Brunswick, N.J.: Rutgers University Press, 1963.

Gide, André. *Journals, 1889–1949.* Selected, edited, and translated by Justin O'Brien. London: Pelican, 1967.

———. *Pretexts: Reflections on Literature and Morality.* Selected, edited, and translated by Justin O'Brien. London: Secker & Warburg, 1959.

Girard, René. *Deceit, Desire, and the Novel: Self and Other in Literary Structure.* Translated by Yvonne Freccero. Baltimore: Johns Hopkins University Press, 1965.

———, ed. *Proust: A Collection of Critical Essays.* Englewood Cliffs, N.J.: Prentice-Hall, 1962.

Grossvogel, David I. "Proust: *Remembrance of Things Past.*" In *Limits of the Novel: Evolutions of a Form from Chaucer to Robbe-Grillet.* Ithaca, N.Y.: Cornell University Press, 1968.

Hardy, Barbara. *Tellers and Listeners: The Narrative Imagination.* London: Athlone, 1975.

Hindus, Milton. *The Proustian Vision.* New York: Columbia University Press, 1954.

Houston, John Porter. *The Shape and Style of Proust's Novel.* Detroit: Wayne State University Press, 1982.

Hughes, Edward J. *Marcel Proust: A Study in the Quality of Awareness.* New York: Cambridge University Press, 1983.

Humphries, Jefferson. *The Otherness Within: Gnostic Readings in Marcel Proust, Flannery O'Connor, and François Villon.* Baton Rouge, La.: Louisiana State University Press, 1983.

Jauss, Hans Robert. *Zeit und Erinnerung in Marcel Prousts* A la Recherche du temps perdu: *Ein Beitrag zur Theorie des Romans.* Heidelberg: C. Winter, 1955.

Jay, Paul. "Joyce and Proust: The Theory of Fictional Autobiography." In *Being in the Text: Self-Representation from Wordsworth to Roland Barthes,* 142–53. Ithaca, N.Y.: Cornell University Press, 1984.

Jephcott, E. F. N. *Proust and Rilke: The Literature of Expanded Consciousness.* New York: Barnes & Noble, 1972.

Johnson, J. Theodore. "Proust's 'Impressionism' Reconsidered in the Light of the Visual Arts of the Twentieth Century." In *Twentieth-Century French Fiction: Essays for Germaine Brée,* edited by George Stambolian, 27–56. New Brunswick, N.J.: Rutgers University Press, 1975.

Joiner, Lawrence D. *The Art of the Proustian Novel Reconsidered.* Rock Hill, S.C.: Winthrop College, 1979.

Kamber, Gerald, and Richard Macksey. " 'Negative Metaphor' and Proust's Rhetoric of Absence." *MLN* 85, no. 6 (1970): 858–83.

Kassell, Walter. *Marcel Proust and the Strategy of Reading.* Philadelphia: J. Benjamins, 1980.

Kilmartin, Terence. *A Reader's Guide to* Remembrance of Things Past. New York: Random House, 1983.

Kopp, Richard L. *Marcel Proust as a Social Critic.* Rutherford, N.J.: Fairleigh Dickinson University Press, 1971.

Ladimer, Benthany. "The Narrator as Voyeur in *A la Recherche du temps perdu.*" *Critical Quarterly* 19, no. 3 (1977): 5–20.

Levin, Harry. *The Gates of Horn: A Study of Five French Realists.* New York: Oxford University Press, 1963.

March, Harold. *The Two Worlds of Marcel Proust.* Philadelphia: University of Philadelphia Press, 1948.

Mauriac, François. *Proust's Way.* Translated by Elsie Pell. New York: Philosophical Library, 1950.

Maurois, André. *Proust: Portrait of a Genius.* Translated by Gerard Hopkins. New York: Harper, 1950.

———. *The World of Marcel Proust.* Translated by Maura Budberg with the assistance of Barbara Creed. New York: Harper & Row, 1974.

May, Derwent. *Proust.* New York: Oxford University Press, 1983.

Mehlman, Jeffrey. *A Structural Study of Autobiography: Proust, Leiris, Sartre, Lévi-Strauss.* Ithaca, N.Y.: Cornell University Press, 1974.

Melnick, Daniel. "Proust, Music, and the Reader." *Modern Language Quarterly* 41, no. 2 (1980): 181–92.

Moss, Howard. *The Magic Lantern of Marcel Proust: A Critical Study of* Remembrance of Things Past. Boston: Nonpareil Books, 1963.

Murray, Jack. *The Proustian Comedy.* York, S.C.: French Literature Publications, 1980.

Nordlinger-Riefstahl, Marie. "Proust as I Knew Him." *London Magazine* 1, no. 7 (August 1954): 51–61.

Ortega y Gasset, José. "Time, Distance, and Form in Proust," translated by I. Singer. *The Hudson Review* 11, no. 4 (1958): 504–13.

Painter, George D. *Proust.* 2 vols. Boston: Little, Brown, 1959–65.

Peyre, Henri. *Marcel Proust.* New York: Columbia University Press, 1970.

Pinter, Harold. *The Proust Screenplay.* London: Eyre-Methuen, 1978.

Poulet, Georges. *Proustian Space.* Translated by Elliott Coleman. Baltimore: Johns Hopkins University Press, 1977.

Price. Larkin B., ed. *Marcel Proust: A Critical Panorama.* Urbana: University of Illinois Press, 1973.

Proust, Marcel. *Letters of Marcel Proust to Antoine Bibesco.* Translated by Gerard Hopkins. London: Thames & Hudson, 1953.

———. *Marcel Proust et Jacques Rivière: Correspondance, 1914–1922.* Edited by Philip Kolb. Paris: Plon, 1955.

———. *Marcel Proust: Selected Letters, 1880–1903.* Edited by Philip Kolb, translated by Ralph Manheim. Garden City, N.Y.: Doubleday, 1983.

Quennell, Peter, ed. *Marcel Proust. 1871–1922: A Centennial Volume.* New York: Simon & Schuster, 1971.

Revel, Jean Fraçois. *On Proust.* Translated by Martin Turnell. New York: Library Press, 1972.

Riffaterre, Michael. "Descriptive Imagery." *Yale French Studies,* no. 61 (1981): 107–25.

Rivers, J. E. *Proust and the Art of Love: The Aesthetics of Sexuality in the Life, Times, and Art of Marcel Proust.* New York: Columbia University Press, 1981.

Sansom, William. *Proust and His World.* London: Thames & Hudson, 1973.

Schehr, Lawrence R. "Proust's Musical Inversions." *MLN* 97, no. 5 (1982): 1086–99.

Scott-Moncrieff, Charles Kenneth, ed. *Marcel Proust: An English Tribute.* London: Chatto & Windus, 1923.

Shattuck, Roger. *Marcel Proust.* Princeton, N.J.: Princeton University Press, 1982.

———. *Proust's Binoculars: A Study of Memory, Time, and Recognition in* A la Recherche du temps perdu. New York: Random House, 1963.

Slater, Maya. *Humor in the Works of Proust.* New York: Oxford University Press, 1979.

Spalding, Philip Anthony. *A Reader's Handbook to Proust: An Index Guide to Remembrance of Things Past.* Rev. ed. New York: Barnes & Noble, 1975.

———. *Proust's Recherche: A Psychoanalytic Interpretation.* Boston: Routledge & Kegan Paul, 1981.

Stambolian, George. *Marcel Proust and the Creative Encounter.* Chicago: University of Chicago Press, 1972.

Taylor, Elisabeth Russell. *Marcel Proust and His Contexts: A Critical Bibliography of English Language Scholarship.* New York: Garland, 1981.

Taylor, Rosalie. "The Adult and World Childhood in *Combray.*" *French Studies* 22, no. 1 (1968): 26–36.

Ullmann, Stephen. "The Metaphorical Texture of a Proustian Novel." In *The Image in the Modern French Novel: Gide, Alain-Fournier, Proust, Camus,* 124–238. Cambridge: Cambridge University Press, 1960.

———. "Transpositions of Sensations in Proust's Imagery." In *Style in the French Novel,* 189–209. Cambridge: Cambridge University Press, 1960.

Vigneron, Robert. "Structure de *Swann*." *Modern Philology* 45 (1948): 185–207.

Wharton, Edith. "Marcel Proust." *Yale Review* 14 (1925): 209–22.

Wilson, Edmund. "Marcel Proust." In *Axel's Castle*, 132–90. New York: Scribner's, 1931.

Woolf, Virginia. "Phases of Fiction." In *Granite and Rainbow*, 93–145. New York: Harcourt, Brace & World, 1958.

Yale French Studies, no. 34 (June 1965). Special Marcel Proust issue.

Zimmerman, Eugenia N. "Death and Transfiguration in Proust and Tolstoy." *Mosaic* 6, no. 2 (1973): 161–72.

———. "The Metamorphoses of Adam: Names and Things in Sartre and Proust." In *Twentieth-Century French Fiction: Essays for Germaine Brée*, edited by George Stambolian, 57–71. New Brunswick, N.J.: Rutgers University Press, 1975.

Acknowledgments

"Memory Habit, Time" (originally entitled "Proust") by Samuel Beckett from *Proust: The Collected Works of Samuel Beckett* by Samuel Beckett, © 1970 by Grove Press, Inc. Reprinted by permission of the Grove Press, Inc. (and John Calder Ltd.) All rights reserved. This essay was first published in 1931.

"The Closed Door" by Germaine Brée from *Marcel Proust and Deliverance from Time* translated by Catherine Jandine Richards and Anne D. Truitt, © 1955 (renewed 1969) by the Trustees of Rutgers College in New Jersey. Reprinted by permission of Rutgers University Press, New Brunswick, New Jersey.

"The Image of Proust" by Walter Benjamin from *Illuminations*, edited and with an introduction by Hannah Arendt, translated by Harry Zohn, © 1955 by Suhrkamp Verlag, Frankfurt am Main; English translation © 1968 by Harcourt Brace Jovanovich, Inc. Reprinted by permission of Harcourt Brace Jovanovich, Inc. and Joan Daves.

"The Worlds of Proust" by Rene Girard from *Deceit, Desire and the Novel*, translated by Yvonne Freccero, © 1961 by Editions Bernard Grasset; © 1965 by the Johns Hopkins University Press, Baltimore/London. Reprinted by permission.

"The Windows" by Howard Moss from *The Magic Lantern of Marcel Proust* by Howard Moss, Macmillan Publishing Company, 1962; David Godine, 1979; © 1963 by Howard Moss. Reprinted by permission of the author.

"Proust's Binoculars" by Roger Shattuck from *Proust's Binoculars: A Study of Memory, Time and Recognition in* A la recherche du temps perdu by Roger Shattuck, © 1963 by Roger Shattuck. Reprinted by permission of Random House, Inc., and Joan Daves.

"Signs and Thought" (originally entitled " 'Signs' and 'The Image of Thought' ") by Gilles Deleuze from *Proust and Signs*, translated by Richard Howard, © 1972 by George Braziller, Inc. Reprinted by permission.

"Time and Narrative in *a la recherche du temps perdu*" by Gérard Genette from *Aspects of Narrative: Selected Papers from the English Institute*, edited by J. Hillis Miller, © 1971 by Columbia University Press. Reprinted by permission of Columbia University Press.

"Proust and the Art of Incompletion" by Leo Bersani from *Aspects of Narrative: Selected Papers from the English Institute,* edited by J. Hillis Miller, © 1971 by Columbia University Press. Reprinted by permission of the author and Columbia University Press.

"Reading (Proust)" by Paul de Man from *Allegories of Reading* by Paul de Man, © 1979 by Yale University. Reprinted by permission of Yale University Press.

"Writing and the Return to Innocence: Proust's 'La Confession d'une jeune fille' " by Walter Kasell from *The Art of the Proustian Novel Reconsidered,* edited by Lawrence D. Joiner, © 1979 by Winthrop Studies on Major Modern Writers. Reprinted by permission.

"Proust, Joyce and the Theory of Metaphor" by Randolph Splitter from *Literature and Psychology* 29, nos. 1 and 2 (1979), © 1979 by Morton Kaplan. Reprinted by permission.

"Proust: A Retrospective Reading" by Jean Ricardou, and translated by Erica Freiberg from *Critical Inquiry* 8, no. 3 (Spring 1982), © 1982 by Jean Ricardou and Erica Freiberg. Reprinted by permission of Jean Ricardou and Erica Freiberg. All rights reserved.

"Clothes as Masks" by Diana Festa-McCormick from *Proustian Optics of Clothes: Mirrors, Masks, Mores* by Diana Festa-McCormick, Stanford French and Italian Studies 29 (1984): 86-126, © 1984 by ANMA Libri and Co., Saratoga, California. Reprinted by permission.

Index